Praise, Praise, Praise for Diabetes For Dummies!

"As one of the country's leading endocrinologists, Alan Rubin could be expected to know a lot about diabetes. But the surprising thing about his new book is how well he says it, and his support of the glycemic index shows in particular that he is current with the latest thinking on how to deal with diabetes."

— Rick Mendosa, Diabetes Journalist,
`www.mendosa.com/diabetes.htm`

"*Diabetes For Dummies* is a wonderfully written book and will become the companion book for all people with diabetes and their families. It is very clearly written so that it can be readily understood by younger diabetics as well as elderly diabetics, and it will be especially important for a newly diagnosed diabetic. It is also a must-read for diabetic educators."

— Michael D. Goldfield, M.D.
Assistant Clinical Professor of Psychiatry,
University of California Medical Center,
San Francisco, California

"At last, a diabetes book for everyone. Dr. Rubin is superb at translating the medical issues of diabetes into plain English. He does a terrific job of covering just about every conceivable aspect of diabetes in clear, concise, and readable text with a touch of humor. A must-read."

— G. Robert Hampton, M.D.
Retinal Specialist on the American Academy of
Ophthalmology's Public Information Committee,
Syracuse, New York

"Dr. Rubin provides a marvelous face-lift with this fun, very readable, and practical book. You'll learn ten myths about diabetes that you can forget, and hundreds of powerful tips that you'll long remember. Filled with wit and wisdom, this book will teach you the Ten Commandments of Diabetes Care which can add life to your years . . . and years to your life."

— Dr. Joel Goodman, Director,
The HUMOR Project, Inc.,
Saratoga Springs, New York

"When it comes to diabetes, almost everyone is a dummy — including, alas, a number of health care professionals! This lively and lucid tell-it-all guide will provide you with the information you need to leap from the valley of diabetes ignorance to the peaks of understanding. (We particularly appreciate the extensive and inspiring list of famous people in all walks of life who have diabetes.)"

— June Biermann and Barbara Toohey
Founders and Editors-in-Chief
of www.DiabetesWebSite.com

"I would recommend this book to parents, adolescents, and children with diabetes. It presents a clear, straightforward, and honest discussion of diabetes and does this within the context of understanding developmental tasks and processes."

— Sal Lomonaco, M.D.
Associate Clinical Professor of Psychiatry,
Division of Child-Adolescent Psychiatry

Praise from Readers:

"I really appreciate your new 'Dummy' book. I think it's great for those of us who have had diabetes for years, and those who know nothing! Thanks."

— Laura Shapiro,
Albuquerque, New Mexico

"I have been a diabetic for almost 30 years. I bought your book yesterday, knowing that I already knew a lot, but also knowing there was much to learn! Thank you very much for the book!"

— Brent Clisby,
Ontario, Canada

Diabetes Cookbook For Dummies®

Cheat Sheet

Determining Your Ideal Weight, Body Mass Index, and Kilocalorie Intake

The following is a general rule for calculating your ideal weight:

- A man should weigh 106 pounds for 5 feet and 6 pounds more for every inch over 5 feet.
- A woman should weigh 100 pounds for 5 feet and 5 pounds more for every inch over 5 feet.

The range of appropriate weights is the ideal weight plus or minus 10 percent.

Body mass index is a formula to determine a person's body weight relative to height. This number is a good indicator of the amount of fat in your body. To obtain your body mass index (BMI):

1. **Multiply your weight in pounds by 705.**
2. **Divide this number by your height in inches.**
3. **Divide again by your height in inches.**

   The result is your BMI.

A body mass index under 20 is slim, 20 to 25 is normal, 25 to 30 is overweight, and greater than 30 is obese.

To figure your daily calorie needs:

1. **Multiply your ideal weight in pounds by 10.**
2. **If you get no exercise, multiply the result of Step 1 by 10% or 0.1. If you exercise moderately, multiply the result of Step 1 by 20% or 0.2. If you get heavy exercise, multiply this number by 40% or 0.4.**
3. **Add the result of Step 2 to the result of Step 1.**

   This number is the amount of calories you should consume every day in order to maintain your ideal weight.

Government Definitions for Fat Content

- Fat-free is less than 0.5 grams of fat per serving.
- Lowfat is less than 3 grams of fat per serving.
- Lean meat has less than 10 grams of fat, less than 4 grams of saturated fat, and less than 95 milligrams of cholesterol.
- Cholesterol-free means less than 2 milligrams of cholesterol per serving.

Diabetes Cookbook For Dummies®

Cheat Sheet

Cooking Terms That Indicate Low or High Fat Content in a Food

If you are overweight, you must be able to evaluate recipes for their fat content.

These terms indicate a low fat content:

- Baked
- Broiled
- Cooked in its own juice
- Poached

These terms indicate a high fat content:

- Buttered or in butter sauce
- Creamed
- Deep fried
- Fried
- In plum sauce
- In cheese sauce
- Sautéed
- Sweet and sour

Eyeballing Portion Size

To determine the size of a portion, compare it to something you see regularly. For example:

- Three ounces of meat is the size of a deck of cards.
- A medium fruit is the size of a tennis ball.
- A medium potato is the size of a computer mouse.
- A medium bagel is the size of a hockey puck.
- An ounce of cheese is the size of a domino.
- A cup of fruit is the size of a baseball.
- A cup of broccoli is the size of a light bulb.

Ten Simple Steps to Improve Your Diet

Here are ten steps that aren't very difficult to do but that will make a difference in your health.

- Keep a food diary.
- Avoid missing a meal; eat at regular times.
- Use water in place of caloric drinks.
- Cook with half the fat you usually use.
- Don't add salt.
- Flavor with condiments, herbs, and spices.
- Include vegetables in all meals.
- Sit down for meals.
- Remove all visible fat.
- Cook by the B's: Braise, broil, or boil.

Cheat Sheet $2.95 value. Item 5230-9.
For more information about IDG Books, call 1-800-762-2974.

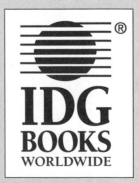

Diabetes Cookbook FOR DUMMIES®

Diabetes Cookbook FOR DUMMIES®

by Alan L. Rubin, M.D.,
with Fran Stach, R.D., C.D.E.,
and Chef Denise C. Sharf

IDG BOOKS WORLDWIDE

IDG Books Worldwide, Inc.
An International Data Group Company

Foster City, CA ◆ Chicago, IL ◆ Indianapolis, IN ◆ New York, NY

Diabetes Cookbook For Dummies®

Published by
IDG Books Worldwide, Inc.
An International Data Group Company
919 E. Hillsdale Blvd.
Suite 400
Foster City, CA 94404
www.idgbooks.com (IDG Books Worldwide Web site)
www.dummies.com (Dummies Press Web site)

Library of Congress Catalog Card No.: 99-69725

ISBN: 0-7645-5230-9

Printed in the United States of America

10 9 8 7 6 5 4 3 2 1

1O/RS/QW/QQ/IN

Distributed in the United States by IDG Books Worldwide, Inc.

Distributed by CDG Books Canada Inc. for Canada; by Transworld Publishers Limited in the United Kingdom; by IDG Norge Books for Norway; by IDG Sweden Books for Sweden; by IDG Books Australia Publishing Corporation Pty. Ltd. for Australia and New Zealand; by TransQuest Publishers Pte Ltd. for Singapore, Malaysia, Thailand, Indonesia, and Hong Kong; by Gotop Information Inc. for Taiwan; by ICG Muse, Inc. for Japan; by Intersoft for South Africa; by Eyrolles for France; by International Thomson Publishing for Germany, Austria and Switzerland; by Distribuidora Cuspide for Argentina; by LR International for Brazil; by Galileo Libros for Chile; by Ediciones ZETA S.C.R. Ltda. for Peru; by WS Computer Publishing Corporation, Inc., for the Philippines; by Contemporanea de Ediciones for Venezuela; by Express Computer Distributors for the Caribbean and West Indies; by Micronesia Media Distributor, Inc. for Micronesia; by Chips Computadoras S.A. de C.V. for Mexico; by Editorial Norma de Panama S.A. for Panama; by American Bookshops for Finland.

For general information on IDG Books Worldwide's books in the U.S., please call our Consumer Customer Service department at 800-762-2974. For reseller information, including discounts and premium sales, please call our Reseller Customer Service department at 800-434-3422.

For information on where to purchase IDG Books Worldwide's books outside the U.S., please contact our International Sales department at 317-596-5530 or fax 317-572-4002.

For consumer information on foreign language translations, please contact our Customer Service department at 1-800-434-3422, fax 317-572-4002, or e-mail rights@idgbooks.com.

For information on licensing foreign or domestic rights, please phone +1-650-653-7098.

For sales inquiries and special prices for bulk quantities, please contact our Order Services department at 800-434-3422 or write to the address above.

For information on using IDG Books Worldwide's books in the classroom or for ordering examination copies, please contact our Educational Sales department at 800-434-2086 or fax 317-572-4005.

For press review copies, author interviews, or other publicity information, please contact our Public Relations department at 650-653-7000 or fax 650-653-7500.

About the Authors

Alan L. Rubin, M.D., is one of the nation's foremost experts on diabetes. He is a professional member of the American Diabetes Association and the Endocrine Society and has been in private practice specializing in diabetes and thyroid disease for over 25 years. Dr. Rubin was Assistant Clinical Professor of Medicine at University of California Medical Center in San Francisco for 20 years. He has spoken about diabetes to professional medical audiences and nonmedical audiences around the world. He has been a consultant to many pharmaceutical companies and companies that make diabetes products.

Dr. Rubin was one of the first specialists in his field to recognize the significance of patient self-testing of blood glucose, the major advance in diabetes care since the advent of insulin. As a result, he has been on numerous radio and television programs, talking about the cause, the prevention, and the treatment of diabetes and its complications. His first book, *Diabetes For Dummies,* is a basic reference for any nonprofessional who wants to understand diabetes.

Fran Stach, R.D., C.D.E., is a registered dietitian and a certified diabetes educator. She has been training people with diabetes to eat appropriate foods for over 30 years. She has a B. S. in Dietetics from Texas Woman's University and is the consulting dietitian and diabetes educator in several hospitals and medical practices. She has given numerous community education programs on health and nutrition. She complements her educational activities by cooking for family and friends and by a program of regular exercise that keeps her physically fit at all times.

Chef Denise C. Sharf, who created many of the breakfast, lunch, and appetizer recipes in this book and who kitchen-tested many other recipes from the various hotels and restaurants, is a Certified Chef de Cuisine through the American Culinary Federation. She specializes in personal chef services throughout south Florida and has previously held positions as an Executive Chef and Chef de Garde Manger for several major hotel chains and restaurants. Chef Sharf has achieved recognition as a culinary competitor, judge, and presenter of seminars. She also writes food and wine articles regularly for print, Web, and radio, and can be reached by e-mail at `ChefDeni@aol.com`.

ABOUT IDG BOOKS WORLDWIDE

Welcome to the world of IDG Books Worldwide.

IDG Books Worldwide, Inc., is a subsidiary of International Data Group, the world's largest publisher of computer-related information and the leading global provider of information services on information technology. IDG was founded more than 30 years ago by Patrick J. McGovern and now employs more than 9,000 people worldwide. IDG publishes more than 290 computer publications in over 75 countries. More than 90 million people read one or more IDG publications each month.

Launched in 1990, IDG Books Worldwide is today the #1 publisher of best-selling computer books in the United States. We are proud to have received eight awards from the Computer Press Association in recognition of editorial excellence and three from Computer Currents' First Annual Readers' Choice Awards. Our best-selling *...For Dummies®* series has more than 50 million copies in print with translations in 31 languages. IDG Books Worldwide, through a joint venture with IDG's Hi-Tech Beijing, became the first U.S. publisher to publish a computer book in the People's Republic of China. In record time, IDG Books Worldwide has become the first choice for millions of readers around the world who want to learn how to better manage their businesses.

Our mission is simple: Every one of our books is designed to bring extra value and skill-building instructions to the reader. Our books are written by experts who understand and care about our readers. The knowledge base of our editorial staff comes from years of experience in publishing, education, and journalism — experience we use to produce books to carry us into the new millennium. In short, we care about books, so we attract the best people. We devote special attention to details such as audience, interior design, use of icons, and illustrations. And because we use an efficient process of authoring, editing, and desktop publishing our books electronically, we can spend more time ensuring superior content and less time on the technicalities of making books.

You can count on our commitment to deliver high-quality books at competitive prices on topics you want to read about. At IDG Books Worldwide, we continue in the IDG tradition of delivering quality for more than 30 years. You'll find no better book on a subject than one from IDG Books Worldwide.

IDG BOOKS WORLDWIDE

John Kilcullen
Chairman and CEO
IDG Books Worldwide, Inc.

VIII WINNER
Eighth Annual Computer Press Awards 1992

IX WINNER
Ninth Annual Computer Press Awards 1993

1994 COMPUTER CURRENTS 1995 READERS' CHOICE

X WINNER
Tenth Annual Computer Press Awards 1994

XI WINNER
Eleventh Annual Computer Press Awards 1995

IDG is the world's leading IT media, research and exposition company. Founded in 1964, IDG had 1997 revenues of $2.05 billion and has more than 9,000 employees worldwide. IDG offers the widest range of media options that reach IT buyers in 75 countries representing 95% of worldwide IT spending. IDG's diverse product and services portfolio spans six key areas including print publishing, online publishing, expositions and conferences, market research, education and training, and global marketing services. More than 90 million people read one or more of IDG's 290 magazines and newspapers, including IDG's leading global brands — Computerworld, PC World, Network World, Macworld and the Channel World family of publications. IDG Books Worldwide is one of the fastest-growing computer book publishers in the world, with more than 700 titles in 36 languages. The "...For Dummies®" series alone has more than 50 million copies in print. IDG offers online users the largest network of technology-specific Web sites around the world through IDG.net (http://www.idg.net), which comprises more than 225 targeted Web sites in 55 countries worldwide. International Data Corporation (IDC) is the world's largest provider of information technology data, analysis and consulting, with research centers in over 41 countries and more than 400 research analysts worldwide. IDG World Expo is a leading producer of more than 168 globally branded conferences and expositions in 35 countries including E3 (Electronic Entertainment Expo), Macworld Expo, ComNet, Windows World Expo, ICE (Internet Commerce Expo), Agenda, DEMO, and Spotlight. IDG's training subsidiary, ExecuTrain, is the world's largest computer training company, with more than 230 locations worldwide and 785 training courses. IDG Marketing Services helps industry-leading IT companies build international brand recognition by developing global integrated marketing programs via IDG's print, online and exposition products worldwide. Further information about the company can be found at www.idg.com.

1/26/00

Dedication

This book is dedicated to the great chefs and restaurant owners, especially the ones in this book, who spend all their time and creative energy producing delicious and nutritious food in a beautiful environment and make sure that it is served in a way that complements the taste.

Authors' Acknowledgments

Acquisitions editors Tami Booth, who believed that the idea of great chefs producing wonderful food for people with diabetes could be made into a book, and Linda Ingroia, who used her in-depth knowledge of producing such books to bring it to completion, deserve special commendation. Our project editor, Christine Beck, along with copy editors Diane Smith, Corey Dalton, Patricia Yuu Pan, and Tina Sims, made certain that the book is understandable and readable in the great *...For Dummies* tradition.

Chef Denise Sharf produced most of the recipes for breakfast, lunch, and appetizers, and tested many of the recipes from the restaurants. Her help has been invaluable, and she has set an example for really nutritious food.

Molly Siple, R.D., is responsible for most of the discussions of food and the organization of the recipes in the book. Her tremendous skill in doing so is apparent in this book and in her own book, *Healing Foods For Dummies.* Molly has a Master of Science in Nutritional Science.

Recipe tester, Laura Pensiero, has not only checked every recipe to verify that it can be successfully prepared and tastes very good, but has offered numerous suggestions for replacing or reducing ingredients so that the finished product is a perfect fit for a person with diabetes.

Reviewer Lea Ann Holzmeister, R.D., C.D.E., did a fantastic job of assuring that the information in the book is accurate.

Dr. Rubin's wife, Enid, has shown great patience, perseverance, and love in providing the time and the environment in which he could write this book.

Fran Stach thanks her husband for his encouragement, enthusiastic tasting of the recipes she prepared, and uncomplaining washing of the dishes.

Publisher's Acknowledgments

We're proud of this book; please register your comments through our IDG Books Worldwide Online Registration Form located at `http://my2cents.dummies.com`.

Some of the people who helped bring this book to market include the following:

Acquisitions, Editorial, and Media Development

Project Editor: Christine Meloy Beck

Executive Editor: Tammerly Booth

Acquisitions Editor: Linda Ingroia

Copy Editors: Corey Dalton, Patricia Yuu Pan, Tina Sims, Susan Diane Smith

Acquisitions Coordinator: Karen S. Young

Recipe Tester: Laura Pensiero

General Reviewer: Lea Ann Holzmeister, R.D., C.D.E.

Editorial Manager: Jennifer Ehrlich

Media Development Manager: Heather Heath Dismore

Editorial Assistant: Laura Jefferson

Production

Project Coordinator: Emily Perkins

Layout and Graphics: Joe Bucki, Barry Offringa, Tracy K. Oliver, Brent Savage, Jacque Schneider, Brian Torwelle

Proofreaders: Corey Bowen, John Greenough, Susan Moritz, Marianne Santy

Indexer: Johnna VanHoose

Special Help

Amanda M. Foxworth

General and Administrative

IDG Books Worldwide, Inc.: John Kilcullen, CEO

IDG Books Technology Publishing Group: Richard Swadley, Senior Vice President and Publisher; Walter R. Bruce III, Vice President and Publisher; Joseph Wikert, Vice President and Publisher; Mary Bednarek, Vice President and Director, Product Development; Andy Cummings, Publishing Director, General User Group; Mary C. Corder, Editorial Director; Barry Pruett, Publishing Director

IDG Books Consumer Publishing Group: Roland Elgey, Senior Vice President and Publisher; Kathleen A. Welton, Vice President and Publisher; Kevin Thornton, Acquisitions Manager; Kristin A. Cocks, Editorial Director

IDG Books Internet Publishing Group: Brenda McLaughlin, Senior Vice President and Publisher; Sofia Marchant, Online Marketing Manager

IDG Books Production for Branded Press: Debbie Stailey, Director of Production; Cindy L. Phipps, Manager of Project Coordination, Production Proofreading, and Indexing; Tony Augsburger, Manager of Prepress, Reprints, and Systems; Laura Carpenter, Production Control Manager; Shelley Lea, Supervisor of Graphics and Design; Debbie J. Gates, Production Systems Specialist; Robert Springer, Supervisor of Proofreading; Kathie Schutte, Senior Page Layout Supervisor; Michael Sullivan, Production Supervisor

Packaging and Book Design: Patty Page, Manager, Promotions Marketing

◆

The publisher would like to give special thanks to Patrick J. McGovern, without whom this book would not have been possible.

◆

Contents at a Glance

Recipes at a Glance

Cartoons at a Glance

By Rich Tennant

"Don't use that excuse on me, Wayne. Ain't no good reason why a man with diabetes can't help himself to some of Earl's fried mealworms."

page 291

"Give me 2 carbohydrate exchanges, 1 protein exchange, and if I have any room left, I'll take a ½ fat exchange."

page 263

"I forgot to time my insulin intake correctly, so if you don't mind, I'll just nibble on the centerpiece until dinner's served."

page 7

"Well, yes, my blood sugar is a little low..."

page 319

"It's nearly a perfect meal. I've got 40% fat, 30% protein, 20% carbohydrates and 10% guilt for the 40% fat."

page 61

Fax: 978-546-7747

E-mail: richtennant@the5thwave.com

World Wide Web: www.the5thwave.com

Table of Contents

THE INFORMATION IN THIS REFERENCE IS NOT INTENDED TO SUBSTITUTE FOR EXPERT MEDICAL ADVICE OR TREATMENT; IT IS DESIGNED TO HELP YOU MAKE INFORMED CHOICES. BECAUSE EACH INDIVIDUAL IS UNIQUE, A PHYSICIAN MUST DIAGNOSE CONDITIONS AND SUPERVISE TREATMENTS FOR EACH INDIVIDUAL HEALTH PROBLEM. IF AN INDIVIDUAL IS UNDER A DOCTOR'S CARE AND RECEIVES ADVICE CONTRARY TO INFORMATION PROVIDED IN THIS REFERENCE, THE DOCTOR'S ADVICE SHOULD BE FOLLOWED, AS IT IS BASED ON THE UNIQUE CHARACTERISTICS OF THAT INDIVIDUAL.

Introduction

People with diabetes *can* eat great food! We don't have to prove that statement anymore. The recipes in Dr. Rubin's previous book, *Diabetes For Dummies* (published by IDG Books Worldwide, Inc.), show that people can follow a diabetic diet at home or anywhere they travel and still enjoy a five-star meal. They just have to know how to cook it or where to go to get it.

More and more eating is being done away from home or, if at home, from food in the form of take-out from a local supermarket or restaurant, and people with diabetes want to know what they can and can't eat.

If you bought *Diabetes For Dummies,* you know that you can find such food in Chicago, New York City, Santa Monica, and San Francisco. But what about the rest of the world? This book is both a cookbook that shows you how to prepare great foods in your own home and a guide to eating out in restaurants and fast-food places.

When you get to the restaurants featured in this book, how will you know which dishes are approved for a person with diabetes? We have asked the restaurants to put the letters *MD,* which stand for "meal for diabetes," next to a healthy dish. We can't guarantee that they will comply with our request, but the level of health awareness that we have found among the chefs and restaurant owners with whom we worked leads us to believe that they will.

Is diet important for a person with diabetes? Do salmon swim upstream? The Diabetes Control and Complications Trials showed that a good diabetic diet could lower the hemoglobin A1c, a test of overall blood glucose control, by over 1 percent. That much improvement will result in a reduction of complications of diabetes such as eye disease, nerve disease, and kidney disease by 25 percent or more. The progression of complications that have already started to occur can be significantly slowed.

Of course, there's much more to managing diabetes than diet alone. In this book, you can discover the place of diet in a complete program of diabetes care.

About This Book

You wouldn't read a cookbook from cover to cover, and this book is no exception to that rule. There's no reason to read about setting up your kitchen if you simply want a place to eat in New York where you can find healthy nutrition for your diabetes. You may want to read the first few chapters to get an overview of the place of diet in your overall diabetes management, but if you just need a great entrée for tonight's supper or a great restaurant wherever you are, go right to that information. The book is written to be understood no matter where you find yourself in it.

Conventions Used in This Book

The recipes in this book are produced in a standard form that tells you what you are cooking, how much you are cooking, and how to cook it. The preparation time, cooking time (which is in addition to the prep time), and *yield,* or number of servings, are all presented at the beginning of the recipe, followed by a list of ingredients. We suggest that you always read through a recipe completely before you start preparing it so that you can make sure you have all the ingredients and equipment you need.

Chefs sometimes use exotic ingredients that may not be easily available to you. With the permission of the chefs, we have tried to substitute more common ingredients. On the other hand, walking into a store that sells special ingredients for a Chinese meal or an Indian meal, for example, can be a fascinating experience. We always define ingredients that are unfamiliar to English-speaking eaters in the introduction to the recipe.

You can find nutrition information and diabetic exchanges at the end of every recipe so that you can incorporate the recipe into your nutrition plan. The nutrition information is always given in the following order:

- Kcalories (see Chapter 1)
- Grams of protein
- Grams of carbohydrate
- Grams of fat
- Grams of saturated fat
- Milligrams of cholesterol
- Grams of fiber
- Milligrams of sodium

If salt is listed in a recipe as an optional ingredient or listed "to taste," it isn't figured into the nutritional information; but if a specific amount of salt is listed in the recipe, that amount is calculated into the nutritional information. Serving sizes are always calculated as the total recipe divided by the number of servings listed at the beginning of the recipe.

You can find more information about the exchange lists in Chapter 2 and a comprehensive list of food exchanges in Appendix B.

Here are a few other guidelines to keep in mind about the recipes:

- All eggs are large.
- All milk is lowfat unless otherwise specified.
- All butter is unsalted. Margarine is not a suitable substitute for butter, because of the difference in flavor and nutritional value. Butter is a natural product, while margarine is man-made and contains trans fatty acids.
- All salt is table salt unless otherwise specified.
- All dry ingredient measurements are level — use a dry ingredient measuring cup, fill it to the top, and scrape it even with a straight object such as the flat side of a knife.

If you need or want vegetarian recipes, scan the list of "Recipes in This Chapter" on the first page of each chapter in Part II. A little tomato in front of the name of a recipe, rather than a triangle, marks that recipe as vegetarian.

This is not a complete book about diagnosing and treating diabetes and its complications. That is found in *Diabetes For Dummies*. Check out that book if you need diagnosis and treatment information.

What You Don't Have to Read

All *...For Dummies* books have shaded areas that we call *sidebars*. They contain interesting but nonessential information. If you aren't interested in the nitty-gritty, you can skip these sidebars. We promise not to include that information on the test.

Foolish Assumptions

The book assumes that you have done some cooking and are familiar with the right knife to use to slice an onion without slicing your finger and how to tell one pot from another. Beyond that, you can find many cooking terms in Appendix C at the end of the book.

How This Book Is Organized

The book is divided into five parts to help you incorporate the benefits of a good diet into your diabetes management program, while showing you that the food can be great.

Part I: Building a Healthy Lifestyle

This part takes you on the road to long life and great health as you incorporate the needs of being a person with diabetes into the rest of your life. It begins by showing you all aspects of a healthy lifestyle and continues by focusing on food and its importance to you. When you cook for a person with diabetes, you must keep some special considerations in mind, but this part shows you that a diet for diabetes is an excellent diet for anyone. We guide you around the kitchen and take you to the supermarket to find out about meal-enhancing ingredients, as well as the ones to bypass as you navigate the aisles.

Part II: Healthy Recipes That Taste Great

This part presents recipes from A to Z (apples to zucchini) and everything in between. The chapters take you through your eating day, starting with your breakfast, providing snacks for midmorning and midafternoon, and offering larger meals at lunch and dinner. They end, naturally, with wonderful desserts, which show that you're not "doomed" to give up what you may consider the best part of the meal. You just need to be careful about calories. In this part we feature the recipes from the great restaurants that have participated in the book.

Part III: Eating Out for the Person with Diabetes

In this book, we can't cover every city and every restaurant you may visit. What do you do if you find yourself without a suggestion from this book? Part III tells you how to eat well and stay healthy wherever you are. You can always visit a fast-food franchise, but a lot of that food isn't good for you. If you pick and choose well, however, you will be able to select a meal even when your only choice is the one fast-food restaurant off the next exit on the freeway.

Part IV: The Part of Tens

We love to help you solve your problems in groups of ten. If you have 13 problems, you'll just have to wait for the next book to solve the last three. In this part, we provide ten steps to improve your diet and ten food substitutions that you can easily make within a recipe. You can explore ten strategies to normalize your blood glucose and ten ways to promote healthy eating in children.

Part V: Appendixes

Appendix A provides you with the restaurants that gave us many of the delicious recipes found in the book. You find out about their particular style of cooking and the chefs who make this possible. Appendix B contains exchange lists for the person with diabetes. In Appendix C you find a glossary of key cooking terms. Appendix D offers guidelines if you want to substitute other sweeteners for sugar, as well as cooking equivalents like how many tablespoons make up a cup. In Appendix E you find other resources in books and on the World Wide Web for recipes and nutritional information for people with diabetes.

Icons Used in This Book

The icons are like bookmarks, pointing out essential and nonessential information. You may adopt one particular icon, such as the Anecdote, and find it wherever it appears. The Anecdote icon points you to a lot of interesting stories about others with diabetes and how they cope with their diets. The icons used in this book include

We use this icon whenever we tell a story about our patients.

The Jargon Alert icon marks paragraphs where we define terms.

Whenever we want to emphasize the importance of the current information to your nutritional plan, we use this icon.

When you see the Remember icon, pay special attention because the information is essential.

This icon flags situations when you should see your doctor (for example, if your blood glucose level is too high or you need a particular test done).

This helpful Tip icon marks important information that can save you time and energy.

Watch for this icon; it warns about potential problems (for example, the possible results if you don't treat a condition).

Where to Go from Here

Where you go from here depends on your immediate needs. If you want an introduction to the place of nutrition in diabetes management, start with Chapter 1. If you are hungry and want some lunch, go to Chapter 8 or 9. If you are about to travel or eat out, head for Part III. At any time, the Part of Tens can provide useful tips for healthy eating. Finally, the Appendixes help you with cooking for yourself or choosing a restaurant. Feel free to jump around, but take the time to go through Part II so you will realize that diabetes and great food are not mutually exclusive.

Part I
Building a Healthy Lifestyle

"I forgot to time my insulin intake correctly, so if you don't mind, I'll just nibble on the centerpiece until dinner's served."

In this part . . .

Diabetes is a disease with which you can live. In this part, we show you not just how to live with diabetes, but how to thrive with diabetes. It requires that you think about every aspect of your lifestyle, and we try to cover all the issues. But it starts with the way you eat, because diet is central to a healthy lifestyle. We show you what to eat, how much to eat, and, especially, how to prepare your food so that the fact that you have diabetes doesn't prevent you from enjoying a variety of delicious cuisine.

Chapter 1

A Healthy Lifestyle for People with Diabetes

In This Chapter

- Defining diabetes
- Eating for health
- Exercising and resting
- Finding out about diabetes
- Controlling your glucose
- Keeping blood pressure normal
- Deciding whether to drink alcohol
- Staying away from illegal drugs
- Controlling other areas of your life

We now use the term *person with diabetes* rather than *diabetic* because we recognize that diabetes is only one small part of what makes up a complex human being. In this chapter, you find out how to manage most of the obstacles that diabetes brings to your lifestyle and also about some of the challenges that everyone faces. Don't focus on diabetes alone, risking sickness or death from some other source. That would be like the 70-year-old man who decided he wanted to live a long life. He started to diet and exercise and gave up smoking. He lost his potbelly, his body firmed up, and, finally, he bought a toupee to cover his bald scalp. Then he walked out in the street one day and was hit by a car. As he lay dying, he called, "God, how could you do this to me?" God replied, "To tell you the truth, I didn't recognize you."

Use this advice to bring your blood glucose under control and avoid diabetes complications, but don't neglect the rest of your lifestyle.

Understanding Diabetes

In order to put the place of diet into perspective, you need to understand what diabetes is all about. This section defines the different kinds of diabetes, provides some insight into how diabetes can damage your health, and introduces you to various treatments. Dr. Rubin's previous book, *Diabetes For Dummies* (published by IDG Books Worldwide, Inc.), provides this information in great detail. This section offers a much briefer introduction to the subject.

The diagnosis

A diagnosis of diabetes is made when blood tests show that the amount of glucose in your blood is above a particular level. The glucose level that warrants a diagnosis of diabetes has changed in the last few years and may change in the future as we in the field of medicine refine our understanding of this disease. For now, a diagnosis of diabetes is made if one of the following conditions is present:

- A *casual* (any time of day or night) blood glucose of 200 mg/dl or greater accompanied by some of these symptoms: fatigue; frequent urination and thirst; blurred vision; slow healing of skin, gums, and urinary infections; genital itching (particularly in women); and obesity
- A *fasting* (no food for eight hours) blood glucose of 126 mg/dl or greater
- A blood glucose of 200 mg/dl or greater two hours after consuming 75 grams of glucose

The term *mg/dl* is the abbreviation for *milligrams per deciliter* and describes how much glucose is present in a specific amount of blood. A reading of 70 to 140 mg/dl after eating is considered to be within the normal range. The mg/dl glucose measurement is used in the United States. Most of the rest of the world uses the International System (SI), in which the units are mmol/L (millimoles per liter). To find your mmol/L level, divide mg/dl by 18 (for example, 200 mg/dl is 11.1 mmol/L).

To make a diagnosis of diabetes, it's not enough for one of these conditions to be present on only one occasion. The same one or one of the other two conditions must be found another time.

Types of diabetes

There are two major types of diabetes:

- **Type 1 diabetes:** Once called *juvenile diabetes,* this disease usually begins in childhood and results from destruction of the cells of the pancreas that produce insulin. Insulin is the key chemical in the body responsible for getting glucose (blood sugar) into cells where it can be used for energy. Storage of food for energy depends on the presence of insulin.
- **Type 2 diabetes:** Formerly called *adult-onset diabetes,* this disease often begins in adults, usually after age 40. It results not from an absolute lack of insulin, like type 1, but from a resistance to the action of insulin, called *insulin resistance.* People with type 2 diabetes are often overweight, but this type can occur regardless of whether a person is overweight. The pancreas of people with type 2 diabetes often makes more than the normal amount of insulin to keep up with the demands of the body.

So the major difference between the two types is that no insulin is found in the body in type 1 diabetes, but a normal to increased amount of insulin is found in people with type 2 diabetes.

A less frequent but important type of diabetes is *gestational diabetes,* which occurs during pregnancy in women who didn't have diabetes before they became pregnant. This disease results when tissues associated with pregnancy make a large amount of different chemicals that oppose the action of insulin. Gestational diabetes is more like type 2 than type 1 diabetes. Gestational diabetes is important not just because it can lead to premature and difficult birth, but because a woman who has it is at higher risk of developing type 2 diabetes later in life. The diabetes generally disappears after the baby is born but can reappear during later pregnancies and even without a pregnancy.

Consequences of diabetes

Before insulin became available in 1922, people with type 1 diabetes rarely lived a normal life span. Unable to store fat or glucose, the diabetic body begins to break down its lean tissue, mostly muscle, and the person wastes away. Insulin was a lifesaver, but its properties allowed people to live long enough to suffer the consequences of untreated high blood glucose. These consequences are divided into three major groups: the irritations of diabetes, the short-term complications of diabetes, and the long-term complications. All three sets of problems may occur in type 1 or type 2 diabetes, although the short-term complications are more severe in type 1, resulting from the total lack of insulin.

Irritations of diabetes

The irritations of diabetes are the signs and symptoms that accompany a high blood glucose level. The glucose level is not high enough to be life-threatening, but it definitely affects the lifestyle of the person with diabetes.

These irritations may be so mild that they aren't even thought of as signs or symptoms of a disease. The most important of these irritations include the following:

- Blurred vision
- Fatigue
- Frequent urination and thirst
- Genital itching, particularly in women
- Gum and urinary infections
- Obesity
- Slow healing of skin

Short-term complications

Among the short-term complications are

- **Ketoacidosis:** Insulin is the key that permits glucose to enter cells. If you lack insulin, your cells can't use glucose for energy, so you begin to burn body fat instead. The process of breaking down fat for energy creates *ketones*. The accumulation of large amounts of ketones makes the blood acidic. Ketoacidosis happens in type 1 diabetes but rarely in type 2.
- **Hyperosmolar syndrome:** Because of advanced age or other factors, your kidneys may have trouble removing glucose from your body. If you happen to lose a large amount of fluid due to sickness or neglect, your blood volume decreases, which makes it even harder for your kidneys to remove glucose. Your blood glucose level can skyrocket. Eventually, the level of blood glucose becomes so high that the blood is like syrup. This complication happens in type 2 diabetes when severe dehydration is present.
- **Hypoglycemia or low blood glucose:** This complication results from excessive treatment with agents that lower blood glucose levels, not eating enough when these agents are used, or excessive exercise.

Long-term complications

People who have any type of diabetes are subject to long-term complications. These complications are broken down into two groups: *microvascular* (small blood vessels) and *macrovascular* (large blood vessels).

The microvascular complications include

- **Diabetic retinopathy:** Eye damage that can lead to blindness if untreated
- **Diabetic nephropathy:** Kidney damage that can lead to kidney failure if not treated
- **Diabetic neuropathy:** Nerve damage resulting in many different symptoms, the most common of which is loss of sensation, tingling, and numbness in the feet and hands

The macrovascular complications consist of

- **Arteriosclerotic heart disease:** The blood vessels that supply blood to heart tissue are blocked. This is the most common cause of death in people with diabetes, just as it is in people who do not have diabetes.
- **Arteriosclerotic cerebrovascular disease:** The arteries to the brain are blocked, leading to stroke or sometimes loss of intellectual function.
- **Arteriosclerotic peripheral vascular disease (PVD):** The arteries that carry blood to the legs become narrowed or clogged. If blood flow ceases completely, amputation may be necessary.

Treatment of diabetes

Three measures form the foundation for the treatment of diabetes and the prevention of complications. All three are directed toward keeping the blood glucose as close to normal as possible without going too low. They include

- Diet
- Exercise
- Medication

This book is all about the place of diet in the management of diabetes. *Diabetes For Dummies* covers the subjects of exercise and medication extensively.

Eating in Moderation

Just as the three most important factors in the value of a house are location, location, and location, the three most important factors in diet for people with diabetes are moderation, moderation, and moderation. The majority of people who develop type 2 diabetes are either overweight or obese. If these people were able to reduce their weight, in most cases their blood glucose levels would return to normal, and they wouldn't suffer the irritations or complications we describe in the preceding section. This weight loss requires a significant reduction in intake of calories. Unfortunately, this moderation in calorie intake doesn't happen often enough and especially not in restaurants. Many European chefs who work in the United States are amazed at the amount of food U.S. customers expect on their plates. In Europe, by contrast, the portions are much smaller. This cultural difference explains, at least in part, the increasing incidence of obesity in the United States.

A key to eating in moderation is monitoring your portion sizes. If you can't weigh each serving (for example, if you are in a restaurant), then eyeball the food and compare it with the amount you know to be an average portion, or plan to eat only half of everything and take the rest home. The following are the approximate sizes for various portions:

- An ounce of meat is the size of a matchbox.
- 3 ounces of meat is the size of a deck of cards.
- A medium fruit is the size of a tennis ball.
- A medium potato is the size of a computer mouse.
- A bagel is the size of a hockey puck.
- An ounce of cheese is the size of a domino.
- A cup of fruit is the size of a baseball.
- A cup of broccoli is the size of a light bulb.

Try to visualize these sizes and compare them with the amounts you usually eat. Even better, weigh or measure your food several times until you are confident that you can eyeball a serving of each of the foods you most often eat. Then compare those serving sizes to the serving sizes that you get in a restaurant, as we have done in Figure 1-1. You will be amazed at how much larger the portions in the restaurant are than you are supposed to eat. No wonder you may be gaining weight.

Figure 1-1: Eating in moderation means the portion sizes on the left, rather than the portions on the right.

Getting Your Exercise (But Don't Forget to Rest)

Exercise plays a huge role in maintaining a healthy lifestyle for anyone, not just a person with diabetes. For a person with diabetes, it is especially important because diabetes is associated with a higher incidence of coronary heart disease, not to mention strokes and disease of the blood vessels of the legs. Exercise protects against these problems while it lowers blood glucose to prevent the complications of eye disease, nerve disease, and kidney disease.

An exercise program doesn't need to be extremely strenuous. The best program is one that is done every day for 20 to 30 minutes. Brisk walking at 3 to 4 miles per hour is moderate exercise that almost anyone can do. Check out *Fitness Walking For Dummies* for a thorough discussion of the way to achieve fitness by walking. Dr. Rubin's previous book, *Diabetes For Dummies,* and many others can give you more information about checking your body's response to exercise and deciding which exercise to choose.

TIP

Unless you're a self-starter, having an exercise partner may be helpful; making a commitment to a partner forces you to show up.

People who exercise usually do aerobic exercise, which makes the heart beat faster, but few people combine this activity with muscle-maintaining exercise. A workout with light weights three times a week strengthens your arms and back. Three or four different types of exercises will involve different muscle groups. You will increase your stamina as well as develop and maintain a larger mass of tissue to take up and lower your blood glucose. A larger muscle mass also helps your body burn more calories.

Also keep in mind that rest is a very important component of a healthy lifestyle. The body needs seven to eight hours of sleep a night, and a "power nap" in the afternoon isn't a bad idea.

Continuing to Educate Yourself

The pace of advances in diabetes is amazingly rapid at the beginning of the 21st century. You certainly don't want to miss out on a development that can make a big difference in the way that diabetes affects you. For this reason, continuing to educate yourself about every aspect of diabetes is essential. You can pursue information in many ways:

- **Take a course from a certified diabetes educator.** This class can provide you with the information you must know to manage your disease right now. You can also find out about some of the newer drugs and treatments that are on the near horizon.

- **Find ongoing sources of information about diabetes.** An example is the publication of the American Diabetes Association, *Diabetes Forecast.* The association publishes this resource every month, offering useful information for managing diabetes as well as articles about future advances. You can call the ADA at 1-800-DIABETES (342-2383) or find their excellent Web site at www.diabetes.org.

  TIP

  Don't neglect the World Wide Web, which is overflowing with information about every aspect of diabetes. Unfortunately, the Web also contains a lot of wrong information. Appendix C in *Diabetes For Dummies* covers the "reliable" sites on the Web. That appendix also explains how to tell the difference between a site you can trust and one you can't. Or you can go to Dr. Rubin's Web site, drrubin.com, and link from there to some of the best sources of information about diabetes.

- **After a few years of diabetes, go back and take a refresher course.** The pace of advances is so great that most of the material will be new.

REMEMBER

All the people you work with to control your diabetes, from the dietitian to the physician who is a diabetes specialist, can also answer many of your questions.

Controlling Your Glucose

Glucose is the form of sugar that is present in the blood. You can find a thorough discussion of the role of glucose in *Diabetes For Dummies.* Studies of type 1 and type 2 diabetes have shown conclusively that controlling blood glucose prevents the long-term complications of diabetes, especially eye disease, kidney disease, and nerve disease. If the complications have begun already, then blood glucose control slows them down significantly.

Blood glucose control is accomplished by balancing diet, exercise, and medication (if necessary). Any way that you can lower blood glucose helps, and one medication may not be better than any other as long as the result lowers the average blood glucose as shown by the *hemoglobin A1c test.* This is a test that indicates the overall control of the blood glucose for the last 60 to 90 days.

REMEMBER

If you are put on medication for your diabetes, take it as your doctor recommends. Many people with diabetes make the mistake of reducing or stopping medication — which is successfully controlling their disease — when they begin to see much better glucose values with self-testing of blood glucose. The medication is controlling the blood glucose. Without it, control deteriorates and complications develop.

This book focuses on the place of diet in your glucose control, but other strategies such as exercise and medications should also be incorporated into management of your diabetes.

Keeping Your Blood Pressure in the Safe Range

The United Kingdom Prospective Diabetes Study was a major study of how controlling blood glucose levels would affect the complications of diabetes, particularly the long-term complications that we describe in the section, "Consequences of diabetes," earlier in this chapter. At the same time, it looked at the effect of controlling blood pressure on these same complications. Since the United Kingdom Prospective Diabetes Study was published in 1998, we know, for certain, the benefit of lowering blood pressure to prevent long-term complications of diabetes (such as eye disease, kidney disease, nerve disease, coronary artery disease, and stroke). Coronary artery disease and stroke don't seem to respond to improved blood glucose control as much as they do to improved blood pressure control.

Losing weight usually lowers high blood pressure, but if shedding pounds isn't necessary for you or if you are unable to lose weight, antihypertensive drugs may be the answer.

If high blood pressure is your problem, one class of drugs called ACE inhibitors may be the best choice for you with your diabetes. *ACE inhibitors* (angiotensin converting enzyme inhibitors) protect the kidneys while they lower blood pressure. Discuss this option with your doctor.

Deciding Whether to Enjoy Alcohol with Your Food

A little wine with your meal can be a very pleasant addition. Sharing wine with others is certainly a social custom, and studies have shown that a little alcohol can greatly reduce the risk of a heart attack. This effect is even more helpful for the person with diabetes. But alcohol lowers blood glucose. A person who is already taking a glucose-lowering medication can have severe low blood glucose if he or she drinks alcohol without eating food.

Never drink alcohol without food, especially if you are taking a glucose-lowering medication.

A little wine means two 4-ounce glasses for a man or one 4-ounce glass for a woman. Men metabolize alcohol more rapidly than women, and that is the reason for the difference. A 12-ounce bottle of light beer or 1½ ounces of gin,

How alcohol helps heart disease

When taken in moderation, alcohol has a number of effects that help prevent heart disease and heart attacks. Alcohol can

- Decrease insulin resistance
- Increase the level of the good cholesterol, called HDL cholesterol
- Decrease the tendency of blood platelets to form clots that block arteries in the heart
- Increase the tendency of chemicals in the blood to break down clots that form

rum, vodka, or whiskey is the same as a glass of wine in terms of alcohol content. Any one of these choices is considered equal to two fat exchanges (see Appendix B) and contains about 100 *kilocalories* (see the nearby sidebar, "Kilocalories versus calories"). Regular beer has an additional carbohydrate exchange and provides 150 kilocalories. If you have questions about alcohol and your diabetes, contact your physician or dietitian.

If you add mixes such as juice, soda, tonic water, and so forth to your alcohol, you're probably getting much more sugar, unless you add club soda or some other mix that contains no calories.

Remember that alcohol has no nutritional value. It provides no vitamins, minerals, or other important nutrients. The term *empty calories* applies very well here. In addition, if you have never been a drinker, don't interpret this information as a suggestion to start drinking. Alcohol use may not fit your lifestyle.

Of course, drinking too much alcohol is associated with liver disease and raises your blood pressure as well as worsens diabetic neuropathy. Alcohol is also highly addictive. These may be key reasons not to begin using alcohol.

Avoiding Illicit Drugs

Your life is challenging enough already just dealing with diabetes. You don't want to add the problems of illicit drugs to the mixture. Some illegal drugs interact with diabetes medications, causing either hypoglycemia or hyperglycemia. Intravenous illegal drugs may lead to infections, hepatitis, and even AIDS. During the time you are affected by the drug, you are certainly not able to properly manage your diabetes. Get your high by exercising or by losing weight (if you are overweight). These strategies help improve your diabetes while making you feel better in general.

Kilocalories versus calories

We use the term *kilocalories* (or *kcalories*) rather than *calories* because experts in health and medicine measure energy in a diet plan or in food in kilocalories (a kilocalorie is 1,000 times greater than a calorie). Unfortunately, the term *calories* has been established on food labels and in diets, and health officials don't want to confuse the public by attempting to correct this error.

Calorie counts in the text of this book and in the nutritional analyses of the recipes are given in kilocalories.

Paying Attention to the Rest of Your Lifestyle

Your diabetes is just one aspect of your life, although it certainly has a major effect upon your lifestyle. In this section, we discuss some of the other features that make up your lifestyle and how they affect your diabetes. Some you can change and some are fixed, but all determine the quality and the length of your life.

Avoiding tobacco

Whether you smoke it, chew it, or inhale it because someone else is using it, tobacco shortens your life and makes you a prime candidate for many different kinds of cancer. There is nothing positive about using tobacco. It stains your teeth and fingers, gives you horrible breath, and ruins your health, all for just a few dollars a day. If you have diabetes, you run the risk of amputations of your feet and legs by promoting closure of your arteries — just for the sake of a few puffs. Give it up, now!

Driving safely

If you're taking drugs such as the sulfonylureas or insulin, which can lower blood glucose to dangerous levels, test your blood glucose before driving, and raise it to normal before getting behind the wheel. You can't know exactly what your glucose level is without testing. Try guessing your blood glucose and then testing it, and you'll see what we mean. Always carry a source of carbohydrate such as food or glucose tablets in your vehicle to treat low blood glucose.

Wear a seat belt when you drive. It really will prevent major injury if you get into an accident. Of course, you'll be driving no faster than the speed limit, so there's less chance of an accident, but it's the other driver we're concerned about. You can't be sure what he or she is going to do.

Benefiting from relationships

Studies clearly show that people in relationships live longer than solitary individuals. This connection has definitely been established for people with diabetes. Your loved one can help set an example of good eating. He or she can be your exercise partner. And on those rare occasions when you are hypoglycemic and can't help yourself, your loved one is there to help you.

Relationships also help cushion another major life stress: financial difficulties. Your spouse or significant other may be able to keep earning even when you can't.

People who participate in social group activities benefit from the interactions, whether in church, on a ball team, or in a book group. Friends can take much of the stresses out of your daily life.

You may want to join a diabetes support group, both for the friendships you'll make and the information you'll discover.

Keeping your sense of humor

Finding humor in your life will certainly make the inconveniences and complications associated with diabetes much more easy to bear. Norman Cousins, the author of several books on the subject of the healing power of humor, was able to reverse an incurable disease by exposing himself to all kinds of funny experiences.

Plenty of funny things happen in your life all the time. You just have to recognize and appreciate them. If you have trouble finding humor in your life, rent some of the old Marx Brothers videotapes. If they don't do it for you, find something that does.

Dr. Rubin went to a conference on humor recently. The speaker asked each participant to write down the name of his or her favorite comedian. Then the group mingled and shared their selections. Everyone was amazed to find out how many different choices people came up with. Just as there's a man for every woman (or a significant other, to be completely politically correct), there's a comedian for every person. Find the one who makes you smile and laugh and get as much of his or her written and performance material as you can find. When you feel low, read it or watch it.

Chapter 2

The Importance of What, When, and How Much You Eat in Managing Diabetes

In This Chapter

- Starting with total kilocalories
- Coping with carbohydrates
- Selecting protein
- Cutting the fat in your diet
- Eating enough micronutrients (vitamins and minerals)
- Timing your food

In the United Kingdom Prospective Diabetes Study, doctors were able to lower the average hemoglobin A1c test result from 7.9 percent to 7 percent. (The hemoglobin A1c test shows the average amount of glucose in your blood over the last three months.) The people with the lower hemoglobin A1c experienced 25 percent fewer complications than those with higher A1c levels. Doctors know that a careful diet can lower the hemoglobin A1c by more than 1 percent. Therefore, diet can play a major role in prevention of complications.

This chapter tells you how much to eat, what to eat, and when to eat. Because most people with diabetes are overweight, we provide advice about losing some weight. One bit of advice right now: Don't go on a crash diet; you'll come out looking like a wreck. And don't go to a paint store and expect to get thinner there. If you are thick and tired of it, this chapter is for you.

Counting Calories

The first thing you need to know when you plan your diet is how much you should be eating. To find out how many *kilocalories* (commonly called *calories;* see Chapter 1) you need, you have to do a little math. For a man, use 106 pounds for 5 feet of height plus 6 pounds for each inch over 5 feet. Therefore a 5-foot, 4-inch man should weigh about 130 pounds, and a 5-foot, 7-inch man should weigh about 150 pounds. For a woman, the figures are 100 pounds for 5 feet of height plus 5 pounds for each inch over 5 feet. So a 5-foot, 6-inch woman should, ideally, weigh 130 pounds.

REMEMBER

Ideal body weights may not be "reasonable" weight goals for many overweight and obese individuals. Weight goals must be individualized.

To find your *basal,* or minimum, calorie needs, multiply your ideal weight by 10. A woman with an ideal weight of 130 pounds needs at least 1,300 kilocalories. Then add calories for activity. A person who doesn't exercise needs about 10 percent more kilocalories for activity. A person doing moderate exercise needs 20 percent more kilocalories, and a person doing heavy exercise or work may need 40 percent more kilocalories or even more. This woman would then need 1,430 kilocalories, 1,560 kilocalories, or 1,820 kilocalories or more, depending on her level of activity.

TIP

People with special needs, such as pregnant and nursing mothers, need even more kilocalories, and people trying to lose weight need to reduce their daily calorie intake to accomplish this goal.

After you know your total calorie intake objective, break it down into the three sources of energy: carbohydrates, protein, and fat.

Calculating Carbohydrates — Precursors of Glucose

When you eat a meal, the immediate source of glucose in your blood comes from the carbohydrates in that meal. One group of carbohydrates is the starches, such as cereals, grains, pastas, breads, crackers, starchy vegetables, beans, peas, and lentils. Fruits make up a second major source of carbohydrate. Milk and milk products contain not only carbohydrate but also protein and a variable amount of fat, depending on whether the milk is whole, lowfat, or fat-free. Other sources of carbohydrate include cakes, cookies, candies, sweetened beverages, and ice cream. These foods also contain a variable amount of fat.

To determine what else is found in food, check a source such as *The Official Pocket Guide to Diabetic Exchanges,* published by the American Diabetes Association and the American Dietetic Association, or *The Diabetes Carbohydrate and Fat Gram Guide,* also published by the ADA.

How much carbohydrate should you have in your diet? At one time, experts prescribed exact percentages of carbohydrate, protein, and fat calories in the daily diet. Now, we are much more flexible and allow the percentage of carbohydrate to vary. In our own experience, we have found that patients who keep their carbohydrate intake to around 40 percent of calories consumed have less trouble controlling their blood glucose levels and maintaining lower levels of blood fats, so we generally recommend this amount to our patients. Your registered dietitian may recommend more. We wouldn't argue as long as you can maintain satisfactory blood glucose levels while not increasing the level of *triglyceride,* a blood fat.

The various carbohydrate sources differ in the degree to which they raise the blood glucose. This difference is called the *glycemic index,* and it refers to the glucose-raising power of a food compared with white bread. In general, choose foods with a lower glycemic index in order to keep the rise in blood glucose to a minimum. Carbohydrate sources that have lower glycemic indexes are foods such as whole grain breads, unrefined cereals (such as oats), and basmati rice. Cookies, cakes, and muffins made with fruits and whole grains tend to have a lower glycemic index as well.

Many of these lower glycemic index foods contain a lot of fiber. Fiber is a carbohydrate that can't be broken down by digestive enzymes, so it doesn't raise blood glucose and adds no calories.

If a food has a lot of fiber in it (more than 5 grams per serving), you can subtract the grams of fiber from the number of carbohydrates in that food.

The best sources of fiber are fruits, grains, and vegetables. Animal food sources don't provide fiber.

Fiber can be present in two forms:

- **Insoluble:** It doesn't dissolve in water but stays in the intestine as *roughage,* which helps to prevent constipation; for example, fiber found in whole grain breads and cereals, and the skin of fruits and vegetables.
- **Soluble:** It dissolves in water and enters the blood, where it helps lower glucose and cholesterol; for example, fiber found in barley, brown rice, and beans, as well as vegetables and fruits.

TIP

For years, doctors told their patients with diabetes not to eat sugar. Now we know that many foods, such as corn and potatoes, raise blood glucose just as fast as table sugar, and we would never ban those foods. The recommendations have changed. You can take a spoonful of sugar in your coffee and have a little sugar in your food, but be aware of the number of calories you are adding.

Getting Enough Protein (Not Just from Meat)

Protein comes from meat, fish, poultry, milk, and cheese. It can also be found in beans, peas, and lentils, which we mention in the carbohydrate discussion in the preceding section. Meat sources of protein can be low or very high in fat, depending on the source. Because we are trying to keep the fat content of our diets fairly low, lowfat sources of protein, such as skinless white meat chicken or turkey, flounder or halibut, and fat-free cheese are preferred. Beans, peas, and lentils, which can be very good sources of protein, don't contain fat but do contain carbohydrate.

How much protein should you eat? We recommend that 40 percent of your calories should be carbohydrate, and in the next section, we suggest that you limit your fat intake to 30 percent of your calories. The remaining 30 percent is protein.

Protein doesn't cause an immediate rise in blood glucose, but it can raise glucose levels several hours later, after your liver processes the protein and converts some of it into glucose. Therefore, protein isn't a good choice if you want to treat low blood glucose, but a snack containing protein at bedtime may help prevent low blood glucose during the night.

Focusing on Fat

These days, just about everyone knows his or her cholesterol level. If you have ever had blood tests ordered by a doctor, the chances are good that a cholesterol check was part of that chemical profile. You can also have a cholesterol reading performed at a local health fair. You usually find out your total cholesterol level, a combination of so-called good cholesterol and bad cholesterol. If your total is high, much of that cholesterol may be the good kind — *HDL (high-density lipoprotein) cholesterol*. If you're interested in knowing the balance between good and bad cholesterol in your body, talk with your medical practitioner, who may recommend a lipid panel that delivers more details.

The Framingham Study, an ongoing study of the health of the citizens of Framingham, Massachusetts, has shown that the total cholesterol amount divided by the good cholesterol figure gives a number that is a reasonable measure of the risk of a heart attack. People who had results that were less than 4.5 were at lower risk of heart attacks, while those with results of more that 4.5 were at higher risk. The risk increases as the number rises.

WARNING!

Most foods don't contain much cholesterol — with the exception of eggs. The daily recommendation for cholesterol is less than 300 milligrams, and one egg almost reaches that level. Some doctors say that eating an egg two or three times a week won't hurt you, but this isn't true if you have diabetes. Avoid eggs and foods such as organ meats that are high in cholesterol. But just as important is avoiding saturated fat, the fat you see on fatty meats, dairy fats, and some processed foods. Always cut away visible fat from meat and use lowfat or fat-free dairy products and processed foods.

Fat has concentrated calories, so don't eat too much fat in your diet. However, monounsaturated fats seem to protect against heart disease. The best examples of monounsaturated fats are canola oil and olive oil. The increased intake of olive oil by people living around the Mediterranean Sea may be the reason for their lower incidence of heart disease.

Although vegetable sources of fat are generally better than animal sources, the exceptions are palm oil and coconut oil, which are highly saturated fats.

NUTRITION SPEAK

Here's our bottom line recommendation: No more than 30 percent of your kilocalories should come from fat, and of that, no more than a third should come from saturated fats. For a person eating 1,500 kilocalories a day, this recommendation would mean 450 kilocalories from fat, and 150 of those kilocalories from saturated fat.

TIP

Use vegetable oils, preferably canola oil and olive oil, as your primary sources of fat, because these lower cholesterol.

You, like many people, may be concerned about the fat in your diet, and it may be worthwhile to understand the government definitions for words describing the amounts of fat in various foods.

JARGON ALERT

Here are the definitions:

- **Fat-free:** Less than 0.5 grams of fat per serving
- **Lowfat:** Less than 3 grams of fat per serving
- **Reduced fat:** 25 percent less fat when compared with a similar food
- **Lean meat:** Less than 10 grams of fat, less than 4 grams of saturated fat, and less than 95 milligrams of cholesterol per serving
- **Low saturated fat:** 1 gram or less of saturated fat and no more than 15 percent of calories from saturated fat

- **Cholesterol-free:** Less than 2 milligrams of cholesterol per serving or 2 grams or less of saturated fat per serving
- **Low cholesterol:** Less than 20 milligrams of cholesterol or less than 2 grams of saturated fat per serving
- **Reduced cholesterol:** At least 25 percent less cholesterol compared to a similar food and 2 grams or less of saturated fat

Trying to understand these definitions gets complicated. Save yourself the trouble and choose fish or poultry as your source of protein in order to avoid consuming too much fat along with your protein. If you remove the skin from chicken, you'll get little fat. Fish actually has certain fatty acids that lower cholesterol.

There's a little danger in eating too much salmon, however. One man ate so many salmon croquettes, salmon steaks, and salmon salads that he had to fight the urge to go north and spawn.

Figuring Out Your Diet

After you know how much to eat of each energy source (carbohydrate, fat, and protein), how do you translate this into actual foods? You can use three basic approaches. In this section, we describe each one.

Using the food guide pyramid

The federal government, with the assistance of many experts, has come up with a simple way for you to eat a good, balanced diet: the food guide pyramid (see Figure 2-1).

The food guide pyramid presents all your food choices. The foods that should be eaten the most are at the base of the pyramid, and it rises to a point because you should eat less of the foods higher in the pyramid. For example, you should eat 6 to 11 servings of grains, beans, and starchy vegetables every day but only 3 to 5 servings of other vegetables and 2 to 4 servings of fruits. You should eat about the same number of servings, 2 to 3, of milk as you eat of meat. Eat only small amounts of fats, sweets, and alcohol.

NUTRITION SPEAK

The key to using the food guide pyramid is to know what a food serving really represents. Here are the serving sizes referred to in the food guide pyramid:

- **Bread, cereal, rice, and pasta:** A serving is 1 slice of bread; or 1 ounce of ready-to-eat cereal; or ½ cup of cooked cereal, rice, or pasta.
- **Fruit:** A serving is 1 medium apple, banana, or orange; or ½ cup of chopped cooked or canned fruit; or ¾ cup of fruit juice.

- **Vegetables:** A serving is 1 cup of raw leafy vegetables; or ½ cup of other vegetables, cooked or chopped raw; or ¾ cup of vegetable juice.
- **Meat, poultry, fish, dry beans, eggs, and nuts:** A serving is 2 to 3 ounces of cooked lean meat, poultry, or fish; or ½ cup of cooked dry beans; or 1 egg. Two tablespoons of peanut butter count as 1 ounce of meat.
- **Milk, yogurt, and cheese:** A serving is 1 cup of milk or yogurt, or 1½ ounces of natural cheese, or 2 ounces of processed cheese.

Notice that the food guide pyramid permits an egg, which is not recommended on a daily basis for people with diabetes.

The food guide pyramid is probably a good tool for a person with type 2 diabetes who doesn't tend to gain weight, but the person with type 1 diabetes or the person who is obese with type 2 diabetes needs to know the specific number of calories and particularly the carbohydrate calories that he or she is eating. That's the reason we provide information about diabetic exchanges and carbohydrate counting in the next sections.

For more information on the food guide pyramid, go to the government's official Web site at `www.nal.usda.gov:8001/py/pmap.htm` or check the ADA publication, *Diabetes Meal Planning Made Easy: How to Put the Food Pyramid to Work for Your Busy Lifestyle.*

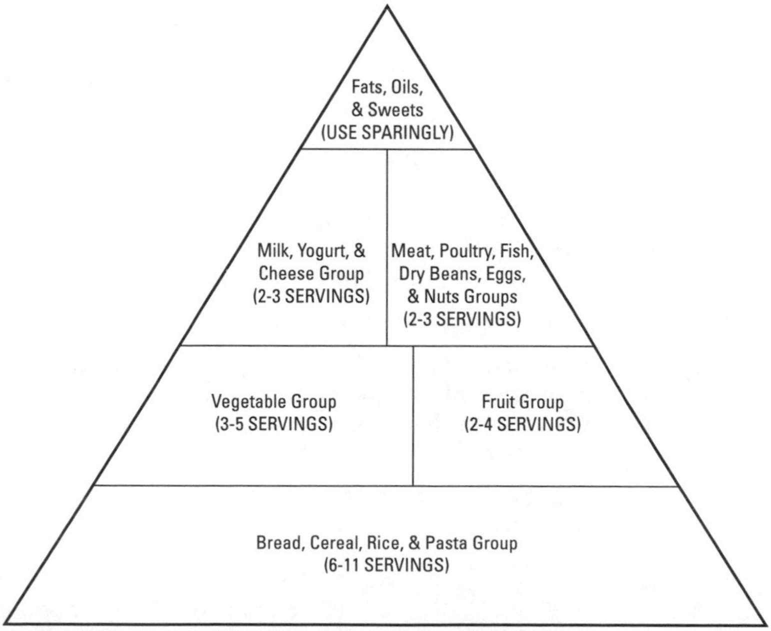

Figure 2-1: The government food guide pyramid.

Source: U.S. Department of Agriculture/U.S. Department of Health and Human Services

Working with diabetic exchanges

Despite the huge variety of foods that you can make from the various ingredients available, all foods can be placed in one of several *exchange* groupings so that a given quantity of that food has approximately the same calorie count and content of carbohydrate, protein, and/or fat. For example, ½ small bagel can replace 1 slice of bread, ½ hot dog bun, 1 small roll, a 6-inch tortilla, or ½ cup of bran cereal. In Appendix B, all foods that contain the same kilocalorie count coming from the same amounts of carbohydrate, protein, and fat are shown in the various exchange lists.

The exchange lists consist of starches, fruits, milks, other carbohydrates, vegetables, meats and meat substitutes, fats, and *free foods,* those that contain no calories and can be eaten "freely." When you know how many calories of each energy source you can eat, you can create a diet for yourself. Because balancing all the information — and the foodstuffs — may be complicated, you probably will want the help of a dietitian.

Using the percentages we offer in the preceding sections, here's how the exchange system works for a man who should eat 1,800 kilocalories per day:

- **Carbohydrate:** He can eat 40 percent of his kilocalories as carbohydrate, which gives him around 720 kilocalories of carbohydrate. Because each gram of carbohydrate is 4 kilocalories, he can eat 180 grams of carbohydrate. As you can see in the Appendix B exchange lists, one exchange of carbohydrate is 15 grams, so he can eat 12 carbohydrate exchanges in a day.

  Carbohydrate is found in milk, fruit, starch, vegetable, and other carbohydrate groups.

- **Protein:** He can eat 30 percent of his diet, or 540 kilocalories, as protein. A gram of protein is 4 kilocalories, so he can eat 135 grams of protein. Each meat or meat substitute exchange has 7 grams of protein in it. Therefore, he can eat about 19 protein exhanges each day, which corresponds to about 19 ounces of protein daily.

  Protein is found not just in meat but in milk, starch, and some vegetables.

- **Fat:** He can eat no more than 30 percent, or 540 kilocalories, of fat per day. A gram of fat is 9 kilocalories, so he can eat no more than 60 grams of fat per day. A fat exchange is 5 grams of fat, so he can eat 12 fat exchanges in a day.

  Fat is found in milk, meat, and the other carbohydrate groups as well as pure fats like butter.

Table 2-1 provides a visual perspective of this 1,800-kilocalorie per-day diet and its exchange system particulars.

Table 2-1 Exchange System for 1,800-Kilocalories Per Day

Energy Source	*Percent of Daily Diet*	*Daily Amount of Kcalories*	*Kcalories Per Gram*	*Total Grams Per Day*	*Grams in One Exchange*	*Number of Exchanges Per Day*
Carbo-hydrate	40%	720	4	180	15 grams	12
Protein	30%	540	4	135	7	19
Fat	30%	540	9	60	5 grams	12

The following sample of an 1,800-calorie diet shows proportions of 40 percent carbohydrate, 30 percent protein, and 30 percent fat.

Breakfast:

1 fruit exchange

1 starch exchange

1 medium-fat meat exchange

2 fat exchanges

1 lowfat milk exchange

Lunch:

3 lean-meat exchanges

1 vegetable exchange

2 fat exchanges

2 starch exchanges

2 fruit exchanges

½ lowfat milk exchange

Dinner:

4 lean-meat exchanges

2 starch exchanges

2 vegetable exchanges

1 fruit exchange

3 fat exchanges

Snack:

2 starch exchanges

2 lean-meat exchanges

½ lowfat milk exchange

Using the exchange lists in Appendix B, you can figure exchanges by the food it represents. For example, the fruit exchange for breakfast could be ½ grapefruit, ⅓ small cantaloupe, or ½ glass of fruit juice. The four lean-meat exchanges for dinner could be 4 ounces of tuna, or 4 ounces of dark meat turkey or chicken, or 1 cup of cottage cheese.

REMEMBER

This technique of creating a diet gives you an infinite variety. In the second part of the book, where we show you actual recipes, we break down the recipes into food exchanges so that you can fit them into your exchange plan. Remember that you can take exchanges from one meal and move them to another so that a recipe that doesn't fit into a single meal can borrow some exchanges from other times of day. This approach makes for a very flexible diet program.

Counting carbohydrates and constant carbohydrates

SEE YOUR DOCTOR

People with type 1 diabetes and those with type 2 diabetes who take insulin may find the technique of counting carbohydrates to be the easiest for them. You still need to know how much carbohydrate you should eat in a given day. You divide the total into the meals and snacks that you eat and then, with the help of your doctor or certified diabetes educator, you determine your short-acting insulin needs based upon that amount of carbohydrates and the blood glucose that you measure before that meal.

For example, suppose that a person with diabetes is about to have a breakfast containing 60 grams of carbohydrate. He has found that each unit of lispro insulin controls about 20 grams of carbohydrate intake in his body. Figuring the proper amount of short-acting insulin can be accomplished by a process of trial and error: knowing the amount of carbohydrate intake and determining how many units are needed to keep the blood glucose level about the same after eating the carbohydrate as it was before. (The number of carbohydrate grams that each unit of insulin can control differs for each individual, and another person might control only 15 grams per unit.)

In this example, the person's measured blood glucose is 150 mg/dl (milligrams per deciliter). This result is about 50 mg/dl higher than he wants it to be. He knows that he can lower his blood glucose by 50 mg/dl for every unit of insulin he takes. Therefore, he needs 3 units of lispro for the carbohydrate intake and 1 unit for the elevated blood glucose for a total of 4 units. For more information on lispro and other types of insulin, see *Diabetes For Dummies* (IDG Books Worldwide, Inc.) by Dr. Rubin, one of the authors of this book.

He has a morning that is more active than he expected. When lunchtime comes, his blood glucose is down to 60 mg/dl. He's about to eat a lunch containing 75 grams of carbohydrate. He takes 4 units of lispro for the food but reduces it by 1 unit to a total of 3 units because his blood glucose is low.

At dinner, he is eating 45 grams of carbohydrate. His blood glucose is 115 mg/dl. He takes 2 units of lispro for the food intake and needs no change for the blood glucose, so he takes only 2 units.

TIP

There are two keys to making carbohydrate counting successful:

- You must have an accurate knowledge of the grams of carbohydrate in the food you are about to eat and how many units of insulin you need for a given number of grams of carbohydrate.
- You must measure your blood glucose and know how your body responds to each unit of insulin.

TIP

For more information on determining individual insulin sensitivity, consult *Diabetes For Dummies.*

JARGON ALERT

This calculation can be made a little easier by using *constant carbohydrates,* which means that you try to choose carbohydrates so that you are eating about the same amount at every meal and snack. This approach makes determining proper amounts of insulin less tricky; just add or subtract units based upon your blood glucose level before that meal. A few sessions with your physician or a certified diabetes educator can help you gain comfort with counting carbohydrates.

Monitoring Your Micronutrients

Food contains a lot more than just carbohydrate, protein, and fat. Most of the other components are *micronutrients* (present in tiny or micro quantities), and they are essential for maintaining the health of human beings. Examples of micronutrients include vitamins (such as vitamin C and vitamin K) and minerals (such as calcium, magnesium, and iron). Most micronutrients are needed in such small amounts that it's extremely unlikely that you would ever suffer a deficiency of them. A person who eats a balanced diet by using the pyramid technique or the exchange technique doesn't have to worry about getting sufficient quantities of micronutrients — with a few exceptions, which follow:

- Adults need to be sure to take in at least 1,000 milligrams of calcium each day. If you are a young person still growing, you are pregnant, or you are elderly, you need 1,500 milligrams daily.
- Some menstruating women lose more iron than their bodies can spare and need to take iron supplements.
- You probably take in 20 to 40 times more salt (sodium) than you need and would be better off leaving added salt out of your diet.

For more information on micronutrients, check out *Diabetes For Dummies.*

Recognizing the Importance of Timing of Food and Medication

SEE YOUR DOCTOR

If you take insulin, the peak of your insulin activity should correspond with the greatest availability of glucose in your blood. To accomplish this, you need to know the time when your insulin is most active, how long it lasts, and when it is no longer active.

- *Regular insulin,* which has been around for decades, takes 30 minutes to start to lower the glucose level, peaks at 3 hours, and is gone by 6 to 8 hours. This insulin is used before meals to keep glucose low until the next meal. The problem with regular insulin has always been that you have to take it 30 minutes before you eat or run the risk of becoming hypoglycemic at first, and hyperglycemic later when the insulin is no longer around but your food is providing glucose.

- *Rapid-acting lispro insulin* is the newest preparation and the shortest acting. Lispro insulin begins to lower the glucose level within 5 minutes after its administration, peaks at about 1 hour, and is no longer active by about 3 hours. Lispro is a great advance because it frees the person with diabetes to take a shot only when he or she eats. Because its activity begins and ends so quickly, lispro doesn't cause hypoglycemia as often as the older preparation.

Given a choice, because of its rapid onset and fall-off in activity, we recommend lispro as the short-acting insulin of choice for people with type 1 diabetes and those with type 2 diabetes who take insulin.

If you are going out to eat, you rarely know when the food will be served. Using lispro, you can measure your blood glucose when the food arrives and take an immediate shot. This preparation really frees you to take insulin when you need it. It adds a level of flexibility to your schedule that didn't exist before.

If you take regular insulin, keep to a more regular schedule of eating. Most people who take insulin rely on an intermediate-acting insulin, such as NPH or Lente, as well as the short-acting preparation (regular or lispro, as described earlier in this list). The reason is to ensure that some insulin is always circulating in order to keep the body's metabolism running smoothly. Because intermediate-acting preparations have their peak activity around 6 to 8 hours after an injection, you need to be sure that some glucose is around to balance the activity of the insulin. That is where snacks can be very helpful. Ideally, what people with diabetes need is a long-acting insulin that can provide a low level of activity for 24 hours after a shot. Such a preparation is being developed and should be available to patients by 2001.

Each person responds in his or her own way to different preparations of insulin. You need to test your blood glucose to determine your individual response.

An additional factor affecting the onset of insulin is where you make the injection. The abdomen is the site that provides the most regular activity from shot to shot. If you use the arms or legs, the insulin will be taken up faster or slower, depending on whether you exercise or not.

The depth of the injection also affects the onset of activity. A deeper injection results in a faster onset of action. If you use the same length needle and insert it to its maximum length each time, you'll ensure more uniform activity.

You can see from the discussion in this section that a great deal of variation is possible in the taking of an insulin shot. It's no wonder that people who must inject insulin tend to have many more ups and downs in their blood glucose. But with proper education, these variations can be reduced.

If you take oral medication, in particular the sulfonylurea drugs like micronase and glucotrol, the timing of food in relation to the taking of your medication must also be considered. For a complete explanation of this balance between food and medication, see *Diabetes For Dummies.*

Chapter 3

Meal Planners to Get You Started

In This Chapter

- Figuring how many calories to eat
- Losing weight quickly at 1,200 kilocalories
- Dropping weight more slowly at 1,500 kilocalories
- Maintaining your weight at 1,800 kilocalories
- Moving exercise into the equation

If you follow our advice and try the recipes in this book, you will discover such wonderful foods that you could be tempted to eat too heartily. This chapter is about eating well, but smartly, for your nutritional needs. You can continue to eat great food, but you must limit your portions. We show you how to plan three different daily levels of *kilocalories* (the more proper term for what most people call *calories*). You can lose weight rapidly, lose more slowly, or maintain your weight. We prefer the slower approach to losing weight. With this method, you'll probably feel less hungry, and cutting back a few hundred kilocalories a day doesn't cause a major upheaval in daily life. Also, maintaining a weight loss may be easier if you lose the weight slowly.

Patients often worry that they are going to feel hungry if they take in fewer calories than they need. Does a bear feel hungry as it lives off its fat all winter long? No, it sleeps. One of our favorite tasks is to point out how many calories of energy are stored in the body of an overweight or obese person. Each pound of fat contains 3,500 kilocalories. If you are 25 pounds overweight, you have 87,500 kilocalories (25 times 3,500) of stored energy in your body. We can give you an idea of what you could do with that much energy. You need 100 kilocalories to walk 20 minutes at 4 miles an hour. So a walk of 1⅓ miles (one-third of 4 miles) burns 100 kilocalories. Your stored energy — 87,500 kilocalories — would take you about 1,100 miles (87,500 divided by 100 times 1⅓)! The point is not to suggest that you stop eating and fast for any length of time in order to lose weight, but that you recognize that your stored energy, in the form of fat, will provide all the calories necessary to continue your daily activities without fatigue and often without hunger.

Before planning a nutritional program, you need to know how much you need to eat on a daily basis to maintain your current weight. Then you can figure how rapidly a deficit of calories will get you to your goal.

Figuring Your Daily Caloric Needs

Start by determining your ideal weight for your height. Obviously, this is a range and not a single weight at each height, but we will use numbers that give us a weight in the middle of that range. Because people have more or less muscle and larger or smaller frames, you are considered normal if your weight is plus or minus 10 percent of this number. For example, a person who is calculated to have an ideal weight of 150 pounds is considered normal at a weight of 135 (150 minus 10 percent) to 165 (150 plus 10 percent) pounds.

TIP

Because no two people, even twins, are totally alike in all aspects of their lives, we can only approximate your ideal weight and the number of calories you need to maintain that weight. You will test the correctness of the approximation by adding or subtracting calories. If your daily caloric needs are 2,000 kilocalories, and you find yourself putting on weight, try reducing your intake by 100 kilocalories and see if you maintain your weight on fewer kilocalories.

If you are a male, your approximate ideal weight is 106 pounds for 5 feet of height plus 6 pounds for each inch over 5 feet. If you are a female, your ideal weight is 100 pounds for 5 feet plus 5 pounds for each inch over 5 feet tall. Table 3-1 shows the ideal weights for females and males from 4 feet, 10 inches to 6 feet, 2 inches in height.

Table 3-1 Ideal Weight (Pounds) at Each Height (Feet, Inches)

Height	*Male*	*Female*
4'10"	94	90
4'11"	100	95
5'	106	100
5'1"	112	105
5'2"	118	110
5'3"	124	115
5'4"	130	120
5'5"	136	125
5'6"	142	130
5'7"	148	135
5'8"	154	140
5'9"	160	145

Height	*Male*	*Female*
5′10″	166	150
5′11″	172	155
6′	178	160
6′1″	184	165
6′2″	190	170

Now you know your ideal weight for your height. What a surprise! Yes, we know. You have big bones, but bear with us. It is amazing how often we have seen big bones melt away as weight is lost.

The next step is to figure out how many calories you need to maintain your ideal weight. Start by multiplying your ideal weight by ten. For example, if you are a male, 5 feet, 6 inches tall, your ideal weight is 142 pounds. Your daily kilocalorie allowance is about 1,400. But this number is ideal only if you don't take a breath or have a heartbeat. It is considered your *basal* caloric need. You must increase your calorie intake depending upon the amount of physical activity you do each day. Table 3-2 shows this graduated increase.

Table 3-2 Kilocalories Needed Based on Activity Level

Level of Activity	*Kilocalories Added*	*5′6″ Male*
Sedentary	10% more than basal	1,540 kilocalories
Moderate	20% more than basal	1,680 kilocalories
Very active	40%+ more than basal	1,960+ kilocalories

The "Very active" line displays a plus sign because some people doing hard manual labor need so many extra calories that they should not be held to only 40 percent more than their basal calorie intake. This requirement becomes clear as the person gains or loses weight on his or her food plan.

You gain weight when your daily intake of kilocalories exceeds your daily needs. Each pound of fat has 3,500 kilocalories, so when the excess has reached that number of calories, you are a pound heavier. On the other hand, you lose weight when your daily expenditure of calories exceeds your daily intake. You lose a pound of fat each time you burn up 3,500 kilocalories more than you take in, whether you do it by burning an extra 100 kilocalories per day for 35 days or an extra 500 kilocalories per day for 7 days.

Now you can create a nutritional program and fill in the blanks with carbohydrates, proteins, fats, and real foods.

Losing Weight Rapidly at 1,200 Kilocalories

As figured in the preceding section, if you are a moderately active male, 5 feet, 6 inches tall, you need 1,680 or approximately 1,700 kilocalories daily to maintain your weight. If you eat only 1,200 kilocalories daily, you will have a daily deficit of approximately 500 kilocalories. By dividing the kilocalories in a pound of fat (3,500) by 500, you can see that you will lose 1 pound per week (3,500 divided by 500 is 7, so the loss will take 7 days).

You can use the exchange system to create a nutritional plan providing 1,200 kilocalories per day with a breakdown of about 40 percent carbohydrate, 30 percent protein, and 30 percent fat. You can find the various food exchange lists in Appendix B, and Chapter 2 explains the exchange system. You will definitely want the help of a registered dietitian as you set up your plan.

Each item in an exchange list — for example, the fruits list — is considered to have the same nutrient content as any other item in that list and can, therefore, be exchanged for one another in the plan. For example, a small apple is the same as 4 apricots or 12 cherries or ½ cup of grape juice.

Table 3-3 shows the exchanges for a 1,200-kilocalorie diet. If you are a woman you will probably want to add some calcium in the form of tablets.

Table 3-3 Exchanges for 1,200-Kilocalorie Diet

Breakfast	*Lunch*
1 fruit exchange	3 lean-meat exchanges
1 starch exchange	1 starch exchange
1 medium-fat meat exchange	1 vegetable exchange
1 fat exchange	1 fruit exchange
1 lowfat milk exchange	1 fat exchange
Dinner	***Snack***
3 lean-meat exchanges	1 starch exchange
1 starch exchange	½ lowfat milk exchange
1 vegetable exchange	
1 fruit exchange	
2 fat exchanges	
½ lowfat milk exchange	

The plan provides about 480 kilocalories of carbohydrate, 360 kilocalories of protein, and 360 kilocalories of fat.

After you know the various exchanges and the breakdown of exchanges in a specific nutritional plan, you can fill in the blanks with whatever food you prefer. Table 3-4 shows an example of a 1,200 kilocalorie diet.

Table 3-4 A Sample Menu

Breakfast	***Lunch***
½ cup apple juice	3 ounces skinless chicken
1 slice toast	2 breadsticks
1 ounce lowfat cheese	1 cup of green beans
1 teaspoon margarine	1 small pear
1 cup 1% milk	2 walnuts
Dinner	***Snack***
3 ounces fresh salmon	¼ cup lowfat granola
1 slice whole-wheat bread	½ cup 1% milk
1 cup of broccoli	
1 slice honeydew melon (10 ounces)	
¼ (2 ounces) avocado	
½ cup 1% milk	

Because you can exchange many food items, you can make up an entirely different menu plan that provides the same number of calories. Table 3-5 offers another 1,200-kilocalorie diet using entirely different selections.

Table 3-5 Another Sample 1,200-Kilocalorie Menu

Breakfast	***Lunch***
½ grapefruit	3 ounces fresh tuna
½ cup bran cereal	1 ounce roll
1 egg	1 cup of salad greens
1 tablespoon sunflower seeds	½ cup canned peaches
1 cup 1% milk	1 teaspoon margarine

(continued)

Table 3-5 *(continued)*

Dinner	*Snack*
3 ounces turkey	3 cups popcorn, no fat added
3 ounces french-fried potatoes	½ cup 1% milk
1 cup cauliflower	
½ cup fruit cocktail	
½ cup 1% milk	

Notice that the dinner in the second sample menu didn't contain two separate fat exchanges. The potatoes contain the fat, so it's not added separately. A french-fried potato is a simple example of a combination food. Understanding combination foods gets much more complex when you or a restaurant creates a dish containing multiple energy sources. Here are a few examples:

- Chow mein (2 cups) with no noodles or rice is 1 starch and 2 lean-meat exchanges.
- Pizza (2 slices of 10-inch size) with a meat topping is 2 starches, 2 medium-fat meats, and 2 fat exchanges.
- Turkey (11 ounces) with gravy, mashed potatoes, and dressing is 2 starches, 2 medium-fat meats, and 2 fat exchanges.
- Lasagna (8 ounces) is 2 starches and 2 medium-fat meat exchanges.

That is why it is so important to check the food labels, as explained in Chapter 5, to find out how much carbohydrate, protein, and fat the food actually contains.

The portions on all food labels are based on a 2,000-kilocalorie diet. Not one of the diets in this chapter allows you to eat that many calories. Such a portion may be much too large for a person on a 1,200 kilocalorie diet.

Losing Weight More Slowly at 1,500 Kilocalories

The smaller the deficit of calories between what you need and what you eat, the more slowly you will lose weight. If your daily needs are 1,700 kilocalories and you eat 1,500, you will be missing 200 kilocalories each day. Because a pound of fat is 3,500 kilocalories, you will lose a pound in about 17 days (3,500 divided by 200). You will lose almost 2 pounds a month or 24 pounds in a year. You can accomplish this loss by reducing your daily intake only by the equivalent of a piece of bread and two teaspoons of margarine. Put that way, losing the weight doesn't seem difficult at all.

Table 3-5 shows the appropriate exchanges for a 1,500-kilocalorie diet. As you can see, it differs from the diet in the preceding section by having two more lean-meat exchanges, one additional starch exchange, one additional vegetable exchange, one more fat exchange, and one more fruit exchange.

Table 3-6 Exchanges for a 1,500-Kilocalorie Diet

Breakfast	***Lunch***
1 fruit exchange	3 lean-meat exchanges
1 starch exchange	1 vegetable exchange
1 medium-fat meat exchange	2 fat exchanges
1 fat exchange	1 starch exchange
1 lowfat milk exchange	2 fruit exchanges
Dinner	***Snack***
4 lean-meat exchanges	1 bread exchange
2 starch exchanges	½ lowfat milk exchange
2 vegetable exchanges	1 lean-meat exchange
1 fruit exchange	
2 fat exchanges	
½ lowfat milk exchange	

In this plan you are eating 600 kilocalories of carbohydrate, 450 kilocalories of protein, and 450 kilocalories of fat.

With the exchange lists in Appendix B in front of you, you can create an infinite number of daily menus.

As you create your meals, you will be amazed at how small the portions really are. Three ounces of lean meat aren't much compared to what most people are used to eating at home or in restaurants. Eating proper portions is very important because it will ultimately make the difference between weight gain and weight maintenance or loss. Portion size may also be the difference between controlling your blood glucose and not controlling it.

TIP

Think of the money you will save if — each time you go to a restaurant — your knowledge of portion sizes allows you to take home half of your meal to eat another day.

Maintaining Your Weight at 1,800 Kilocalories

Suppose that you have finally reached a weight (not necessarily your "ideal" weight that we calculate in the section "Figuring Your Daily Caloric Needs") that allows your blood glucose levels to remain between 80 and 140 mg/dl all the time. Now, you want to maintain that weight. You want to eat about 1,800 kilocalories, up another 300 from the previous diet in this chapter. Compared to the 1,200 kilocalorie diet, this may seem like a lot of food.

The differences between this plan and the 1,500-kilocalorie diet are 2 additional fat exchanges, 2 additional starch exchanges, and 1 additional lean-meat exchange. The exchange list looks like Table 3-6.

Table 3-7 Exchanges for an 1,800-Kilocalorie Diet

Breakfast	***Lunch***
1 fruit exchange	3 lean-meat exchanges
1 starch exchange	1 vegetable exchange
1 medium-fat meat exchange	2 fat exchanges
2 fat exchanges	2 starch exchanges
1 lowfat milk exchange	2 fruit exchanges
Dinner	***Snack***
4 lean-meat exchanges	2 starch exchanges
2 starch exchanges	2 lean-meat exchanges
2 vegetable exchanges	½ lowfat milk exchange
1 fruit exchange	
3 fat exchanges	
½ lowfat milk exchange	

Exercise for prevention

A study published in the October 20, 1999, edition of *The Journal of the American Medical Association* showed that walking may prevent the onset of diabetes. Among a large group of nurses, the occurrence of diabetes was less for those who walked compared with those who were sedentary. The women who walked most briskly had the lowest incidence of diabetes.

This plan provides 180 grams of carbohydrate, 135 grams of protein, and 60 grams of fat, maintaining the 40:30:30 division of calories.

If you have type 2 diabetes, this plan is an excellent way for you to eat the right amount of calories in the right ratios of energy sources. If you have type 1 diabetes, or you have type 2 and take insulin, you need to know the grams of carbohydrate in each meal in order to determine your insulin needs for that meal.

Benefiting from Exercise

A final but very important point is that exercise can help speed up weight loss or permit you to eat more and still lose weight. Twenty minutes of walking burns up 100 kilocalories, and 30 minutes of walking will burn up 150 kilocalories. Walk for 30 minutes a day, and you lose about ⅓ of a pound per week (7 times 150 equals 1,050 kilocalories divided into 3,500) — without reducing your calories. That activity amounts to an annual weight loss of 17 pounds in a year. Who says you can't lose weight by exercising but not dieting?

Chapter 4

Cooking Healthy Meals

In This Chapter

- Working with your own diet
- Having a plan for eating
- Keeping the right ingredients at hand
- Choosing the best tools
- Making modifications for better diabetic control
- Getting through the holidays

Say that you're getting ready to cook. How can you really enjoy your food and not feel deprived? This question was one of the main reasons for this book, to show you that you can eat great food and remain on your diabetic diet. You can find recipes to prove this premise in the next part. You can also use all kinds of tricks to substitute what is good for you for what will not help your diabetes. That's what this chapter is all about.

We wish we could eliminate the word "diet" from the diabetic vocabulary. The word implies taking something away or having to suffer somehow in order to follow it. This is not the case at all. You can eat great food and enjoy the taste of every ethnic variety, provided you concentrate on the amount of food and its breakdown into the sources of energy, keeping fats and carbohydrates in control. Perhaps the phrase "nutritional plan" would be better than "diet."

Stop dieting and start eating delicious foods. It may take a lot of willpower, but you can give up dieting if you try hard enough.

Choosing from Familiar Foods

If you become diabetic, you don't have to give up the kinds of food you have always eaten. You can eat the same foods but decrease the portions, particularly if you are obese. Every ethnic group has its own cuisine, and most of the people in that group are normal in weight. They are doing two things that you need to do as well: They are eating smaller portions, and they are keeping physically fit with exercise.

After you receive a diagnosis of diabetes, try to find a dietitian who treats many members of your ethnic group. This person will be best trained to show you how to keep eating what you love, while altering it slightly to fit your needs. The alteration may be no greater than simply reducing the amount of food that you eat each day. Or it may involve changing ingredients so that a high fat source of energy is replaced by a lowfat energy source with no loss in taste.

Esmeralda Cruz is an example of a patient with a particular diet whose diabetes could be managed successfully with minor alterations in her nutritional regime. She is a 46-year-old woman with type 2 diabetes, which has been diagnosed for five years. She is 5 feet, 2 inches tall and weighs 156 pounds. Her blood glucose averages 176 mg/dl, and she has a hemoglobin A1c of 8.6 percent.

Esmeralda follows a typical Filipino diet and has found that she has gained at least 3 to 6 pounds each year for the last four years. She comes from a region of the Philippines called Pampanga, which is considered by many to be the culinary capital of the country. Analysis of her diet reveals that she eats a lot of food fried in lard. She also eats too much rice for the calories and carbohydrate that is planned for her diet. Another problem is her tendency not to trim the fat from the meat that she eats.

Her dietitian advised her to cut off visible fat from her meats. She reduced the amount of frying and began broiling and roasting instead. She switched to canola oil in place of lard, while reducing the amount of fat she used. One of her dishes, a pork dish called Tortung Babi, was made with three eggs, but reducing the number to two didn't diminish the taste. Similar alterations were made in many of her favorite dishes, also without affecting the food's appeal. She began to eat more fish and poultry, still using her favorite recipes but with healthy modifications. She significantly reduced the amount of rice that she ate each day and tried to eat a low glycemic type of rice such as basmati.

As a result, she began to lose weight without feeling that she had to give up her native food. She gradually lost 12 pounds over the next six months and her blood glucose began to fall to the point that it averaged 132 mg/dl with a hemoglobin A1c of 6.9 percent. Because she has made these changes for all members of her family, everyone has benefited.

This patient profile, and many others like it, proves that you don't have to give up your mother's favorite recipes.

Following Your Eating Plan

Your diabetes medication may require you to have three meals a day, but if not, having three meals is still important. This approach spreads calories over the day and helps you avoid coming to a meal extremely hungry. Try not to skip breakfast, even though our society doesn't encourage taking the time for this meal. Making your own lunch as often as possible gives you control over what you eat. The fast lunches that are eaten out may not provide the lowfat nutrition that you think you're getting. For example, salads are often covered with a lot of oil. It may be the right type of oil, but it still provides a lot of fat calories.

Before you cook, make sure that the recipes fit into your eating plan. If you have already eaten your carbohydrate portions for the day, make sure that the food you are about to eat has little carbohydrate in it. The same is true for protein and, of course, fat. If you think "moderation" as you make your meal plan, you will keep to the portions you need to eat and no more.

Chapter 2 describes how to divide your food into the proper number of kilocalories from carbohydrate, protein, and fat. You can translate those numbers into exchanges and pick out the food that is the delicious end point of all the calculating. Make sure that your choices come from a variety of foods rather than eating the same thing over and over. You will be much more likely to stay on your program if you aren't bored with what you eat.

Seasonal foods should play a primary role in your eating plan for several reasons:

- Seasonal foods are the freshest foods in the market.
- They are the least expensive foods.
- The recipes you can prepare with these fresh foods are some of the most delicious. The recipes in this book show the tremendous influence that fresh ingredients have had on the imaginations of the best chefs in the United States and Canada.

In addition, time is an important factor in your eating plan. You may not have a great deal of time to prepare your food, and some of the recipes in this book may take more time than you can spare. Choose the meals that fit into your schedule. But remember that once you have prepared a recipe a few times, preparation is much faster and easier. Consider the time you spend preparing delicious, healthy food an investment in your well-being. Take the time to eat properly now so that later you won't have to give up your time being sick.

As a person with diabetes, especially if you have type 1 diabetes, your plan also has to include the timing of your food. You need to eat when your medications will balance your carbohydrates. This process is much easier with the new rapid-acting insulin, lispro, but if you're still using regular insulin, you will have to eat about 30 minutes after you take your shot.

Another essential part of your planning is what to do when you feel hungry but shouldn't eat. You can prepare a low-calorie snack for such occasions, or you can provide yourself with some diversion, whether it is a hobby or a movie or, best of all, some exercise. Examples of low-calorie snacks might be baby carrots, cherry tomatoes, a piece of fruit, or lowfat pudding.

Stocking Up with the Right Ingredients

Some common ingredients are used in many different recipes. Having them at hand is convenient, thus avoiding more trips to the market and more exposure to foods you don't need.

Some of the foods that belong in every kitchen or pantry (if you are a vegetarian, make the appropriate substitutions) include the following:

For the freezer:

Chicken breasts

Egg substitute

Frozen fruit

Fruit juice concentrate

Loaf of bread

Soft margarine or butter

For the pantry:

Canned fruit

Canned tomatoes

Canned tuna, salmon in water

Catsup

Dried fruit, unsugared

Evaporated skim milk

Fat-free salad dressing

Fresh garlic

Fruit spreads

Grains (rice, couscous)

Legumes (peas, beans, lentils)

Mustard

Nonfat dry milk

Nonstick cooking sprays

Oils (olive, canola, peanut)

Onions

Pasta

Pasta sauce

Peanut butter

Potatoes

Red and white cooking wine

Reduced-calorie mayonnaise

Reduced-sodium broths

Reduced-sodium soy sauce

Sugar-free cocoa mix

Tomato paste

Vinegars

Worcestershire sauce

For baking:

Baking powder
Baking soda
Cocoa powder
Cornstarch
Cream of tartar
Dry bread crumbs
Extracts (vanilla, lemon, almond)
Flour (all purpose, whole wheat)
Rolled oats
Semi-sweet chocolate
Sugar-free gelatin
Unflavored gelatin

Sweeteners:

Artificial sweeteners
Honey
Light maple syrup
Molasses
Sugar

Seasonings:

Dried herbs
Fresh herbs and spices
Pepper
Salt

With these ingredients, you're ready for just about any of the recipes in the book. The exceptions are exotic ingredients, such as ethnic foods that can be bought in specialty stores as you need them.

Prepare a list of these ingredients and make multiple copies so that you can check off what you need before you go to the market. Leave a little space for the perishables such as fresh fruits, vegetables, milk, meat, fish, and poultry. In the next chapter, we tell you more about the process of shopping for these ingredients.

Using the Right Tools

Just as you wouldn't try to bang in a nail with a shoe (especially with your foot inside), don't try to cook without the right tools. Spending a little more at the beginning pays huge dividends later on. For example, get the best set of knives you can afford. They make all cutting jobs much easier, and they last a long time. Buy good nonstick pans; they make cooking without oils much easier.

Here's the basic equipment that all kitchens should have in order to turn out delicious meals:

Chopping boards

Food processor

Knives

Measuring cups and spoons

Microwave

Mixer with dough hook

Pots and pans

Salad spinner

Scales

Steamer with double boiler

Thermometers (for roasts and turkey)

Making Simple Modifications

You can make all kinds of simple modifications that will reduce calories and reduce the amounts of foods (such as those containing cholesterol) that you are trying to keep in check. You can easily

- Use skim milk instead of whole milk.
- Use cuts of meat that are low in fat instead of high fat meats. Lowfat meats include lean beef, lean pork, and skinless white meat poultry.
- Trim all visible fat off meats and poultry.
- Stay away from packaged luncheon meats, which tend to be high in fat.
- Select foods that are low in sodium and saturated fats (check the label on the food).
- Choose high fiber foods like whole fruits, vegetables, and grains.
- Enjoy nonfat yogurt instead of sour cream.
- Have dressings, sauces, and gravies served on the side.
- Substitute lentils and beans for meat, fish, and poultry.
- Replace butter with olive oil, herbs, spices, or lemon juice.
- Prepare foods by baking, broiling, and so on — any method other than frying.

Use your imagination to come up with your own unique ways to cut calories and fat.

Taking Holiday Measures

This is a particularly good heading for this section, because the key to getting through a holiday in good diabetic control is to control the portions of everything you eat during the holidays. Eating too much is easy.

If you encounter a buffet table, vow to make only one trip. You will probably fill your plate with more food than you need, so plan to leave a large portion on the plate. Focus on the foods that you should eat and avoid high fat and high sugar foods, particularly desserts. Stick to fruits for high fiber, low calorie desserts.

If you're invited to a potluck dinner, make something that you know will work for your nutritional plan. You can certainly find something in this book that fits for you. These recipes have all been taste-tested and are delicious, so you don't have to think that you're bringing something inferior. We suggest that you have a snack before you go to a party so that you don't arrive feeling hungry.

Most important of all, try to forget the all-or-nothing mindset. If you go off your nutritional plan once or twice, put the lapse behind you and get back to doing the things you know are right for you. The benefits will be immediate in the form of a general feeling of well-being and, of course, long-term in the fact that you won't develop the long-term complications of diabetes.

Chapter 5

A Grocery Store Guide to Healthy Ingredients

In This Chapter

- Planning for the market
- Reading food labels
- Checking your choices

Every trip to the market is an adventure. This chapter is about coping with the challenge of going grocery shopping without being lured into buying items that aren't good for your diabetes nutritional plan. But it's also about overcoming your natural desire to take home what you know isn't good for you.

You deserve the best, and that holds true for the food you eat as much as anything else. Of course, you could be like the man whose doctor told him that the best thing he could do for himself would be to get on a really good diet, stop chasing women, and stop drinking so much alcohol. The patient replied: "I don't deserve the best. What about second best?" We hope you won't settle for second best.

Going to the Market with a Plan

If you have a hobby, you have probably developed a series of steps by which you can accomplish your hobby in the most efficient manner, whether it's painting pictures or raising tomatoes. If you paint pictures, you certainly wouldn't start painting without deciding on a subject and buying the right paints, brushes, and canvas. If you raise tomatoes, you prepare the soil, add amendments such as manure, and buy the seeds or, more likely, the plants. You use a watering system as well as tomato cages to hold up your crop.

Your excursion to the market should be planned in the same careful manner. Decide in advance what you need that complies with your nutritional plan. In Chapter 4, we give you a list of recommendations for the staples you should have at home. You can use those suggestions to make a shopping list to make sure that you purchase what you need. To that list, add the perishables that you will use immediately, such as meat and poultry or fish, milk and other diary products, and, of course, fruits and vegetables.

Eat something before you go to the market so that you aren't hungry as you walk down the isles.

A market is like a huge menu set up to entice you. Most markets are set up in the same way. This setup is not by accident. It's arranged to encourage you to buy. What people buy on the impulse of the moment is often the most calorie-concentrated and expensive food that is least appropriate for them. You will find that all the perishable food is arranged around the perimeter of the market. The high calorie foods are in the aisles. Unless you want to take the long way around, you must go through the aisles to get to the meat, milk, fruit, and vegetables. You pass the loose candies, the cookies, the high sugar cereals, and all the other no-nos. If you prepare a list and buy only from the list, you won't purchase any of those foods. Walking into the market hungry and without a list is dangerous for your health.

Sometimes the market employs a person who is trained to help people with medical conditions avoid bad choices. Check with your market to find out whether such a person is on staff, and spend some time touring the aisles with him or her. You'll get some valuable insights that will make handling a shopping trip easier.

Some keys to shopping the market most effectively include the following:

- Shop at the same market each time.
- Shop as seldom as you can.
- Go to the market when it is not crowded.
- Do not walk every aisle.
- Don't be tempted by free samples. They are usually high in calories to appeal to your taste buds.
- If you bring your kids (not advisable) to the store, make sure that they aren't hungry.
- Be especially careful in the checkout lane, where stores force you to run a gauntlet of goodies — none of which are good for you.

Most markets offer a variety of sections. Each one presents a different challenge and requires a different strategy.

The deli counter

A deli counter offers luncheon meats and prepared foods. These foods often contain a lot of salt and fat. You probably want to avoid most of the foods in this area (with the exception of prepared chicken, which is often spit-roasted and very tasty). Even the lowfat meats in this section are rich in salt. The pickled foods may also contain a great deal of salt, despite being low in calories and free of fat.

If you choose salads from this area, pick out those that contain oil instead of cream. Don't be afraid to question the counterperson about the exact ingredients in these prepared foods. In some cases, lower fat versions are available. People often prefer fatty foods — and the grocery obviously wants people to buy the food — so the market caters to those preferences.

Fresh meat and fish counter

The fresh meat and fish counter provides some good choices for your protein needs. Don't forget that lentils and other legumes can provide protein as well. At the meat counter, buy no more than a normal serving for each member of the family. Just because the meat attendant has cut a 12-ounce piece of swordfish doesn't mean that you have to buy the whole thing. You are entitled to get just the piece you want. For convenience, you can get two servings at one time if you know you have the willpower to save the second serving for another meal. Ask the attendant to cut the fish in half so you aren't tempted to eat the whole thing.

Look for lowfat cuts of meat. The best choices for you are top round, sirloin, and flank steak. These tend to be the leanest cuts of meat. They are also very tasty. When buying chopped meat (for hamburgers, for example), consider how you will cook it. If you like meat cooked well done, you don't always have to choose the package with the lowest fat content because the fat may be cooked out. Otherwise, look for lower-fat chopped meat.

Try to buy skinless poultry to eliminate a major source of the fat in chicken. You may have to cook it a shorter time, or you can barbecue the chicken using an indirect method (place the coals along the sides of the chicken instead of underneath). The chicken will be much more juicy and not dried out.

TIP

Try to eat fish at least twice a week because of the positive effect it has on blood fats. Remember that a "fatty" fish such as salmon is good for you but adds extra fat calories.

The fresh meat and fish counter usually offers breaded or battered fish to make your life easier; you only have to put it in the oven. The problem is that the breading or batter often contains too much butter, fat, and salt. Ask the person serving you for a list of the ingredients in the breading or batter. Or better yet, skip the prepared fish and head for the fresh. If you notice a very fishy smell, then the fish is not very fresh.

Dairy case

At the dairy case, you can make some very positive diet modifications. Go for the lowest fat content you can eat, but don't neglect the dairy part of the food guide pyramid. That's where you get calcium. Try to find lowfat cheeses, yogurt, and cottage cheese. You can even buy cheeses that aren't lowfat if you use them sparingly.

Bakery

You can really make a dent in your diet in the bakery section, where all the desserts are on display. These foods usually contain too much fat and carbohydrate; however, you don't have to give up all your "treats." The key is to figure a rich dessert into your overall 24-hour meal plan, but only on an occasional basis. Remember to keep the portion small, in any case.

Muffins and pastries are usually high in fat, but, in deference to the popular belief that fat makes us fat, stores now sell lowfat muffins and pastries. The problem is that these still contain many calories, so don't overdo it. Try a smaller portion or share your muffin with a friend. A popular choice is angel food cake, which is totally fat-free but filled with calories.

Produce

Fruits and vegetables are in the produce section. Stores continue to offer the usual apples, pears, and bananas, but more and more they stock fruits and vegetables that you may never have seen before. Here is where you can add some real variety to your diet. Try some of these new tastes. They may replace cakes, pies, and other concentrated calorie foods. For example, you can try all kinds of new varieties of melons; they are sweet and have a great texture.

The other benefit to trying new fruits and vegetables is that you get a variety of vitamins and minerals from the different sources. Each differently colored vegetable provides different vitamins, so pick out a variety of colors.

To prolong their season, you can freeze some of the fruits, especially the berries, and use them as you need them.

Remember that dried fruits have very concentrated carbohydrate and should be used sparingly.

Root vegetables need no refrigeration but must be kept in a cool, dry place. Most of the others must go in the refrigerator.

Frozen foods

When the season for fresh fruits and vegetables is over, the frozen food area of the market may provide your fruits and vegetables, but with fresh food coming in from all over the world, you may not need this area much.

Food manufacturers are producing a variety of frozen foods, which you can heat in the microwave oven. These meals are often high in fat and salt. Be sure to read the food label, which we explain in the next section. Avoid frozen foods mixed with cream or cheese sauces.

Canned and bottled foods

Canned and bottled foods can be healthful and can help you quickly make recipes calling for ingredients such as tomato sauce. Check the Nutrition Facts label to determine what kind of liquid a food is canned in. Oil adds a lot of fat calories, so look for the same food canned in water.

Watch for this marketing trick: Stores often display higher priced canned foods at eye level and lower priced products on lower shelves. Also, store brands are often less expensive and just as good as name brands.

Bottled foods include fruit juice drinks. These are high in sugar and low in nutrition. You are better off drinking pure fruit juice rather than a juice drink diluted with other ingredients.

The same principle is true for bottled and canned soda. It has no nutritional value and lots of calories. Substitute water for this expensive and basically worthless food that really doesn't quench your thirst (they often leave an aftertaste, especially the diet drinks). You might add lemon or lime to your water or use the flavored calorie-free water drinks.

You can find lowfat or fat-free salad dressing and mayonnaise in this area. Better yet, try using mustard and some of the other condiments to spice up your salads without adding many calories.

The supermarket is not the only place where you can find good food. Check out your local farmer's market. Most areas have these markets, and many are open all year. And be sure to look into specialty food stores where you can find some of the more exotic ingredients.

Deciphering the Mysterious Food Label

Most packaged foods have a food label. The Nutrition Facts label is not so mysterious if you know how to interpret it. It was designed to be understood. Figure 5-1 shows a typical food label. The contents of the Nutrition Facts label are regulated by the Food and Drug Administration.

Nutrition Facts
Serving Size 1/2 cup (113g)
Servings Per Container 4

Amount Per Serving	
Calories 120 Calories from Fat 15	
	% Daily Value
Total Fat 1.5g	3%
Saturated Fat 1.0g	5%
Cholesterol 10mg	3%
Sodium 290mg	12%
Total Carbohydrate 15g	5%
Dietary Fiber 0g	
Sugars 14g	
Protein 10g	10%

Figure 5-1: A Nutrition Facts food label.

The label in Figure 5-1 is from a 1-pound container of cottage cheese with fruit. You can find the following information on the label:

- **Serving Size:** Note the size because it may not be the same as an exchange (see Chapter 2 for an explanation of exchanges and check out Appendix B for a comprehensive list). The serving size on this food label is ½ cup, but an exchange of lowfat cottage cheese (which you can find in the "Very lean meat and substitutes" list) is ¼ cup. Therefore, one serving is two exchanges. In this case, one of the exchanges is carbohydrate and one is protein, which you can tell from the number of grams of carbohydrate and protein on the label.
- **Servings Per Container:** At ½ cup, this container holds 4 servings. If you were to use the exchange list serving size of ¼ cup, this container would serve 8.
- **Calories:** The number of kilocalories in a serving — in this case, 120 kilocalories.

- **Calories from Fat:** The number of fat kilocalories in each serving.
- **% Daily Value:** The nutrient amounts appear in grams or milligrams and also as % Daily Value. % Daily Value refers to the percentage of the daily value for a person on a 2,000-kilocalorie-per-day diet.
- **Total Fat:** The total fat is 1.5 grams, of which 1.0 is saturated fat. The fact that there's less than 3 grams of fat allows the producer to refer to this product as *lowfat.*
    - **Saturated Fat:** The amount of the fat in each serving that is saturated.
- **Cholesterol:** This food provides little cholesterol. Therefore, the producer could call it "low cholesterol" because that term applies if the product provides less than 20 milligrams of cholesterol and 2 grams or less of saturated fat per serving (see Chapter 2 for more information).
- **Sodium:** At 290 milligrams of sodium, this food provides 12% of the sodium allowed in a 2,000-kilocalorie-a-day diet.
- **Total Carbohydrate:** As a person with diabetes, you need to know the grams of carbohydrate in a serving, both to fit it into your nutritional plan and to determine insulin needs if that is what you take.
    - **Dietary Fiber:** This food provides no fiber, so all the carbohydrate is digestible. If fiber were present, you could subtract the fiber grams from the total grams of carbohydrate to get the actual grams from carbohydrate absorbed.
    - **Sugars:** The fact that 14 of the 15 grams of carbohydrate come from sugar means that the sugar will be absorbed rapidly.
- **Protein:** As a person with diabetes, you are most concerned with the grams of protein in a portion. The figure for % Daily Value doesn't help you in planning your diet.
- **Vitamins and Minerals:** Usually, the label provides the % Daily Value for vitamin A, vitamin C, calcium, and iron. Some food labels follow that information with a list of ingredients, but this information is not required as part of the Nutrition Facts label.

Calculating Exchanges from the Food Label

The Nutrition Facts label isn't required to contain the exchanges that make up the food, but this information would certainly be helpful to people with diabetes or anyone trying to plan and maintain a good diet. If you need to determine the exchange value of a food, follow these guidelines:

- If the food is mostly carbohydrate (cereals, grains, pasta, bread, dried beans, peas, and lentils), divide the grams of carbohydrate by 15, because each starch exchange contains 15 grams of carbohydrate. Remember that starch exchanges also contain 3 grams of protein. A fruit exchange also contains 15 grams of carbohydrate but no fat or protein.
- If the food is mostly protein (meat and meat substitutes), divide the grams of protein by 7, because each meat exchange contains 7 grams of protein. Remember that it is a lean-meat exchange if it contains 3 grams or less of fat, a medium-fat meat exchange if it contains 4 to 5 grams of fat, and a high-fat meat exchange if it contains 8 or more grams of fat.
- If the food is mostly fat (avocado, margarine, butter, nuts, and seeds), divide the grams of fat by 5 to calculate the fat exchanges.
- Milk exchanges contain 12 grams of carbohydrate, 8 grams of protein, and a variable number of grams of fat — 0 grams in the case of skim and very lowfat milk (skim milk or nonfat yogurt, for example), 5 grams for reduced fat milk (2% milk or plain lowfat yogurt), and 8 grams for whole milk. Calculating the exchanges in food with several energy sources can get complicated, so get some help from your dietitian.
- Vegetable exchanges contain 5 grams of carbohydrate and 2 grams of protein per exchange.

Evaluating Your Selections

The best way to verify that your trip to the market has been successful is to evaluate the contents of your grocery sacks. The division of the contents should look similar to the food guide pyramid (see Chapter 2). Most of the choices should come from the bread, cereal, rice, and pasta group. Vegetables should appear about half as often and fruit slightly less often than the veggies. Foods from the milk group, including cheese and yogurt, should be present slightly less often than the fruit group. The meat, poultry, and beans group should be about the same as the milk group. Finally, fats, oils, and sweets should be a very small part of your grocery purchases.

Part II

Healthy Recipes That Taste Great

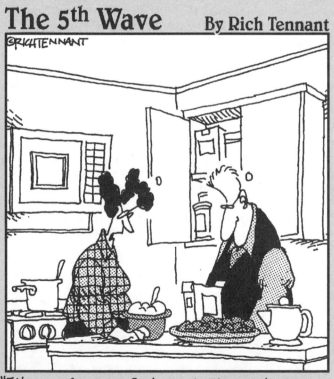

The 5th Wave — By Rich Tennant

"It's nearly a perfect meal. I've got 40% fat, 30% protein, 20% carbohydrates and 10% guilt for the 40% fat."

In this part . . .

Your first impression when you were told that you have diabetes was that you were doomed to bland, uninteresting food for the rest of your life. This part shows that impression could not be more wrong. Starting with your breakfast and working through the day with lunch, snacks, main courses, and desserts, your food can be just as exciting, exotic, and full of taste as it has always been, perhaps even more so.

We have gathered together the creativity of some of the best chefs in the United States and Canada and put them at your disposal. You can choose from simple recipes, requiring few ingredients, or more complicated and time-consuming recipes, sometimes with many more ingredients. We guarantee that all will be delicious, because we have tested all of them, not once but twice to make sure that you will enjoy them and can cook them yourself.

Chapter 6

The Benefits of Breakfast

In This Chapter

- Balancing breakfast foods
- Choosing whole fruit over juice
- Selecting protein foods
- Savoring baked goods and healthy grains
- Enjoying crunchy breakfast treats

Recipes in This Chapter

- Bagel with Warm Veggie Spread
- Apple Banana Pancakes
- Soy Waffles
- Vegetable Omelet
- Breakfast Pizza
- Potato Biscuits
- Crispy Corn French Toast

For the person with diabetes, breakfast is an especially important meal. Having breakfast breaks the fast of the long night that can send blood glucose levels downward. The wait between dinner and breakfast can be 12 hours or more, a long period of time for a person with diabetes to go without food. Eating for diabetes requires regular and frequent meals. Some individuals can keep their blood glucose levels within the normal range simply by eating three meals a day, while others must also have between-meal snacks and a snack at bedtime. But whatever pattern is followed, eating a breakfast that supplies a proper balance of nutrients is always a requirement.

Giving Yourself a Balanced Breakfast

One good way to manage blood glucose is to include some protein, some fat, and some carbohydrate in every meal or snack you eat. With this mix, you are more likely to have a steady supply of energy as these macronutrients break down and are assimilated into your system. Carbohydrates, which include starches and sugars, break down the quickest and can increase blood glucose levels within the hour. Protein breaks down more slowly and begins to affect blood glucose levels after about an hour and a half. Fat generally doesn't contribute to blood glucose after a meal.

Having a bagel (a source of carbohydrate) topped with a slice of smoked salmon (a source of protein) and a smear of cream cheese (a source of fat) for breakfast helps you stave off hunger pangs throughout the morning and keeps you from having low blood glucose soon after eating. Of course, this morsel is relatively high in fat because of the combination of fish and cheese.

If you're trying to curb the number of calories from fat in your diet because you're watching your weight, you may want to experiment with this alternative: a bagel topping made with fat-free cheese, which supplies just a smidgen of fat (only ½ gram per serving). Make up a batch of the following classic deli veggie spread and see how it works for you.

Bagel with Warm Veggie Spread

Cream cheese mixed with chopped vegetables is a deli specialty, but you can easily whip up some in your own kitchen. This mouth-watering spread is especially good on whole-grain bagels, complemented by the crunch of green pepper and the bite of red onion and chives.

Preparation time: *15 minutes*

Cooking time: *3 minutes*

Yield: *4 servings (4 bagels with spread, plus extra spread)*

8 ounces fat-free cream cheese

4 ounces fat-free ricotta cheese

2 tablespoons green pepper, cored, seeded, and finely chopped

2 tablespoons red onion, finely chopped

2 tablespoons chives, chopped

1 teaspoon freshly squeezed lemon juice

4 whole wheat or multigrain bagels, 3 ounces each, sliced in half

1 In a bowl and using a fork, beat together the cream cheese and ricotta. Fold in the green pepper, onion, chives, and lemon juice.

2 Place bagel halves, cut side up, on the rack of a toaster oven. Toast at highest setting. When bagels are golden brown, transfer to a serving plate, spread bagel halves with the cheese mixture, and enjoy.

Nutrient analysis per serving: *244 kcalories, 16 grams protein, 40 grams carbohydrate, 2.6 grams fat, 0.4 grams saturated fat, 5 milligrams cholesterol, 8 grams fiber, 454 milligrams sodium*

Exchanges: *2½ starch, 1 very lean meat*

Enjoying Whole Fruit Rather than Juice

What could be healthier than having a glass of orange juice in the morning? Well, if you have diabetes, having a slice of orange would be healthier. Whole fruit, such as a slice of orange or an orange segment, contains fiber, and this fiber needs to be digested in the stomach before it can pass into the intestines where it is absorbed. Because digestion happens gradually, sugars are freed and absorbed somewhat more slowly, and more gradually enter the bloodstream. As a result, eating a piece of fruit, compared with drinking fruit juice, is less likely to cause a dramatic rise in blood glucose.

In contrast, fruit juice enters your body fiber-free! Yes, country-style orange juice does contain a little pulp, but it's in bits and doesn't significantly slow absorption of the juice sugars.

If you do want to enjoy a glass of juice, have a small one, and along with it have some protein and fat, for example, apple juice with cheese and crackers.

Getting more nutrients by eating whole fruit

Whole fruit beats out fruit juice every time because when you eat whole fruit, you are more likely to consume the full range of nutrients that the fruit naturally contains. For example, after an orange is squeezed and the juice is exposed to the air, the oxygen destroys at least half of the vitamin C within a half hour. Light and heat also cause a loss of vitamin C.

Shopping for whole fruit

Certain fruits cause less of a rise in blood glucose than others. A list of these fruits, which have a lower glycemic index, follows. Of course, serving size is also critical. In terms of the Food Exchange Lists for diabetes, 2 tablespoons of raisins are equivalent to 7 apricot halves or a third of a cantaloupe. (For more guidance on deciding on portion size, take a look at Appendix B.)

Fruits with a low glycemic index include

- Apples
- Cherries
- Grapefruit
- Grapes

- Peaches
- Pears
- Plums

TIP

When you eat a piece of fruit including the skin, this food is digested and absorbed more slowly than if you were to eat the fruit without the skin. However, the outside surface also harbors most of the pesticides and other toxins, if the fruit was raised by standard commercial means. You may want to consider buying organic fruits, which, because of increasing demand, are now showing up in supermarkets as well as natural food stores. Or alternatively, keep a bottle of fruit and vegetable wash within easy reach by your sink. Soak conventionally raised fruit in a solution of this wash to remove pesticides, waxes, fungicides, and herbicides. A solution of 2 drops dish soap to 1 pint water is also very effective.

You can add whole fruit to an assortment of breakfast foods. Top corn flakes with blueberries. Top oatmeal with bananas. Slip some chopped dried apricots into muffins. Or add fruit to pancake batter. Get started by cooking a batch using the following recipe.

Apple Banana Pancakes

Top these pancakes with fruit instead of maple syrup. You'll be more likely to limit the amount of sugars you are eating and better control your blood glucose.

Preparation time: *15 minutes*

Cooking time: *10 minutes*

Yield: *4 servings (12 pancakes — 3 per person)*

¾ cup all-purpose flour

½ cup whole wheat flour

2 teaspoons baking powder

¼ teaspoon salt

1½ teaspoons applesauce

2 teaspoons apple juice concentrate

1¼ cups lowfat milk

3 egg whites

2 overripe bananas, mashed well

Nonstick cooking spray

1 In a bowl, combine all-purpose flour, whole wheat flour, baking powder, and salt. Set aside.

2 In another bowl, combine applesauce, apple juice concentrate, milk, egg whites, and bananas. Stir well. Add flour mixture. Stir until smooth. (Pancake batter thickens as it sits. If you do not immediately cook the pancakes, or if the cooking extends over a period of time, you may need to thin the batter with a little more milk as you cook each batch.)

3 Coat a large, well-seasoned or nonstick skillet with cooking spray. Heat skillet over medium heat until hot. For each pancake, spoon ¼ cup of batter onto skillet. When bubbles form on top of pancakes, after about 1 to 1½ minutes, turn them over (see Figure 6-1). Cook until bottom of each pancake is golden brown. Serve immediately, topped with fruit of your choice.

Figure 6-1: Bubbles on the top of the pancake remind you to turn the pancake over.

Nutrient analysis per serving: *245 kcalories, 10 grams protein, 49 grams carbohydrate, 1.6 grams fat, 0.7 grams saturated fat, 3 milligrams cholesterol, 4 grams fiber, 409 milligrams sodium*

Exchanges: *3 starch*

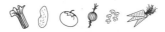

Giving whole-grain baked goods a try

Whole grains have a lower glycemic index than refined grains. That is, whole grains are less likely to send your blood glucose soaring and then dipping. The protein, fat, and fiber in whole grains slows their absorption into the bloodstream. If you're convinced that you like only white bread, not the brown stuff, please give whole grains another try. Today, all sorts of delicious whole-grain baked goods are available in markets, from whole-grain croissants to whole-grain English muffins and bagels, not to mention appetizing loaves of country bread. You may find the chewier texture and more substantial taste of whole grains somewhat heavy, but stick with them for a while. After a few weeks of enjoying these far more nutritious products, you may find the fluffy white stuff much less appealing.

Also search out some of the new whole-grain dried and cooked breakfast cereals. You can find exotic whole grains such as millet and amaranth combined with wheat and oats. Cream of barley, cream of buckwheat, and cream of brown rice are also good bets.

Another breakfast basic that features grain is waffles. Although waffles can give you a dose of carbohydrates, especially if you eat them swimming in syrup, you can adjust most waffle recipes to suit a diabetic diet. Substitute some of the grain flour with soy flour. A cup of soy flour contains 26.4 grams of protein, while enriched wheat flour contains only 11.6 grams of protein. To sample soy waffles, just try the following recipe.

Soy Waffles

Because these waffles are made with some soy flour, this recipe gives you more protein than usual. The batter needs to rest a while before cooking, so these waffles are best served for a late brunch. Enjoy them topped with sautéed vegetables and herbs, with curried chicken, or as a dessert, served with crushed berries and lowfat yogurt.

Preparation time: *5 minutes plus 1½ hours to sit*

Cooking time: *12 minutes*

Yield: *4 servings*

Nonstick cooking spray

¼ cup soy flour

¾ cup whole wheat flour

1 teaspoon active dry yeast

1 cup evaporated skim milk

½ teaspoon orange zest

1 In a large bowl, mix together the soy flour, whole wheat flour, yeast, milk, and orange zest. Let sit for 1½ hours.

2 Prepare a waffle iron by lightly coating it with an oil such as canola and preheat it. Spread a ladle-full of soy waffle batter onto the iron and cook until the waffle is done, 3 to 5 minutes, depending on the waffle iron.

Nutrient analysis per serving: *150 kcalories, 11 grams protein, 26 grams carbohydrate, 1 gram fat, 0 grams saturated fat, 2 milligrams cholesterol, 4 grams fiber, 76 milligrams sodium*

Exchanges: *1½ starch, ½ lowfat milk*

Choosing Your Breakfast Protein

If you want to add protein to your breakfast, the first food you are likely to think of is eggs. This simple food is an ideal source of protein, containing all essential amino acids. Eggs are also a source of B complex vitamins, vitamin A, vitamin D, vitamin E, selenium, and zinc.

However, egg yolks also contain a significant amount of cholesterol. Consequently, low-cholesterol diets restrict the number of eggs allowed each week. If you have elevated blood levels of cholesterol and have become an egg counter, here's a recipe that lets you fiddle with the arithmetic. Yes, this omelet is made with 12 egg whites, but only 4 egg yolks, the portion of the egg that contains all the cholesterol. This recipe makes a lighter omelet than if you made it with all the yolks, especially if you beat some air into the whites before adding them to the whole eggs.

Vegetable Omelet

Enjoy this omelet for breakfast or any other time of day or night when you want a satisfying little meal. This version is easy to prepare, just a matter of mixing and pouring. Add fresh, seasonal vegetables, and perhaps some fresh herbs, for maximum nutrition. Whet your appetite for this tasty dish by checking out the photo of it in the color section of this book.

Preparation time: *10 minutes*

Cooking time: *10 minutes*

Yield: *4 servings*

Nonstick cooking spray

½ medium zucchini

4 mushrooms

½ bell pepper

½ medium onion

2 broccoli florets

4 whole eggs

8 egg whites

1 medium plum tomato, seeded and chopped

1 *To prepare vegetables:* Cut zucchini and pepper into thin strips. Cut mushrooms into quarters and finely chop onion. Chop broccoli florets.

2 Coat a large skillet (preferably nonstick) with cooking spray and place over medium heat. Sauté vegetables, stirring often, until tender.

3 In a bowl, mix together eggs and egg whites and season with pepper. Pour egg mixture over vegetables in skillet. Add tomatoes to skillet. Cover pan and cook over low heat until eggs are cooked and puffy, 5 to 7 minutes. Serve immediately.

(continued)

Nutrient analysis per serving: *134 kcalories, 15 grams protein, 6.7 grams carbohydrate, 5.5 grams fat, 1.6 grams saturated fat, 212 milligrams cholesterol, 2 grams fiber, 183 milligrams sodium*

Note: *If you choose to season your omelet with salt and pepper, you increase the sodium level of this recipe.*

Exchanges: *1 vegetable, 2 lean meat*

This same ratio of whole eggs to egg whites is specified in the following recipe for Breakfast Pizza. What's special about this dish is that it's really a mini-meal. The eggs supply protein, the butter and cheese provide fat, and the bread and vegetables give carbohydrate. These three macronutrients together help ensure stable blood glucose levels. Combining these ingredients to make pizza doesn't hurt either. Healthy food can be fun food.

Breakfast Pizza

As any cook knows, eggs can be served in so many ways — incorporated into salads, added to sauces and meat loaf, and in this recipe, used as the filling for an inventive sandwich that was inspired by the pleasures of pizza. A small amount of shredded cheese is made to stretch, supplying plenty of flavor without all the calories of America's favorite fast food!

Preparation time: *15 minutes*

Cooking time: *20 minutes*

Yield: *4 servings*

1 loaf French or Italian bread

Nonstick cooking spray

1 tablespoon unsalted butter

½ small onion, finely chopped

4 medium red potatoes, boiled, diced small

⅛ teaspoon garlic powder

⅛ teaspoon black pepper

4 whole eggs

8 egg whites

½ cup shredded reduced-fat cheddar cheese

1 Preheat oven to 350 degrees Fahrenheit.

2 Cut bread in half lengthwise. Scoop out half of soft center. Place bread crust cut side up on a baking sheet coated with cooking spray, and spread bread with butter. (See Figure 6-2.)

Breakfast Pizza
1. Cut bread in half, lengthwise.
2. Scoop out half of the soft center.
3. Place bread crust, CUT side up, on a baking sheet coated with cooking spray...
4. and spread with butter.
BUTTER
5. Spoon egg mixture into bread...
...and sprinkle cheese on top.

Figure 6-2: The steps to preparing breakfast pizza.

3 Coat a large, well-seasoned or nonstick skillet with cooking spray and place over medium heat. Sauté onions, stirring often, until tender, about 5 minutes. Spray the pan again with oil if necessary and add potatoes, garlic powder, and pepper. Sauté for 5 minutes.

4 In a bowl, whisk together eggs and egg whites. Add to onion-potato mixture. Cook over medium heat, stirring to scramble, until eggs are cooked.

5 Spoon egg mixture into bread. Sprinkle cheese on top. Bake 8 to 10 minutes until cheese melts. Cut each half of the bread in half again, crosswise. Serve immediately.

Nutrient analysis per serving: *447 kcalories, 25 grams protein, 58 grams carbohydrate, 13 grams fat, 5.5 grams saturated fat, 225 milligrams cholesterol, 4 grams fiber, 632 milligrams sodium*

Exchanges: *4 starch, ½ fat, 2 medium-fat meat*

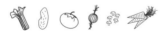

Finding Good Protein Beyond Eggs

Of course, you have more to choose from than eggs when you need to add some kind of protein to your breakfast. Consider these foods, too:

- Canadian bacon
- Cheese wedge
- Egg substitutes
- Herring in tomato sauce
- Lowfat cottage cheese

- Nuts added to cereal
- Salmon, smoked
- Steak (last night's leftovers)
- Turkey sausage
- Whitefish, smoked
- Yogurt

Discovering Fresh-Baked Biscuits and Other Morning Delights

If it's been a while since you've treated yourself to freshly baked biscuits in the morning, now's the time. You'll be surprised at how little effort they take, and you'll be savoring your first mouthful within minutes!

Potato Biscuits

Instead of buying baked goods for breakfast, cook your own by using this quick recipe — a good way to be sure of the quality of the ingredients and the calories. Buttermilk is relatively low in fat but delivers rich flavor. (See the sidebar "About the fat in milk.")

Preparation time: *22 minutes*

Cooking time: *12 minutes*

Yield: *4 servings (total 12 biscuits, or 14 biscuits if you use the trimmings)*

2 cups all-purpose flour (Substitute whole wheat pastry flour for higher amounts of vitamins and minerals.)

2½ teaspoons baking powder

¼ teaspoon baking soda

¼ teaspoon salt

2 tablespoons unsalted butter, cold, cut into small cubes

¾ cup nonfat buttermilk

⅔ cup mashed cooked potatoes

Nonstick cooking spray

1 Preheat oven to 425 degrees Fahrenheit.

2 In a bowl, combine flour, baking powder, baking soda, and salt. With a pastry blender or fork, work in butter until mixture is coarse, as shown in Figure 6-3.

Figure 6-3: Using two pastry blenders to speed up the work.

3 In another bowl, combine buttermilk and mashed potatoes. Add to dry ingredients; mix until just combined.

4 Transfer dough to lightly floured surface. Knead two or three times, as shown in Figure 6-4, until smooth. Roll out dough ½-inch thick. Using a 2-inch biscuit cutter dipped in flour, cut out 12 rounds.

Kneading Dough
To knead dough, press down with your palm...
Fold the dough over and rotate 1/4 turn
Repeat steps 1+2 until dough is soft and elastic.
voila!

Figure 6-4: Knead dough by pushing down, folding, and rotating ¼ turn.

5 Arrange rounds on a baking sheet, coated with cooking spray. Bake for 10 to 12 minutes until golden brown.

Nutrient analysis per serving: *335 kcalories, 8 grams protein, 56 grams carbohydrate, 8 grams fat, 4 grams saturated fat, 17 milligrams cholesterol, 2 grams fiber, 550 milligrams sodium*

Exchanges: *4 starch, 1 fat*

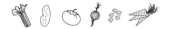

About the fat in milk

The Potato Biscuits recipe uses buttermilk, a dairy product that is relatively low in fat — good to know if you are watching your weight. You may already be making a special effort to buy lowfat dairy products, but be aware that labels can be deceiving.

A few years ago, the way manufacturers of dairy products labeled their milk made news. People began to look more closely at how fat content was listed, and they discovered that lowfat milk was not that low in fat after all. The percentage of fat stated on a milk carton refers to the weight of the fat, not the percent of calories that the fat contributes. Fat is not particularly heavy — remember, cream floats to the top of a bottle of milk — so the numbers for percentage of fat by weight are relatively small.

Type of Milk	% Fat by Weight	% Calories from Fat	Grams of Fat in One Cup
Whole milk	3.25	49	8
Lowfat 2% milk	2.00	35	4.7
Lowfat 1% milk	1.00	21	2.6
Buttermilk	0.5 to 1.00	20	2.2
Skim milk	0.5	4	0.4

Enjoying Something Crunchy in the Morning

Having a good chew in the morning can be very satisfying. Crunchy foods that require a great deal of jaw action are wake-up foods, hence the popularity of toast and noisy breakfast cereal. The following version of French toast is made with an American classic, crunchy corn flakes, but experiment with other dried breakfast cereals, too, including those made with whole grains.

Crispy Corn French Toast

This recipe, pictured in the color section of this book, is a new twist on an old favorite. The orange and vanilla flavors give a hint of sweetness, so you don't need to add sugary syrup to enjoy this recipe.

Preparation time: *10 minutes*

Cooking time: *10 minutes*

Yield: *4 servings (total 8 slices)*

2 egg whites, lightly beaten

⅔ cup lowfat milk

1 teaspoon grated orange rind

1 teaspoon vanilla extract

1⅓ cup corn flakes, crushed

8 thin slices whole wheat or multi-grain bread

1 tablespoon unsalted margarine

1 In a shallow bowl large enough to hold a slice or two of bread flatly, whisk egg whites, milk, orange rind, and vanilla extract until blended.

2 Place corn flakes in another similar, large bowl. Dip each slice of bread into egg mixture, allowing the bread to absorb some of the moisture but without letting the bread become soggy. Then coat each side of the bread slices with corn flakes.

3 Melt ¼ of margarine in a large, nonstick or well-seasoned cast-iron skillet, over medium heat. Place two coated bread slices in the skillet; cook approximately 2 minutes or until lightly browned. Turn and cook other side until golden brown.

4 Prepare remaining bread slices in same manner. Enjoy with ginger tea for a stimulating but caffeine-free start to the day.

Nutrient analysis per serving: *186 kcalories, 9 grams protein, 32 grams carbohydrate, 4 grams fat, 1 gram saturated fat, 2 milligrams cholesterol, 7 grams fiber, 394 milligrams sodium*

Exchanges: *2 starch, 1 very lean meat*

Chapter 7

Hors d'Oeuvres and First Courses: Off to a Good Start

In This Chapter

- Beginning with paté and other savory nibbles
- Diving into dips
- Starting off with salsas
- Launching lunch with homemade fun foods

Recipes in This Chapter

- Portobello Paté
- Black Olive Pesto (Tapenade)
- Roasted Red Pepper Dip
- Eggplant Salsa
- Black Bean Salsa
- Crab and Artichoke Dip
- Salad of Smoked Salmon with Horseradish Dressing
- Seasoned Sweet Potato Chips
- Wild Mushroom Tacos

Any meal can be healthy, starting with the first bite — no need for oily cocktail nibbles or fat-laden patés. Choose instead among the many nutritious foods you can use to create delicious first courses. The recipes in this chapter introduce you to the many ways of enjoying these ingredients. Imagine garlicky olives, mushrooms turned into paté, sweet roasted red peppers, and smoked salmon laid out before you to whet your appetite. You may find it difficult to save room for the main course!

Examples of healthy appetizers abound in traditional cuisines from cultures around the world. In the Middle East, meals begin with an offering of chickpea hummus (a source of calcium), along with raw radish, scallion, and fennel with a yogurt dip, all of which promote good digestion. In Indonesia, skewered pieces of grilled chicken are served with peanut sauce, both excellent sources of protein. In Mexico, avocado is mashed and made into guacamole, a dish that supplies monounsaturated fats and folic acid, which are both important for heart health.

As you plan your evening's dinner or the menu for a party, use the starter course as a way to add quality ingredients to your meals. (Interesting starter courses are also ways of sneaking healthy ingredients into the mouths of loved ones!) These dishes, designed to be eaten in small portions, also make great mini-meals. If you have any leftovers, you can enjoy them as between-meal snacks to help maintain normal blood glucose levels.

Special Spreads and Dips

Party food usually includes some sort of chopped, minced, or puréed mixture of distinctively flavored ingredients, which is meant to be smeared on a cracker or used as a dip for vegetables. Experiment with the entertaining nibbles and amusing foods in this chapter — made with healthy ingredients — and include them in meals, whether or not you're having guests.

Making vegetable paté

Books on vegetarian cooking almost always include a recipe for vegetable paté, based usually on beans, lentils, or nuts. These foods supply sufficient fat and protein to make up for the liver or other meats omitted in the recipe. Another good candidate for vegetarian paté is mushrooms, featured in the paté recipe that follows. However, the type of mushroom you decide to use makes a difference.

Time to buy a portobello mushroom! These huge, rich-tasting fungi are sold, often two to the pack, in the produce section of most supermarkets. Portobellos are fully mature cremini mushrooms (see the two compared in Figure 7-1), easily measuring 6 inches in diameter. Because portobellos are older, the gills on the underside are fully exposed, causing some of the mushroom's moisture to be lost. Consequently, this drying-out process concentrates the flavor and produces a dense and meaty texture, making the portobello an excellent choice for paté.

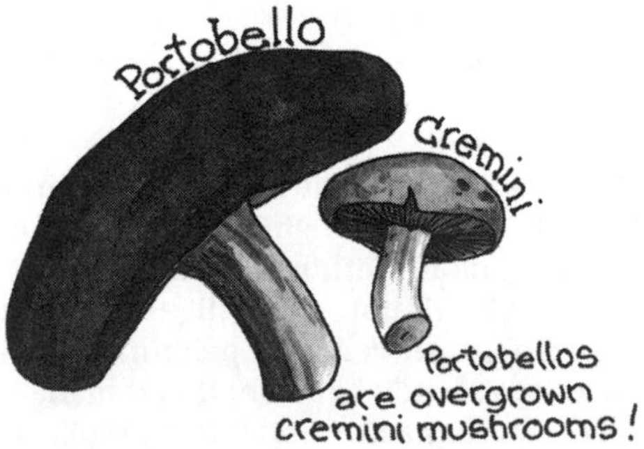

Figure 7-1: Use larger, more mature portobello mushrooms for paté.

Although the typical liver paté delivers ample amounts of saturated fat, this mushroom paté contains only a half gram per serving, an important difference if you are overweight and have concerns about heart health.

Portobello Paté

Savor this meaty and satisfying mushroom paté, a perfectly acceptable substitute for duck liver paté, but with little or no fat or calories.

Preparation time: *30 minutes*

Cooking time: *20 minutes (included in the preparation time)*

Yield: *4 servings*

2 cups portobello mushrooms, chopped

2 tablespoons extra-virgin olive oil

4 cloves garlic, minced

2 tablespoons white wine

¼ teaspoon white pepper

¼ teaspoon salt

1 tablespoon fat-free sour cream

1 Combine mushrooms, oil, and garlic in small saucepan. Cover and cook over low heat for 10 to 12 minutes until the mushrooms are tender and fragrant and only a small amount of liquid remains in the pan.

2 Add wine. Cook for 2 minutes.

3 Add pepper and salt.

4 Transfer to food processor. Add 1 tablespoon fat-free sour cream to facilitate processing. Process until smooth.

5 Serve with pita, bagel chips, or French bread slices.

Note: *To boost your nutrient intake, serve this paté with whole-grain crackers. A good brand is ak-mak, which you can find in natural food stores.*

Nutrient analysis per serving: *91 kcalories, 20 grams protein, 4 grams carbohydrate, 7.6 grams fat, 1 gram saturated fat, 0 milligrams cholesterol, 1 gram fiber, 154 milligrams sodium*

Exchanges: *1 fat, 1 vegetable*

Trying tapenade

Yes, Americans have long served olives as a before-meal morsel. An accomplished hostess in the 1950s would be sure to own what was referred to as an "olive dish." And today, canned olives usually show up as a nicety at Thanksgiving dinner. But for most people, that's where olive sophistication ends. The various olives and the special ways they are marinated and flavored in the cuisines of other cultures go untasted. When did you last eat an olive marinated in herbs and garlic, or a dry-cured olive with a dense flavor and wrinkly skin? Did you know that olives — from Italy, Greece, and Spain — come stuffed with almonds, chilies, and onions? And are you familiar with tapenade?

The French invented a way of turning olives into a sumptuous paste called *tapenade* (pronounced TA-puh-nahd or ta-pen-AHD). Traditional ingredients include capers, anchovies, olive oil, lemon juice, seasonings, and sometimes pieces of tuna. The following recipe gives you a chance to taste tapenade, minus the salty capers and anchovies, in case you are watching your blood pressure. You are in for a treat and about a half gram of fat per olive. Fortunately, most of this fat is monounsaturated, the type that benefits the heart. The walnuts, too, contain fats that help normalize cholesterol levels, and they also provide texture and richness.

Black Olive Pesto (Tapenade)

This recipe comes from Papillon Café in Denver (see Appendix A). Tapenade is a handsome dish with a rich, charcoal-gray coloring, beautiful when served on an orangy-yellow plate, a classic color of Provençe. In this recipe, squid ink is added to darken the tapenade. Squid, which are members of the mollusk family and related to octopus, have ink sacs. In Italy, the ink is removed from these sacs and used to color pasta and added to other dishes as well. Squid ink can sometimes be purchased at seafood markets and specialty food stores. Enjoy this olive pesto spread on a slice of crusty country bread, or use it as a garnish on grilled salmon — a little goes a long way.

Preparation time: *10 minutes*

Cooking time: *0 minutes*

Yield: *2½ cups or 10 ¼-cup servings*

3 cloves garlic, peeled

2 cups pitted black olives, drained

1 cup pitted kalamata or Greek olives

½ cup olive oil

1 tablespoon squid ink, optional

½ cup Parmesan cheese, grated

white pepper to taste

½ cup walnuts, chopped

1 Place garlic and olives in food processor and chop fine.

2 Add olive oil and squid ink and process until well combined.

3 Add cheese and white pepper and pulse to combine.

4 Add walnuts and process.

5 Store in plastic container and chill.

Nutrient analysis per serving: *205 kcalories, 3 grams protein, 4 grams carbohydrate, 20 grams fat, 3.4 grams saturated fat, 4 milligrams cholesterol, 2 grams fiber, 445 milligrams sodium*

Exchanges: *4 fat*

Inventing a dip

You can start with all sorts of nutritious ingredients and end up with a delicious dip. Have some yogurt on hand? Add garlic and herbs, a touch of mustard or lemon juice, and you are on your way. Salad dressings and marinades can make great starting points, as can salsas. You can also experiment with the many spice and herb mixes that are now part of standard brands of seasonings. Look for evocative names such as Caribbean Rub, Lemon Curry, Barbecue Grill Spice, Cajun Creole Seasoning, and Jamaican Jerk Blend. Add any of these to lowfat yogurt or mayonnaise, or a combination of both, and you'll quickly have a terrific dipping sauce. Many of these seasonings specify on the label that they are salt-free.

And if you want wonderful flavor that you won't find in a bottle, start by roasting some red peppers! The next recipe tells you how.

TIP

When you shop for peppers, choose those that are firm and have a glossy skin. Be sure to select red peppers and not green, which are fully developed but not completely ripe and may be difficult to digest. Fresh peppers can be stored in the refrigerator for up to a week.

Roasted Red Pepper Dip

Don't wait until you give a party to whip up some dip. This mix of red peppers makes a mouth-watering snack food. As the peppers roast and char, they develop wonderful flavor. Scoop out some dip with a slice of raw turnip, a cucumber spear, or any other vegetable, an easy way to increase your intake of vegetables.

Preparation time: *30 minutes*

Cooking time: *8 minutes (included in the preparation time)*

Yield: *4 servings (1½ cups)*

(continued)

3 red peppers

Nonstick cooking spray

⅓ cup lowfat sour cream

⅓ cup nonfat mayonnaise

¼ cup nonfat plain yogurt

⅛ teaspoon white pepper

⅛ teaspoon salt

1 Stem and seed the red peppers and then cut them in half lengthwise, as shown in Figure 7-2.

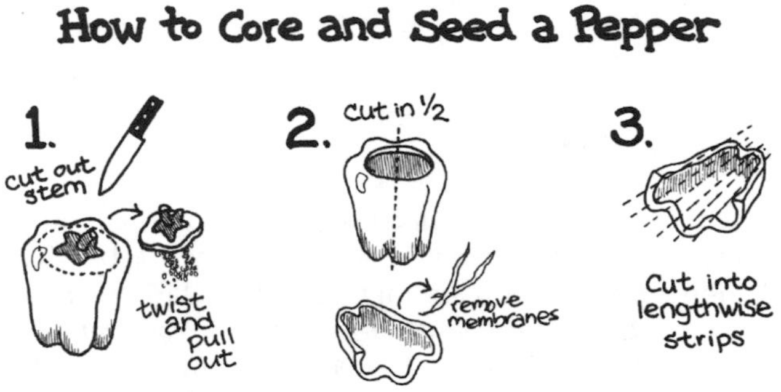

Figure 7-2: How to stem and seed peppers.

2 Use one of the following methods to cook the red peppers:

To oven-roast peppers: Preheat oven to 500 degrees Fahrenheit. Lightly coat the peppers with oil. Put them on a roasting pan and place the pan on an upper rack in the oven. Roast, shaking the pan occasionally, until peppers are browned and have collapsed, about 30 minutes. Proceed to Step 3.

To broil peppers: Preheat broiler. Lightly coat the peppers with oil. Place the peppers in a roasting pan and set it under the broiler, 3 to 4 inches from the heat. Broil, turning occasionally, until they are evenly browned and blistered, about 10 minutes. Some charring is fine, but don't let the peppers burn too badly. Proceed to Step 3.

To grill peppers: Preheat grill. Lightly coat the peppers with oil and place them on the grill. Cover and cook, turning occasionally, until the peppers are blistered and have collapsed, about 10 minutes. Some charring is fine, but don't let the peppers burn too badly. Proceed to Step 3.

3 Transfer the peppers to a bowl, cover tightly with foil or plastic wrap, and set aside until they are cool enough to handle. Peel the skin from the peppers.

4 Add red peppers, sour cream, mayonnaise, yogurt, pepper, and salt to food processor and process until smooth.

5 Transfer dip to a bowl, and cover and chill.

6 Serve with fresh vegetables such as broccoli florets, cauliflower florets, carrot sticks, celery sticks, cherry tomatoes, radishes, scallions, and zucchini.

Nutrient analysis per serving: *72 kcalories, 2 grams protein, 12 grams carbohydrate, 2.5 grams fat, 1.5 grams saturated fat, 8 milligrams cholesterol, 2 grams fiber, 252 milligrams sodium*

Exchanges: *2 vegetable, 1 fat*

Savoring Salsas

Salsa, a recent import into the U.S. kitchen, is so popular that salsa sales now exceed sales of catsup. In trendy restaurants, tomato salsa shows up on scrambled eggs and as a condiment for hamburgers. And variations on this classic salsa abound. Order grilled swordfish when you are dining out, and the fish may arrive garnished with some sort of fruit salsa made with mango or pineapple. (Check out the Shrimp and Papaya Enchilada with Avocado-Tomatillo Salsa from Star Canyon in Chapter 12.)

Salsa has stood the test of time because of its exciting flavor and also, no doubt, because of its ingredients: tomatoes, chili peppers, onions, and garlic.

Eggplant Salsa

The salsa of this recipe is reminiscent of *babaganoush,* a Middle-Eastern appetizer made with oily sesame seeds. Here's a slimming variation that contains a minimum of fat.

Preparation time: *35 minutes*

Cooking time: *20 minutes (included in the preparation time)*

Yield: *4 servings*

(continued)

1¼ pounds unpeeled eggplant

Nonstick cooking spray

1 tablespoon extra-virgin olive oil

1¼ cups diced celery (2 large stalks)

½ cup finely chopped onion (1 small)

1 large clove garlic, minced

1¼ cups coarsely chopped tomato (1 large or 2 medium)

3 tablespoons low- or no-salt tomato sauce

2 tablespoons red wine vinegar

2 tablespoons chopped ripe olives

1 tablespoon capers

⅛ teaspoon salt

¼ teaspoon pepper

1 tablespoon chopped fresh parsley

1 Preheat oven to 500 degrees Fahrenheit.

2 Coat a baking sheet with cooking spray. Peel eggplant and cut into about ⅓-inch thick slices lengthwise and arrange it in a single layer on the baking sheet. Using oil sprayer, lightly coat eggplant with oil. Bake eggplant for 5 minutes. Using tongs, turn over eggplant and bake for an additional 5 minutes. Dice eggplant, transfer to a large bowl, and set aside to cool.

3 Coat a large skillet with cooking spray and place over medium heat until hot. Add celery, onion, and garlic. Sauté, stirring often, until softened. Add tomato, tomato sauce, vinegar, olives, and capers. Season with salt and pepper. Continue to cook, stirring occasionally, for approximately 8 to 10 minutes. Remove from heat.

4 Stir in the baked eggplant and parsley. Place mixture in a bowl, cover, and chill.

5 Serve with pita, bagel chips, or French bread slices.

Nutrient analysis per serving: *103 kcalories, 3 grams protein, 16 grams carbohydrate, 4 grams fat, 0 grams saturated fat, 0 milligrams cholesterol, 5.6 grams fiber, 219 milligrams sodium*

Exchanges: *1 starch, 1 fat*

Another variation on basic tomato salsa is salsa made with beans, or *frijoles* in Spanish. Scoop up a tortilla-full of this dip and you'll increase your fiber intake, thanks to the *frijoles.*

Black Bean Salsa

This salsa, made with black beans, is a low-fat source of protein. Dip in with oven-baked corn chips — which are available commercially — or, if you prefer, enjoy with the Seasoned Sweet Potato Chips later in this chapter. You can find a photo of this tempting treat in the color section of this book.

Preparation time: *15 minutes*

Cooking time: *0 minutes*

Yield: *4 servings*

2 tablespoons extra-virgin olive oil

2 tablespoons vegetable juice (V-8 or low-sodium tomato juice)

2 tablespoons balsamic vinegar

1 tablespoon freshly squeezed lemon juice

1 teaspoon freshly squeezed lime juice

1 clove garlic, minced

1 tablespoon chopped fresh basil

1 teaspoon chopped fresh thyme

½ teaspoon ground cumin

½ teaspoon chili powder

¼ teaspoon fresh ground black pepper

¼ teaspoon salt

1 can (15 ounces) black beans, rinsed and drained

⅓ cup red pepper, cored, seeded, and finely chopped

⅓ cup red onion, minced

⅓ cup cucumber, diced, unpeeled

2 tablespoons celery, diced

2 tablespoons jalapeño pepper, minced

1 In a medium bowl, combine olive oil, vegetable juice, vinegar, lemon juice, lime juice, garlic, basil, thyme, cumin, chili powder, pepper, and salt.

2 To this olive oil mixture, add the beans, red pepper, onion, cucumber, celery, and jalapeño pepper. Using a wooden spoon, stir well. Cover and chill before serving.

Nutrient analysis per serving: *126 kcalories, 4 grams protein, 16 grams carbohydrate, 7 grams fat, 1 gram saturated fat, 0 milligrams cholesterol, 5 grams fiber, 359 milligrams sodium*

Exchanges: *1 starch, 1 fat*

Starting with Seafood

One way to increase the nutritional value of a meal is to include seafood. Fish is a source of protein and healthy oils that help lower cholesterol. Splurge on mineral-rich shrimp, crab, and lobster. They are pricey per pound, but you won't need to buy as much if you are preparing them for a first course.

For example, try this Crab and Artichoke Dip, a creamy mix of nutritious ingredients and a good choice when you are having friends over for cocktails before going out to dinner. Artichokes, too, supply essential nutrients for diabetic patients — B vitamins that nourish the nervous system, and fiber.

Crab and Artichoke Dip

This combination of crab and artichoke sends a message of luxury and abundance, even though the calories in this dish are trimmed. Using lowfat dairy products and mayonnaise in this recipe keeps the calories down where they belong.

Preparation time: *10 minutes*

Cooking time: *6 minutes*

Yield: *2 cups (6 to 8 servings)*

1 can (14 ounces) artichoke hearts, drained

¼ pound fresh lump crabmeat, shell pieces removed

¼ cup lowfat sour cream

¼ cup nonfat mayonnaise

1 tablespoon grated fresh Parmesan cheese

1 teaspoon freshly squeezed lemon juice

1 teaspoon prepared horseradish

½ teaspoon Worcestershire sauce

1 small clove garlic, minced

1 Preheat oven to 350 degrees Fahrenheit.

2 Chop artichoke hearts, and in a medium bowl, combine with crabmeat, sour cream, mayonnaise, Parmesan cheese, lemon juice, horseradish, Worcestershire sauce, and garlic.

3 Transfer mixture into a casserole or other oven-proof dish.

4 Bake for approximately 20 to 25 minutes, until warm throughout.

5 Serve with pita, bagel chips, or French bread slices.

Note: *Many commercial foods contain hidden sugars. Sweet pickles and catsup are good examples. Nonfat mayonnaise may also contain sugar, although it may not taste particularly sweet. If sugar intake is of concern to you, become a savvy label reader.*

Nutrient analysis per serving: *58 kcalories, 5.4 grams protein, 6 grams carbohydrate, 1 gram fat, 1 gram saturated fat, 15 milligrams cholesterol, 0 grams fiber, 285 milligrams sodium*

Exchanges: *½ starch, 1 very lean meat*

Another easy way to start a meal with fish is by serving smoked salmon. Chef Gordon Hamersley of Hamersley's Bistro in Boston (see Appendix A) devised the following recipe for this showy first course. He rolls and fans the salmon slices into roses. (Don't worry. If you're all thumbs, you can serve the slices as is, and they will still taste the same!) Salmon is one of several fish that are high in essential fatty acids (EFAs), which are vital for heart health. These fats keep blood platelets from getting too sticky and lower elevated blood triglycerides and blood pressure. Essential fatty acids found in fish also nourish the nervous system, which can become damaged as diabetes progresses. Essential fatty acids are found abundantly in nerve relay stations,called *synapses*, that permit the flow of information from nerve to nerve.

EFAs are found in other oily fish as well, including the following:

- Anchovies
- Herring
- Mackerel
- Sardines
- Tuna

Salad of Smoked Salmon with Horseradish Dressing

Roses made of sliced salmon, creamy horseradish dressing, and pumpernickel croutons turn this stylish first course into a little masterpiece of flavor — take a look at it in the color section of this book. The croutons add satisfying crunch. Buy them in the supermarket or make your own by cutting thick slices of bread into cubes and toasting them in the oven until golden. Be sure to search out radicchio rather than ordinary greens. This Italian type of chicory has appealing red-tinged leaves.

(continued)

Preparation time: *20 minutes*

Cooking time: *None*

Yield: *6 servings*

6 cups assorted bitter greens including watercress, Belgian endive, and radicchio

2 tablespoons lemon juice

3 tablespoons olive oil

½ teaspoon fresh dill, chopped

½ teaspoon salt and pepper to taste

1½ teaspoons prepared horseradish, drained

¼ cup heavy cream

2 tablespoons lemon juice

1 tablespoon extra-virgin olive oil

2 teaspoons capers, drained

8 slices packaged smoked salmon (3 ounces)

2 ounces homemade or unseasoned commercial croutons

1 Wash and dry all the greens and toss together. Refrigerate until needed.

2 To prepare lemon vinaigrette: Whisk together lemon juice, olive oil, dill, salt, and pepper. Reserve.

3 To prepare dressing: In a small bowl, whisk together horseradish, heavy cream, lemon juice, olive oil, salt, and pepper. Stir in the capers, cover, and refrigerate.

4 Beginning with one end, start rolling up salmon slice to form a coil. When almost all of the salmon has been rolled, sit it on its base and curl the last piece of salmon around to form the rose, as shown in Figure 7-3. (Alternatively, the salmon can simply be draped over the greens.)

Salad of Smoked Salmon with Horseradish Dressing
Roll slices of salmon up, starting at one narrow end and then....
turn up on that end. They should resemble small roses.

Figure 7-3: Rolling salmon slices into roses.

5 Sprinkle the greens with lemon vinaigrette, and place on individual plates. On each plate, place a salmon rose, resting on the greens, or drape the salmon slices over greens. Lightly drizzle the creamy horseradish dressing over the greens and salmon. Sprinkle with pumpernickel croutons.

Nutrient analysis per serving: *190 kcalories, 15 grams protein, 12 grams carbohydrate, 14 grams fat, 4 grams saturated fat, 17 milligrams cholesterol, 3 grams fiber, 263 milligrams sodium*

Exchanges: *2 vegetable, 3 fat*

Making Healthy Fun Foods

In real life, rather than starting on some salmon to satisfy your first pangs of hunger, you are more likely to reach for such common fixes as oily, salted cocktail peanuts or potato chips. Nuts are an excellent source of minerals and healthy fats, but eating them raw — not toasted, salted, and sugar-coated — is better. Many commercial roasted nuts have actually been fried, a process that degrades the quality of their oils, although cooking does produce a rich and tawny flavor that is hard to resist. Enjoy raw almonds and walnuts, and if you must have peanuts, which do not taste good raw, have them roasted but not salted or honey-dipped.

TIP: If you want toasted nuts, cook them yourself in a skillet or scattered on a baking sheet placed in a moderately warm oven until they turn fragrant and light brown. This way you have some control over the cooking temperature, time, and the quality of the oils you are eating.

You can also make your own potato chips. The following section shows you how.

Introducing the new and improved potato chip!

What is junky about junk foods is often not the ingredients themselves but the way the food is prepared. After all, potato chips start with nutritious potatoes that have kept generations alive.

Even if you are watching your fat and sodium, you can still have these crispy little nibbles by cooking them yourself in the oven. No need for the store-bought, fried-in-fat versions. You can control the amount of salt sprinkled on them, which is helpful if you are concerned about sodium intake and hypertension. In addition, by eating potatoes, you'll increase your intake of potassium. Potassium works with sodium to normalize the heartbeat and assists in the conversion of glucose to glycogen, the form in which glucose can be stored in the liver.

Seasoned Sweet Potato Chips

Why buy potato chips that are fried when home-cooked chips such as these have great taste with far fewer calories and much less salt? For best results, be sure to cut the potatoes into uniform slices. You can buy a mandoline — an ideal slicing tool for this task — at most kitchen stores for under $40.

Preparation time: *15 minutes*

Cooking time: *10 minutes*

Yield: *4 servings*

⅛ teaspoon cinnamon

⅛ teaspoon nutmeg

⅛ teaspoon freshly ground black pepper

Pinch of salt

4 sweet potatoes

2 tablespoons extra-virgin olive oil

Nonstick cooking spray

1 Preheat oven to 375 degrees Fahrenheit.

2 Peel the sweet potatoes and slice thin, using a mandoline or food processor fitted with the slicing blade to make uniform ⅛ inch slices.

3 In a small bowl combine cinnamon, nutmeg, pepper, and salt. In a large bowl, coat sweet potato slices with oil. Add the seasonings and toss to combine.

4 Arrange potatoes on a baking sheet coated with cooking spray. Bake until potatoes are cooked through and lightly browned, 20 to 25 minutes. Halfway through the cooking time, turn the pan ¼ turn for even browning. The chips will further crisp as they cool.

Nutrient analysis per serving: *177 kcalories, 2 grams protein, 28 grams carbohydrate, 7 grams fat, 1 gram saturated fat, 0 milligrams cholesterol, 3 grams fiber, 84 milligrams sodium*

Exchanges: *2 starch, 1 fat*

Tempting tiny tacos

Why not start a meal with miniature tacos, a crowd-pleaser at parties and a fitting start to any dinner when made with elegant ingredients. The tacos in this recipe are filled with exotic mushrooms. Tacos are particularly satisfying because they require a bit of chewing, thanks to the taco shell and the iceberg lettuce. Many refined and processed foods in the standard American diet lack crunch. These tacos will get your jawbone working!

TIP

The recipe calls for wild mushrooms, which are richly flavored, not button mushrooms. Select from the following exotic varieties that many supermarkets now carry:

- Cremini mushroom
- Oyster mushroom
- Portobello mushroom
- Shiitake mushroom
- Straw mushroom

Wild Mushroom Tacos

This appetizer, from Anasazi Restaurant in Santa Fe (see Appendix A), is a fun, spicy start to a meal. Because it's low in carbohydrate, you have a lot of leeway in choosing foods for the rest of your meal. These tacos are featured in the color section of this book.

Preparation time: *15 minutes*

Cooking time: *25 minutes*

Yield: *4 servings*

1 tablespoon olive oil

½ cup minced onion

2 tablespoons minced garlic

2 cups mixed (assorted) sliced mushrooms, such as cremini and shiitake

Optional: 1 to 2 tablespoons Chipotles en Adobo, chopped (hot peppers in a smoky tomato sauce, available in markets that carry Mexican foods)

¼ cup beer

¼ cup chicken broth

2 tablespoons cilantro, chopped

¼ teaspoon salt

Lime juice to taste

½ cup shredded iceberg lettuce

8 mini taco shells, 2½-inch diameter

1 Heat olive oil in heavy-bottomed sauté pan. Sauté onion until caramelized, about 15 minutes. Add garlic and mushrooms. Sauté about 5 minutes. Add chopped Chipotles and beer. Bring to a boil (about 2 minutes) and reduce beer by ½ volume. Add chicken broth and simmer mushroom mixture until slightly thickened, about 3 to 5 minutes. Add cilantro, salt, and lime juice to taste.

(continued)

2 (*Optional:* Heat taco shells in 350-degree Fahrenheit oven for 2 to 3 minutes before filling.) Place shredded lettuce in bottom of taco shells. Spoon mushroom compote on top and serve.

Nutrient analysis per serving: *115 kcalories, 3 grams protein, 13 grams carbohydrate, 6 grams fat, 1 gram saturated fat, 0 milligrams cholesterol, 2 grams fiber, 290 milligrams sodium*

Exchanges: *½ starch, 1 vegetable, 1 fat*

Chapter 8

Soup, Beautiful Soup

In This Chapter

- Discovering the basic steps for creating great soup
- Starting a soup with leftovers
- Thickening soup the healthy way
- Enhancing flavor without using salt
- Ordering soup in restaurants
- Adding flavor by adding stock
- Enjoying soup for dessert

Recipes in This Chapter

For a diabetic patient, soup is an ideal food because its makeup is so flexible. There's almost no limit to the range of ingredients that can go into it. You can easily tailor the amount of protein, carbohydrate, and fat a soup contains to suit your specific metabolic needs. Want more protein? Add some chunks of beef or shreds of chicken, along with some beans. Boost the carbohydrate content with noodles, rice, and potatoes. For added fat, drizzle in some olive oil or add a slice of butter. It's your call.

In addition, you don't have to follow any rules about when and how to eat it. Soup makes a great main course for lunch or dinner. (The Japanese even eat soup for breakfast.) Or you can sip soup as a between-meal snack, if your diabetic treatment plan recommends eating small amounts more frequently.

Given the advantages of soup, you would expect it to be a standard part of the average diet. In fact, most people forget to have it. Most people don't think that they have time to cook soup, and when they eat a meal out, they tend not to order soup and have salad instead, which can be lower in calories and is less filling. Soup is beginning to show up on the menus of fast-food eateries where a person is more likely to order just a single dish — a far better choice than eating a food that has been deep-fried. However, prepared soups are often very high in sodium, a concern for individuals with high blood pressure.

An Old-Fashioned Food

Soup was a staple of home cooking in earlier times. Any day, you might find a pot of soup bubbling contentedly on the back burner as its ingredients simmered to perfection. But with today's emphasis on quick cooking methods and foods that can be prepared in minutes, making soup may seem hopelessly old-fashioned to you. Who has time? Who has the patience? But consider these points:

- No one is asking you to sit and watch the soup as it cooks. Soup does fine all by itself. If you work at home, start a soup while you are preparing breakfast. Keep it cooking while you telecommute, and you'll have a luscious and nourishing fresh soup for lunch! Or after dinner, brew a broth while you are watching television and then make soup the next day, using this stock to speed up the process.
- Soup doesn't need to take a long time to make. If you purée vegetables leftover from dinner and add milk or chicken broth, you can have a freshly made soup in 10 minutes.
- Soup keeps. Make it on a weekend in spare moments and enjoy a bowlful on a weekday when your schedule is more hectic, allowing no time for cooking.
- Soups freeze well. Make a potful and fill portion-size plastic containers with the results. Label the container, or you'll regret not knowing the contents later, and tuck away the soup in your freezer. When you want to defrost some soup, just put the frozen block into a pot over medium heat and let it melt into a delicious concoction, ready to eat.
- Another convenient way of preparing soup is to cook it in a crockpot on low heat over several hours. Flavors blend to produce a rich and satisfying soup.

To be sure to have leftovers, prepare a double recipe of the soup you are making, such as the following recipe for carrot soup. It calls for various elegant ingredients — white wine, leeks, and blood orange — that you probably don't cook with on a daily basis. But what a wonderful brew to find in your freezer because you've gotten around to making it once in a while.

Why blood oranges are special

Blood oranges have a sweet and tart taste and are zesty and full-flavored, but they are especially prized for the jewel-like colors of their flesh. The fruit may be flecked with scarlet, rust, purple, or garnet or be colored throughout with these hues. Segments make a stunning garnish, as you can see if you follow the instructions for preparing Carrot Soup with Leek and Blood Orange.

This glamorous member of the citrus family is native to Italy and Spain where blood oranges are a standard fruit. Here in America, they are still considered exotic and are in short supply. Unfortunately, their often high price per pound reflects their scarcity. California produces some, and also Florida, but many kinds are imported. Look for Ruby Blood and also Moro varieties, which orange connoisseurs particularly favor. These are juicy but firm, without seeds, and the fruit has a deep raspberry aftertaste.

Blood oranges are likely to be available in stores beginning in December but can show up as late as June, depending upon their origin. Most blood oranges are small or medium in size. As with any orange, gauge freshness by weight. You want the heftiest. The skin may be smooth or tinted and look like common oranges or have a red tint.

Carrot Soup with Leek and Blood Orange

This recipe, from Erna's Elderberry House in Oakhurst, California (see Appendix A), is shown in the color section of this book. The root vegetables that it contains, carrots and parsnips, are durable vegetables that freeze well. Carrots and parsnips are good sources of soluble fiber, which helps normalize blood glucose. You can benefit from both by enjoying this recipe for an elegant soup, garnished with orange segments and *zest,* the outer skin of the citrus fruit.

Preparation time: *25 minutes*

Cooking time: *45 minutes*

Yield: *6 servings*

1 small carrot, sliced paper thin

½ medium leek, pale green inner stalk, cut into thin slices

1 small onion, sliced

1 tablespoon unsalted butter

1 pound (about 5 medium) carrots, peeled and chopped

1 medium parsnip, peeled and chopped

¼ cup dry white wine

5 cups chicken broth, reduced-sodium or homemade

Juice of 5 blood oranges (or substitute ¾ cup orange juice)

salt, white pepper, and ground caraway to taste

1 blood orange, zested, peeled, and sectioned

1 tablespoon chopped parsley

(continued)

1 Blanch the sliced carrot and leek in a medium saucepan of boiling, salted water until tender but not limp, about 2 minutes. Set aside.

2 In another medium saucepan, sauté the onion in the butter over medium heat until slightly softened. Add carrots and parsnips and cook, stirring often, for 5 minutes. Add the wine, stirring to dissolve any flavorful browned particles adhering to the bottom of the pan. Add broth and orange juice and bring to a boil. Reduce heat and let simmer until the carrots are tender enough to be easily crushed between two fingers, about 35 minutes.

3 Transfer to a blender or food processor in batches and purée. Strain through sieve into a clean saucepan and reheat. Season with salt, white pepper, and caraway to taste.

4 Ladle the carrot soup into individual warmed soup bowls. Top with sliced carrots and leek, orange sections, zest, and parsley.

Nutrient analysis per serving: *125 kcalories, 5 grams protein, 21 grams carbohydrate, 2 grams fat, 1 gram saturated fat, 5 milligrams cholesterol, 5 grams fiber, 493 milligrams sodium*

Exchanges: *1 starch, 1 vegetable*

Preparing Soup: Basic Techniques

In many recipes for soup, the first few steps ask you to sauté some vegetables to bring out their flavor. You may heat and stir together a combination of vegetables such as onions, carrots, and celery, along with herbs and spices, in a small amount of fat. The fat may be oil or butter, or even a bit of fatty smoked meat such as bacon. What happens next is caramelization. As the ingredients begin to turn brown, they will *caramelize,* developing a rich and nutty flavor.

Next, add liquid, perhaps some vegetable broth, chicken or beef broth, wine, or water. First, add just a half-cup or so of liquid to *deglaze* the pot. In this procedure, any bits of caramelized vegetables stuck to the bottom are gently dislodged, preferably using a wooden spoon. You want these flavorful morsels to blend in with the other flavors of the soup. Then add the remainder of the liquid and any other ingredients, bring to a boil, and turn down for a long, slow cook.

To get a feel for these procedures, cook your way through the following delicious soup, which is accented with garlic and Italian herbs.

Zucchini Soup with Herbs and Spices

Clever lowfat cooking relies on herbs and spices for the flavor spark. This recipe, from Hamersley's Bistro in Boston (see Appendix A), combines curry and Italian herbs. The Italian herbs are sold premixed, or you can concoct your own formula by combining basil, oregano, thyme, sage, rosemary, and marjoram.

Preparation time: *40 minutes*

Cooking time: *25 minutes*

Yield: *6 servings*

4 tablespoons cooking oil

3 onions, chopped

1 potato, peeled and diced

4 cloves garlic, peeled and minced

8 pounds zucchini, chopped

1 tablespoon curry powder

1 tablespoon mixed Italian herbs

2 cups white wine

8 cups chicken stock

salt and pepper to taste

1. In a medium saucepan, heat oil over medium heat and sauté onions, potato, and garlic until they are translucent. Add zucchini, potato, curry powder, and Italian herbs and cook, stirring, until the zucchini begins to release its juices (about 7 minutes).
2. Add wine and chicken stock, bring to a boil, and then simmer over low to medium heat for approximately 20 minutes, until zucchini is fully cooked. Allow to cool.
3. Transfer the soup, in batches, to the bowl of a food processor or blender, and purée until smooth. Season with salt and pepper to taste. Serve the zucchini soup chilled.

Nutrient analysis per serving: *258 kcalories, 12 grams protein, 29 grams carbohydrate, 10 grams fat, 1.2 grams saturated fat, 0 milligrams cholesterol, 8 grams fiber, 761 milligrams sodium*

Exchanges: *1 starch, 3 vegetable, 2 fat*

Using Leftovers: Making Hunter Soup

In Italian, *cacciatore* means "hunter," and Italian dishes prepared "al cacciatore" contain ingredients that a hunter might find in the countryside, such as mushrooms, onions, and herbs. Usually, the cook also adds some wine. You can also make soup al cacciatore, but in this case, it can mean something different. The hunt won't have taken place in fields and forests, but inside the refrigerator when you search for leftovers, which can be used as the makings for great soups.

If you went to your refrigerator right now, you'd probably find enough fixings to concoct some sort of soup or broth. The best place to start searching is in the vegetable drawers. Perhaps you'll come across the last few carrots from a bunch, some forgotten celery, and an onion rolling around at the back. If you are lucky, you may also discover some leftover meat or chicken, or a lone sausage from breakfast. Adding a few bay leaves and some pepper never hurts. Throw it all into the pot. The results are sure to be unique and tasty, as well as slimming if the majority of the ingredients are vegetables.

Even if you only find a cucumber in the fridge — and you happen to have some yogurt and some milk — add a dash of dill, and you can make a passable cucumber soup with a Danish flavor. Or plan ahead, shop for the ingredients you need, and make the following elegant version.

Chilled Cucumber Soup

Make cucumber soup even more refreshing by adding naturally tart yogurt. Yogurt, plus the nonfat sour cream in this recipe, makes this soup a substantial and satisfying starter course for lunch or dinner.

Preparation time: *35 minutes*

Cooking time: *15 minutes (included in the preparation time)*

Yield: *4 servings*

Nonstick cooking spray

1 large or 2 small cucumbers, peeled, seeded, and cut into ¼-inch slices (2 cups)

2 shallots, minced

¼ cup white wine

2 cups low-sodium chicken broth

¼ teaspoon pepper

⅛ teaspoon salt

½ cup nonfat sour cream

½ cup plain nonfat yogurt

4 fresh dill weed sprigs

1 Coat a large skillet with cooking spray and place over medium heat until hot. Sauté cucumber and shallots, tossing or stirring frequently until soft and translucent (about 5 minutes).

2 Stir in wine and chicken broth. Bring to a boil and simmer for 10 minutes. Add pepper and salt. Continue to simmer for 2 minutes. Remove from heat.

3 Place contents of skillet in an electric blender or the bowl of a food processor, cover, and process until smooth.

4 Pour mixture into a bowl. Let cool slightly. With a wire whisk, stir in sour cream and yogurt. Cover and chill. Garnish with dill weed sprigs.

Nutrient analysis per serving: *91 kcalories, 6 grams protein, 15 grams carbohydrate, 0 grams fat, 0 grams saturated fat, 0 milligrams cholesterol, 1 gram fiber, 315 milligrams sodium*

Exchanges: *1 starch*

Slimming Ways to Thicken Soup

Adding cream to a soup will give it a nice body but may not do much to benefit yours! Cream is loaded with saturated fat, which can lead to elevated blood lipids and heart disease, a condition that often affects people with diabetes. However, certain soups — especially those made from puréed vegetables — can turn into an unappealing slush unless you add some form of thickening agent. You can use any of the following ingredients to thicken a soup and enhance its texture.

- Beans
- Bread
- Cornstarch
- Flour
- Peas
- Potatoes
- Rice
- Yuca

In particular, beans, peas, and yuca (see the sidebar, "Is yuca for you?") are good choices for thickeners in a diabetic soup because these foods contain soluble fiber, which helps maintain normal blood glucose levels. For example, if your soup contains beans, remove some of them after the soup is cooked and purée these in a food processor. Add the puréed beans back as a thick paste, and they act as a thickening agent. You can use many other ingredients in the same way.

Some thickeners such as potato and bread have a high glycemic index and are more likely to elevate blood glucose, making them less desirable in a diabetic diet.

The following recipe for vegetable soup gives you an opportunity to experiment with yuca, an ingredient that may not be familiar to you. Yuca both absorbs juices and acts as a thickening agent. Cutting yuca into small pieces, as called for in this recipe, creates more surface area and maximizes the effect of this root vegetable on the texture of your soup.

Hearty Vegetable Soup

The U.S. Department of Agriculture's Dietary Guidelines for Americans suggests at least five servings of fruits and vegetables every day to ensure adequate intake of vitamins, minerals, and fiber. Enjoying a bowlful of vegetable soup such as this recipe is a delicious way to meet your quota.

When you prepare vegetable soup, first add the items that require longer cooking (such as beets or carrots), and later add quick-cooking ingredients (such as spinach and tomatoes). You'll have all your vegetables just where you want them, done to perfection when your soup is finished. However, this procedure does require your time and attention. Another way to make sure that all the vegetables finish cooking about the same time is to cut the longer-cooking ones (such as potatoes) into smaller pieces and the faster-cooking types (such as squash) into larger chunks.

Preparation time: *15 minutes*

Cooking time: *30 minutes*

Yield: *4 servings*

Nonstick cooking spray

½ cup diced onions

½ cup diced celery

½ cup diced carrots

1 cup diced fresh yuca

½ cup diced fresh tomatoes

½ cup diced zucchini

1 bay leaf

⅛ teaspoon thyme

½ teaspoon oregano

2 cups low-sodium chicken broth

⅛ teaspoon white pepper

1 Choose a large pot with a tightly fitting lid. Coat the pot with nonstick spray and cook, stirring constantly, onion, celery, and carrots until onions are translucent — about 5 to 7 minutes. You can spray the pot with additional cooking spray or add a little stock or water if the vegetables begin to stick or burn. Add remaining ingredients and stir to combine.

2 Bring vegetable soup to a boil over high heat, uncovered, and then simmer covered for 20 minutes.

3 Serve immediately as a light lunch or mini meal.

Note: *Adding salt is optional, but it does increase the sodium level.*

Nutrient analysis per serving: *33 kcalories, 2 grams protein, 6 grams carbohydrate, 0 grams fat, 0 grams saturated fat, 0 milligrams cholesterol, 2 grams fiber, 212 milligrams sodium*

Exchanges*: ½ starch*

Is yuca for you?

Yuca, which is pronounced "YOO-ka," not "YUK-ka," is more commonly known in the United States as *cassava,* the Spanish term for this root vegetable. If you have ever eaten tapioca, you've eaten yuca, the source of that thickener. The taste can be sweet, buttery, and nicely bland. The texture is waxy, tacky, and glutinous. Yuca may be an acquired taste for most people in the United States, but much of the world relishes yuca. It is in the native soups and stews of a wide range of countries, including Brazil, Venezuela, Cuba, Colombia, Puerto Rico, and in East Africa, Asia, and the South Pacific.

Yuca are shaped like long, narrow sweet potatoes. The outside is rough and brown and looks like bark. Inside is flesh that is dense, hard, and white. Yuca is available year-round in Hispanic markets and in supermarkets in cities that have sizeable Hispanic populations. Look for yuca that is as completely covered with bark as possible. Avoid those that have any sliminess or mold, or hairline cracks, which indicate dryness. Yuca should smell clean and fresh. Ask the produce person to cut open a yuca to check for freshness. You should not see any darkening near the skin.

Yuca spoils rapidly. It's best to use up the amount you've bought in one cooking. Store it in the refrigerator, but for no more than four days. Yuca also freezes well. Peeled and cut into chunks, yuca can be kept frozen for several months.

Adding Salt to Your Soup

A diabetic diet is likely to be a low-sodium diet, to curb elevated blood pressure that is often associated with complications of diabetes. Many standard soup recipes call for salt and do need some sort of flavor enhancer. If you are salt-sensitive and need to watch your intake, try any of these condiments to spark flavors:

- Chilies
- Fresh herbs
- Freshly ground black pepper
- Garlic
- Honey
- Lemon juice
- Onion
- Salt-free seasoning mixes
- Vinegar

TIP

Fats are flavor carriers. If you've made a soup that is virtually fat-free, it probably tastes flat. But you can remedy this lack of flavor easily by adding something fatty, such as a bit of butter or a splash of extra-virgin olive oil. You'll be surprised at how little is required to deliver flavor.

No wonder the following recipe for gazpacho is so tasty! It contains all sorts of flavor enhancers: garlic, salt, cayenne, olive oil, onion, vinegar, honey, black pepper, and cilantro. If you need to omit the salt when you make this soup, you probably won't miss it.

Farmer Tomato Gazpacho

To make a good gazpacho, start with great tomatoes. Some consider the organic tomatoes of Missouri and eastern Kansas to be the best in the world — hence the popularity of this recipe, which comes from Cafe Allegro in Kansas City (see Appendix A), in the heart of tomato country. The dark rich soils of the riverbeds in combination with the extremely long and hot summers produce a sweet, meaty, deep-red tomato ideal for gazpacho. Your local variety of fresh tomatoes, in season, will do fine as well. And don't be afraid to make a large amount of this recipe. This soup is even better a day or two after you make it, so this recipe is written for eight servings to give you some leftovers.

Preparation time: *35 minutes*

Cooking time: *20 minutes*

Yield: *8 servings*

5 farmer or local tomatoes, peeled, seeded, and diced

7 cloves garlic, minced

2 teaspoons kosher salt

1 teaspoon cayenne pepper

2 tablespoons extra-virgin olive oil

2 red onions, small diced

½ red pepper, small diced

2 cucumbers, peeled, seeded, and small diced

8 ounces San Pellegrino or sparkling water

¼ cup sherry vinegar

⅛ cup honey

cracked black pepper to taste

Garlic Croutons

½ baguette bread, cut into ¾-inch slices (whole-grain baguette bread provides more vitamins, minerals, and flavor than white-flour baguette)

5 cloves garlic, minced

¼ cup olive oil

2 tablespoons fresh parsley, chopped

pinch cracked black pepper

2 tablespoons cilantro, chopped

1 In a large bowl, combine tomatoes, garlic, salt, and cayenne. Slowly pour in extra-virgin olive oil, constantly stirring. This mixture creates the base of the soup and gives it a velvety finish. Add onions, red peppers, cucumbers, sparkling water, vinegar, and honey. Season with pepper, and adjust seasoning with salt if necessary. Mix well and chill.

2 *To make garlic croutons:* Preheat oven to 350 degrees Fahrenheit. In a large bowl, toss together the baguette slices with the remaining garlic, olive oil, parsley, salt, and pepper. (If you need to conserve fat, the croutons can be misted with olive oil spray or brushed with 1 tablespoon of oil and then tossed with herbs and seasonings.) Bake for 20 minutes or until golden brown. Let cool.

3 Serve soup in ice-cold bowls, topped with garlic croutons and chopped cilantro.

Nutrient analysis per serving: *192 kcalories, 3 grams protein, 22 grams carbohydrate, 11 grams fat, 1.6 grams saturated fat, 0 milligrams cholesterol, 2.6 grams fiber, 580 milligrams sodium*

Exchanges: *1 starch, 1 vegetable, 2 fat*

If your physician or dietitian has given you any instructions at all about watching your salt, you've probably been told about the high sodium content of canned soup. You may be on a standard 3,000-milligram-a-day regimen, recommended for most individuals, or a 2,000-milligram-a-day sodium-restricted diet. Table 8-1 shows some sample amounts of the milligrams of sodium in a single serving of some common soups.

Table 8-1 Canned Soups and Sodium

Soups	*Serving Size*	*Sodium in Milligrams*
Chicken Broth (Campbell's)	4 ounces (condensed soup)	770
Low Sodium Chicken Broth (Campbell's)	10½ ounces	140
Chicken Broth (Health Valley)	8 ounces	150
Chicken Noodle instant soup (Knorr)	8 ounces	910
Tomato (Campbell's)	4 ounces (condensed soup)	760
Low Sodium Tomato (Campbell's)	10½ ounces	60
Lentil (Progresso)	8 ounces	750
Vegetable Beef (Campbell's)	4 ounces (condensed soup)	890
Chunky Beef (Campbell's)	10¾ ounces	1,130
Clam Chowder (Campbell's)	4 ounces (condensed soup)	960
Onion Soup Mix (Lipton)	8 ounces (or 1 tablespoon mix)	610

Ordering Soup When You Eat Out

If you are at a loss for what to order when you eat out, you usually can't go wrong by ordering soup. Although you won't know for sure how much fat or sodium the soup contains, in general, soups are one of the most wholesome foods you can order in a restaurant. The soup may have been made with a spectacular stock, the result of simmering pounds of trimmings that are available to only a restaurant chef producing volumes of food. Such soup can be rich in nutrients. In addition, soup is prepared in healthy ways such as boiling and simmering, not deep-frying. And because soup can fill you up at the start of a meal, it makes you less likely to eat more fattening foods.

Various types of restaurants, such as ethnic eateries, each have their soup specialties. Look for these on menus:

- Pea, bean, and beef with barley soups at diners and coffee shops
- Lentil, bean, minestrone, and escarole soups at Italian restaurants
- Mulligatawny (lentil) at Indian establishments
- Miso (soybean) at Japanese restaurants
- Tom ka gai at Thai establishments
- Borscht (beet) at Russian restaurants
- Egg drop, wonton, and sweet and sour at Chinese restaurants

You can also try your hand at preparing any of the following soups at home.

Braised Leek and Shiitake Hot and Sour Soup

This recipe comes from Cafe Allegro in Kansas City (see Appendix A). Enjoy this soup as the starter course, followed by stir-fried chicken and broccoli. Or turn this soup into a meal in itself by adding tofu, a good source of protein. The bland tofu will take on the many flavors of the other ingredients, including the serrano chili. This very hot and savory chili is about 1½ inches long and is slightly pointed. When young, it is bright green, but it turns red and then yellow as it matures. Jalapeño chili pepper may be substituted.

Preparation time: *20 minutes*

Cooking time: *20 minutes*

Yield: *4 servings*

2 tablespoons sesame oil

2 leeks, washed, white part only, split in half and sliced ½-inch thick

1 celery stalk, diced

1 small carrot, diced

1 serrano chili pepper, seeded and minced

2 cloves garlic, minced

1 teaspoon ginger, minced

3 cups mushroom broth, such as Wild Mushroom Broth (see the following recipe), or reduced sodium chicken broth

1 cup shiitake mushrooms, sliced

5 tablespoons "lite" (low-sodium) soy sauce

⅓ cup rice wine vinegar

2 tablespoons cracked black pepper

8 scallions, slanted cut ¼-inch thick

8 large cilantro leaves

(continued)

1 In a medium saucepan, heat sesame oil over low heat. Add leeks, and cover and cook slowly for about 10 minutes (this allows the leeks to develop a very buttery flavor). Uncover and add celery, carrot, chili pepper, garlic, and ginger. Raise heat to medium and cook, stirring often, until vegetables are slightly soft, about 5 minutes.

2 Add broth and shiitake mushrooms, and bring to a simmer. Taste, and then add soy sauce and rice wine vinegar. Taste again to determine whether the soup needs more salt (add more soy sauce) or sour (add more vinegar), and adjust accordingly. After you balance the flavor, add black pepper.

3 Ladle into bowls and garnish with scallions and cilantro leaves.

Nutrient analysis per serving: *177 kcalories, 6 grams protein, 24 grams carbohydrate, 7 grams fat, 1 gram saturated fat, 0 milligrams cholesterol, 3 grams fiber, 890 milligrams sodium*

Exchanges: *1 starch, 1 vegetable, 1 fat*

Wild Mushroom Broth

Cafe Allegro in Kansas City (see Appendix A) contributed this rich broth for use in mushroom-based soups and sauces, including two in this book: Braised Leek and Shiitake Hot and Sour Soup (see the preceding recipe) and Truffled Wild Mushroom Gravy (see Chapter 14).

Preparation time: *20 minutes*

Cooking time: *1 hour*

Yield: *10 servings*

1 yellow onion, thinly sliced

1 leek, darker green part, washed and chopped

1 clove garlic, in skin, crushed with side of knife

½ pound shiitake mushrooms

1 teaspoon salt

1½ teaspoons whole black peppercorns

1 pound whole portobello mushrooms, washed and cut in half

2 carrots, chopped

3 parsley sprigs, chopped

3 thyme sprigs

2 oregano sprigs

2 sage sprigs

2 bay leaves

3 quarts cold water

1. Place all ingredients in a large saucepan. Over high heat, bring to a boil. Reduce heat to medium-low and simmer broth, uncovered, for 1 hour.

2. Strain through a fine strainer. Discard vegetables and reserve broth for use in Truffled Wild Mushroom Gravy or other recipes.

Nutrient analysis per serving: *34 kcalories, 2 grams protein, 6 grams carbohydrate, 0 grams fat, 0 grams saturated fat, 0 milligrams cholesterol, 0 grams fiber, 244 milligrams sodium*

Exchanges: *½ starch*

Making Stocks

You can begin a soup using water, but making a soup with real depth of flavor calls for stock. Basically, a *stock* is a liquid in which solid ingredients are cooked and then usually strained out. The flavors of these ingredients end up in the final broth.

You can make a basic stock by simmering together aromatic vegetables such as onion and celery with carrots, which add sweetness, plus some parsley and a bay leaf. You only need to cook this mixture for about 20 minutes. In fact, longer cooking can cause the broth to have a trace of bitterness.

TIP

Add strong-flavored vegetables such as broccoli, cauliflower, and asparagus cautiously or they will overpower the other ingredients.

Dried mushrooms will also enrich a stock and are easy to keep on hand for an impromptu soup-making session. Garlic is another kitchen staple that you may decide to add to your stock. But before you do, make sure that its flavors really suit the soup you're making. After you've added garlic, you can't cover over it or make it go away.

Most markets carry various brands of chicken and beef stock that offer good flavor. These are adequate for making everyday soups and are well worth keeping on hand. However, such broths can be loaded with sodium, so be sure to search out low-salt versions. You can always add more salt to your soup if it needs it and your diet permits.

TIP

Experiment with vegetable stock mixes. Some lines of herbs and spices also include these, and you can find them in the open bin sections of natural food stores. Some are better than others; the flavor can overtake your soup.

Both of the following recipes use stock. The better the stock, the better the soup.

Pumpkin Soup

Pumpkins are not just for Halloween. Use fresh pumpkin to make this seasonal soup from Barbetta in New York (see Appendix A). Or you can use canned pumpkin to enjoy its autumnal flavor year-round.

Preparation time: *20 minutes*

Cooking time: *45 minutes*

Yield: *6 servings*

1 tablespoon sweet butter

1 tablespoon canola oil

2 leeks, finely chopped

1 small pumpkin (about 2½ pounds), peeled, seeded, and diced (or substitute canned pumpkin without flavorings or sugar)

5 cups reduced sodium chicken stock

Salt and pepper to taste

1 Combine butter and oil in a medium saucepan (or pot) and place over medium heat. When the butter has melted, add the leeks and cook, stirring often, until they are golden, about 10 minutes. Add pumpkin and cook another 5 minutes, stirring frequently to prevent sticking.

2 Add chicken stock, salt, and pepper, and simmer, uncovered, until the pumpkin is very tender, about 45 minutes.

3 Purée half of the soup mixture in a food processor or blender, or pass it through a food mill. Add the purée to the remaining pumpkin soup in the saucepan. Bring to a simmer, adjust seasoning if necessary, and serve.

Nutrient analysis per serving: *120 kcalories, 5 grams protein, 17 grams carbohydrate, 4 grams fat, 2 grams saturated fat, 5 milligrams cholesterol, 1 gram fiber, 470 milligrams sodium*

Exchanges: *1 starch, ½ fat*

Roasted Butternut Squash Soup

A well-balanced diet should include a variety of vegetables, including those that are colored orange, a sign that they are an excellent source of vitamin A. Winter is the time to enjoy the golden-colored squashes such as acorn, Hubbard, and butternut, the squash featured in this tantalizing spiced soup from Cafe Allegro in Kansas City (see Appendix A).

Preparation time: *30 minutes*

Cooking time: *1 hour, 30 minutes*

Yield: *10 servings*

2 small butternut squash, about 1½ pounds each

2 tablespoons vegetable oil

2 medium yellow onions, thinly sliced

pinch of salt

2 tablespoons minced garlic

1 tablespoon minced ginger

2 tablespoons chili powder

2 tablespoons cumin, ground

1 carrot, thinly sliced

½ gallon (2 quarts) vegetable broth or water

¼ teaspoon salt and pepper to taste

¼ cup roasted pumpkin seeds

1 Preheat oven to 350 degrees Fahrenheit.

2 Cut butternut squash into halves, lengthwise. Scoop out seeds and discard. Place squash, inside down, on a flat baking pan. Bake for approximately 50 minutes, or until a fork can easily be inserted into the vegetable. Set aside to cool. After the squash cools, use a large spoon to scoop out the insides and discard the rind. Set aside.

3 In a large saucepan, heat oil over medium heat. Add onions and season with salt. Sauté, stirring occasionally until transparent, about 5 minutes. Stir in the garlic, ginger, chili powder, cumin, and carrot. Cook for 2 to 3 minutes. Add broth or water and the reserved squash, bring to a boil and simmer uncovered for 30 minutes.

4 Pour the mixture into a food processor, and purée until smooth. Season with salt and pepper. Garnish with toasted pumpkin seeds.

Nutrient analysis per serving: *116 kcalories, 4 grams protein, 15 grams carbohydrate, 5 grams fat, 1 gram saturated fat, 0 milligrams cholesterol, 3 grams fiber, 68 milligrams sodium*

Exchanges: *1 starch, 1 fat*

Serving Soup for Dessert

If you've ever been treated to the experience of a traditional Chinese feast, you know that this meal of many courses ends with a bowl of thick, sweet bean paste soup. The warm, glutinous broth can feel soothing after overindulging — if you can manage to find the room for yet another dish.

Scandinavians, too, serve soup for dessert, in this case fruit soup that may include cherries, berries, and citrus. And in Germany, in summertime, fruit soup is served chilled to begin a meal. The following soup recipe gives you a chance to sample such a dish. Both cherries and berries contribute to its wonderful crimson color.

Red Fruit Soup

Fruit soups eaten as starter courses are not appealing to most palettes when the soup is overly sweet. This soup, from Barbetta in New York City (see Appendix A), offers tartness along with the sweet taste. With only ½ tablespoon of sugar per serving, the recipe is also designed to fit into a diet that limits carbohydrate intake. This soup gives you a reason to buy some arrowroot, a thickener, if you don't already have this staple in your kitchen. Arrowroot is a very fine powder made from a tropical root. Arrowroot is preferable to cornstarch, which can give a dish a chalky taste, while arrowroot has no taste at all. In addition, arrowroot becomes absolutely clear when cooked. In supermarkets, arrowroot is sold in the section for herbs and spices.

Preparation time: *10 minutes*

Cooking time: *10 minutes*

Yield: *4 servings*

1½ cups red wine

1 lemon, juice only

2 tablespoons sugar

6 ounces sour cherries, frozen, thawed

6 ounces raspberries, fresh or frozen, thawed

6 ounces strawberries, fresh

3 tablespoons cold water

1 teaspoon arrowroot

1 Place wine, lemon juice, and sugar in a medium saucepan, and bring to a boil. Add the cherries, raspberries, and strawberries and stir to combine the fruit mixture. Bring to a boil for a second time. Turn off heat.

2 In a small saucepan and using a fork or a whisk, combine water and arrowroot. Over medium heat, warm arrowroot mixture until arrowroot dissolves, about 1 minute.

3 Pour the arrowroot over the fruit, stir and cook over medium heat for 1 minute. Remove from heat and cool the fruit soup before serving.

Nutrient analysis per serving: *120 kcalories, 1 gram protein, 21 grams carbohydrate, 0 grams fat, 0 grams saturated fat, 0 milligrams cholesterol, 4 grams fiber, 7 milligrams sodium*

Exchanges: *1½ fruit*

Chapter 9

Taking Salad Seriously

In This Chapter

- Choosing salad greens
- Using fruit to enliven a salad
- Enjoying salad as a main course

Recipes in This Chapter

- Simple Green Salad with Citrus and Herbs
- Riviera Salad
- Jícama and Belgian Endive Salad with Tequila-Orange Vinaigrette
- Field Greens with Bay Shrimp
- Oriental Portobello Salad
- Mango-Tortilla Salad
- Chicken Salad with Gorgonzola Mayonnaise and Walnuts
- Tarragon Chicken Salad
- Mango Crab Salad
- Greek Salad with Swordfish
- Grilled Lobster with Green Bean, Corn, and Tomato Salad
- Steak Salad Niçoise
- Oriental Beef and Noodle Salad

Salad can be more than lettuce and tomatoes. Having a nice green salad on the side, along with your main course or a bowl of soup, can be very pleasant, but these days, restaurant chefs and creative home cooks have turned salads into a main course.

This chapter walks you through some great ways to prepare magnificent, served-at-room-temperature meals that qualify as salads. Some are composed entirely of vegetables, while others incorporate meat, fish, or poultry to increase the protein content. Add a little dressing to supply some fats, and you have a balanced meal, as well suited for a diabetic diet as any dinner you may take the time to plan.

Starting with Salad Greens

Whether greens are an important part of the salad you're making or added just for garnish, using special and novel greens makes your salad stand out. Skip the pale green iceberg lettuce and buy some darker green lettuces like romaine and leaf lettuce instead. The greener the leaf, the more nutrients it contains, especially magnesium, a mineral important for heart and bone health.

TIP

Iceberg lettuce does have one virtue. It stays crisp for a long time, whether wedged inside a hamburger or coated with sesame oil and used to make Chinese chicken salad. Iceberg adds bulk when you cut a wedge of iceberg lettuce crosswise. The result could pass for packing material, what the French call a *chiffonade,* which translated literally means "made of rags."

When you go shopping, consider picking up some of these types of greens:

- Arugula, also called *rocket* and *roquette*
- Boston lettuce, also called *butterhead*
- Chicory, including radicchio, escarole, and frisée
- Dandelion
- Endive
- Watercress

Simple Green Salad with Citrus and Herbs

The dressing on this salad, from Heartbeat in New York (see Appendix A), makes use of regular lemons and naturally sweet Meyer lemons. If Meyer lemons aren't available, substitute with ruby red grapefruit, which adds rosy color to this salad. Enjoy it with some cheese and crackers for a light but balanced meal.

Preparation time: *15 minutes*

Cooking time: *None*

Yield: *4 servings*

¼ cup freshly squeezed Meyer lemon juice or ruby red grapefruit juice

2 tablespoons freshly squeezed lemon juice

2 teaspoons finely sliced fresh chives

1 tablespoon finely sliced fresh chervil

1 teaspoon finely sliced flat parsley leaves

¼ cup lemon oil

¼ cup Meyer lemon segments or ruby red grapefruit segments, divided use

¼ teaspoon salt and freshly ground pepper to taste

1 head Bibb or Boston lettuce

4 cups loosely packed baby greens or baby lettuce

1 In a medium mixing bowl, make the dressing by combining the Meyer lemon juice, regular lemon juice, chives, chervil, parsley leaves, lemon oil, and half the Meyer lemon segments. Toss gently and season with salt and pepper.

2 Separate the leaves of the Bibb or Boston lettuce from the head. Gently wash them, keeping them whole; dry gently and set aside. Place the baby greens or baby lettuce in a medium mixing bowl.

3 Stir the dressing well and drizzle enough over the baby greens or baby lettuce to lightly moisten. Gently toss the greens until well coated.

4 Brush each Bibb or Boston lettuce leaf with some of the dressing. Arrange the four largest leaves in the center of four chilled salad plates. Mound some of the baby greens atop the Boston leaves. Place the next largest leaves atop the baby greens. Repeat until you have three layers of Boston lettuce leaves with the final layer covered with baby greens.

5 Place the remaining Meyer lemon segments around the salad. Serve immediately.

Nutrient analysis per serving: *153 kcalories, 2 grams protein, 11 grams carbohydrate, 14 grams fat, 1 gram saturated fat, 0 milligrams cholesterol, 4 grams fiber, 154 milligrams sodium*

Exchanges: *2 vegetable, 3 fat*

An arugula salad is standard fare in most upscale Italian restaurants. Remember to order one sometime if you've never tasted this somewhat bitter salad green with its peppery, mustard flavor. Or prepare at home the splendid arugula salad that follows.

Riviera Salad

The Dining Room at the Ritz-Carlton, San Francisco, contributed this recipe (see Appendix A). An extremely colorful dish, Riviera Salad is worth the effort. You'll need to search out such specialty ingredients as *fava beans,* which resemble very large lima beans (available at specialty markets and some specialty foods shops); *haricot vert,* slim string beans used in French cooking; and *English cucumber,* which can be up to 2 feet long and is virtually seedless. If fava beans are unavailable, you can substitute frozen lima beans that you have thawed. The olive tapenade is also available in some supermarkets and gourmet specialty stores. Those of you watching your salt intake, note the amount of salt in this recipe.

This recipe also gives you a reason to go out and buy a *mandoline* a hand-operated gadget with adjustable blades that allows you to slice foods very thinly. You can always use a sharp paring knife, but the mandoline helps you keep the thickness of the slices all the same.

Preparation time: *60 minutes*

Cooking time: *60 minutes*

Yield: *4 servings*

(continued)

1 English cucumber, peeled, seeded, and cut into large pieces

½ cup shelled fresh fava beans

2 medium-size tomatoes

1 red bell pepper

1 yellow bell pepper

4 anchovy fillets, canned, drained

1 tablespoon lemon juice

Pinch pepper

4 eggs

2 baby artichokes

1 lemon

¼ pound haricot vert

1 bulb fennel

1 celery stalk

4 French breakfast radishes

4 scallions

4 cups mesclun greens

2 ounces olive tapenade

2 tablespoons olive oil

2 tablespoons chopped fresh basil

½ cup of your favorite oil-and-vinegar-based vinaigrette

1 Preheat oven to 225 degrees Fahrenheit.

2 Put the cucumber in a colander set over a bowl and season with salt to remove moisture.

3 Cook beans in a large pot of boiling, salted water until crisp-tender, about 2 minutes. Immediately transfer with slotted spoon to ice water to stop cooking. Drain beans and gently peel away outer skins.

4 Place tomatoes into boiling water and blanch until their skins loosen, 30 seconds to 1 minute. Using a slotted spoon, remove them and peel away the skins. Keep the water simmering in the pot. Cut the tomatoes into quarters, removing the seeds. Slice the quarters of one tomato to yield 12 strips. Place the four quarters of the other tomato on a cookie sheet. Drizzle with olive oil. Bake at 225 degrees Fahrenheit for 1 hour. Cool and slice the quarters into 12 strips. Increase oven temperature to broil.

5 Meanwhile, blanch the haricot verts in the simmering water until just tender, about 3 to 5 minutes. Drain and transfer to a bowl filled with ice water. Drain again and set aside.

6 Slice off the top and bottom of the red and yellow peppers and remove the seeds and pulp with a serrated knife. Cut each pepper in half vertically. In a small, shallow roasting pan, broil peppers about 4 inches from heat, turning every 5 minutes, until skins are blistered and charred, about 12 minutes. Transfer peppers to a bowl and let steam, covered, until cool. Peel the peppers and slice each into 12 strips.

7 In a small bowl, combine the anchovy fillets and the lemon juice and season with pepper. Set aside to marinate. Meanwhile, place the eggs into a small saucepan, cover with water, and boil until hard-cooked, about 8 minutes. When the eggs are cool enough to handle, peel them and set aside.

8 Cut off top half of each artichoke and discard. Cut off stem of artichoke. Starting at base, bend tough outer leaves back and snap them off where they break naturally, leaving tender inner leaves. Using a small, sharp knife, trim the outside of the base until no dark green areas remain. Rub trimmed area with lemon half and then slice the artichokes using a mandolin. Set aside.

9 Trim the bottom and any stalks from the fennel bulb. Remove the tough outer layer of the bulb and then, using a mandolin, slice thinly. Transfer fennel slices to a bowl filled with ice water and set aside. Using the edge of a knife, scrape off the tough outer fibers of the celery stalk and thinly slice the celery stalk with a mandolin. Place in the ice water with the fennel.

10 Trim the radishes, slice into rounds, and reserve in water. Remove the greens and roots of the scallions, leaving 1½ inches of white. Cut each into four slices. Set aside in ice water.

11 Combine the olive tapenade, olive oil, and basil. Mix until creamy. Set aside.

12 In a large bowl, place the cucumber, fava beans, tomato, red and yellow peppers, anchovies, eggs, sliced artichokes, radishes, and scallions with 2 tablespoons of vinaigrette. Toss gently to combine.

13 Drain the fennel, celery, and scallions and place them in a small bowl with the haricot verts and 2 tablespoons of the vinaigrette. In a large bowl, toss the mesclun with the remaining vinaigrette. Place mesclun in a neat mound in center of each plate. Top with a generous spoonful of the cucumber and fava bean mixture, followed by the celery, fennel, scallions, and haricot verts. Finally, dollop the tapenade around the plate.

Nutrient analysis per serving: *390 kcalories, 14 grams protein, 30 grams carbohydrate, 25 grams fat, 4 grams saturated fat, 215 milligrams cholesterol, 9 grams fiber, 770 milligrams sodium*

Exchanges: *1 starch, 3 vegetable, 1 medium-fat meat, 4 fat*

Storing salad greens

Store your salad greens in the vegetable bin of your fridge. Store romaine with the head intact because the outer leaves keep the inner leaves moist. However, loose-leaf lettuce has a shorter shelf-life. To store this type of lettuce, remove the leaves and wash and drain them. Gather and wrap them in a clean, damp paper towel or two and then store in a plastic bag. The leaves will stay fresh for a couple of days, but not much longer.

Enticingly edible endive

Endive is another salad green used by professional cooks. A head of Belgian endive, also known as French endive, is about 6 inches long and cigar-shaped. The leaves are a fashionable pale chartreuse. They are kept from turning green by growing the endive in complete darkness, a labor-intensive procedure. The darling of caterers, endive's long, scooplike leaves can be used to hold all sorts of treats, like a bit of caviar and lowfat sour cream, to serve as hors d'oeuvres. The elegant, pointed leaves also make a wonderful garnish. In this recipe, they are arranged in a spoke pattern to form a star.

Jícama and Belgian Endive Salad with Tequila-Orange Vinaigrette

Dallas's Star Canyon (see Appendix A) contributed this beautiful plate, featured in the color section of this book. Orange sections add color, while jícama gives the salad a satisfying crunch. Jícama, shown in Figure 9-1, is a bulbous root vegetable, native to Mexico, and has a sweet, nutty flavor.

If you omit the tablespoon of dressing over the endive leaves, you cut the fat in half. This high-fiber dish also reduces total available carbohydrates by 13 grams, a bonus for carbohydrate counters. And if you need to avoid alcohol, you can alter this recipe further by substituting lime juice for the tequila.

Preparation time: *35 minutes*

Cooking time: *None*

Yield: *6 servings*

The vinaigrette:

¼ cup fresh orange juice

2 tablespoons tequila

1 tablespoon white wine vinegar

½ small shallot, peeled and chopped

½ cup corn oil

¼ cup olive oil

½ teaspoon salt and freshly ground white pepper to taste

The salad:

2 heads Belgian endive, rinsed, dried, and leaves separated

3 oranges, peeled with a knife and sections removed

2 medium jícamas, peeled and julienned

Chives, snipped for garnish

Figure 9-1: Jícama has a thin brown skin and white, crunchy flesh.

1 *To make the vinaigrette:* Place the orange juice, tequila, vinegar, and shallot in a blender and blend at high speed for 10 seconds.

2 Slowly add the oils through the opening in lid while still blending. (If you don't have a blender with a lid that has an opening, make vinaigrette in a food processor fitted with a metal blade, following the same steps as for the blender, and add the oil through the tube opening in the lid.) Blend for 10 or 15 seconds.

3 Add salt and white pepper. Makes about 1¼ cups.

4 *To assemble the salad:* On each plate, arrange the endive leaves, tip pointing out. Scatter the orange sections over the endive.

5 Toss the jícama with 6 tablespoons of the vinaigrette and mound in the middle of each plate. Ladle 1 tablespoon of the vinaigrette over the endive on each plate and sprinkle with the chives.

Nutrient analysis per serving with 2 tablespoons dressing: *268 kcalories, 2 grams protein, 29 grams carbohydrate, 16 grams fat, 2 grams saturated fat, 0 milligrams cholesterol, 13 grams fiber, 125 milligrams sodium*

Exchanges: *3 vegetable, 1 fruit, 3 fat*

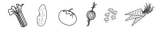

Munchable mesclun

Pronounced MEHS-kluhn, mesclun is simply a mix of young, small salad greens, typically radicchio, arugula, sorrel, frisée (free-ZAY), dandelion, oak leaf lettuce, and such exotics as mizuna (a delicate, feathery salad green from Japan) and mâche (a tangy, nutlike green, native to Europe). While the following recipe calls for "field greens," you're not expected to go foraging! Just head for your local supermarket and buy a package of precut mixed greens, preferably mesclun, which is pricey but worth it.

Field Greens with Bay Shrimp

Anthony's Fish Grotto in San Diego (see Appendix A) contributed this refreshing salad, which makes a great entrée. Not only does it taste good, but the presentation of the food clearly indicates that you're eating something special. Here's a chance to vary your diet, a step that's always good for health, by incorporating a mix of greens.

Preparation time: *17 minutes*

Cooking time: *None*

Yield: *2 servings*

The Pesto Balsamic Vinaigrette:

¼ cup of your favorite oil and vinegar dressing

1 teaspoon pesto sauce

1 teaspoon balsamic vinegar

The salad:

2 cups field greens

1 cup romaine hearts (the pale green leaves at the core of each head of lettuce)

4 ounces bay shrimp, cooked and peeled

1 tablespoon sun-dried tomatoes, julienned

2 thin slices red onion, divided into rings

1 tablespoon pine nuts, sliced and toasted

2 tablespoons feta cheese, crumbled

1 Heat a small sauté pan over medium heat and cook pine nuts, stirring continuously, until they begin to turn golden, about 3 minutes. Remove from heat and reserve.

2 *For the vinaigrette:* In a small bowl, whisk together the dressing, pesto, and balsamic vinegar.

3 *For the salad:* Combine the greens, romaine hearts, shrimp, tomatoes, and onion with the Pesto Basil Vinaigrette. Mound in a large pasta bowl. Top with the pine nuts and feta cheese.

Nutrient analysis per serving: *251 kcalories, 11 grams protein, 6 grams carbohydrate, 20 grams fat, 4.8 grams saturated fat, 9 milligrams cholesterol, 2 grams fiber, 433 milligrams sodium*

Exchanges: *3 vegetables, 1 medium-fat meat, 3 fat*

Portobellos: The inside story

Growers of cremini mushrooms had a problem. Each season, part of the crop would mature into extremely large mushrooms that no one wanted to buy. But in the 1980s, the growers came up with a great marketing concept: Give these giant creminis a new name, a fashionable-sounding one at that, and customers will feel they are buying something special. Enter the portobello, today sold widely in gourmet stores and supermarkets.

The posh portobello

Portobellos are very large mushrooms, sometimes 6 inches across. Because these mushrooms are fully mature, the gills on the underside are exposed, causing the mushrooms to lose moisture. However, as the mushrooms begin to dry out, their flavor becomes more concentrated and rich, exactly the reason these meaty mushrooms are prized. Sometimes portobellos are served whole, like a New York steak, or they are sliced, sautéed, and served with salad greens and roasted sweet red peppers. Yum! Ideal for a diabetic diet, mushrooms are considered free foods because they have an insignificant effect on blood glucose.

Oriental Portobello Salad

Portobello mushrooms are popping up on every restaurant menu. Here is another filling but low-calorie appetizer that features these meaty fungi. This dish has an Asian accent, thanks to the addition of Japanese enoki mushrooms, which come in clumps of spaghetti-like stems about 3 inches long. When served, the clumps are broken apart and the stems are used in a bunch as a garnish or scattered through a salad.

Preparation time: *15 minutes*

Cooking time: *None*

Yield: *4 servings*

The dressing:

2 teaspoons low-sodium soy sauce

¼ teaspoon ground ginger

2 teaspoons rice wine vinegar

2 teaspoons sesame oil

1 teaspoon Dijon mustard

1 clove garlic, minced

⅛ teaspoon white pepper

(continued)

The salad:

½ pound portobello mushrooms (1 large cap)

2 tablespoons minced red onion

2 tablespoons thinly sliced green onions

2 tablespoons finely chopped red pepper

2 tablespoons finely chopped yellow pepper

The garnishes:

2 ounces enoki mushrooms, brushed clean, separated if attached at the base

2 teaspoons chopped fresh parsley

1 teaspoon toasted sesame seeds (see note)

1 *To make the dressing:* In a large bowl, whisk together the soy sauce, ginger, vinegar, sesame oil, mustard, garlic, and white pepper. Reserve.

2 *To make the salad:* First, clean the portobello mushrooms. Shave off the bottom gills with a sharp paring knife and, if the cap "skin" is tough (as is often the case with larger mushrooms), peel it off. Cut the cap into quarters and then thinly slice the quarters.

3 Add the portobello mushrooms, red onion, green onion, red peppers, and yellow peppers to the bowl with the dressing. Toss well.

4 Garnish with the enoki mushrooms, parsley, and sesame seeds.

Note: *In a small sauté pan, over medium heat, toast the sesame seeds, stirring continuously, until golden, about 1 minute.*

Nutrient analysis per serving: *58 kcalories, 3 grams protein, 5 grams carbohydrate, 3 grams fat, 0.4 grams saturated fat, 0 milligrams cholesterol, 3 grams fiber, 117 milligrams sodium*

Exchanges: *1 fat*

Adding Fruit to Salads

Everyone knows how refreshing fruit salad can taste, made with three or four of the season's best crops. But in a diabetic diet, fruit, which is full of natural and easily absorbed sugars, needs to be counted in the meal plan. How can you still include the juicy pleasures of fruit in a diabetic diet? By cooking with small amounts and combining it with other foods, as in the following Mango Tortilla Salad. Mango is combined with raw jícama and bell pepper, and olive oil adds fat to balance the carbohydrates in the fruit.

Mango-Tortilla Salad

This salad comes from Star Canyon in Dallas (see Appendix A). When you have a choice of flour or corn tortillas, choose corn. They supply calcium, a mineral that helps regulate the heartbeat. Specially tinted tortillas and the green vinaigrette turn this recipe into a festive dish. If you can't find the red and blue tortillas, use ordinary corn tortillas. They aren't as colorful, but the nutrient content is the same.

Preparation time: *15 minutes*

Cooking time: *10 minutes*

Yield: *8 servings*

The garnish:

Vegetable oil for frying tortilla strips (about 3 cups)

2 yellow corn tortillas, julienned

1 red corn tortilla, julienned

1 blue corn tortilla, julienned

The vinaigrette:

4 small limes, juice only

½ cup olive oil

½ teaspoon salt

The salad:

1 large jícama, peeled and julienned

½ mango, peeled, pitted, and diced

½ red bell pepper, julienned

¼ cup cilantro leaves

1 *To make the garnish:* Heat the vegetable oil in a large sauté pan until almost smoking. Fry the yellow, red, and blue julienned tortillas until crisp, about 2 to 3 minutes. Watch carefully to prevent burning. They should not brown.

2 Using a skimmer, remove the tortilla strips from the oil and drain on several layers of paper towels.

3 *To make the dressing:* Place the lime juice in a medium-sized bowl. Slowly drizzle in the olive oil while whisking until well combined. Season with salt.

4 *To prepare the salad:* Combine the jícama, mango, red bell pepper, and cilantro in a large bowl. Toss with ¼ cup of the vinaigrette.

5 Divide among eight plates and garnish each with a few of the tortilla strips. Drizzle each plate with an additional ½ tablespoon of vinaigrette to garnish.

(continued)

Nutrient analysis per serving: *182 kcalories, 2 grams protein, 21 grams carbohydrate, 11 grams fat, 1.5 grams saturated fat, 0 milligrams cholesterol, 5 grams fiber, 150 milligrams sodium*

Exchanges: *1 starch, 1 vegetable, 2 fat*

Having Salad as a Main Course

When a salad contains several ounces of protein foods, such as chicken, fish, meat, and cheese, plus several vegetables and some healthy oils, you can consider it a complete meal — just what you need to keep blood glucose steady. Each recipe in this section makes a fine main course, and if you want to increase the carbohydrates, all you need to add is a fresh piece of your favorite bread to round out the meal.

A bonus of eating this way is that meals tend to be lower in calories than if you have a dinner of many courses. You'll be filling up on vegetables and healthy vegetable oils in the salad dressing.

One of the healthiest oils to use to make salad dressing is extra-virgin olive oil, which lends wonderful flavor. Adding a garlic clove or two doesn't hurt either!

Sprucing up chicken breast

Salads topped with grilled chicken breast have become an enormously popular main course dish. They're a frequent choice of dieters, especially individuals who are attempting to adopt a high-protein, low-carb way of eating for weight loss. Typical salad ingredients, such as lettuce, celery, and radishes, contribute only a meager amount of starches, while the chicken breast is a source of protein with only a modest amount of fat (considered a lean meat in the Food Exchange Lists for diabetes).

As anyone who goes out of his way to eat this standard chicken salad again and again can tell you, this combination soon tastes bland and boring. However, you can add all sorts of ingredients to spruce up the flavors. The simple taste of lettuce and light-meat chicken welcomes many other ingredients, as you can see in the following recipe for Chicken Salad with Gorgonzola Mayonnaise and Walnuts. Let the ingredients in that recipe be your inspiration. Citrus, mustard, Tabasco, cheese, and nuts all lend their distinctive flavors. Make your own version of the salad by using some or all of the ingredients.

TIP

All sorts of nuts make terrific additions to salads — almonds, walnuts, and peanuts, to name a few. Buy them raw to make sure they're fresh, and then you do the roasting. Lightly roast them in the oven or in a sauté pan to develop their flavor. They're done when they just begin to turn a light, golden brown. Nuts add protein, oil-soluble vitamins, important minerals, and healthy oils.

Chicken Salad with Gorgonzola Mayonnaise and Walnuts

This salad, from Chef Marc Bianchini of Osteria del Mondo in Milwaukee (see Appendix A), makes a complete meal and a wonderful luncheon entrée, providing protein, carbohydrates, and fat in proportions suitable to a diabetic diet. The recipe incorporates a useful technique. Nuts are toasted in a pan lined with *parchment paper,* a heavy, grease- and moisture-resistant paper often used to line baking pans. The parchment paper acts as a barrier between the nuts and the high temperature of the heated pan and helps prevent the nuts from burning.

Preparation time: *20 minutes*

Cooking time: *20 minutes*

Yield: *6 servings*

1 egg yolk

1 tablespoon fresh lemon juice

½ teaspoon dry mustard

⅓ cup olive oil

⅓ cup corn oil

⅓ cup walnut oil (or additional corn oil)

Tabasco to taste

Pinch of salt, optional

pepper to taste

1 ounce Gorgonzola cheese, crumbled

1½ pounds boneless, skinless chicken breasts

1 tablespoon olive oil

2 ounces walnut halves

1 tablespoon honey

1 pound endive or other salad greens

1 *For the mayonnaise:* Whisk the egg yolk, lemon juice, and mustard together in a large bowl. Slowly add the olive, corn, and walnut oils to the mix, whisking quickly, until thick, creamy, and emulsified. Add the salt and pepper and Tabasco. Add the Gorgonzola cheese and mix in. Serving size is 1 tablespoon.

2 *For the chicken:* Heat a grill until very hot. Brush the chicken lightly with the olive oil and place on the grill. Cook for 6 to 8 minutes on one side. Season with salt and pepper. Turn and grill on second side for 4 to 5 minutes. (The chicken is done if the juices run clear when you pierce the chicken with the tip of a sharp knife.) Slice into ½-inch strips and reserve.

(continued)

3 *For the honey-glazed walnuts:* Put the nuts in a sauté pan lined with parchment paper. Toast over low heat until they are fragrant, about 3 minutes. Add the honey and cook, stirring constantly, until it caramelizes, about 1 or 2 minutes. Remove from heat and transfer nuts to a baking sheet to cool.

4 *To assemble the salad:* Combine the endive, 6 tablespoons of the Gorgonzola mayonnaise, the grilled chicken strips, and the honey-glazed walnuts and divide among six large salad plates.

Nutrient analysis per serving: *408 kcalories, 37 grams protein, 5 grams carbohydrate, 25 grams fat, 4 grams saturated fat, 108 milligrams cholesterol, 3 grams fiber, 268 milligrams sodium*

Exchanges: *5 lean meat, 1 vegetable, 2 fat*

Tarragon Chicken Salad

Add interest to chicken breast by preparing it with *tarragon,* a particularly aromatic herb with a flavor reminiscent of anise. Tarragon is widely used in classic French cooking. This recipe keeps calories and fat low by using only white meat. Have a piece of bread to add carbohydrates.

Preparation time: *18 minutes (includes cooking time)*

Cooking time: *10 minutes*

Yield: *4 servings*

2 boneless, skinless chicken breasts (about 10 to 12 ounces)

2 cups low-sodium chicken broth

½ small red onion, minced

4 medium stalks celery, minced

¼ cup lowfat sour cream

¼ cup nonfat mayonnaise

2 teaspoons crushed dried tarragon

¼ teaspoon white pepper

1 In a medium saucepan, place the chicken breasts and chicken broth, which should cover the poultry. Cook, covered, over medium heat, until the chicken is firm and cooked through, 12 to 15 minutes. Remove the chicken from the broth and allow to cool (see note).

2 Cut the chicken into bite-size pieces. In a bowl, combine the chicken with the onion, celery, sour cream, mayonnaise, tarragon, and white pepper.

3 Serve over greens or as a sandwich filling.

Note: *If you have time to cook the chicken more slowly, cool the breasts in the broth to keep the meat moist and prevent the chicken from drying out.*

Nutrient analysis per serving: *128 kcalories, 17 grams protein, 5 grams carbohydrate, 4 grams fat, 1.6 gram saturated fat, 49 milligrams cholesterol, 1 gram fiber, 197 milligrams sodium*

Exchanges*: 2 lean meat, 1 vegetable*

Showing off seafood

American chefs have become very creative in recent years in how they prepare fish, taking inspiration from cuisines from Latin America and the Caribbean. Fish is treated to the sweetness of fruit, the tartness of vinegar and citrus, and the fiery flavor of chilies.

One of the tastiest and trendiest ways of eating fish is in an exotic salad. The two recipes that follow give you a chance to try your hand at these. The mix of ingredients, which include a significant amount of protein, turn these salads into well-balanced meals that fit the requirements of a diabetic diet.

Be forewarned, if you haven't shopped for fresh fish lately, that most seafood, including the crabmeat for the Mango Crab Salad, is pricey. Save up for this special treat. It's worth it.

Mango Crab Salad

The sea is full of minerals and so are the plants and creatures that dwell in its waters. This crab salad gives you a succulent way of increasing your intake of these essential nutrients.

Preparation time: *15 minutes*

Cooking time: *None*

Yield: *4 servings*

(continued)

The dressing:

¼ cup lowfat sour cream

¼ cup nonfat mayonnaise

2 tablespoons finely chopped celery

2 tablespoons chopped fresh cilantro

2 teaspoon freshly squeezed lemon juice

1 teaspoon freshly squeezed lime juice

2 teaspoons minced jalapeño pepper

The salad:

1 cup peeled and diced mango

1 pound fresh lump crabmeat, shell pieces removed

The presentation:

4 cups mixed greens, or 4 pita pockets

2 tablespoons slivered almonds, toasted

1 *To make the dressing:* Combine the sour cream, mayonnaise, celery, cilantro, lemon juice, lime juice, and pepper in a large bowl. Stir well.

2 Fold the mango and crabmeat into the dressing. Toss to combine.

3 Divide the salad greens among four individual dinner plates. Top with the mango-crabmeat mixture. Sprinkle with almonds. Alternatively, fill pita pockets with the mango-crab mixture. Enjoy a luxurious mouthful!

Nutrient analysis per serving: *209 kcalories, 22 grams protein, 14 grams carbohydrate, 4 grams fat, 1 gram saturated fat, 72 milligrams cholesterol, 1.5 grams fiber, 470 milligrams sodium*

Exchanges*: 3 lean meat, 1 fruit*

Greek Salad with Swordfish

This recipe comes from Anthony's Fish Grotto in San Diego (see Appendix A) and is featured in the color section of this book. The hearty flavors of a classic Greek salad, with its feta cheese, olives, and cucumbers, are a perfect match for meaty swordfish. Go out of your way to use kalamata olives, as this recipe specifies, because they have a rich, fruity flavor. You'll find kalamata olives in specialty food markets. Swordfish can be grilled, as in this recipe, or oven-broiled or pan-fried if you like. Just be sure not to overcook the fish to preserve its moistness.

Preparation time: *20 minutes*

Cooking time: *6 minutes*

Yield: *4 servings*

The dressing:

8 tablespoons olive oil

2 teaspoons dried oregano

1 teaspoon pepper

3 tablespoons lemon juice

The salad:

1 large head romaine lettuce, trimmed, washed, and cut into bite-size pieces

1 long, seedless cucumber or 2 medium cucumbers, seeded, cut into half moons

12 kalamata olives

6 ounces feta cheese

The swordfish:

1 pound swordfish, fillets, cut in 1-ounce thin slices

The presentation:

3½ ounces shredded cooked beets (see note)

8 tomato wedges

1 small red onion, sliced into rings

4 pita bread pockets, cut into wedges (optional)

1 *To prepare dressing:* In a small bowl, combine the olive oil, oregano, pepper, and lemon juice. Whisk together and set aside.

2 *To prepare swordfish:* Preheat grill. Lightly brush swordfish with oil, season with salt, and place on a baking pan. Cook for 2 to 3 minutes on each side, until nicely browned and just a touch of translucence remains. Do not overcook.

3 With a spatula, remove the swordfish from the grill and cut into ½-inch strips.

4 *To prepare salad:* Toss the romaine lettuce, cucumber, olives, and feta cheese with the dressing in a medium bowl. Divide between four large plates or bowls.

5 Garnish salad with beets, tomatoes, onion, and pita bread.

6 Lay swordfish on top of salads and serve.

Note: *For convenience, substitute 1 small can shredded beets.*

Nutrient analysis per serving: *627 kcalories, 28 grams protein, 38 grams carbohydrate, 42 grams fat, 11 grams saturated fat, 66 milligrams cholesterol, 7 grams fiber, 960 milligrams sodium*

Exchanges: *2 starch, 1 vegetable, 4 medium-fat meat, 4 fat*

Grilled Lobster with Green Bean, Corn, and Tomato Salad

This salad, pictured in the color section of this book, comes from Hamersley's Bistro in Boston (see Appendix A). It is a pièce de résistance that features grilled lobster, along with midsummer favorites — fresh corn, tomatoes, and basil. After you've readied the lobster, cooking it is no different from grilling hamburgers. For best flavor, cook the lobster on a charcoal, wood, or gas grill. This salad makes a delectable summer supper.

Preparation time: *65 minutes*

Cooking time: *15 minutes*

Yield: *4 servings*

4 1¼ pound lobsters

3 tablespoons butter, melted

1 teaspoon chopped oregano

1 teaspoon chopped basil

1 clove garlic, chopped

½ teaspoon white pepper

3 oranges (16 orange segments)

½ tablespoon Dijon mustard

2 tablespoons lime juice

1 pinch crushed red pepper flakes

1 pinch fennel seeds

1 teaspoon chopped tarragon

12 tablespoons olive oil (¾ cup)

salt and pepper to taste

2 cups mixed summer greens, such as mesclun, mizuna, red oak leaf, or mâche

1 pound green beans, ends trimmed, lightly cooked (see note)

4 large ripe tomatoes, sliced

4 ears corn, scraped off the cob and lightly cooked (see note)

1 Heat grill to medium heat.

2 *To prepare the lobsters (each lobster should be prepared separately):* Lay the live lobster on a cutting board with the softer side of the body facing down. (A good way to hold the lobster is to first lay a towel over the head of the lobster. Then, if you are right-handed, hold the lobster with your left hand firmly over the head.) With a large chef's knife, cut into the lobster and split it from the point where the body meets the tail, cutting up toward the head. Turn the lobster and split the tail portion. The lobster should be split entirely in half. Remove the "lady," a hard sac near the head, and the intestinal tract that runs through the middle of the underside of the tail meat, and discard. (Save the *roe,* or eggs, for another use if desired.) Crack the claws with a nutcracker, small hammer, or the back of a chef's knife.

(Considered by some a more humane method of killing the lobster, you can also begin by poking a hole behind the lobster's eyes, right at the cross-hatch, using a thin, sturdy, pointed knife. Then to halve the lobster, cut up through the head and down through the tail.)

3 In a small bowl, combine butter, oregano, basil, garlic, and white pepper. Brush the lobster halves, meat, and shells with this herb butter. Place lobsters on a large pan and place in the refrigerator until ready to grill.

4 *To prepare dressing:* Peel the oranges. Separate segments and peel membranes from all but three of these. Set aside the peeled segments. Squeeze the juice of the three remaining segments into a small bowl, to yield 4 tablespoons of orange juice. Set aside. In a small mixing bowl, combine mustard, orange juice, lime juice, red pepper flakes, fennel seeds, and tarragon. Add olive oil in a steady stream, whisking until it is incorporated. Season with salt and pepper and reserve. (This makes 1 cup of dressing, enough for this salad, plus nearly a half cup left over to enjoy another time.)

5 Oil grill lightly. Salt and pepper lobsters and place them shell-side down on the grill surface. Cover them with aluminum foil and cook for 7 to 8 minutes, until tail meat is firm. Using oven mitts for protection, remove the claws from the body and continue to cook the claws for an additional 2 minutes.

6 On four large platters, evenly divide greens. In a medium bowl, drizzle ⅓ cup salad dressing over green beans, tomatoes, and corn and arrange over the greens. Arrange the two halves of each lobster on the platter and drizzle with a tablespoon more of dressing. Garnish with orange segments. Serve extra vinaigrette on the side.

Note: *Blanch green beans for 3 to 4 minutes. For the corn, if cooked on the cob, it should be boiled for about 8 minutes. If removed from the cob first, the kernels should be cooked for about 3 minutes in boiling water and then drained.*

Nutrient analysis per serving: *608 kcalories, 36 grams protein, 60 grams carbohydrate, 27 grams fat, 8 grams saturated fat, 159 milligrams cholesterol, 10 grams fiber, 698 milligrams sodium*

Exchanges: *2 starch, 3 vegetable, 3 fat, 4 lean meat, 1 fruit*

Making the most of meat

In the diabetic diet, meat portion-size is a modest 3 to 4 ounces, to limit the intake of saturated fat. The beauty of having salad as a main course is that a small amount of meat can seem like much more when it's mixed with all the other ingredients. For example, the following Steak Salad Niçoise includes just 2 ounces of sirloin steak per serving.

Steak Salad Niçoise

The term *Niçoise* refers to the type of cooking done in and around the city of Nice, one of the seaside towns on the French Riviera. Not surprisingly, salad Niçoise is usually made with tuna, but in this Americanized version, the featured protein is red meat. A little goes a long way when incorporated into a salad — an acceptable way to include red meat in a low saturated-fat diet. The salad dressing also cuts calories by relying on chicken broth as the primary liquid. A piece of fruit for dessert will provide more carbohydrate. Check out the color section of this book for a look at this entrée salad.

Preparation time: *40 minutes*

Cooking time: *15 minutes*

Yield: *4 servings*

The steak:

8 ounces boneless top sirloin steak, trimmed of fat, cut 1 inch thick

The salad:

1 pound small red new potatoes, scrubbed and quartered

¼ pound green beans, ends trimmed

1 small red onion, thinly sliced

6 pitted ripe olives, chopped

8 cherry tomatoes, sliced lengthwise in half

The dressing:

1 cup low-sodium chicken broth

¼ cup white wine vinegar

2 tablespoons extra-virgin olive oil

1 tablespoon lemon juice

1 clove garlic, minced

1 teaspoon Dijon mustard

¼ teaspoon black pepper

1 teaspoon chopped dried thyme

The garnish:

1 large head leaf lettuce, such as Boston lettuce or red leaf lettuce

2 teaspoons chopped fresh herbs such as thyme, marjoram, and tarragon

1 *For the steak:* Pan-fry steak over high heat until medium rare, about 1 to 2 minutes per side. Chill. Slice on the bias into ¼-inch thick slices.

2 *For the salad:* Place the potatoes in a small saucepan with enough water to cover. Bring to a boil, reduce heat to simmer, and cook for 10 minutes or until potatoes are tender. Drain and chill.

3 In another saucepan, cook the green beans in boiling, salted water until tender but still crisp, about 5 minutes. Drain and chill.

4 In a large bowl, combine the steak, potatoes, green beans, red onions, olives, and cherry tomatoes and toss.

5 *For the dressing:* In a small bowl, whisk together the chicken broth, vinegar, olive oil, lemon juice, garlic, mustard, and pepper. Pour over the steak mixture and toss gently (see note).

6 Wash the lettuce. Tear the leaves into small pieces. Divide and arrange on plates. Divide the steak mixture; spoon on top of lettuce.

Note: *This recipe yields a cup of vinaigrette, but you may find that using less is quite sufficient, for flavor and in terms of calories.*

Nutrient analysis per serving: *273 kcalories, 16 grams protein, 30 grams carbohydrate, 10 grams fat, 2 grams saturated fat, 27 milligrams cholesterol, 4 grams fiber, 201 milligrams sodium*

Exchanges*: 2 starch, 2 lean meat*

Oriental Beef and Noodle Salad

If you have a craving for Chinese take-out, satisfy your hunger with this healthy, lowfat version, full of Asian flavor. Using a minimum of meat with lots of vegetables is typical of Chinese cooking. Although this style of cooking evolved by necessity, due to a scarcity of meat, the result of this hardship was the creation of an exceptionally healthy cuisine. A good example is this beef and noodle salad, made with lean meat and a minimum of cooking oil.

Preparation time: *25 minutes*

Cooking time: *None*

Yield: *4 servings*

(continued)

8 ounces thin spaghetti

4 teaspoons sesame oil

Nonstick cooking spray

1 pound boneless top sirloin steak, trimmed of fat, cut 1 inch thick, and cut into slices about ¼-inch thick

2 teaspoons low-sodium soy sauce

2 teaspoons red wine vinegar

1 teaspoon Dijon mustard

¼ teaspoon ground ginger

1 clove garlic, minced

⅛ teaspoon white pepper

2 tablespoons thinly sliced green onion

2 tablespoons finely chopped red bell pepper

2 teaspoons chopped fresh cilantro

1 Bring a large pot of water to boil. Salt the boiling water and cook the spaghetti according to package directions, typically 5 to 6 minutes. Drain, rinse under cold running water, and drain again. Transfer to a large bowl and toss with the sesame oil and set aside.

2 Coat a large cast-iron or nonstick skillet with cooking spray and place over medium-high heat until hot. Add steak slices and cook until medium rare, about 1 minute per side. Add the steak to the bowl with the pasta.

3 In a small bowl, whisk together the soy sauce, vinegar, mustard, ginger, garlic, and white pepper. Add the green onions and red pepper and toss well. Add to the bowl with the spaghetti and steak and toss well.

4 Divide among four serving plates, sprinkle with cilantro, and serve.

Nutrient analysis per serving: *460 kcalories, 42 grams protein, 43 grams carbohydrate, 12 grams fat, 3 grams saturated fat, 82 milligrams cholesterol, 1.5 grams fiber, 180 milligrams sodium*

Exchanges*: 4½ lean meat, 3 starch*

Chapter 10

Stocking Up on Grains and Legumes

In This Chapter

- Shopping for quality grains
- Discovering gourmet whole grains
- Getting your grain from pasta
- Learning to like legumes
- Making soup with legumes

Recipes in This Chapter

- Wild and Brown Rice Pilaf with Toasted Pecans
- Barley Pilaf
- Kasha and Brown Rice Pasta
- Risotto with Seasonal Green Vegetables (Risotto con Verdure)
- Grits and Cheese Casserole
- Cappellini with Moose's Winter Tomato Sauce
- Spicy Eggplant Tomato Sauce
- Butterfly Pasta with Sun-Dried Tomatoes and Artichoke Hearts
- Seafood Farfalle Salad
- Cabbage, Bean, and Bacon Soup
- Black Bean Soup with Salsa Mexicana
- Cool Minestrone Soup (Minestrone Freddo)
- Basil and Onion Pea Soup
- Gordon Hamersley's Hearty Lentil Soup

Grains and legumes, two broad categories of food, are rarely given the attention they deserve. In the American diet, grains for the most part have been reduced to refined wheat, white rice, and an occasional bowl of oats, while *beans* usually refers to navy beans prepared in a sugar sauce and served with spareribs. Yet these two food groups are potentially so nutritious that they can make up the bulk of the diet, which they do in countries where meat is scarce.

Eating Quality Grains

The nutritional difference between refined and whole grains is enormous. Whole grains still retain all their parts: the *germ* of the grain that contains healthy fats and oil-soluble vitamins; the *bran*, which is an excellent source of fiber; and the starchy bulk of the kernel, the *endosperm*. Consequently, whole grains are a terrific source of B vitamins, vitamin E, magnesium, selenium, and zinc, as well as many other nutrients.

Thumbs up for oats

Oatmeal is one of the few whole grains that is a common part of the American diet. It's also an ideal choice for diabetes, as oats are a source of soluble fiber. This form of fiber helps in the management of blood glucose. In addition, fiber is especially effective when consumed with complex carbohydrates such as whole grains.

Unfortunately, when a grain is refined, the germ and the bran are removed, along with many nutrients and fiber. (Of course you can buy wheat germ to add to your cereal in the morning, if you want to pay for the portion of the grain the manufacturer removed in the first place!) Enriched wheat flour does replace some nutrients, but only 5 out of the 20 or more vitamins and minerals that have been tampered with.

TIP

When shopping for the healthiest form of wheat in baked goods, look for the words "whole grain," not "whole wheat," which refers to refined wheat flour.

The difference between whole and refined grains is especially important to the person with diabetes. Refined flour, which is mostly starch with little fiber, can have a more dramatic effect on blood glucose levels than whole grains, with their fats and fiber, which the digestive system breaks down and absorbs more slowly. Of course, you still can't eat all you want of whole grains, especially those like millet and rice (brown and white), which have a higher glycemic index. Portion control still matters.

Introducing Whole Grains

If an unappealing pile of brown rice comes to mind when you think of whole grains, think again. Savory rice pilafs, flavored with herbs, can be made with whole grains. Barley and kasha, which is buckwheat *groats* (buckwheat that has been hulled and crushed), can be turned into delicious side dishes to serve with meats and poultry. You'll find a great selection of whole grains, sold in bulk and in packaged mixes, in natural food stores. Markets are also now beginning to carry baked goods, including croissants, muffins, and bagels, made with unrefined flour.

Pleasing pilafs

A meal in the Middle East and India is not complete without pilaf. Just as potatoes are so frequently used as a source of starch in the West, pilaf is a primary source of starch in places like Turkey and all the regions of the Indian continent. A classic pilaf is typically made of rice or bulgur wheat. In a classic pilaf, the grain is first browned in butter or oil and then cooked in stock. Other ingredients are often added, including vegetables, meats, and spices. The next time you plan to cook rice, add some complementary foods such as nuts and herbs, and rather than have everyday steamed rice, treat yourself to a savory pilaf.

Rice and other grains aren't "cooked" so much as they are steamed, as shown in Figure 10-1. To prepare these grains, bring the water or stock to a boil, add the grain, and then cover and reduce heat.

Figure 10-1: Rice and grains steam rather than cook.

TIP

All sorts of ingredients can be added to pilafs. Besides adding nuts, try mixing in dates, raisins, or currants, all sources of soluble fiber.

Wild and Brown Rice Pilaf with Toasted Pecans

Try this pilaf made with brown rice and wild rice, which is not really a grain at all but comes from marsh grass native to the northern Great Lakes. The tawny flavor of toasted pecans is the perfect flavor complement to these whole grains. Nuts also increase the fat content of this dish, helping to balance the starchy carbohydrates of the grains.

Preparation time: *10 minutes*

Cooking time: *45 minutes*

Yield: *4 servings*

(continued)

1 orange, preferably organic

⅔ cup brown rice

⅓ cup wild rice

2 ½ cups lowfat chicken broth

¼ cup pecan halves

1 Using a zester, peel off small strips of orange peel. Place on a cutting surface and chop fine.

2 In a medium-size pot with a tightly fitting lid, combine the orange zest, brown rice, wild rice, and chicken broth. Bring to a boil over high heat and cover. Reduce heat to low and cook, covered, until tender and all of the liquid has been absorbed, about 45 minutes.

3 Cut the pecans lengthwise. Place a small sauté pan over medium-high heat and add the pecans. Heat the pecans, stirring constantly, until aromatic and slightly browned, about 2 minutes. Transfer to a small bowl and let cool to room temperature.

4 When the pilaf has finished cooking, add the pecans, toss, and serve immediately.

Nutrient analysis per serving: *230 kcalories, 6 grams protein, 40 grams carbohydrate, 5 grams fat, 0.5 grams saturated fat, 0 milligrams cholesterol, 3 grams fiber, 356 milligrams sodium*

Exchanges: *2½ starch, ½ fat*

Barley Pilaf

Barley that still retains the bran takes a long time to cook, so manufacturers *pearl* the barley, which means they remove the bran. Pearled barley is the kind you usually find in supermarkets. Look for barley with grains that are oval, not round, a sign that the bran is mostly intact. In comparison with rice and wheat, barley has significantly less effect on blood glucose. Barley is also tasty added to soups.

Preparation time: *10 minutes*

Cooking time: *50 minutes*

Yield: *6 servings*

1 6-ounce piece smoked ham hock

2 stalks celery, cut into 2-inch lengths

2 bay leaves

½ teaspoon dried sage

Freshly ground black pepper, to taste

4 cups water

1 medium onion, chopped

1 tablespoon safflower oil

1 cup pearled barley

The best way to store grains

Have you ever bought a whole collection of decorative glass jars to hold grains and put them on display, turning where you cook into a country kitchen? A pleasing sight, but not so good for the grains! Grains contain natural oils, which can go rancid when exposed to heat or light. After you buy grains and bring them into your home, store them in your refrigerator or, even better, in the freezer. This is a good practice, especially for storing flour. And don't worry, because you don't have to defrost grain before cooking with it.

1 In a large pot, put the ham hock, celery, bay leaves, sage, pepper, and water. Over high heat, bring to a boil, lower heat to medium, and cook, uncovered, for 20 minutes. Volume of the broth will reduce by about 1 cup

2 In a medium pot, heat the safflower oil over medium heat. Cook, stirring occasionally, until soft, about 5 minutes. Add the barley and cook, stirring for 1 minute.

3 When the ham hock stock is prepared, pour the broth through a sieve into the barley. Bring to a boil.

4 Turn the heat to low, cover the pot, and cook the barley until tender and all the liquid is absorbed, about 30 minutes. If the barley is not quite done, add 1 or 2 tablespoons water and continue to cook. And if the barley is cooked, but liquid remains, turn off heat and let the barley rest in the covered pot while the grain continues to absorb the liquid.

Nutrient analysis per serving: *169 kcalories, 7 grams protein, 28 grams carbohydrate, 4 grams fat, 1 gram saturated fat, 8 milligrams cholesterol, 6 grams fiber, 220 milligrams sodium*

Exchanges: *2 starch*

Kasha and Brown Rice Pasta

Sometimes simple food, such as this delicious combination of kasha and pasta, tastes the best. The flavors are mellow and nutty with just a hint of mushroom, a step beyond blandness but still quiet, comfort food. This mixture is meant to be a background dish, served with savory foods such as a chicken roasted with herbs or slow-cooked flank steak prepared with onion and dried fruits. This merger of whole grains and pasta is especially favored in Eastern European and Russian cooking.

(continued)

Preparation time: *10 minutes*

Cooking time: *25 minutes*

Yield: *6 servings*

2 teaspoons safflower oil

1 medium onion, chopped

1 egg, slightly beaten

1 cup kasha (buckwheat groats)

½ cup sliced button mushrooms

2 cups boiling vegetable broth or water

Freshly ground black pepper

Sea salt (optional)

4 cups water

1½ cups brown rice rotini (Lundberg brand)

1. In a heavy medium saucepan, heat the oil and sauté the onion until translucent, 5 to 7 minutes.
2. Beat the egg in a small bowl. Add the kasha and mix together, coating each grain with the egg. Add to the onions. Cook the kasha while stirring until the grains are dry and separated.
3. Add the mushrooms, broth, pepper, and sea salt, if desired. Cover the skillet and simmer until all the liquid is absorbed, about 15 minutes.
4. In the meantime, bring the 4 cups water to a boil in a large pot. Add the rotini and cook for 6 minutes, or until tender but still firm. Drain and, if necessary, keep warm while the kasha finishes cooking.
5. When the kasha is fully cooked, fluff with a fork and stir in the rotini.

Nutrient analysis per serving: *240 kcalories, 7 grams protein, 44 grams carbohydrate, 4 grams fat, 1 gram saturated fat, 35 milligrams cholesterol, 4 grams fiber, 109 milligrams sodium*

Exchanges: *3 starch*

When only white rice will do

In terms of taste, Chinese food and Indian curry seem to call for the lighter texture and blander flavor of white rice. It's much less nutritious than brown rice, but in its favor, the protein in the grain is more available because the bran and germ are removed. In addition, important to diabetics, some rices have less of an effect on blood glucose than others. One such rice is *basmati,* the delectable, fragrant grain of India.

Risotto with Seasonal Green Vegetables (Risotto con Verdure)

This risotto recipe comes from Spiaggia restaurant in Chicago (see Appendix A) and is pictured in the color section of this book. Risotto is an Italian specialty made by stirring hot stock into a mixture of rice and, often, chopped onions that have been sautéed in butter. The liquid is added a half-cup at a time, and the mixture is stirred continuously. Traditionally, arborio rice is used to make risotto. The shorter and fatter grains are high in starch, giving this dish its sought-after creamy texture.

An elaborate risotto such as this one can be served as a main course. However, when meal planning for diabetes, a main course supplying this amount of starch is not recommended. Better to enjoy this risotto as a side dish, with chicken or turkey. This recipe makes 8 servings, enough to feed a family for dinner, plus some for lunch the next day. Be sure to start the Vegetable Stock before making the risotto, or to save time, substitute with commercial vegetable stock. However, for fine flavor, it's best to make your own stock.

Vegetable Stock

Preparation time: *10 minutes*

Cooking time: *45 minutes*

Yield: *1½ quarts*

1 carrot, coarsely chopped

1 onion, coarsely chopped

2 celery stalks, coarsely chopped

4 white field mushrooms, quartered

1 fennel bulb, coarsely chopped

1 thyme sprig

10 black peppercorns

3 bay leaves

2½ quarts water

1 In a large pot, put the carrot, onion, celery, mushrooms, fennel, thyme, peppercorns, bay leaves, and water. Simmer over medium-low heat for 45 minutes.

2 Strain the broth, pushing the vegetables through the sieve. Keep at a low simmer until ready to use.

Risotto

Preparation time: *45 minutes*

Cooking time: *35 minutes*

Yield: *8 servings*

(continued)

1 small zucchini, cut into cubes

5 brussels sprouts, ends trimmed, peeled and quartered with root intact

5 asparagus spears, stems peeled and cut in 1-inch lengths, tips reserved separately

10 string beans, cut in half

5 snap peas, ends trimmed

½ medium onion, finely chopped

4 tablespoons butter, divided use

4 tablespoons extra-virgin olive oil, divided use

2¼ cups Vialone Nano or arborio rice

1½ cups dry white wine

1 quart vegetable stock (see accompanying recipe)

½ cup freshly grated Parmigiano-Reggiano cheese (see note)

1 In a medium pot, bring 2 quarts of salted water to a boil. Blanch the vegetables by plunging the zucchini, brussels sprouts, asparagus stems, green beans, and snap peas into the water for about 2 minutes. Then shock the vegetables by draining them and placing them in a large bowl of ice-cold water to stop them from cooking further. (See Figure 10-2.) When the vegetables have cooled, drain and set aside.

Figure 10-2: Vegetables are blanched and placed in an ice-cold water bath.

2 Heat 2 tablespoons of the butter and 2 tablespoons of the olive oil in a heavy, nonreactive pot over medium heat. Add the onion and cook, stirring, until limp, about 5 minutes. Add the rice and toast it for approximately 2 minutes.

3 Add the wine and boil until most of the liquid has evaporated or been absorbed by the rice. Continue stirring, adding 1 cup of the simmering stock. Cook, stirring, until the rice again absorbs most of the liquid. Continue adding simmering stock, ½ cup at a time, until the rice is tender but firm; the total cooking time of the rice should not exceed 18 minutes. The rice should have movement but no excess liquid. If it requires more cooking, add a touch more liquid and cook for another 1 to 2 minutes. You may not need to use all the stock.

4 When the risotto is done, add the vegetables to the pan and gently stir the rice and vegetables together for about 1 minute or until the vegetables are heated through. Remove the pot from the stove and stir in the remaining 2 tablespoons butter, the remaining 2 tablespoons olive oil, and the Parmigiano-Reggiano cheese. Serve.

Note: *The flavor of Parmigiano-Reggiano is subtle and delicious, but this cheese is expensive. Tasty and more economical substitutes include regular Parmesan and Grana Padana cheeses.*

Nutrient analysis per serving: *579 calories, 12 grams protein, 82 grams carbohydrate, 19 grams fat, 8 grams saturated fat, 27 milligrams cholesterol, 4 grams fiber, 230 milligrams sodium*

Exchanges: *5 starch, 1 vegetable, 3 fat*

Grits and Cheese Casserole

Here's a homey dish that, like risotto, also makes the most of grain and cheese, but this one requires less time and effort. By using lowfat cheese and lowfat milk, you can watch your weight and still enjoy the rich flavors of this dish.

Preparation time: *20 minutes*

Cooking time: *45 minutes*

Yield: *4 servings*

1½ cups lowfat milk

1½ cups low-sodium chicken broth

⅔ cup hominy grits

¼ teaspoon salt

¾ cup shredded reduced-fat cheddar cheese

1 whole egg

2 egg whites

⅛ teaspoon white pepper

Nonstick cooking spray

1 Preheat oven to 350 degrees Fahrenheit.

2 In a saucepan, over medium heat, bring the milk and chicken broth to a boil. Stir in the grits and salt. Reduce heat to low. Cook, stirring, until thick, approximately 5 minutes. Remove from heat. Mix in the cheese. Let cool slightly.

3 In a bowl, whisk together the egg, egg whites, and white pepper. Slowly fold the egg mixture into the grits mixture.

(continued)

4 Transfer the mixture to a baking dish (one that holds about 1½ quarts), coated with cooking spray. Bake, uncovered, until lightly browned, 35 to 40 minutes.

Nutrient analysis per serving: *228 kcalories, 14 grams protein, 25 grams carbohydrate, 7 grams fat, 4 grams saturated fat, 70 milligrams cholesterol, 2 grams fiber, 555 milligrams sodium*

Exchanges: *1 starch, ½ lowfat milk, 1 lean meat*

Enjoying Grain in the Form of Pasta

Who needs bread? You can add a serving of carbohydrate to your meals by having pasta, with your favorite sauce. Eat Italian-style, with pasta as the first course. One diabetic exchange of pasta is one-half cup. Do the math and relish the portion size you can afford for the day.

Cappellini with Moose's Winter Tomato Sauce

Moose's in San Francisco (see Appendix A) contributed this cappellini recipe for our book. This dish is adapted for lowfat and low-salt diets. If you prefer more of a homemade tomato sauce, substitute the bottled sauce with a 28-ounce can of organic whole tomatoes (Muir Glen brand is tops), but remember to increase the cooking time an additional 2 hours. In this recipe, you can use any soy sauce, but the chef prefers Ohsawa Nama Shoyu (*Ohsawa* is the importing company, *Nama* means *the fresh one,* and *Shoyu* means *soy sauce*). This sauce is aged, so it has more complex flavor, and it contains less sodium.

Preparation time: *20 minutes*

Cooking time: *60 minutes*

Yield: *4 servings*

½ teaspoon black pepper

1½ tablespoons extra-virgin olive oil

½ cup chopped onion

4 cloves garlic, minced

Soya-water mix for spraying (1 part organic Ohsawa Nama Shoyu and 3 parts water, premixed in a spray bottle)

2 cups Muir Glen bottled Fat-free Tomato Sauce

6 ounces tomato juice

2½ teaspoons tomato paste

2 tablespoons apple juice concentrate

2 sprigs oregano

5 quarts water

10 ounces dry-weight cappellini (angel hair pasta) (2½ ounces per portion)

4 sprigs fresh basil or Italian parsley, julienned

1 Grind the pepper into a medium saucepan, placed over medium heat. Add the olive oil and warm it. Add the onion and garlic and spray lightly with the soya-water mix. Lay a piece of waxed paper or parchment directly atop the onion. Cover the pan and reduce the heat to low. Cook for 5 minutes. The onion should soften without browning.

2 In a small bowl, whisk together the tomato paste and the apple juice concentrate. Add the tomato sauce and the oregano. Stir. Cover the pan and simmer for 1 hour, stirring occasionally.

3 After 40 minutes of cooking the tomato sauce, bring 5 quarts of water to a boil, which takes 20 minutes, and cook the cappellini for 3 minutes. Drain well, using a sieve, and return the pasta to the pot.

4 Toward the end of the cooking time of the sauce, taste to decide whether more salt is needed. If so, lightly spray the sauce with soya-water. Add the sauce to the drained cappellini, toss to combine, and serve immediately, sprinkled with fresh basil or Italian parsley.

Nutrient analysis per serving: *378 kcalories, 12 grams protein, 68 grams carbohydrate, 7 grams fat, 1 gram saturated fat, 0 milligrams cholesterol, 4 grams fiber, 288 milligrams sodium*

Exchanges: *4 starch, 2 vegetable, 1 fat*

Spicy Eggplant Tomato Sauce

Denver's Papillon Café (see Appendix A) is the home of this sauce. A standard part of Italian antipastos is grilled and marinated eggplant, a great addition to tomato sauce as well. Eggplant gives this sauce substance and adds some soluble fiber to your meal. Try this spicy tomato sauce with whole-grain pastas, available in a wide variety of forms. Garnish this pasta with strips of broiled chicken to add protein for a balanced meal.

Preparation time: *25 minutes*

Cooking time: *25 minutes*

Yield: *4 servings*

(continued)

1 tablespoon olive oil

2 tablespoons chopped garlic

1 medium red onion, chopped

1 teaspoon crushed red pepper

½ teaspoon chili powder

½ teaspoon ground cumin

1 medium eggplant, peeled and diced

3 cups tomatoes, peeled, seeded, and diced

1 cup white wine

2 teaspoons lemon juice

¼ teaspoon salt and pepper to taste

1 Heat a medium saucepan over medium heat. Add the oil and garlic and sauté, stirring, until soft, not brown, about 2 minutes. Add the onions and cook, stirring often, until translucent, about 5 minutes. Add the red pepper, chili powder, cumin, half of the eggplant, and 1½ cups tomato. Sauté for 2 to 3 minutes.

2 Add the white wine and lemon juice to the saucepan and simmer for 5 minutes. Add the remaining half of the eggplant and the remaining 1½ cups tomatoes. Bring to a boil, reduce heat to low, and simmer the sauce for 10 minutes. Remove saucepan from heat. Add salt and pepper. Serve over pasta of choice.

Nutrient analysis per serving: *132 kcalories, 3 grams protein, 21 grams carbohydrate, 4 grams fat, 0.6 grams saturated fat, 0 milligrams cholesterol, 6 grams fiber, 170 milligrams sodium*

Exchanges: *1 starch, 1 vegetable, 1 fat*

TIP

In Italy, they serve pasta *al dente*, a term that means "to the tooth." Such pasta offers a slight resistance when you bite into it, adding a pleasing texture to a dish.

Butterfly Pasta with Sun-Dried Tomatoes and Artichoke Hearts

The few ingredients that this simple recipe calls for complement each other perfectly, as you can see from the photo in the color section. The dish is a certified crowd-pleaser, full of color and flavor, and ideal for entertaining. The pasta is best served at room temperature, so you can make it hours in advance, freeing you for the last-minute details of throwing a party.

Preparation time: *15 minutes*

Cooking time: *10 minutes*

Yield: *4 servings*

2 ounces sun-dried tomatoes, chopped

½ cup extra-virgin olive oil

3 cloves garlic, minced

½ cup finely chopped basil leaves, plus extra whole leaves for garnish

1 15-ounce jar marinated artichoke hearts, drained

8 ounces butterfly pasta

Salt and freshly ground black pepper, optional

Grated Parmesan cheese, optional

1 In a shallow bowl, combine tomatoes, olive oil, garlic, and basil. Let rest overnight to allow tomatoes to rehydrate.

2 Transfer tomato mixture to a large bowl and add artichoke hearts. Lightly toss together.

3 Bring a large pot of water to boil and cook the pasta according to the directions on the package until the pasta is *al dente,* cooked but not soft. Drain and add to the tomato artichoke mixture. Adjust seasoning with salt and pepper.

4 Serve at room temperature, garnished with whole basil leaves and Parmesan cheese on the side.

Nutrient analysis per serving: *540 kcalories, 10 grams protein, 56 grams carbohydrate, 33 grams fat, 4 grams saturated fat, 0 milligrams cholesterol, 6 grams fiber, 505 milligrams sodium*

Exchanges: *4 starch, 6 fat*

Seafood Farfalle Salad

It's no surprise that in Italy, a country with many port cities, many pasta dishes include fish. The Italians have even figured out how to use the black ink of octopus in one special pasta dish. This recipe is much tamer, however. It's a low-calorie but quite satisfying combination of seafood and pasta. Using *farfalle,* pasta shaped like a butterfly or a bowtie (shown in Figure 10-3), adds eye appeal. If you have access to a specialty Italian food market, you may even be able to find *farfallini,* the smallest butterflies, or *farfallone,* the largest.

(continued)

Figure 10-3: Farfalle is butterfly or bowtie pasta.

Preparation time: *25 minutes*

Cooking time: *20–25 minutes (in prep)*

Yield: *4 servings*

8 ounces farfalle pasta

Nonstick cooking spray

½ pound bay scallops

½ pound cooked baby shrimp

1½ teaspoons white wine vinegar

1 tablespoon extra-virgin olive oil

1 teaspoon freshly squeezed lemon juice

1 teaspoon dried thyme leaves

1 clove garlic, minced

2 teaspoons chopped fresh parsley

⅛ teaspoon freshly ground black pepper

½ cup plum tomatoes, peeled, seeded, and diced

1 small cucumber, peeled, seeded, and diced

2 tablespoons seeded and finely chopped green pepper

1 Bring a large pot of water to a boil. Salt the boiling water and cook the farfalle according to package directions. Drain, rinse under cold running water, and drain again. Set aside.

2 Meanwhile, coat a medium nonstick skillet with cooking spray or 2 teaspoons of canola oil and place over medium heat until hot. Add the scallops and shrimp, a few at a time, and sauté, turning them as they brown, allowing 1½ to 2 minutes per side; remove them to a bowl as they finish.

3 In a large bowl, whisk together the vinegar, olive oil, lemon juice, thyme, garlic, parsley, and pepper. Add the tomatoes, cucumber, and green pepper and mix thoroughly. Combine the pasta, scallops (and their released juices), and shrimp and toss well.

Nutrient analysis per serving: *398 kcalories, 32 grams protein, 48 grams carbohydrate, 7.5 grams fat, 1 gram saturated fat, 131 milligrams cholesterol, 2.4 grams fiber, 363 milligrams sodium*

Exchanges: *3 starch, 3 very lean meat*

Developing a Liking for Legumes

Legumes — beans, peas, and lentils — can be very satisfying foods. They supply protein without much fat and are full of minerals. You can also flavor them all sorts of ways. Beans are a tasty way of managing blood glucose, thanks to the soluble fiber they contain. A legume-rich diet is beneficial to good health.

When you eat some beans along with some grains, you're giving yourself a high quality protein, equivalent to meat. (Turn to Chapter 14 for more information.)

Beans, peas, and lentils make hearty soups, as the legumes cook and break down, thickening the broth. You can make the soup even creamier by purée-ing part of the batch and returning it to the pot. You can also add a meaty flavor to the brew with the addition of ham hocks, bacon, or prosciutto. Such brews can make a satisfying main course or a substantial start to an evening meal. Even if your diet has been lacking in legumes up to now, once you taste these scrumptious soups, you're likely never to go without legumes again.

In terms of the Exchange Lists for diabetes, most beans qualify as 1 very lean meat exchange, plus 1 or 2 starch exchanges, the beginnings of a meal. Have a green salad with a bowl of bean soup, and you are eating well and watching your weight at the same time.

If one of the reasons you rarely eat beans is the gas that they can generate, the solution is a product called Beano. It supplies the missing enzyme needed to break down the offending sugars in the bean. You can also try a host of traditional remedies for the problem, such as adding certain herbs to the cooking water when you prepare beans, but these methods are only mildly beneficial by comparison. Another way to prevent the problem of gas is to eat more beans so you'll build up a tolerance.

Many people never get around to cooking beans because they don't want to bother soaking them for hours. But actually, you can cook dried beans as is. Cooking time increases by 15 minutes to a half hour, but this difference is easy to plan for.

Either of the following two soups would make an excellent supper.

Cabbage, Bean, and Bacon Soup

This fortifying soup, from Hamersley's Bistro in Boston (see Appendix A), is an excellent source of fiber, thanks to the beans, turnips, carrots, and cabbage.

Preparation time: *45 minutes*

Cooking time: *90 minutes*

Yield: *6 servings*

4 tablespoons cooking oil

6 slices bacon, diced

1 onion, diced

2 cloves garlic, chopped, divided use

½ head green cabbage, halved and cut into ¼-inch thick slices

2 turnips, peeled and diced

2 carrots, peeled and diced

2 teaspoons fresh thyme leaves, removed from sprigs

½ cup white wine

12 cups chicken stock, or 1 quart stock and 2 quarts water

3 cups white beans

1 Heat the cooking oil in a medium saucepan over medium heat. Add the bacon and sauté for 3 minutes or until bacon is cooked. Add the onion, half of the garlic, cabbage, turnips, and carrots. Cook, stirring, over medium heat for 5 minutes.

2 Add the thyme, white wine, and chicken stock. Bring to a boil and then lower heat and simmer for 15 minutes.

3 Meanwhile, in another saucepan, cover the beans with water, bring to a boil, and then add the remaining garlic, lower the heat, and simmer for approximately 5 minutes. Drain the beans. Add the beans to the saucepan with the vegetables and simmer for 75 to 90 minutes, until beans are thoroughly cooked and can be easily mashed between two fingers.

4 Serve in large warmed soup bowls.

Nutrient analysis per serving: *500 kcalories, 29 grams protein, 70 grams carbohydrate, 13 grams fat, 2 grams saturated fat, 5 milligrams cholesterol, 18 grams fiber, 535 milligrams sodium*

Exchanges: *2 lean meat, 4 starch, 1 vegetable, 1 fat*

Black Bean Soup with Salsa Mexicana

This soup and salsa combination comes from Anasazi Restaurant in Santa Fe (see Appendix A). A serving of this soup contains 43 grams of carbohydrate. But when you have a bowlful, only 33 grams of the total are available for your body to turn into glucose. The fiber in the beans is the reason. Fiber reduces the effect carbohydrates have on your blood glucose.

Preparation time: *40 minutes*

Cooking time: *3 hours*

Yield: *8 servings*

The Black Bean Soup

1 pound black beans

2 tablespoons vegetable oil

1 onion, chopped

1 small leek (white part only), chopped

4 cloves garlic, chopped

3 jalapeño chilies, seeded and membranes removed

½ bunch cilantro

1½ cups dark beer

1 quart chicken broth

1 quart water

1 smoked ham hock or smoked pork neck bones

½ teaspoon salt

Juice of 1 lime

The Salsa Mexicana

1 tablespoon minced garlic

3 tablespoons minced jalapeño

⅓ cup minced onion

⅓ cup red tomato, diced

⅓ cup yellow tomato, diced

2 tablespoons chopped cilantro

3 tablespoons fresh lime juice

1 tablespoon extra-virgin olive oil

1 Rinse the beans, removing stones and shriveled beans. Soak beans in enough cold water to cover 8 hours or overnight. Drain.

2 Heat the vegetable oil in a large pot over medium heat. Add the onion and the leeks and sauté, stirring until soft, about 4 minutes. Stir in the garlic and jalapeños and cook another minute. Add the drained beans, cilantro, beer, chicken stock, water, and ham hocks or neck bones. Bring to a boil. Lower heat and simmer, stirring occasionally, until the beans are very soft, about 2 hours. Skim off any foam that rises to the surface, as shown in Figure 10-4.

(continued)

Figure 10-4: Skim off the foam that rises to the surface of the soup.

3 While the beans cook, prepare Salsa Mexicana. In a medium bowl, combine the garlic, jalapeño, onion, red and yellow tomatoes, cilantro, lime juice, and olive oil, adding salt to taste (see note).

4 When the beans are soft, remove the ham hock or neck bones. Pour the beans into a blender or food processor, dividing into batches if necessary, and blend until smooth. Season to taste with salt and lime juice. The soup should be fairly thick, but pourable. If soup is too thick, thin with additional hot chicken stock or water.

5 Serve soup in warm bowls garnished with Salsa Mexicana.

Note: *If you're on a low-salt diet, omit this added salt and this soup will still have plenty, thanks to the salty ham hock.*

Nutrient analysis per serving: *313 kcalories, 16 grams protein, 43 grams carbohydrate, 8 grams fat, 1 gram saturated fat, 7 milligrams cholesterol, 10 grams fiber, 660 milligrams sodium*

Exchanges: *3 bread/starch, 1 lean meat*

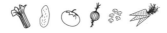

Cool Minestrone Soup (Minestrone Freddo)

Eating a variety of vegetables is essential for good nutrition. Here's your chance to do so, Italian-style, from New York City's Barbetta (see Appendix A). This recipe for a classic soup has an intriguing twist — minestrone served at room temperature, something like gazpacho, the tomato-based soup of Spain that's usually served chilled.

This minestrone is made with specialty ingredients you may find in your local supermarket and for certain in a market specializing in Italian foods. Cranberry beans, also called *shell beans,* are large beige beans, splotched with red that is lost during the cooking process. Cranberry beans must be shelled before cooking. Prosciutto is Italian ham that is salt-cured and air-dried. Arborio rice is Italian short-grain rice. Pecorino cheese is sheep's milk cheese.

Preparation time: *30 minutes*

Cooking time: *2½ hours*

Yield: *6 servings*

⅓ cup arborio rice, cooked

⅓ cup fresh cranberry beans, shells removed, soaked for 4 hours, or ⅓ cup reduced-sodium canned pinto beans

1 prosciutto bone or beef bone, or a ham bone or hock

2½ quarts water

2 tablespoons olive oil

4 to 6 slices prosciutto, chopped (about 2 ounces)

1 medium onion, chopped

1 clove garlic, minced

½ pound string beans, cut in 1-inch pieces

2 ripe tomatoes, diced

4 medium potatoes, diced

4 carrots, diced

4 small zucchini, diced

4 stalks celery, diced

½ head cabbage, shredded

¾ cup pecorino cheese

1 tablespoon pesto sauce

1 Cook the rice according to instructions on the package (a standard ratio of liquid to rice is usually 2:1 and the cooking time is 18 minutes). Set aside.

2 Remove the cranberry beans from their pods and rinse them. In a large saucepan, combine the cranberry beans, prosciutto bone, and water, bring to a boil, and simmer for 60 minutes.

3 In a medium saucepan, heat the olive oil over medium-high heat. Add the chopped prosciutto, onions, and garlic and sauté, stirring often, until golden brown. Stir in the string beans, tomatoes, potatoes, carrots, zucchini, celery, and cabbage.

4 Remove the bone from the cooked meat and beans, and add the beans and broth to the sautéed vegetables. Simmer partially, stirring occasionally, for 90 minutes. If necessary, add up to another 2 cups of liquid during cooking.

5 Remove from heat; add the reserved cooked rice, cheese, and pesto sauce. Cool and serve at room temperature, not chilled. Adjust seasoning if necessary.

Nutrient analysis per serving: *320 kcalories, 13 grams protein, 47 grams carbohydrate, 10 grams fat, 3 grams saturated fat, 17 milligrams cholesterol, 9 grams fiber, 440 milligrams sodium*

Exchanges: *2 starch, 3 vegetable, 1 lean meat, 1 fat*

Basil and Onion Pea Soup

If you've been wanting the taste of homemade soup but think you never have the time to prepare such a luxury, look no farther than this recipe from Osteria Del Mondo in Milwaukee (see Appendix A). Fresh peas cook quickly, and within the hour, you can be sipping on this gourmet soup. Rich and creamy, this yummy soup is an elegant beginning to a meal. It should be paired with a lowfat entrée, such as a grilled chicken sandwich.

Preparation time: *15 minutes*

Cooking time: *20 minutes*

Yield: *6 servings*

¼ cup chopped onion

1 tablespoon olive oil

2 cups fresh peas (or frozen peas)

1 bunch fresh basil, leaves only

1 cup vegetable broth or stock

½ cup light whipping cream

¼ teaspoon salt

¼ teaspoon white pepper, or to taste

1 In a medium saucepan, sauté the onions in the oil over medium heat until tender, about 5 minutes. Add the peas and cook for about 3 minutes, then stir in the basil. When this mixture is hot, add the vegetable broth and cream. Season with the salt and white pepper. Bring to a simmer and cook for 10 minutes.

2 Remove from heat. Blend the soup in a blender or a food processor fitted with a metal blade in batches until smooth and return to the saucepan to heat. Ladle into 6 large, individual soup bowls and serve.

Nutrient analysis per serving: *121 kcalories, 3.5 grams protein, 8 grams carbohydrate, 9 grams fat, 4 grams saturated fat, 22 milligrams cholesterol, 2 grams fiber, 324 milligrams sodium*

Exchanges: *½ starch, 2 fat*

Gordon Hamersley's Hearty Lentil Soup

Lentils belong in every well-stocked kitchen. They are an excellent source of fiber, just like beans, but offer a cooking advantage. Lentils don't require presoaking and cook up quickly. Start preparing this soup from Hamersley's Bistro in Boston (see Appendix A) in the late morning, and you'll be enjoying it for lunch. If you can't find Herbes de

Provence in the market, you can substitute with a combination of sage, marjoram, rosemary, basil, oregano, and thyme. And if you want a spicy version of this soup, substitute the herbs with 2 tablespoons of curry powder when you are cooking the vegetables. To reduce the relatively high sodium content of this soup, use half the bacon, still a sufficient amount to enhance flavor, and only a very light sprinkling of cheese.

Preparation time: *20 minutes*

Cooking time: *55 minutes*

Yield: *6 servings*

1 tablespoon olive oil

1 tablespoon butter

1 medium onion, diced

2 carrots, peeled and diced

6 cloves garlic, peeled and smashed

6 slices smoked bacon, diced

2 teaspoons Herbes de Provence (see note)

2 cups lentils, washed and checked for stones

8 cups water or low-sodium chicken stock

Optional salt and pepper to taste

2 ounces Asiago cheese

6 large croutons, toasted

1 Heat the olive oil and butter in a soup pot. Add onion, carrots, garlic, bacon, and herbs, and cook over medium heat for 5 minutes, stirring occasionally.

2 Add the lentils and water or chicken stock, and raise the heat. Bring to a boil. Skim the foam from the surface, reduce heat to low, and simmer for 50 minutes, or until lentils are cooked. Season with salt and pepper.

3 Grate the cheese.

4 Heat large soup bowls. Ladle soup into each bowl, top with a crouton, and sprinkle with cheese. Serve immediately.

Note: *Herbes de Provence can be found in most markets, but if you can't find this mix, substitute with Fines Herbes or Italian Herbs.*

Nutrient analysis per serving: *390 kcalories, 28 grams protein, 46 grams carbohydrate, 11 grams fat, 4.5 grams saturated fat, 21 milligrams cholesterol, 21 grams fiber, 1023 milligrams sodium*

Exchanges: *3 bread, 3 lean meat*

Chapter 11

Adding Veggies to Your Meals

In This Chapter

- Converting vegetables into Food Exchanges
- Fitting starchy vegetables into your diet
- Finding out about foods that contain soluble fiber
- Avoiding fat by steaming and baking
- Filling up with phytonutrients
- Giving dark leafy greens a try
- Going for variety

Recipes in This Chapter

- Sweet Cabbage and Apples
- Caramelized Cauliflower
- Mashed Potatoes with Parmesan
- Julienned Parsnips with Tomatoes, au Gratin
- Minted Carrots with Feta
- Caribbean-style Okra with Shrimp
- Creamed Greens with Cardamom
- Spaghetti Squash with Fresh Basil
- Braised Fennel (Finocchio)
- Sautéed Broccoli with Red Peppers
- Spiced Chopped Kale and Potatoes
- Braise of Spring Vegetables
- Tagliarini alla Primavera

While the Dietary Guidelines for Americans recommends that you eat at least three servings a day of vegetables, 80 percent or more of Americans never manage to meet this quota. Of course, you've probably heard repeatedly that eating vegetables is a good idea if you want to be healthy, but you may find that getting around to eating vegetables can be a challenge. Fast-food outlets focus on meats and starches, the vegetables served in coffee shops are often bland and waterlogged, and vegetable side-dishes in most eateries are often pricey. In these circumstances, many people, perhaps including you, simply never have the chance to develop a liking for vegetables. But that's all going to change now, with the mouthwatering recipes in this chapter. We guide you through various healthy ways of preparing vegetables and give you tempting recipes to practice.

TIP

Eating your vegetables raw

According to the American Diabetes Association Food Exchange Lists, you can have even more of a vegetable, per exchange, if you eat the vegetable raw! Introduce *crudités* (the French version of raw vegetables served with some sort of sauce or dip) into your diet. Many vegetables commonly included in crudités are "free" vegetables, such as celery, cucumber, endive, radishes, zucchini, and mushrooms — another reason to enjoy this healthy invention.

A platter of raw vegetables has become common party fare, but don't forget to enjoy crudités as a snack. Whip up a simple dip such as lowfat yogurt mixed with a bit of mayonnaise and herbs. If you are spending hours working at your computer, munch on crunchy vegetables instead of greasy corn chips.

While all sorts of raw vegetables qualify as healthy foods, the same is not true for dips. At parties, your hostess, in a generous spirit, is likely to have splurged on the ingredients because she's cooking for a special occasion. Party dips are likely to be high in fat and calories, so more is not better.

Translating Vegetable Servings into Exchanges

For people with diabetes, not all vegetables are created equal. The starchy vegetables, such as corn and potatoes, are so high in carbohydrates that they count as a starch, not a vegetable, in the American Diabetes Association Food Exchange Lists. Then there are the many common vegetables that actually count as vegetables — the string beans and tomatoes of everyday eating. Finally, a few vegetables, which typically have a high water content, don't count at all! They contain so little fat, protein, or carbohydrates that you can consider them freebies. You can have up to two cupfuls of these with little effect on your blood glucose.

Following are lists of vegetables to help you keep straight the different categories of vegetables:

- **Starchy vegetables:** Corn; potatoes; sweet potatoes; winter squash, including acorn, butternut, buttercup, and Hubbard; parsnips; pumpkin; plantain; and legumes, including beans, lima beans, peas, and lentils
- **Vegetables that count as a single vegetable exchange:** Artichokes, asparagus, bamboo shoots, bean sprouts, beets, beet greens, broccoli, brussels sprouts, carrots, chard greens, dandelion greens, eggplant, green pepper, jícama, kale, kohlrabi, leeks, mustard greens, okra, onions, pea pods, rutabaga, sauerkraut, spinach, string beans, tomatoes, turnips, turnip greens, and water chestnuts

- **Free vegetables:** Alfalfa sprouts, cabbage, celery, chicory, Chinese cabbage, cucumber, endive, escarole, green onions, hot peppers, lettuce, mushrooms, radishes, rhubarb, summer squash such as zucchini, and watercress

Cabbage is another "free" food, and 150 years ago was one of the two most frequently eaten vegetables, along with potatoes. Today, cabbage isn't served as often as it should be, given how healthy a food it is and how good it can taste. Sample the following recipe!

Sweet Cabbage and Apples

This dish has German origins. Enjoy the sweet-sour flavors that taste so good with wintry roast pork and egg noodles. You'll be surprised at how vegetable haters lap up this cabbage-apple mix.

Preparation time: *10 minutes*

Cooking time: *40 minutes*

Yield: *4 servings*

2 teaspoons butter

1 medium onion, chopped

1 small head red cabbage (about 1 pound), cored and thinly sliced

1 apple, peeled, quartered, cored, and thinly sliced

¼ cup apple juice

¾ cup water

1 tablespoon red wine vinegar

Freshly ground black pepper to taste

1 In a large sauté pan, melt the butter over low heat. Add onion and over medium heat, sauté briefly, about 1 minute.

2 Add the cabbage and apple. Cook over medium heat, stirring occasionally, for 5 minutes.

3 In a small bowl, combine apple juice, water, vinegar, and pepper. Pour this mixture into the sautéed cabbage. Cover skillet tightly and cook over low heat for 30 minutes.

4 Serve cabbage mixture warm as a side dish or cold as a cooked slaw.

Nutrient analysis per serving: *87 kcalories, 2 grams protein, 16 grams carbohydrate, 2.5 grams fat, l gram saturated fat, 5 milligrams cholesterol, 4 grams fiber, 34 milligrams sodium*

Exchanges: *1 vegetable, ½ fruit, ½ fat*

Caramelized Cauliflower

The deeply browned cauliflower in this recipe from Heartbeat in New York City (see Appendix A) is an unexpected treat. The caramelization gives character to an otherwise bland vegetable. What's great about this side dish is that you can prepare it completely in advance and then reheat the cauliflower on a baking sheet in the oven shortly before serving.

Preparation time: *5 minutes*

Cooking time: *10 minutes*

Yield: *4 servings*

1 large head cauliflower

2½ tablespoons grapeseed oil

¼ teaspoon coarse salt and freshly ground pepper

1 Remove the green leaves and stem from the cauliflower. Cut out enough of the central core so the vegetable can stand upright. Cut down through the center of the cauliflower to divide the middle into four large slices ¾ to 1 inch thick. Use the florets from either side another time for soup or crudités. Gather up all the tiny bits of cauliflower you find on the cutting board and reserve them.

2 In a large skillet, preferably cast-iron, heat 1 tablespoon oil over medium-high heat. Add the cauliflower slices in a single layer and scatter the bits around. Season lightly with salt and pepper. Place another heavy skillet on top of the slices to weight them down and press gently. Cook, rotating the cast-iron skillet and pressing down occasionally, 5 minutes, or until the cauliflower slices are deeply browned on the bottom.

3 Stir the bits. Drizzle about ½ teaspoon oil over each cauliflower slice, turn over and brown on the second side, 4 to 5 minutes. Lower the heat slightly if the cauliflower seems to be browning too fast. Serve immediately or set aside and reheat in the oven for 15 minutes at 300 degrees Fahrenheit.

Nutrient analysis per serving: *111 kcalories, 5 grams protein, 6 grams carbohydrate, 9 grams fat, 1 gram saturated fat, 0 milligrams cholesterol, 6 grams fiber, 193 milligrams sodium*

Exchanges: *1 vegetable, 2 fat*

Adding Starchy Vegetables to Your Diet

Two of the most commonly eaten starchy vegetables, potatoes and corn, rank among the foods with the highest glycemic index (see Chapter 2). Processed versions of these foods, such as instant mashed potatoes and cornflakes, which enter the bloodstream more quickly than foods in their natural state, rank right up there, along with lowfat ice cream.

Potatoes and corn can have a place in a diabetic diet, but you need to eat these in smaller portions and balance their carbohydrate content with protein and fat in other foods at the same meal.

Mashed Potatoes with Parmesan

Maintaining balance is the strategy in this recipe. We combine the potatoes with cheese and milk to increase the protein and fat in this dish. One way to enjoy the flavor of a fine cheese, without adding a lot of calories because of the fat it contains, is to use cheese as a flavoring rather than a major ingredient. A trail of Parmigiano-Reggiano flows through these mashed potatoes, Italian style. This cheese is more expensive than regular Parmesan cheese, but its granular texture and quality are well worth the higher price.

Preparation time: *10 minutes*

Cooking time: *30 minutes*

Yield: *6 servings*

6 medium boiling potatoes (about 1½ pounds), quartered (see note)

Water

3 tablespoons freshly grated Parmigiano-Reggiano cheese

⅛ teaspoon freshly ground pepper

½ teaspoon salt

½ cup lowfat warm milk

1 Cover potatoes with filtered water in a saucepan. Over moderate heat, bring to a boil. Cover and reduce heat to low. Simmer potatoes until tender, about 20 minutes.

2 Using a colander, drain the potatoes and return to the saucepan. Mash the potatoes using a potato masher. With a wooden spoon, beat in the cheese, salt, and pepper. Add milk and beat potatoes until nearly smooth. Leaving a few lumps can add interest and has recently come into fashion, although your mother may not agree.

Note: *To peel or not to peel: If the potatoes are not organic, peel them. If they are organic, leave some or all of the skins, for added fiber and a nice country feel to the final dish.*

(continued)

Nutrient analysis per serving: *102 kcalories, 4 grams protein, 18 grams carbohydrate, 1 gram fat, 1 gram saturated fat, 3 milligrams cholesterol, 2 grams fiber, 254 milligrams sodium.*

Exchanges: *1 starch*

Choosing Foods That Contain Soluble Fiber

Fiber in vegetables comes in two forms: insoluble fiber, which makes foods like celery crunchy; and soluble fiber, the reason why certain foods like okra have a viscous texture.

Beans and oats are excellent sources of soluble fiber. Both contain *pectins,* the type of fiber that binds with fatty substances and promotes their excretion, a reason why they are credited with lowering cholesterol levels in the blood.

Soluble fibers are also able to help regulate the body's use of sugar, of importance in managing diabetes. How this happens isn't fully understood. It may be that fiber slows the emptying time for the stomach and, consequently, the rate of glucose absorption from the intestinal tract into the bloodstream may slow, too. Vegetables that contain soluble fiber include

- Okra
- Carrots
- Eggplant
- Parsnips

Nopales cactus, cooked as a vegetable in Mexican cooking, is also an excellent source of soluble fiber. If your city has a large Latin community, you may find the fresh cactus paddles in the produce section of your supermarket. Also look for canned, cooked strips of nopales in the ethnic foods aisle. And for sure you'll find all forms of nopales sold in Mexican grocery stores. Nopales tastes something like string beans and is excellent served as a salad, along with tomatoes, onions, and avocado, in a lime vinaigrette.

Getting to like parsnips

Never touch parsnips? Try this recipe that includes tomato, cheese, and herbs. Who says you can't learn to like parsnips?

Julienned Parsnips with Tomatoes, au Gratin

Parsnips arrived on the American shore in the early 1600s, brought to the New World by Europeans. Despite their long history, parsnips never really caught on. These pleasantly sweet root vegetables are usually boiled and mashed like potatoes, but they can be the basis of a gourmet dish like this one.

Preparation time: *15 minutes*

Cooking time: *20 minutes*

Yield: *6 servings*

1 pound parsnips, peeled and cut into sticks

1 medium onion, thinly sliced

½ teaspoon dried thyme

½ cup canned reduced sodium, fat-free chicken broth, plus extra

1 teaspoon unrefined safflower oil to coat the bottom and sides of a baking pan (see note)

1 large tomato

2 tablespoons minced fresh parsley

⅓ cup grated Pecorino-Romano cheese

1 In a large pot, combine parsnips, onion, thyme, and chicken broth. Cook covered, over medium heat, until the parsnips are tender, about 15 minutes. Add more chicken broth if the liquid boils away before the parsnips are fully cooked.

2 Coat a 10-inch baking dish with the oil. Using a pair of tongs or a large spoon that allows juice to be drained, transfer the cooked parsnips to the baking dish.

3 Preheat broiler.

4 With a paring knife, remove the core of the tomato and slice in half crosswise. Gently squeeze the tomato to remove seeds and juice. Cut horizontally into thin slices.

5 Evenly distribute the tomato slices over the parsnips. Sprinkle with parsley and the grated cheese.

6 Broil vegetables about 4 inches from the heat source until cheese melts and the tomatoes cook through and begin to brown.

Note: *You'll find unrefined cooking oils, including safflower, sold in natural food stores.*

(continued)

Nutrient analysis per serving: *87 kcalories, 3 grams protein, 16 grams carbohydrate, 2 grams fat, 1 gram saturated fat, 4 milligrams cholesterol, 4 grams fiber, 110 milligrams sodium*

Exchanges: *1 starch*

Playing it safe with carrots

If you aren't feeling too adventurous, start with carrots. While you know from their crunch that they contain plenty of insoluble fiber, carrots also contain soluble pectin. This recipe accents the carrots with cheese — but an unusual kind, feta.

Traditionally made of sheep's or goat's milk, large commercial producers often make feta from cow's milk. Cheese makers cure and store this cheese in brine, which gives it a salty, tangy taste.

Although these days you can find feta in the cheese section of most supermarkets, go out of your way to buy this cheese in the smaller specialty foods stores that feature traditional Greek and Middle Eastern foods. You can sample all the wonderful varieties and choose among the different flavors. Search out mild, French feta, which is easy to like.

TIP

Avoid the packaged, crumbled feta sold in supermarkets. The crumbled version often has a flat taste and is dried out. Instead, buy feta only in block form; it's usually packaged in brine to prevent drying.

Minted Carrots with Feta

Ho-hum carrots perk up with the addition of lemon and feta. These carrots are treated to a bit of flaxseed oil, a source of essential fatty acids that can lower cholesterol. If you want to make this dish even more nutritious, chop some of the carrot tops (they taste like mild parsley) and add these to the pot along with the carrots. You'll be increasing your intake of greens with little extra effort. This recipe is featured in the color section of this book.

Preparation time: *15 minutes*

Cooking time: *15 minutes*

Yield: *6 servings*

Vegetable Omelet
(Chapter 6); Crispy Corn
French Toast (Chapter 6)

Clockwise from top left: Shrimp Cakes (Chapter 15); Feta Bruschetta (Chapter 15); Wild Mushroom Tacos (Chapter 7); Salad of Smoked Salmon with Horseradish Dressing (Chapter 7)

Carrot Soup with Leek and Blood Orange (Chapter 8)

Spinach Pie (Chapter 15); Jícama and Belgian Endive Salad with Tequila-Orange Vinaigrette (Chapter 9)

Steak Salad Niçoise (Chapter 9)

Cowboy Shrimp with Jalapeño Cornsticks (Chapter 12)

Greek Salad with Swordfish (Chapter 9)

Grilled Lobster with
Green Bean, Corn, and
Tomato Salad (Chapter 9)

Snapper Veracruzana (Chapter 12); Black Bean Salsa (Chapter 7); Sautéed Broccoli with Red Peppers (Chapter 11)

Sautéed Breast of Chicken with Smoke-Flavored Tomato Sauce (Chapter 13); Grilled Spring Vegetables (Chapter 13)

Chicken with Lemon, Spinach, and Ham (Chapter 13); Risotto with Seasonal Green Vegetables (Chapter 10); Spaghetti Squash with Fresh Basil (Chapter 11)

Squab alla Piemontese (Chapter 13); Butterfly Pasta with Sun-Dried Tomatoes and Artichoke Hearts (Chapter 10)

Char-Grilled Double-Cut Pork Chops with Black-Eyed Pea Relish and Sweet Potato Fries (Chapter 14)

Stewed French Lamb Shanks with White Beans (Chapter 14); Minted Carrots with Feta (Chapter 11)

Apple Crisp (Chapter 16)

6 sprigs fresh mint, stems removed and leaves minced (2 tablespoons)

juice of ½ lemon (2 tablespoons)

2 tablespoons flaxseed oil or canola oil

1 bunch carrots, tops removed (1¼ pounds)

2 ounces freshly crumbled feta cheese

1 In a small bowl, using a fork, mix together mint, lemon juice, and flaxseed oil. Set dressing aside.

2 Peel carrots and halve each carrot crosswise, and cut each half into sticks.

3 Using a saucepan with a tight-fitting lid, insert a basket steamer. Place carrots on the steamer and cook, covered, until tender, about 15 minutes.

4 Transfer cooked carrots to a serving bowl and drizzle with dressing. Add feta and toss to combine ingredients. Serve hot or at room temperature.

Nutrient analysis per serving: *105 kcalories, 2 grams protein, 10 grams carbohydrate, 6 grams fat, 2 grams saturated fat, 8 milligrams cholesterol, 3 grams fiber, 137 milligrams sodium*

Exchanges: *2 vegetable, 1 fat*

Giving okra a try

Here's a third way to increase your intake of soluble fiber, an okra recipe that is inspired by cuisines of the Caribbean, where this vegetable shows up in lots of dishes.

TIP

You can find fresh okra in stores May through October, but in the southern United States, okra is available fresh year-round.

Caribbean-style Okra with Shrimp

This inventive combination of okra and shrimp originated in the Dominican Republic. With the addition of protein in the shellfish, it makes a complete and balanced meal. Taste as you combine the ingredients — you may want to add fire with more chilies and punch with more garlic and cinnamon.

Preparation time: *15 minutes after shrimp has been prepped*

Cooking time: *15 minutes*

Yield: *4 servings*

(continued)

3 tablespoons olive oil

1 medium onion, finely chopped

¾ pound okra, cut into ¼-inch slices (2 cups)

3 underripe bananas, peeled and cut into ½-inch slices

2 medium tomatoes, peeled and chopped

¼ cup lemon juice

2 small fresh hot red or green peppers, seeded and chopped

6 sprigs cilantro (1 tablespoon)

1 clove garlic

½ teaspoon ground cinnamon

¼ teaspoon sea salt and freshly ground black pepper

1 pound medium-sized shrimp, shelled and deveined

1 In a large skillet, heat the oil over medium-high heat. When hot, add the onion and sauté the onion until it becomes soft, about 5 minutes. Add the okra and sauté for 2 to 3 minutes. Add the banana, tomatoes, lemon juice, hot pepper, cilantro, garlic, and cinnamon, and season with salt and pepper. Simmer this mixture, stirring occasionally, until the okra is tender, about 5 minutes.

2 Add the shrimp and cook until shrimp turn pink, about 2 minutes. Serve with rice made with a squirt of lemon juice and a garlic clove in the cooking water.

Nutrient analysis per serving: *346 kcalories, 26 grams protein, 35 grams carbohydrate, 13 grams fat, 2 grams saturated fat, 172 milligrams cholesterol, 6 grams fiber, 327 milligrams sodium*

Exchanges: *1 vegetable, 2 fruit, 3 medium-fat meat*

Cooking Veggies with a Minimum of Fat

Look no further than steaming and baking if you want to know the healthiest ways of cooking vegetables. These techniques require no added fat and instead make the most of the natural flavor of the food.

Steaming

Every kitchen should be equipped with a collapsible basket steamer, which easily fits into a variety of pots. For successful steaming, you also need a pot with a tight-fitting lid so that the steam cannot escape. Steamed vegetables are especially nutritious — they don't come into contact with the cooking liquid so the nutrients tend to remain in the food.

Overcooked steamed vegetables, such as cauliflower, can taste bland and lose all texture. Steamed vegetables are best when they still have some crunch.

To enhance the flavor of steamed vegetables, toss them with a squeeze of lemon juice and pepper or cook them on a bed of fresh herbs. You can also serve vegetables with a low-calorie dipping sauce made with low-sodium soy sauce and ginger.

You can also steam vegetables by cooking them in a small amount of liquid. When the liquid boils, the portion of the vegetables higher than the liquid gets steamed. This is the lazy way to steam and it works just fine. Try it out with this recipe for kale.

Creamed Greens with Cardamom

You'll be surprised just how tasty this dish is, flavored with cardamom, a classic curry spice. The addition of yogurt gives you the luxury of a creamed vegetable but with much less saturated fat. Here's a great way to sneak kale onto family dinner plates without anyone knowing!

Preparation time: *15 minutes*

Cooking time: *30 minutes*

Yield: *4 servings*

1 tablespoon extra-virgin olive oil

1 small onion, peeled and chopped (about ½ cup)

½ teaspoon powdered cardamom

¼ teaspoon hot pepper flakes

1 bunch kale, washed and coarsely chopped

½ cup water

½ cup plain yogurt

¼ teaspoon sea salt and freshly ground black pepper

1. Heat the oil in a heavy skillet. Add onion, cardamom, and hot pepper flakes. Cook on medium heat, stirring occasionally, until onions begin to soften, about 4 minutes.
2. Put kale and water in skillet. Cover tightly and steam until kale wilts, about 5 minutes. Remove lid and continue cooking kale mixture over medium heat until tender, about 15 minutes.

(continued)

3 Transfer kale mixture to a food processor fitted with a metal blade. Purée kale.

4 Return puréed kale to the skillet. Add yogurt. Stir ingredients to combine. Season to taste with salt and pepper. Reheat kale mixture over medium-low heat, stirring occasionally, and serve immediately.

Nutrient analysis per serving: *90 kcalories, 4 grams protein,10 grams carbohydrate, 5 grams fat, 1 gram saturated fat, 2 milligrams cholesterol, 2 grams fiber, 196 milligrams sodium*

Exchanges: *2 vegetable, 1 fat*

Baking

Potatoes are baked, but few other vegetables are treated to this effortless way of cooking. Many vegetables are well suited for baking, such as beets, carrots, onions, and squash. Baking retains nutrients and can sweeten vegetables as their sugars caramelize. Use baked vegetables as the main ingredient or to make a delicious vegetable soup.

TIP

If you bake beets and squash whole first, peeling the skin is much easier.

An intriguing squash to experiment with is spaghetti squash, nature's own version of pasta. When you scrape the interior of the cooked vegetable with a fork, the flesh breaks up into long spaghetti-like strands. Give this recipe a try. Adding variety to your diet is good for general health.

Spaghetti Squash with Fresh Basil

Spaghetti squash has a rather bland flavor, so you need to be generous with the seasonings. In this recipe, featured in the color section of the book, the baked squash gets treated to a pasta flavoring.

Preparation time: *10 minutes*

Cooking time: *1 hour*

Yield: *8 servings*

1 medium-size spaghetti squash, about 3 pounds

4 tablespoons extra-virgin olive oil

1 clove garlic, finely minced

¼ cup fresh, chopped basil leaves, loosely packed

Sea salt, optional, and freshly ground black pepper, to taste

8 tablespoons grated Pecorino-Romano cheese

1 Heat the oven to 400 degrees Fahrenheit.

2 Using a skewer or a thin-bladed knife, pierce the spaghetti squash in a few places. Bake the squash whole on a baking sheet until you can easily pierce the flesh with a knife, about 1 hour.

3 Cut the squash in half to reveal the flesh. Using a fork, scrape the squash out of the skin and pile the spaghetti-like strands of vegetable in a large bowl, as shown in Figure 11-1.

Spaghetti Squash with Fresh Basil
Scraped with a fork, the flesh breaks up into long, spaghetti-like strands.....
Cut the squash in half to reveal the flesh.
Using a fork, scrape the squash out of the skin and pile the strands of the vegetable in a large bowl.

Figure 11-1: Scrape the squash out of the skin with a fork and pile the strands into a bowl.

4 In a small bowl, combine the olive oil, garlic, and fresh basil.

5 Drizzle the squash with the olive oil dressing and, using tongs or two forks, lightly toss. Season with salt and pepper.

6 Serve immediately with Pecorino-Romano cheese on the side.

Nutrient analysis per serving: *136 kcalories, 3 grams protein, 12 grams carbohydrate, 9 grams fat, 2 grams saturated fat, 5 milligrams cholesterol, 2 grams fiber, 89 milligrams sodium*

Exchanges: *2 vegetable, 2 fat*

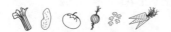

Braising

Dishes cooked by braising develop a rich and substantial flavor, as the vegetables simmer in a small amount of liquid and slowly cook. Braising is the first step of the following recipe. Then the fennel is sautéed and finally baked to create a small masterpiece of flavor.

Braised Fennel (Finocchio)

This recipe comes from Barbetta in New York City (see Appendix A). Fennel seeds are used as an herb in cooking, but the fennel bulb, shown in Figure 11-2, is a deliciously flavored vegetable that has a hint of anise. Fennel makes a good addition to salads but is even better cooked and served as a side dish. Its savory aroma is mouthwatering, starting the digestive juices flowing and consequently increasing the absorption of nutrients.

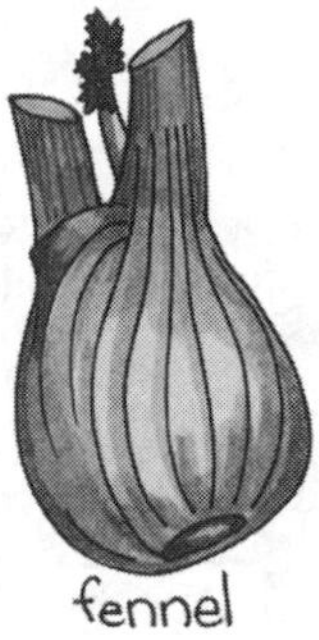

Figure 11-2: If you've never shopped for fresh fennel, here's what to look for in the produce section of your supermarket.

Preparation time: *15 minutes*

Cooking time: *25 minutes*

Yield: *4 servings*

4 medium-size fennel, large stalks removed, bulb only

½ teaspoon salt

2 tablespoons butter

4 tablespoons freshly grated Parmigiano-Reggiano cheese

1 Preheat oven to 450 degrees Fahrenheit. Use a pot large enough to hold all of the fennel and fill ¾ to the top with water. Bring to a boil and season with salt. Add the fennel and cook about 20 minutes, until a paring knife easily pierces the tough bottom core. Drain well. Let cool slightly and then halve lengthwise.

2 Add 1 tablespoon of the butter to a medium skillet and place over medium-high heat. When melted, add the fennel and sauté for 5 minutes, tossing occasionally.

3 Transfer fennel to a roasting pan just large enough to hold them in a single layer. Dot with the remaining butter and sprinkle with Parmigiano-Reggiano cheese. Place the pan in the oven and bake until the cheese is melted and golden brown, 5 to 7 minutes.

Nutrient analysis per serving: *149 kcalories, 5 grams protein, 17 grams carbohydrate, 8 grams fat, 5 grams saturated fat, 20 milligrams cholesterol, 7 grams fiber, 567 milligrams sodium*

Exchanges: *3 vegetable, 2 fat*

Including Vegetables with Phytonutrients

In recent years, scientists have uncovered nutrients in vegetables beyond the well-known vitamins and minerals. Called *phytonutrients,* these compounds appear to play a role in preventing common degenerative diseases such as heart disease and cancer. They are found in a variety of vegetables, underscoring the importance of eating a variety of foods for optimal health.

One category of vegetables that is now required eating is the cruciferous group, which includes cauliflower, brussels sprouts, and broccoli. As you plan your meals to make sure to control blood glucose, remember to cook some cruciferous vegetables for an added bonus of health. You can begin by cooking a batch of this recipe for broccoli.

Sautéed Broccoli with Red Peppers

By keeping cooking time short, this recipe insures that your broccoli turns out emerald green. See it for yourself in the color section of this book.

Preparation time: *10 minutes*

Cooking time: *15 minutes*

Yield: *4 servings*

(continued)

1 bunch of broccoli

1 teaspoon extra-virgin olive oil

2 cloves garlic, minced

1 large sweet red pepper, cut into ⅛-inch strips

½ onion, cut vertically into thin slices

2 tablespoons red wine vinegar or balsamic vinegar

⅛ teaspoon red pepper flakes

Freshly ground black pepper to taste

1 Prepare broccoli by removing tough ends and leaves. Cut off florets, then slice large stalks in thin slices.

2 Fill a large pot with 1 inch of water, cover, and bring to a boil over high heat. Fit the pot with a steamer basket and arrange the broccoli spears on the basket. Cover pot and steam broccoli until it is tender but still has a slight crispness, about 5 minutes. Transfer the broccoli to a bowl and set aside.

3 Remove the steamer from the pot, discard water, and wipe the pot dry.

4 Add the oil to the pot and place over medium heat. Add garlic and sauté until just fragrant, about 30 seconds. Add the peppers and onions. Sauté while stirring frequently, until slightly softened, about 3 to 4 minutes. Add the vinegar and let bubble until nearly evaporated, about 1 minute.

5 Return the broccoli to the pot. Season with red pepper flakes and pepper. Toss vegetable mixture until heated through. Serve immediately or chill and serve as a salad.

Nutrient analysis per serving: *59 kcalories, 4 grams protein, 10 grams carbohydrate, 2 grams fat, 0 grams saturated fat, 0 milligrams cholesterol, 4 grams fiber, 32 milligrams sodium*

Exchanges: *2 vegetable*

Dipping into Dark Leafy Greens

Another category of vegetables vital for health are the dark leafy greens. These include collards, turnip greens, dandelion, mustard greens, chicory, escarole, broccoli rabe, and kale. All of these greens are sources of calcium and magnesium, minerals good for the bones and heart.

Before being washed, these leafy vegetables are often gritty. To make sure you remove all the sand and dirt particles, clean greens by following these steps:

1. **Fill a large bowl full of water.**
2. **Cut off the bottom ends of the stems.**

3. **Put greens into the bowl of water and swish around.**
4. **Lift leaves out into another bowl or colander.**
5. **Discard washing water, rinse bowl, and repeat procedure until the water left in the bowl has no sand or dirt particles.**

Spiced Chopped Kale and Potatoes

Finding good vegetable recipes that are also lowfat is often difficult. This dish from Vij's Restaurant in Vancouver, British Columbia, Canada (see Appendix A) would go well with a hearty entrée such as Chicken in Cilantro, Mint, and Serrano Pepper Curry (see Chapter 13).

Preparation time: *15 minutes*

Cooking time: *30 minutes*

Yield: *4 servings*

2 bunches (about 8 ounces each) fresh kale

1 large potato (8 ounces)

1 tablespoon canola oil

1 tablespoon cumin seeds

1 cup crushed canned tomatoes

½ teaspoon ground turmeric powder

1 teaspoon ground cumin

1 teaspoon ground coriander

1 tablespoon commercial or homemade garam masala (see recipe for garam masala in Kalongi Chicken in Chapter 13)

1 teaspoon salt

½ cup water

1 Cut off and discard the stalks of the kale. Wash leaves in three changes of cool water. Drain in a colander and chop, slicing across the leaves, as shown in Figure 11-3. Set aside. Scrub the potato and chop into ½-inch dice. Set aside.

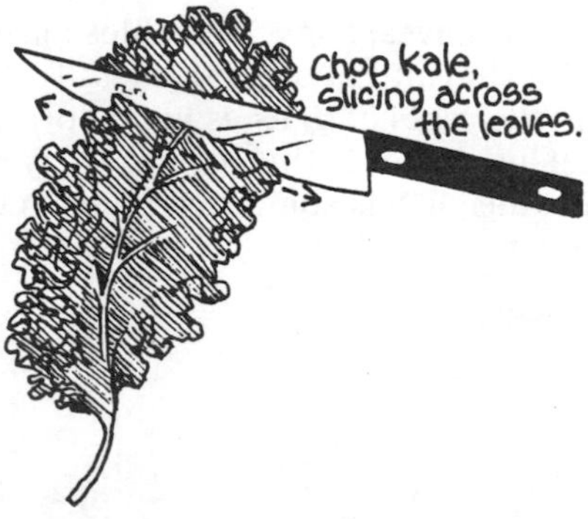
Chop kale, slicing across the leaves.

Figure 11-3: The right way to chop kale.

(continued)

2 In a large, heavy-bottomed cooking pot, heat the canola oil on medium heat for 30 seconds. Add cumin seeds and let them sizzle for 30 seconds. Immediately stir in the crushed tomatoes and all remaining spices. Reduce heat to medium low and while stirring regularly, let simmer for approximately 10 minutes.

3 Add ½ cup water and the diced potato. Cover pot and let cook for 3 or 4 minutes. Remove lid and add the kale. Stir and add another ¼ cup water. Cover pot and let kale cook for approximately 15 minutes or until tender, stirring every 5 minutes and checking that it is not sticking (add another ¼ cup water if needed).

4 Serve as a side dish. It is even better the second day.

Nutrient analysis per serving: *140 kcalories, 6 grams protein, 22 grams carbohydrate, 4 grams fat, 0 grams saturated fat, 0 milligrams cholesterol, 4 grams fiber, 726 milligrams sodium*

Exchanges: *1 starch, 1 vegetable, 1 fat*

The More Vegetables the Merrier

A maxim of healthy eating is that by eating a variety of colors you consume a range of nutrients. The following recipes for a fresh vegetable platter and a version of pasta primavera gives you the opportunity to do just that!

Braise of Spring Vegetables

This recipe from the Dining Room at the Ritz Carlton in San Francisco (see Appendix A) features an array of colorful baby vegetables, diminutive varieties of common vegetables that can be eaten in one or two bites and that often have a sweeter and more intense flavor than the larger versions. In themselves, baby vegetables make wonderful garnishes, but this dish is also adorned with shavings of black truffles. Truffle, which is a fungus that grows under the ground near the roots of trees, is highly prized by gourmets and pricey, definitely an optional ingredient in this recipe. Enjoy this gorgeous array of vegetables as a main course. While this dish is somewhat high in calories, it supplies plenty of fiber to slow down absorption.

Preparation time: *13 minutes*

Cooking time: *30 minutes*

Yield: *2 servings*

1 tablespoon butter

1 tablespoon extra-virgin olive oil

4 baby carrots, peeled

4 green onions, root trimmed and cut to 4 inches

2 baby gold beets, halved

2 baby beets, halved

2 baby turnips

1 baby artichoke, halved

2 fennel bulbs, sliced to 1 inch x ½ inch cubes

a pinch of salt

8 green beans, ends trimmed

1 baby green zucchini, halved lengthwise

2 tablespoons shelling peas

¼ cup chicken stock

1 tablespoon black truffle shavings, optional

1 tablespoon sherry vinegar

1 Preheat oven to 450 degrees. In a sauté pan, melt 1 tablespoon of butter and 1 tablespoon of olive oil over a high heat.

2 Add carrots and cook for 1 minute, then add green onions, beets, and turnips. After another minute, add artichokes, fennel, and a pinch of salt; toss in green beans, zucchini, and peas. Cooking the vegetables in this order will help insure that the green of these vegetables stays bright rather than graying because of overcooking.

3 Sauté vegetables for 1 minute and then add the chicken stock. Bring to a simmer and place in the oven for 2 to 3 minutes or until vegetables are tender.

4 Remove the sauté pan from the oven and place back over a high heat. Reduce liquids until thick.

5 Arrange on a salad plate and add butter if desired. To finish, sprinkle truffles, sherry vinegar, and a pinch of salt and pepper over the dish.

Nutrient analysis per serving: : *259 kcalories, 7 grams protein, 32 grams carbohydrate, 12 grams fat, 5 grams saturated fat, 16 milligrams cholesterol, 12 grams fiber, 340 milligrams sodium*

Exchanges: *1½ starch, 2 vegetable, 2 fat*

Tagliarini alla Primavera

When you shop for the vegetables in this dish from Barbetta in New York City (see Appendix A), graze the produce section of your local supermarket with plenty of plastic bags in hand. Be sure to use very fine pasta to retain the texture of this dish. Shop for *tagliarini,* long, paper-thin ribbon noodles, ⅛-inch wide, or a very fine noodle, *fedelini,* which translates to "little faithful ones." Fedelini is sold boxed. However, avoid using delicate angel hair pasta that doesn't have enough body to support the vegetables.

Preparation time: 20 minutes

Cooking time: 25 minutes

Yield: 4 servings

6 tablespoons extra-virgin olive oil

½ cup grated Parmesan cheese

½ medium onion, diced

4 ounces broccoli (florets only, no stems)

1 sweet red pepper, seeded, cored, and thinly sliced

1 small zucchini, cut in ⅛-inch thick slices

4 ounces string beans, ends trimmed, cut into 1-inch pieces

4 ounces baby peas (fresh or frozen)

½ teaspoon salt and pepper to taste

4 medium tomatoes, seeded and cut into thin strips

12 whole cherry tomatoes

16 fresh basil leaves, removed from stem, sliced into long ribbons if the leaves are large

12 sprigs Italian parsley (leaves only), roughly chopped

8 ounces fresh tagliarini or ½ pound of boxed dried fedelini

½ cup chicken broth

1 In a wide pan, sauté onion in 4 tablespoons of olive oil over medium-high heat for 2 to 3 minutes. Cook, stirring, until golden, 8 to 10 minutes.

2 To the sautéed onion, add broccoli, peppers, zucchini, string beans, and peas. Season with salt and pepper, and cook, stirring or tossing often, about 5 minutes or until vegetables have softened. Add tomatoes, cherry tomatoes, basil, and parsley and cook, stirring often, for another 3 minutes. Set aside.

3 Fill a large pot with water and over high heat, covered, bring to a very fast boil. Put pasta in boiling water and cook according to the box instructions for al dente. (If using fresh pasta, cook about 2 minutes.)

4 Drain pasta and transfer to the pan of sautéed vegetables. Cook, tossing or stirring to evenly incorporate the sauce with the pasta for about a minute, adding remaining olive oil, chicken broth, and Parmesan cheese to blend the vegetables with the pasta and create a smooth consistency. Serve immediately.

Nutrient analysis per serving: *408 kcalories, 14 grams protein, 35 grams carbohydrate, 26 grams fat, 5 grams saturated fat, 28 milligrams cholesterol, 7 grams fiber, 343 milligrams sodium*

Exchanges: *2 starch, 1 vegetable, 5 fat*

TIP

If you are vegetarian and find yourself in a restaurant that doesn't have any meatless dishes on the menu that are appealing, you can always order a plate of vegetables. Ask your waiter to have the chef assemble an assortment of the various vegetable dishes prepared for that day. This offering will probably be tastier than if the vegetables are cooked to order, which is likely to be done by steaming them. What arrives from the kitchen is often a very pleasant surprise.

Chapter 12

Boning Up on Fish Cookery

In This Chapter

- Enjoying the benefits of seafood
- Identifying freshness in fish
- Knowing how to choose safe fish
- Finding out how to prepare fish in healthy ways
- Giving shellfish a second chance

Fish prepared in a restaurant usually tastes much better than fish cooked at home. With the first bite, the flavors just burst in your mouth, and the fish is usually so moist. Wouldn't it be wonderful if you could turn out such mouthwatering dishes right in your own kitchen? You'd probably eat fish more often!

This chapter shows you how to prepare seafood that even a chef would love. Great-tasting fish is all about knowing what to look for when you shop for seafood and how to cook fish to preserve its flavor and texture. The recipes in this chapter give you the chance to cook fish in ways you may never have dared tackle before. You also find out about a whole assortment of flavorings that take fish beyond the ordinary. Forget those soggy, bland fish fillets! You can serve terrific seafood this very night for dinner.

Recipes in This Chapter

Good Reasons to Serve Fish

Like meat and poultry, fish supplies high-quality protein, balancing the fats and carbohydrates in the meal and providing calories that have little effect on blood glucose. But the benefits of eating fish extend beyond this. For instance:

- The oceans are a rich reservoir of minerals, and all creatures that live in the sea are in part made of these minerals. When you eat fish, you are likely also to be consuming iodine, selenium, phosphorus, potassium, iron, and calcium.
- Seafood is a good source of B vitamins, especially niacin, and also contains fat-soluble vitamin A. In addition, fatty fish is one of the few food sources of vitamin D.
- The most important nutrient in fish may well be the omega-3 fatty acids. These polyunsaturated fatty acids are especially high in the fat and oils of fish that live in cold water. (Because these oils stay liquid at room temperature, they may help insulate the fish against the cold.) The omega-3 fatty acids appear to lower the undesirable form of cholesterol, LDL cholesterol, and to raise the desirable form, HDL cholesterol. These fats also have an anti-inflammatory effect. The fish with the highest percentage of these healthy oils are salmon, sardines, tuna, and mackerel.

The two omega-3 fatty acids are *eichosapentaenoic acid* (EPA) and *docosahexanoic acid* (DHA).

The following recipe gives you a chance to sink your teeth into a meaty tuna steak full of healthy oils.

Moose's Barbecued Tuna

This tuna steak recipe comes from Moose's in San Francisco (see Appendix A). Enjoy it with a homemade salsa prepared with roasted tomatoes, and serve alongside thin slices of cold jícama root (sometimes referred to as "the Mexican potato"), dusted with cayenne pepper and garnished with lime wedges.

While fresh tuna can be pricey, you can find a variety of salmon on the market that will fit into your weekly budget. Flash-frozen salmon steaks are great to keep in your freezer for days when you know you won't have time to shop for dinner.

Because tuna oxidizes when it comes into contact with air, store fresh tuna covered with plastic wrap and be sure to wrap tightly if you are freezing the fish.

When thawing frozen fish, thaw the fish in the refrigerator, not at room temperature. Allow about 24 hours of thawing for a pound of fish. If you want to thaw fish more quickly, place the fish in a "zipper-lock" plastic bag and place in a pan of cold water in the refrigerator.

Preparation time: *15 minutes*

Cooking time: *5 minutes*

Yield: *4 servings*

½ teaspoon ground cumin

½ teaspoon ground coriander

½ teaspoon ground white pepper

½ teaspoon ground black pepper

½ teaspoon fennel seed

1 tablespoon sugar

1 tablespoon chili powder

1 tablespoon paprika, sweet or hot

¼ teaspoon dry mustard

¼ teaspoon kosher salt

4 6-ounce tuna steaks

Olive oil, as needed

1 *To prepare barbecue spice mixture:* In a small bowl, combine cumin, coriander, white pepper, black pepper, fennel seed, sugar, chili powder, paprika, dry mustard, and kosher salt, and mix thoroughly.

2 Brush tuna steaks lightly with olive oil and evenly dust on one side with barbecue spice mixture.

3 Brush nonstick sauté pan lightly with olive oil and heat over medium to high heat. Add tuna steaks, spice side down, and sear them for 1 to 2 minutes on the first side, until lightly browned and spices form a crust. Turn steaks over, lower heat, and cook another 3 to 4 minutes for medium-rare. Serve immediately.

Nutrient analysis per serving: *230 kcalories, 40 grams protein, 3 grams carbohydrate, 5 grams fat, 1 gram saturated fat, 76 milligrams cholesterol, 0 grams fiber, 210 milligrams sodium*

Exchanges: *6 very lean meat*

Cold Poached Salmon with Fresh Fruit Chutney and Herb Sauce

This recipe, from Aquavit in New York (see Appendix A), is great for company because it can be prepared ahead of time — and you can rest assured the fish will be moist. Just follow the instructions to cool the cooked salmon in its poaching liquid.

Preparation time: *40 minutes*

Cooking time: *5 to 8 minutes*

Yield: *4 servings*

(continued)

4 cups water

6 tablespoons red vinegar

½ onion, thinly sliced

1 carrot, sliced

1 bay leaf

10 white peppercorns

1 to 2 teaspoons salt

4 pieces salmon fillet, 4 ounces each

The chutney:

1 papaya, peeled and diced finely

1 mango, peeled and diced finely

1 apple, peeled and diced finely

½ small red onion, diced finely

1 bunch cilantro, chopped

1 tablespoon crystallized ginger, minced

Juice from 1 lime

The herb sauce:

1 bunch spinach (about 10 ounces), tough stems removed

1 bunch tarragon or 1 teaspoon dried tarragon

1 bunch parsley, stems removed

1 bunch chives

1 clove garlic

1 cup light sour cream

1 tablespoon Worcestershire sauce

1 Bring the water to a boil in a large skillet and add vinegar, sliced onion, carrot, bay leaf, peppercorns, and salt. Add the salmon fillets, cover, and simmer 2 to 3 minutes. Remove from heat and let the salmon cool in the liquid in the skillet at room temperature.

2 *For the chutney:* Combine the papaya, mango, apple, onion, cilantro, lime juice, and ginger. Mix well; cover and let sit for 2 hours at room temperature or refrigerate if longer.

3 *For the herb sauce:* Bring 3 quarts of salted water to a rolling boil. Blanch the spinach and all herbs for 5 seconds. Drain. Put in blender or food processor with garlic and mince finely. Add sour cream and Worcestershire sauce and purée until smooth. Portion size is 2 tablespoons. Refrigerate unused sauce in a sealed container.

4 Place salmon fillets on individual plates, with a dollop of herb sauce and a spoonful of chutney next to the fish.

Nutrient analysis per serving: *278 kcalories, 29 grams protein, 29 grams carbohydrate, 6 grams fat, 2 grams saturated fat, 42 milligrams cholesterol, 6 grams fiber, 304 milligrams sodium.*

Exchanges: *4 very lean meat, 2 fruit*

Shopping for Fresh Fish

For fresh fish, your best bet is to buy it at a reputable fish market. Pick a busy retailer, one who may also sell wholesale or to restaurants. The store should smell moist and cold, but not fishy! It's fine for a fresh fish to have a faintly ocean or rain smell, but avoid buying fish with an unpleasant, somewhat sour or ammonia-like odor, a sign of significant bacterial growth. While whole fish should be displayed lying directly on a bed of ice chips and also be covered with ice, fish fillets should be lying on ice but not covered with ice chips. Storing fillets this way can leach out the flavor.

When buying whole fish, look for

- A bright outer skin that reflects light.
- Gills that are bright red or pink.
- Flesh that bounces back when gently pressed with a finger.

Clear eyes on a fish are not necessarily a sign of freshness. In some fish, eyes can remain clear for weeks. Trout, for example, loses taste long before the eyes cloud.

When buying fish steaks and fillets, look for

- Fish flesh that is luminous and translucent, as if you could almost see inside.
- Flesh of white fish that is white, not pink, such as halibut, sole, and cod
- Flesh that is firm and elastic to the touch.

Seafood, including fish fillets and shellfish, should be cooked the same day you purchase it or at least within 24 hours of purchase. Once you buy fish, immediately return home and put it in the refrigerator. You don't want to risk the fish turning bad and giving you a dose of seafood poisoning.

Fish stores carry a much wider variety of seafood than supermarkets. You can sometimes find fresh Alaskan cod. When you do, here's a recipe for your catch.

Panko Sautéed Alaskan Cod

Anthony's Fish Grotto in San Diego (see Appendix A) contributed this recipe. This crisp, pan-fried fish is delicious served with a baked potato and fresh asparagus. If you can't find Japanese bread crumbs, substitute with another white, flaky, unseasoned breadcrumb. This recipe makes only one serving, but can easily be doubled or quadrupled. To make two or four servings, double or quadruple all ingredients. For three servings, triple all ingredients except the bread crumbs and egg. One cup bread crumbs and two eggs should be sufficient to coat three fish fillets.

Preparation time: *8 minutes*

Cooking time: *10 minutes*

Yield: *1 serving*

½ cup Panko Japanese bread crumbs

1 egg, well beaten with a drop of water

4 ounces Alaskan cod fillet

1 tablespoon canola oil, olive oil, or cooking spray

1 green onion, sliced

4 lemon wedges

1 Spread the Panko bread crumbs out on a plate. Dip Alaskan cod in egg, gently shake off excess, and place the fillets in the Panko bread crumbs, coating each side.

2 Heat the canola oil over medium heat in a large sauté pan. When hot, lay the cod fillets in the pan; cook until golden brown, then turn and cook on the other side. Total cooking time will be 6 to 8 minutes. Do not overcook, or fish will be tough.

3 Place fish on a large plate, garnish with sliced green onions and lemon wedges, and serve.

Nutrient analysis per serving: *310 kcalories, 25 grams protein, 11 grams carbohydrate, 18 grams fat, 2 grams saturated fat, 155 milligrams cholesterol, 0 grams fiber, 214 milligrams sodium.*

Exchanges: *1 starch, 3 medium-fat meat*

Choosing Fish That Is Safe to Eat

Waters have become polluted and so have fish. You need to consider this fact when selecting seafood. In general, you should favor fish that live far offshore rather than near the land.

Eating farm-raised fish may offer some protection from toxins, but this assertion is controversial. The fish may become polluted with pesticides as ground water run-off from surrounding farmlands enters the pools where fish are raised. Virtually all trout is farm-raised, as is much of the salmon on the market. Fish in lakes and streams may also be exposed to harmful chemicals from farmland run-off and industrial pollution. Hikers report that these days, pure water in mountain streams is rare, even at the highest elevations.

TIP

One way to lower your intake of toxins is to favor white-fleshed fish over fish with dark flesh, such as bluefish. Toxins such as PCBs and heavy metals tend to accumulate in the dark flesh.

Good choices include

- Albacore tuna
- Cod
- Flounder
- Haddock
- Pacific halibut
- Sole

Lemon Sole with Brussels Sprouts

Striped Bass in Philadelphia (see Appendix A) is the home of this recipe. The lemon "marries" the delicate flavor of fish with the stronger flavor of the herbed brussels sprouts beautifully. There's room for some potato or rice as well as a roll or piece of bread to round out this low-calorie meal.

Preparation time: *30 minutes*

Cooking time: *20 minutes*

Yield: *4 servings*

2 6-ounce fillets of sole or flounder

¼ teaspoon salt and pepper to taste

1 cup brussels sprouts, trimmed and quartered

1 tablespoon Dijon mustard

2 tablespoons champagne vinegar (or white wine vinegar)

4 tablespoons grapeseed oil

1 teaspoon butter

1 tablespoon chopped shallots

¼ teaspoon thyme leaves, chopped

½ teaspoon chopped chives

Juice of ½ lemon

(continued)

1 Preheat oven to 400 degrees Fahrenheit.

2 Season sole fillets with salt and pepper and place in baking dish lined with lightly greased foil.

3 Bring 6 quarts water and 2 tablespoons salt to a boil. Add brussels sprouts and cook 3 to 4 minutes, until tender. Drain and refresh in ice water. Drain again.

4 Mix Dijon mustard and vinegar in small bowl. Add salt and pepper if desired. Whisk in oil and set aside.

5 Heat butter in medium sauté pan, then add shallots and thyme. Cook for 1 minute, add brussels sprouts and cook, tossing or stirring, for 2 to 3 minutes. Stir in the chives and remove from the heat. Cover loosely to keep warm.

6 Bake sole fillets for 6 to 8 minutes in oven. Check for doneness by probing a fillet at the thickest part with the tip of a paring knife — the flesh should be opaque inside and pull apart.

7 Place the brussels sprouts in the center of each of four plates. Place the fish on top of the sprouts and squeeze several drops of lemon juice on the fish. Serve immediately.

8 Spoon the Dijon-vinegar-oil mixture around the plate.

Nutrient analysis per serving: *237 kcalories, 17 grams protein, 4 grams carbohydrate, 16 grams fat, 2 grams saturated fat, 43 milligrams cholesterol, 1 gram fiber, 255 milligrams sodium*

Exchanges: *2 medium-fat meat, 1 vegetable, 1 fat*

Preparing Fish in Healthy Ways

No need to deep-fry your catch of the day or to order deep-fried fish when you eat out. Not only is this type of fish loaded with fat, the type of fat is unhealthy. When fats heat to high temperatures, such as in deep-frying, toxic by-products are formed. It is far better to eat seafood prepared by poaching, baking, or grilling — all delicious but slimming ways of cooking fish.

Poaching to perfection

JARGON ALERT

Poaching involves cooking food gently in liquid just below the boiling point. The surface of the poaching liquid should just begin to show some quivering movement. Fish is usually simmered in a *court bouillon,* a broth made by simmering vegetables and herbs in water for 30 minutes. A little vinegar, lemon juice, or wine may also be added.

TIP

To maximize flavor, cool the court bouillon before removing the vegetables.

In the following recipe, a poaching broth is made, starting with a fresh-cooked fish stock to which is added garlic, red pepper, and tomato.

Braised Sea Bass in a Garlic Tomato Broth (Branzino all'Acqua Pazza)

Poaching in a tasty broth is an ideal way of preparing delicately flavored fish fillets. Some cooks prefer to make their own broth using fish bones and seasonings such as bay leaf and peppercorns. However, you can find good quality fish broth in fish stores and some supermarkets, usually sold frozen in pints. Cooking fish in broth insures that the slim fillets won't dry out. Enjoy this dish, from Spiaggia restaurant in Chicago (see Appendix A), with a slice of hearty country-style bread to add carbohydrates to balance the fish protein.

Preparation time: *20 minutes*

Cooking time: *10 minutes*

Yield: *4 servings*

4 sea bass fillets, 6 ounces each

½ teaspoon salt

¼ cup extra-virgin olive oil, plus 6 tablespoons

½ tablespoon garlic, chopped fine

Pinch crushed red pepper

4 cups tomato, seeded and coarsely chopped

2 cups fish broth, hot

4 teaspoons parsley, coarsely chopped

12 bread croutons, rubbed with fresh garlic clove

4 sprigs parsley

1 Season the sea bass fillets with salt and set aside.

2 In a sauté pan, over low heat, place ¼ cup plus 2 tablespoons olive oil, garlic, and crushed red pepper, and cook slowly. Do not brown. Add chopped tomatoes and cook 2 minutes. Add sea bass and cook for approximately 2 minutes, covered. Add the hot fish broth, cover, and continue cooking until the fish easily flakes when probed with a knife, 6 to 8 minutes, depending on the thickness of the fillets. Always remain on low to medium heat. *Do not boil!* When fish is cooked, add the remaining oil and coarsely chopped parsley. Adjust salt to taste.

3 Using a slotted spatula, carefully transfer the fish fillets to shallow bowls. Spoon sauce over top and serve in bowls on a toasted bread crouton rubbed with fresh garlic clove. Garnish with parsley sprig.

(continued)

Nutrient analysis per serving: *409 kcalories, 34 grams protein, 13 grams carbohydrate, 25 grams fat, 4 grams saturated fat, 70 milligrams cholesterol, 2 grams fiber, 473 milligrams sodium*

Exchanges: *1 starch, 4 lean meat, 2 fat*

You can also poach fish fillets in a sauce, as in this next recipe for Red Snapper Veracruzana, a classic Mexican dish that incorporates garlic, tomatoes, lime, hot peppers, and herbs. Usually a whole fish is used, presented in all its glory and decked out in a colorful sauce. But you can also cook fillets Veracruz style, which takes less time but tastes just as good.

Snapper Veracruzana

This recipe comes from Cafe Allegro in Kansas City (see Appendix A). Grilling the tomatoes and green onions prior to adding them to the sauce lends great flavor to this dish because the vegetables char. A similar flavor accent can be achieved by lightly rubbing the vegetables with oil and then placing them under a hot broiler to blacken a bit. You can see a photo of this dish in the color section of this book.

Preparation time: *45 minutes*

Cooking time: *35 minutes*

Yield: *6 servings*

6 tablespoons olive oil

1 white onion, thinly sliced

4 tablespoons garlic, minced

1 red pepper, medium dice

1 green pepper, medium dice

1 jalapeño pepper, seeded, fine dice

2 tomatoes, cut into quarters and grilled

3 green onions, grilled and diced

Juice from 1 lime

4 tablespoons capers, drained

3 cups fish broth

1 bay leaf

3 tablespoons fresh oregano, chopped

2 tablespoons fresh thyme, chopped

3 tablespoons fresh marjoram, chopped

6 5-ounce red snapper fillets

½ teaspoon kosher salt and cracked black pepper to taste

4 corn tortillas, cut into thin strips and fried

1 *To make sauce:* In a large, wide saucepan or braiser, heat olive oil over medium heat. Add white onion and sauté until soft, but not brown. Add garlic and sauté until fragrant, about 30 seconds. Add all peppers and sauté until slightly soft, about 5 minutes. Add tomatoes and green onions and continue cooking another 2 to 3 minutes, stirring often. Add lime juice, capers, fish broth, bay leaf, oregano, thyme, and marjoram. Bring sauce to a simmer. Cook for 10 minutes more. Discard bay leaf.

2 Place snapper fillets in sauce and simmer approximately 8 to 10 minutes.

3 Using a flat skimmer or slotted spatula, carefully remove the fish from the cooking liquid and place on a large serving platter. Season with salt and pepper. Scatter tortilla strips over the top of the fillets and serve immediately.

Nutrient analysis per serving: *421 kcalories, 35 grams protein, 20 grams carbohydrate, 23 grams fat, 3.8 grams saturated fat, 54 milligrams cholesterol, 3 grams fiber, 652 milligrams sodium*

Exchanges: *1 starch, 4 lean meat, 1 vegetable, 2 fat*

Note: *You can reduce the fat and calories of this recipe by baking the tortilla strips instead of frying them. To bake the tortilla strips, preheat oven to 350 degrees Fahrenheit. Put strips on a baking sheet, spray with cooking spray, and bake for 10 minutes or until crisp. You can season the strips with salt before baking, but be aware that doing so will increase the sodium content of this dish.*

Coddling: Extra gentle cooking

Coddling is a method of slow cooking that uses gentle heat. You coddle an egg by placing it in a covered container. You then place the container in simmering water. Alternatively, you can carefully lower a food into a pot of boiling water and then remove the pot from the heat. The food cooks in the cooling liquid.

In this recipe for coddled Wild King Salmon, you place the fish on a layer of steamed leeks and then cook it, covered, over very low heat, to gently steam the salmon. The very slow cooking produces salmon with a luscious, velvety texture and delicate taste.

TIP

The point of cooking fish is to develop its flavor, not to tenderize it. Unlike meat, fish has little connective tissue. Cooking fish only briefly, at moderate temperatures, also retains moistness.

Moose's Coddled Wild King Salmon

Wild King Salmon, called for in this recipe from Moose's in San Francisco (see Appendix A), is a Chinook Pacific Northwest salmon variety. If it is unavailable, farmed Chinook salmon would be a fine substitute. A wonderful way to salt the salmon is to sprinkle on it, just before serving, a tiny pinch of the white snowflake-like salt called Fleur de Se. This caviar of salts is hand-harvested off the coast of Brittany, in France. A favorite brand is Ile de Re. A special soy sauce is also used in this recipe, but any good-quality soy sauce will do.

Preparation time: *8 minutes*

Cooking time: *20 minutes*

Yield: *2 servings*

2 leeks

Canola oil spray

Whole black pepper to taste

Soya-water spray as needed (1 part organic Ohsawa Nama Shoyu soy sauce and 3 parts water, premixed in a spray bottle)

5 to 8 ounces unsalted fish stock or chicken stock

2 6-ounce Wild King Salmon fillets, skin on

Parsley for garnish

1 Cut off and discard the green part of the leek. Halve lengthwise the remaining white part. Hold each half under cold running water, gently lifting up overlapping leaves to release any sand or dirt. Shake dry, lay them on their flat side, and slice about ¼-inch thick.

2 Heat a nonstick sauté pan, spray lightly with canola oil (or brush with oil), and grind pepper into it. Add leeks, a light spray of soya-water, and a few spoonfuls of stock. Over low heat, covered, steam the leeks. As the stock reduces, add more stock, a little at a time, until leeks are creamy soft, about 10 minutes.

3 Grind pepper over the top of the salmon fillets and lay them on the leeks, skin side down. Spray them lightly with soya-water, cover the pan and, over very low heat, steam the fillets until they begin to separate into thick flakes, about 10 minutes. Serve immediately on a base of leeks and garnish with parsley.

Nutrient analysis per serving: *373 kcalories, 37 grams protein, 13 grams carbohydrate, 19 grams fat, 4 grams saturated fat, 112 milligrams cholesterol, 2 grams fiber, 226 milligrams sodium*

Exchanges: *4 medium-fat meat, 3 vegetable*

Grilling for great flavor

The high temperatures of grilling allow for quick cooking. Fish fillets can easily become dry, and quick cooking helps retain moisture. In addition, the charring that occurs during grilling adds intense flavor that invites lively condiments. In the next two recipes, fish is prepared with exotic ingredients from Morocco and the Caribbean.

Grilled Black Grouper with Middle Eastern Couscous

This recipe comes from Cafe Allegro in Kansas City (see Appendix A). It makes a complete meal, a mix of fat, carbohydrates, and a generous amount of protein, 5 ounces per serving. If this serving size exceeds what is recommended in your diet, just reduce the portion and enjoy the leftover fish at another meal, such as for breakfast instead of eggs. If your fish market can't supply you with grouper, a fish found in the Gulf of Mexico and in the North and South Atlantic, you can substitute any thick white fish.

The skin of grouper is very strongly flavored and should always be removed before cooking the fish.

Preparation time: *1 hour, 10 minutes*

Cooking time: *35 minutes*

Yield: *6 servings*

1 tablespoon butter

8 ounces Middle Eastern couscous (1½ cups)

½ teaspoon ground caraway

½ teaspoon ground clover

½ teaspoon ground coriander

½ teaspoon ground cinnamon

1½ teaspoons ground cumin

1¼ cups water

1½ tablespoons olive oil

2 tablespoons garlic, minced

2 carrots, small dice

2 zucchinis, small dice

½ of a 14-ounce can hearts of palm, cut into ½-inch moons

14.75-ounce jar artichoke hearts, quartered

1 pint pearl onions, peeled

1 large tomato, peeled, seeded, and diced

Pinch kosher salt

Pinch cracked black pepper

3 cups low-sodium vegetable broth

6 5-ounce black grouper fillets

1 tablespoon vegetable oil

(continued)

1 In a large skillet, melt butter over low heat. Add couscous and toast over medium heat, stirring occasionally, until golden brown.

2 In a medium saucepan, mix spice blend and cumin in water and bring to a boil over medium heat.

3 In a large mixing bowl, combine couscous and water/spice mixture; cover with plastic wrap and set aside for 20 minutes or until all water is absorbed.

4 In a large, deep sauté pan, heat olive oil and garlic. When garlic begins to brown, add the carrots and zucchini and cook over high heat 3 to 4 minutes, until they begin to brown. Then add the hearts of palm, artichoke hearts, pearl onions, and tomato. Season with pepper. Lower heat slightly and continue cooking the vegetables another 2 to 3 minutes.

5 Add couscous to vegetables and toss. Add vegetable broth and bring to a boil, and then simmer for 3 to 4 minutes.

6 Preheat broiler or grill to medium to high heat.

7 Brush both sides of grouper with vegetable oil and sprinkle with salt and pepper. Place fish on grill and cook for 3 to 4 minutes on each side. Serve with vegetable couscous. Spoon the couscous into a mound in the center of a large platter and arrange the fillets of fish around the rice.

Nutrient analysis per serving: *490 kcalories, 45 grams protein, 54 grams carbohydrate, 11 grams fat, 3 grams saturated fat, 72 milligrams cholesterol, 5 grams fiber, 537 milligrams sodium*

Exchanges: *3 starch, 5 very lean meat, 1 vegetable, 1 fat*

Grilled Red Snapper with Black Bean–Roast Banana Mash

Star Canyon in Dallas (see Appendix A) contributed this recipe for snapper. If you substitute reduced-sodium canned black beans, this dish can be easy and quick to prepare. The banana gives just a hint of sweetness to the beans.

Preparation time: *25 minutes plus 8 hours soaking time for beans*

Cooking time: *1½ hours*

Yield: *6 servings*

1 cup dry black beans (or 3 cups reduced-sodium canned black beans, rinsed and drained)

4 cups chicken stock or reduced sodium chicken broth

2 bananas

3 tablespoons olive oil, divided use

½ small onion, finely diced

½ tablespoon chili powder

1 tablespoon tomato paste

1 clove garlic, chopped

1 tablespoon butter

2 teaspoons lime juice

½ teaspoon salt and pepper to taste

6 6-ounce red snapper fillets

1 Soak dry black beans in 3 quarts water overnight or 8 hours.

2 Drain beans and combine with chicken stock. Cook over medium-high heat until beans are very soft, about 1 hour and 15 minutes, and the stock is almost completely reduced. If beans become too dry, add water a small amount at a time. If canned beans are used, you may omit this step.

3 Preheat oven to 350 degrees Fahrenheit.

4 Roast the bananas in their skins until the fruit is soft and skins are black, about 20 to 30 minutes. When cool enough to handle, peel, chop, and add to cooked beans.

5 In a small sauté pan, heat 2 tablespoons of the olive oil until the oil is very hot but not smoking. Add onion and sauté for 1 minute or until translucent. Add the chili powder, tomato paste, and garlic and continue cooking for 2 minutes, stirring occasionally to prevent sticking. Remove from the heat.

6 Put half of the banana-bean mixture, half of the onion-tomato-spice mixture, 1½ teaspoons butter, and 1 teaspoon lime juice in a food processor fitted with a metal blade. Process until smooth. Repeat this procedure with the remaining half of the ingredients. Season with salt and pepper to taste. Reserve and keep warm.

7 Heat grill until very hot.

8 Salt fillets lightly and brush with 1 tablespoon of the olive oil. Grill fillets for 2 minutes. Carefully turn the fillets 45 degrees with a spatula to make attractive grill marks. Cook 2 more minutes. Turn fish over and repeat the process. Remove from the grill.

9 To serve, place fish on warm plate and spoon Black Bean–Roast Banana Mash alongside. Repeat for each serving. Garnish as desired (finely minced red bell pepper on plate rim looks nice).

Nutrient analysis per serving: *427 kcalories, 44 grams protein, 31grams carbohydrate, 14 grams fat, 3 grams saturated fat, 68 milligrams cholesterol, 6 grams fiber, 580 milligrams sodium*

Exchanges: *5 very lean meat, 2 starch*

Giving Shellfish a Second Chance

When the cholesterol scare was at its height, shellfish were banished from any supposedly healthy diet for fear of developing heart disease because of the cholesterol shellfish contains. But in actuality, shellfish such as scallops and clams have far lower levels of cholesterol than the seemingly innocent light meat of chicken. Three ounces of scallops or clams contain about 29 milligrams of cholesterol, and 3.5 ounces of light-meat chicken contain 84 milligrams of cholesterol. Yes, 3 ounces of shrimp is relatively high in cholesterol, with 130 milligrams, but shrimp, too, is a fine food to eat if your cholesterol levels are normal.

Also, naysayers don't mention that shellfish contains much less fat than meat, and the fat is largely unsaturated and includes heart-healthy omega-3 fatty acids. Add to this benefit the many minerals shellfish contains, and you have a very healthy food to be enjoyed, at minimum, every few weeks. Why not start with the following inventive recipe for scallops?

Seared Scallops in Basil Lemon Broth

This broth, from Striped Bass in Philadelphia (see Appendix A), is a simple dish requiring only warm crusty bread and a crisp green salad to make a quick and satisfying meal. The recipe calls for lemon zest, strips of the outer skin of the fruit. Use an organic lemon to avoid any residues of pesticides, or wash the fruit in water to which has been added a few drops of liquid soap that can help remove the toxins.

Preparation time: *20 minutes*

Cooking time: *12 minutes*

Yield: *4 servings*

2 teaspoons canola oil

1 pound fresh jumbo sea scallops

4 cups low-sodium chicken broth or stock

Zest of 1 lemon

½ cup fresh basil leaves

2 tablespoons extra-virgin olive oil

Salt (optional) and white pepper to taste

Basil sprigs for garnish

1 Heat 1 teaspoon oil in medium nonstick skillet over medium-high heat until it appears wavy. Pat scallops dry and arrange half of them in the skillet, without crowding, and cook until nicely browned and cooked through, 1 to 2 minutes per side. (If necessary, cook in two batches to avoid crowding.) Transfer the scallops to a plate and keep warm. Wipe the skillet clean and repeat the procedure with the remaining teaspoon of oil.

2 Bring chicken broth to a boil in a medium saucepan, add grated lemon zest, and keep hot.

3 Purée basil and olive oil in blender, with salt (optional) and pepper to taste. If the purée needs thinning, add a tablespoon of the stock.

4 To serve, place scallops equally in four large warm soup bowls, pour in hot chicken stock, and spoon basil purée around in broth. Garnish with basil sprigs.

Nutrient analysis per serving: *220 kcalories, 21 grams protein, 4 grams carbohydrate, 13 grams fat, 1 gram saturated fat, 36 milligrams cholesterol, 1 gram fiber, 867 milligrams sodium*

Exchanges: *3 lean meat, 1 vegetable, 1 fat*

Storing Shellfish Until You Cook It

The rule stating that you must cook fish the same day you buy it deserves repeating. This said, how do you refrigerate shellfish after you bring it home?

Before refrigerating live oysters, clams, and mussels, cover them with a clean, damp cloth, a moist paper towel, or lettuce leaves. However, do not place on ice or allow fresh water to come in contact with them, and never place them in an airtight container, because this type of storage will kill them.

Keep freshly shucked oysters, scallops, or clams in their shells and store in the refrigerator at about 32 degrees Fahrenheit, preferably surrounding the package with ice.

Italian restaurants always offer some sort of dish made with clams, a shellfish Americans enjoy, usually in clam chowder. Here's a recipe that gives you a chance to savor clams in a light broth.

Clam and Leek Soup with Parsley (Brodetto di Vongole e Porri al Prezzemolo)

This delectable broth from Spiaggia restaurant in Chicago (see Appendix A) is a little heavy on the fat, so reduce your fat intake during the rest of the day. If you want to add a carbohydrate to balance the fat, have a modest serving of pasta on the side.

Preparation time: *25 minutes*

Cooking time: *35 minutes*

Yield: *2 servings*

(continued)

4 croutons (slices of French bread ½-inch thick)

2 cloves garlic

1 tablespoon unsalted butter

4 ounces extra-virgin olive oil (½ cup)

2 cups leeks, well cleaned, white and light green parts cut into ¼-inch thick slices

1 tablespoon garlic, chopped

1 teaspoon red pepper flakes (peperoncino)

4 bay leaves

4 pounds Manila clams, scrubbed under cold running water

¾ cup dry white wine

¾ cup water

2 tablespoons parsley

Salt (optional) to taste

1 Preheat oven to 350 degrees.

2 To prepare croutons, rub bread slices with garlic clove and place on a small baking pan. Bake until dried and lightly brown, about 15 minutes. Set aside.

3 In a large saucepan, heat half the butter and 3 ounces of the extra-virgin olive oil. Add leeks, chopped garlic, red pepper flakes, and bay leaves. Cook over medium-low heat, stirring often, until leeks are soft, about 7 minutes; do not brown the leeks.

4 Add clams and white wine. Simmer, covered, until all the clams have opened, 10 to 15 minutes. Discard any clams that have not opened.

5 When the clams are open, take them out of the saucepan. Remove clam meat from the shells and discard the shells. Return the clam meat to the broth. Add the water, bring to a simmer, and adjust salt (optional) to taste.

6 Remove from heat and stir in coarsely chopped parsley, and the remaining butter and extra-virgin olive oil.

7 Serve in a soup bowl on top of a bread crouton.

Nutrient analysis per serving: *476 kcalories, 23 grams protein, 16 grams carbohydrate, 32 grams fat, 6 grams saturated fat, 65 milligrams cholesterol, 1 gram fiber, 135 milligrams sodium*

Exchanges: *1 starch, 3 medium-fat meat, 3 fat*

Shrimp and Papaya Enchiladas with Avocado-Tomatillo Salsa

Once there was only shrimp cocktail. Then deep-fried, fast-food shrimp showed up in abundance. Now shrimp has become the darling of gourmet cooks who pair shrimp with fusion flavors from world cuisines. These enchilada and salsa recipes from Star Canyon in Dallas (see Appendix A) have a southwest, Tex-Mex accent. You won't have leftovers!

Enchiladas don't have to be heavy on the cheese. In this dish, the heat of the ancho chili is nicely balanced by the "buttery" texture of the salsa. Canned green chilies can be substituted for the poblano chilies. And be forewarned, the serrano chilies in the sauce are especially fiery. You may want to use less than the two chilies recommended.

The salsa is the perfect accompaniment to the enchiladas. The tomatillos give a unique tang and taste.

Shrimp and Papaya Enchiladas

Preparation time: *1 hour*

Cooking time: *20 minutes*

Yield: *9 servings*

2 tablespoons olive oil

2 onions, diced

2 tablespoons garlic, minced

2 pounds medium raw shrimp, peeled, deveined, and cut into ½-inch dice

3 tablespoons chopped cilantro

6 tablespoons ancho chili purée, divided use

1 papaya, peeled, seeded, and diced

4 poblano chilies, roasted, peeled, seeded, and diced

3½ cups grated reduced-fat Monterey Jack or Chihuahua cheese, divided use

Salt (optional) to taste

Canola oil, for softening the tortillas

18 small corn tortillas

3 tablespoons water

1 cup Avocado-Tomatillo Salsa (recipe follows)

1 Preheat oven to 350 degrees Fahrenheit.

2 Heat the olive oil in a large skillet over medium-high heat until lightly smoking and sauté the onions and garlic for 2 minutes or until lightly browned. Add the shrimp and continue to cook until they just begin to turn pink. Add the cilantro, 4 tablespoons ancho chili purée, the papaya, and poblanos. Cook for 30 seconds, and then remove from heat and add 1½ cups of cheese. Mix all the ingredients thoroughly. Set aside.

(continued)

3 Pour canola oil into a large skillet — the skillet should contain ½ inch of oil. Heat until almost smoking. Submerge the tortillas in the oil one by one for 4 to 5 seconds each, to soften. Place the tortillas on paper towels to drain, and keep warm. Don't stack the tortillas.

4 In a bowl, combine the remaining 2 tablespoons of ancho chili purée and water. Dip the tortillas one at a time into the mixture, lightly coating both sides.

5 To assemble the enchiladas, divide the shrimp-papaya mixture among the tortillas, spreading evenly down the middle. Roll up the tortillas and place seam side down on a baking sheet or in an ovenproof dish, placing them snugly together. Sprinkle the remaining cheese on top. Bake in the oven 3 to 5 minutes, or until the cheese has melted. Serve two enchiladas per plate, together with the Avocado-Tomatillo Salsa in the following recipe.

Nutrient analysis per serving: *485 kcalories, 34 grams protein, 34 grams carbohydrate, 24 grams fat, 10 grams saturated fat, 200 milligrams cholesterol, 4 grams fiber, 550 milligrams sodium*

Exchanges: *2 starch, 4 lean meat, 2 fat*

Avocado-Tomatillo Salsa

Preparation time: *20 minutes*

Cooking time: *None*

Yield: *9 servings*

2 Florida avocados (or California avocados), pitted, peeled, and medium diced

2 teaspoons red bell pepper, diced

2 teaspoons green bell pepper, diced

1 tablespoon scallion, diced

4 tomatillos, husked, rinsed, and diced

1 clove garlic, minced

2 tablespoons cilantro leaves

2 serrano chilies, seeded and diced, or to taste

2 teaspoons fresh lime juice

2 tablespoons olive oil

½ teaspoon salt

1 In a large mixing bowl, combine avocados with bell peppers, scallion, and half of the tomatillos.

2 Place garlic, cilantro, serranos, lime juice, and remaining tomatillos in a blender and purée until smooth. Slowly drizzle in the oil. Pour the purée into the mixing bowl, combine thoroughly, and season with salt to taste.

3 Cover and let stand for 30 minutes or refrigerate until 30 minutes before needed.

4 To serve, divide among nine plates to accompany Shrimp and Papaya Enchiladas.

Nutrient analysis per serving: *108 kcalories, 1 gram protein, 7 grams carbohydrate, 9 grams fat, 1.6 grams saturated fat, 0 milligrams cholesterol, 4 grams fiber, 133 milligrams sodium*

Exchanges: *1 vegetable, 2 fat*

Cowboy Shrimp with Jalapeño Cornsticks

Anasazi in Santa Fe (see Appendix A) contributed this enticing dish. This recipe, pictured in the color section, offers a novel way of preparing shrimp that keeps its fat content low and adds some fiber from the beans. One serving of this recipe provides almost half the recommended daily allowance of sodium. If you are restricting sodium, substitute toast or bread for the cornsticks, use low-sodium cheese and chicken stock, and avoid adding additional salt for flavoring. If using canned pinto beans, rinse to remove some of the sodium. And please note, you do need cornstick molds to make this recipe.

Preparation time: *1½ hours*

Cooking time: *25 minutes*

Yield: *4 servings*

The shrimp:

¼ cup raw bacon, diced

½ cup onion, diced

3 tablespoons garlic, minced

3 tablespoons jalapeño, minced

1 tablespoon ground cumin

¼ cup tomato, diced

1 cup pinto beans, cooked

1 cup chicken stock or low-sodium chicken broth

12 large shrimp (10 to 15 shrimp per pound), peeled and deveined

Optional salt to taste

1 tablespoon olive oil

2 tablespoons fresh thyme, chopped

2 tablespoons cilantro, chopped

Lime juice to taste

2 ounces Queso Cotija, crumbled

Cilantro sprigs for garnish (optional)

(continued)

The cornsticks:

Yield: *8 sticks*

1 cup cornmeal

1 cup flour

1 tablespoon baking powder

1 teaspoon salt (optional)

½ cup buttermilk

½ cup corn purée, cooked (can substitute an 8-ounce can of creamed corn)

3 tablespoons vegetable oil

2 or 3 jalapeños, seeded and minced

1. Heat heavy-bottomed saucepan over medium heat until hot. Cook bacon until crisp, about 3 to 5 minutes.
2. Drain fat, reserving 1 teaspoon. Add onions and garlic to the reserved fat. Cook 2 minutes.
3. Add jalapeño and cumin, sauté 1 minute, and then add tomato, pinto beans, and chicken stock. Simmer for 10 to 15 minutes.
4. Heat 1 tablespoon olive oil in a nonstick sauté pan until it is almost smoking. Sear shrimp until slightly browned, about 1 minute per side.
5. Add chopped thyme and cilantro. Cook until shrimp are just done, about another 1 to 2 minutes. Season with lime juice.
6. Preheat oven to 450 degrees Fahrenheit.
7. Place cornstick molds in oven until hot.
8. In a large bowl, combine cornmeal, flour, baking powder, and salt.
9. In separate bowl, beat together the buttermilk, corn purée, oil, and jalapeños. Add to the dry ingredients and mix until just combined.
10. Spoon the mixture into the cornstick molds and bake 10 to 12 minutes, until lightly browned (a toothpick inserted in the center should come out clean).
11. To serve, place one jalapeño cornstick on plate. Spoon pinto bean mixture onto plate and over cornstick. Lay three shrimp on bean mixture, propped against cornstick. Sprinkle with Queso Cotija and garnish with cilantro sprig, if using.

Nutrient analysis per serving: *484 kcalories, 38 grams protein, 46 grams carbohydrate, 18 grams fat, 2 grams saturated fat, 189 milligrams cholesterol, 7 grams fiber, 950 milligrams sodium*

Exchanges: *4 very lean meat, 3 starch, 2 fat*

Chapter 13

Flocking to Poultry and Game Birds

In This Chapter

- Incorporating poultry into eating for diabetes
- Dressing up chicken
- Selecting the best bird
- Turning to turkey
- Featuring game birds when company comes

Recipes in This Chapter

- Chicken with Lemon, Spinach and Ham (Saltimbocca di Pollo alla Limone con Spinaci)
- Chicken in Cilantro, Mint, and Serrano Pepper Curry
- Sautéed Breast of Chicken with Smoke-Flavored Tomato Sauce and Grilled Spring Vegetables
- Kalongi Chicken
- Roast Chicken with Red Onions and Potatoes
- Roasted Chicken with Spiced Apples and Onions
- Turkey Loaf with Portobello Sauce
- Squab alla Piemontese

Make room for chicken, turkey, and game birds such as squab on your dinner table. These foods are good cooked many different ways, and they are so easy to prepare that even the unpracticed cook can turn out a terrific dish. In this chapter you find recipes for roasted whole chicken, sautéed chicken breasts, simmered chicken pieces, baked turkey loaf, and baked squab.

Poultry is low in fat and saturated fat, making it an ideal meat to include in a diabetic diet. Individuals with diabetes are prone to heart disease, and eating too much saturated fat increases the risk of developing this condition. While a 3½ ounce serving of chicken breast, without the skin, contains only 1½ grams of saturated fat, the same size serving of lean ground beef contains over 7 grams of saturated fat. Most poultry has less total fat than veal, pork, or lamb. Poultry is also a good source of B vitamins, including riboflavin, niacin, vitamin B6, and vitamin B12, and also zinc, magnesium, and iron.

TIP: As poultry loses juices in cooking, B vitamins, which are water-soluble, drip into the pan. However, they are not destroyed by heat. Skim the fat from the drippings and make a sauce from the remaining juice. This way, you won't miss out on these valuable nutrients.

Translating Poultry into Exchanges

How poultry fits into the Food Exchange Lists for diabetes has already been worked out. These foods fall into the two categories of lean meat (3 grams of fat per ounce) and medium-fat meat (5 grams of fat per ounce):

- Lean-meat poultry (without the skin): chicken, turkey, Cornish hen
- Medium-fat poultry (with the skin): chicken, turkey, ground turkey, and capon, as well domestic duck and goose, both well-drained of fat

Nutritionists define a portion as 3.5 ounces. What this serving size looks like on your dinner plate, with chicken for instance, is typically either a half chicken breast or a chicken drumstick and thigh. To reduce the fat content, eat the meat but don't eat the skin. The following recipe is elegant and satisfying and gives you portions that are this modest size.

Chicken with Lemon, Spinach and Ham (Saltimbocca di Pollo alla Limone con Spinaci)

This entrée, shown in the color section, comes from Spiaggia restaurant in Chicago (see Appendix A). The prosciutto, a seasoned and salt-cured dried ham, lends a special earthy flavor. The best tasting prosciutto comes from Italy and is found in Italian markets and some supermarkets. A high quality American ham, labeled country-style or country-cured, makes an acceptable substitute. This chicken dish is low in carbohydrates. Add a couple of starch servings and finish with fruit for dessert.

Preparation time: *15 minutes*

Cooking time: *20 minutes*

Yield: *4 servings*

4 pieces boneless, skinless split chicken breasts, about 4 to 5 ounces each

8 fresh sage leaves

8 slices prosciutto

3 tablespoons extra-virgin olive oil, divided use

8 ounces dry white wine or chicken stock

Juice from 2 lemons

1 pound spinach, tough stems removed, well rinsed and drained

1 tablespoon butter

¼ cup flat Italian or regular parsley, chopped

Optional salt and freshly ground black pepper to taste

1 Preheat oven to 250 degrees Fahrenheit. Place two dinner plates in the oven to warm.

2 Have your butcher cut the chicken breasts in half and pound them thin so that you have eight medallions (or do it yourself, as shown in Figure 13-1). Lay a sage leaf on top of each medallion. Next, lay a piece of prosciutto over the sage, trimming away with kitchen scissors any that extends beyond the edge of the chicken. Press the prosciutto into place, and set chicken aside.

Chicken Cutlets Pounded to an Even Thickness
Place cutlets between two pieces of plastic wrap.
whack!
And pound with a mallet or the bottom of a heavy pan.

Figure 13-1: Pound the chicken breasts into medallions.

3 Heat 1 tablespoon of the oil in a large sauté pan over medium-high heat until hot. Place four of the prepared medallions, prosciutto side down, in the pan. When the bottom of the medallions begins to develop a golden color after approximately 3 minutes, carefully turn them over and cook until done through and golden brown, another 2 to 3 minutes. Transfer to a large roasting pan and place in the warm oven. Add 1 tablespoon oil to the sauté pan and repeat cooking method with the other four medallions using the same pan. When they are cooked, add them to the roasting pan.

4 Pour the wine or chicken stock into the hot sauté pan and scrape all the brown caramelized bits off the bottom, dissolving them in the liquid. Over medium-heat, simmer broth, uncovered, to allow half the liquid to evaporate (about ½ cup liquid should remain) and add the lemon juice to taste. The sauce should be somewhat tart, like a mild vinaigrette. (If you use wine, you may need less lemon juice because of the acidity of wine.) With the broth in the pan boiling, add the parsley and the butter and stir to thicken slightly.

5 Heat the remaining tablespoon of olive oil in a large sauté pan over high heat. Add the spinach, season with salt and pepper and, using kitchen tongs, move the leaves around (from the bottom of the pan to the top) to evenly wilt. When all the leaves have wilted, drain any water from the spinach. Cover to keep warm.

6 Place a mound of spinach in the center of each warmed dinner plate and rest two medallions against it. Spoon the sauce over the chicken. Serve immediately.

Nutrient analysis per serving: *426 kcalories, 34 grams protein, 12 grams carbohydrate, 27 grams fat, 6 grams saturated fat, 104 milligrams cholesterol, 1 gram fiber, 1201 milligrams sodium*

Exchanges: *2 vegetable, 4 medium-fat meat, 1 fat*

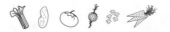

You Can Take Chicken Anywhere

Chicken is that inexpensive food you can trot out, week after week, with a new camouflage every time and not bore your family or friends (or even yourself!). You can serve chicken baked with lemon and herbs one day, and the next day you can grill the chicken and serve it with barbecue sauce. The variations go on and on! If you run out of inspiration, you can refer to the following chart of seasonings. You can go around the world with chicken!

- **Italy:** Garlic, basil, oregano, parsley, rosemary, bay leaves, nutmeg, fennel seeds, red pepper, marjoram, sage
- **France:** Tarragon, chervil, parsley, thyme, rosemary, nutmeg, saffron, bay leaves, garlic, peppercorns
- **Germany:** Caraway seeds, dill, cinnamon, ginger, nutmeg, juniper berries, allspice, mustard seeds
- **Spain:** Saffron, paprika, garlic, parsley, cumin
- **North Africa:** Red pepper, cumin, coriander seeds, cilantro, mint, saffron, garlic, cinnamon, ginger, turmeric
- **Greece:** Oregano, mint, garlic, cinnamon, dill, nutmeg
- **Hungary:** Paprika, poppy seeds, caraway seeds, garlic, white pepper
- **Scandinavia:** Cardamom seeds, nutmeg, dill, white pepper, mustard seeds
- **Russia:** Dill weed, cilantro, parsley, mint
- **Middle East:** Allspice, oregano, marjoram, mint, sesame seeds, garlic, dill, cinnamon, cumin, coriander seeds, cilantro, anise seeds
- **India:** Red pepper, curry powder, chilies, saffron, mint, cumin seeds, coriander seeds, cilantro, garlic, turmeric, nutmeg, cinnamon, ginger, anise seeds, dill, cloves, mace, cardamom seeds, mustard seeds, sesame seeds, fenugreek
- **China:** Ginger, anise seeds, garlic, red pepper, sesame seeds, star anise
- **Indonesia:** Chilies, garlic, red pepper, bay leaves, ginger, coriander seeds, turmeric, curry powder
- **Mexico:** Chilies, oregano, cumin seeds, sesame seeds, cinnamon, cilantro

In addition to these seasonings, all cuisines use onions and black pepper.

Chicken in Cilantro, Mint, and Serrano Pepper Curry

Vij's Restaurant in Vancouver, British Columbia (see Appendix A), contributed this recipe. Here's a good example of how exotic spices can transform a simple chicken breast. Relish the fusion flavors of this chicken entrée. The first step in preparing this recipe is to make a *chutney,* an Indian condiment that classically includes fruit, vinegar, chili, and spices. The recipe also calls for coconut milk, a staple of Indonesian cooking. You can buy canned coconut milk in Asian markets and some supermarkets.

By removing the skin from the chicken, you turn this dish into a lowfat entrée.

Preparation time: *1 hour*

Cooking time: *50 minutes*

Yield: *6 servings*

2 medium red onions, chopped

1 medium tomato, chopped

½ mango, peeled and chopped

4 to 5 serrano chili peppers (for medium spiciness)

½ chopped green cilantro, including stems

¼ cup chopped mint, leaves only

¼ cup coconut milk

4 garlic cloves, crushed

1 3-pound chicken, cut up and skinned

1 cup water

2 tablespoons canola oil

1 teaspoon salt

1 tablespoon ground cumin

1 teaspoon ground turmeric

1 Using a blender, blend the onions, tomato, mango, and chili peppers to produce a chutney with a fairly smooth texture. Empty chutney into a small bowl and set aside. Wash blender, then blend the cilantro, mint, and coconut milk until very smooth. Set aside.

2 In a large saucepan, heat oil over medium heat. Add chicken and cook until it is lightly browned. Remove from the pan to a platter and reserve.

3 Add crushed garlic to the saucepan. When garlic is light brown, add chutney mixture and increase heat to medium-high. Stir frequently to avoid any sticking to the bottom of the pan, about 5 or 6 minutes, and then add the salt, cumin, and turmeric. Cook spices for an additional 1 to 2 minutes.

4 Return the chicken to the pan. Add 1 cup of water, cover, and cook on low heat for approximately 25 to 30 minutes, stirring occasionally to make sure the ingredients are not sticking to the bottom of the pan. Stir in the cilantro-mint mixture. Cover and cook an additional 5 minutes.

(continued)

5 Remove the saucepan from the heat. Let the chicken cool enough to handle. Lift the chicken out of the saucepan, leaving as much sauce in the pan as possible. Debone chicken. Return chicken meat to curry sauce and reheat to serve.

Nutrient analysis per serving: *287 kcalories, 34 grams protein, 11 grams carbohydrate, 12 grams fat, 3.6 grams saturated fat, 103 milligrams cholesterol, 2 grams fiber, 513 milligrams sodium*

Exchanges: *1 starch, 4 lean meat*

Cooking chicken — with the skin or without?

Some people swear that leaving the skin on the chicken while it cooks greatly increases the amount of fat in the final dish. Actually, leaving the skin on the bird (if you are sautéing chicken breasts, for instance) increases the fat by only a minimal amount. More importantly, it keeps the meat from drying out. After the chicken is cooked, you can always remove the skin before you eat the meat.

If you do want to cook chicken without the skin, use a moist-heat cooking method, such as simmering chunks of chicken in sauce. (That's how you prepare the Kalongi Chicken recipe in this chapter.)

Sautéed Breast of Chicken with Smoke-Flavored Tomato Sauce and Grilled Spring Vegetables

This recipe comes from Aquavit in New York (see Appendix A). The roasted flavor of the tomato sauce makes this simple entrée something special, as you can see from the photo in the color section. You can vary the grilled vegetables according to season and personal preference. When this recipe was analyzed for nutritional value and photographed for the book, the vegetables used were 1 corn on the cob, 1 medium red onion, 1 zucchini, and 12 brussels sprouts.

Preparation time: *20 minutes*

Cooking time: *30 minutes*

Yield: *4 servings*

The sauce:

3 slices bacon

2 cloves garlic

14 ounces plum tomatoes or Roma tomatoes (about 5 each)

1 red onion, quartered

½ red bell pepper

4 tablespoons olive oil, divided

½ teaspoon salt

Pepper to taste

The vegetables:

Assorted seasonal vegetables (sweet corn, baby fennel, red onion, zucchini)

The chicken:

4 boneless chicken breasts (about 4 ounces each)

Thyme sprigs, for garnish (optional)

1 *To make the sauce:* Preheat the oven to 350 degrees Fahrenheit.

2 Place bacon, garlic, tomatoes, red onion, and bell pepper on a baking sheet and brush with 1 tablespoon of the olive oil. Roast until browned in color, 30 minutes.

3 Remove baking sheet from oven and let sauce ingredients cool until easy to handle. Blend in blender until smooth. Season with salt and pepper.

4 *To cook the vegetables:* Heat a charcoal or wood-burning grill.

5 Cut seasonal vegetables, except for corn, into ½-inch slices. If using red onion, cut into eight wedges before grilling. If using zucchini, cut into 1-inch slices. If using brussels sprouts, cut lengthwise in half before grilling. Brush vegetables with 1 tablespoon olive oil. If using a gas grill, place over high heat, or the hottest part of a charcoal grill. (If pieces of vegetable are thicker than 1-inch, start these thicker cuts close to the flame and move them a few inches away after the initial browning.) Grill, turning once or twice, until evenly browned on both sides and tender throughout, about 15 minutes.

To grill corn, peel back the husks of the corn, and remove the inner silks. Smooth the husks back in place, or shuck the corn entirely. Grill, turning occasionally. Cooking time is 15 to 20 minutes with husks on and half this time with husks off. The corn is done when some of the kernels char a bit and others are lightly browned. After grilling, cut the corn into 2-inch pieces.

When vegetables are done, remove them to a platter and keep warm while you tend to the chicken.

6 *To cook the chicken:* Heat the remaining 2 tablespoons olive oil in medium nonstick sauté pan over medium heat. Add chicken breasts and sauté chicken for approximately 5 minutes; turn and cook another 2 to 3 minutes or until juices run clear.

7 Serve tomato sauce over chicken. Arrange grilled vegetables on plate, sprinkle with thyme sprigs, if using, and serve.

Nutrient analysis per serving: *389 kcalories, 25 grams protein, 36 grams carbohydrate, 15 grams fat, 3 grams saturated fat, 46 milligrams cholesterol, 6 grams fiber, 725 milligrams sodium*

Exchanges: *1 starch, 4 vegetable, 3 lean meat, 1 fat*

Kalongi Chicken

The complex flavors of this dish from Vij's Restaurant in Vancouver, British Columbia (see Appendix A), develop as you add one spice and then another. Shop in an Indian market for *kalongi,* onion seeds that are colored black, and for the *garam masala,* a classic mix of warming Indian spices. If you have the time and the inclination, you can also prepare homemade garam masala, the first step in this recipe. This spice mixture is also widely available in markets.

Preparation time: *35 minutes*

Cooking time: *30 minutes*

Yield: *4 servings*

The garam masala:

1 tablespoon cumin seed

2 large cinnamon sticks, broken

½ tablespoon cloves

6 pods of black cardamom, seeds only

The chicken:

4 tablespoons canola oil, divided use

3 medium onions, chopped

2 tablespoons onion seeds (kalongi)

1 to 2 tablespoons cumin seeds

6 large cloves garlic, peeled and crushed

2 tablespoons finely chopped fresh ginger

6 small to medium fresh tomatoes, crushed (or 2 cups canned crushed)

1 tablespoon tomato paste

1 teaspoon salt

1 teaspoon turmeric

1 teaspoon cayenne pepper (or less for a milder heat)

1 teaspoon commercial garam masala or homemade (see note)

1 boneless, skinless whole chicken breast (10 to 12 ounces), cut into 1½-inch cubes

¼ cup water

1 bunch fresh cilantro, washed and chopped

1 *For the garam masala:* In a heavy iron skillet, combine 1 cumin seed, cinnamon sticks, cloves, and the cardamom seeds. Cook over medium heat for approximately 2 to 3 minutes or until the cumin seeds turn darker in color. Cool.

2 Place spices in a spice grinder and grind until a powder. Store unused garam masala in an airtight container.

3 *For the chicken:* Heat 3 tablespoons oil in a sauté pan over medium-high heat. Add onion and sauté, stirring often. When browned, transfer onion to a blender or the work bowl of a food processor, and process them until you have a thick paste. Set aside.

4 In a large wok, or a large pot with a heavy bottom, heat the remaining tablespoon of canola oil over medium-high heat. Add the kalongi. When the seeds begin to sizzle, add the cumin seeds and allow both to cook until fragrant and lightly browned, about 30 seconds. Don't let the cumin seeds turn black.

5 Reduce the heat to medium and add crushed garlic. When golden brown, add ginger, crushed tomatoes, and tomato paste. Stir and add salt, turmeric, cayenne, and garam masala. Cook, stirring, about 5 minutes. Add the reserved, cooked onions. Continue to cook 1 to 2 minutes.

6 Add the cubed chicken and cook over medium heat for 10 minutes and then reduce heat to simmer for an additional 20 minutes to allow the chicken to absorb the flavors of the sauce, stirring frequently until chicken is done. Add water a tablespoonful at a time, if needed, to keep chicken mixture from sticking to bottom of the pot.

7 Stir in chopped cilantro and serve the chicken with basmati rice or *naan* (a type of Indian bread).

Note: *A good mail-order source for garam masala is Penzeys Spices, Post Office Box 933, W19362 Apollo Drive, Muskego, Wisconsin 53150, 1-800-741-7787. You can also substitute curry powder for the garam masala. However, this will give a slightly different flavor to the dish.*

Nutrient analysis per serving: *390 kcalories, 22 grams protein, 26 grams carbohydrate, 23 grams fat, 3 grams saturated fat, 60 milligrams cholesterol, 4 grams fiber, 965 milligrams sodium*

Exchanges: *1 starch, 2 vegetable, 2 medium-fat meat, 2 fat*

Chicken by any other name

Do you usually buy just any kind of chicken no matter how you plan to prepare it? Well, the type of chicken you select can make a difference in how dinner turns out. Better to match your bird with how you plan to cook it. Use Table 13-1 as a guide.

Table 13-1 Choosing a Chicken to Suit the Recipe

Type of Bird	*Age in Months*	*Weight in Pounds*	*Best Cooking Method*
Broiler/fryers	2½	3½	Broiled or fried
Roasters	8	2½ to 5	Roasting or rotisserie
Stewing chicken	10 to 18	3 to 6	Stewing or braising
Capons	10	4 to 10	Roasting

TIP

And while we're on the subject of cooking terms, do you know the difference between baking and roasting? Actually, as far as these baking procedures are concerned, there's no real difference at all! According to common usage, a chicken cooked whole is *roasted* while pieces of chicken are *baked*.

The following two recipes show you how versatile a roasted chicken can be. The first has a mustard/herb flavor, while the second is treated to a more exotic combination of spices and herbs.

Roast Chicken with Red Onions and Potatoes

This recipe comes from Hamersley's Bistro in Boston (see Appendix A). This beautiful and decorative platter is an eye-opener! The chicken goes very well with condiments like flavored mustards, pickles, and hot sauces. The red potatoes used in this recipe have a lower starch content than long white and russet potatoes.

Preparation time: *35 minutes*

Cooking time: *75 minutes*

Yield: *4 servings*

2 3-pound chickens

3 tablespoons olive oil

1 tablespoon Dijon mustard

1 teaspoon fresh chopped thyme

1 teaspoon fresh chopped rosemary

½ teaspoon salt and pepper to taste

1 lemon, cut in half

4 medium red onions

8 round red potatoes

4 fresh thyme sprigs

4 fresh rosemary sprigs

1 Preheat oven to 350 degrees Fahrenheit.

2 Wash chickens under cold water. Using dry paper towels or a clean dishcloth, dry them off, and place in a large roasting pan.

3 Mix together oil and mustard. Rub chickens with this mixture. Sprinkle thyme, rosemary, salt, and pepper over the chickens. Squeeze 1 lemon half over the chickens. Cut the squeezed lemon half in two and place these in the cavity of each chicken. Reserve the other lemon half.

4 Peel the onions and cut them into large, thick rounds (about 4 slices per onion). Season with salt and pepper and put them into the pan with the chickens.

5 Wash potatoes and dry them. Rub them with olive oil, salt, and pepper, and put them into the pan along with the chickens and onions.

6 Place the roasting pan in the oven and cook chickens until they are done and potatoes and onions are tender, about 1½ hours. They should finish cooking at the same time. Before removing the chickens from the pan, gently lift one side, tilting to let the juices run out of the cavity. If juice is red, cook another 5 minutes. A thermometer inserted in the thickest part of the thigh should read 160 to 165 degrees Fahrenheit.

7 Allow the chicken to rest for at least 8 minutes before cutting up and slicing. Cut the breast meat off the bone and detach the legs from the carcass. Arrange the chicken on a large serving platter and place the roasted onions and potatoes around it. Squeeze the other half of the lemon over the chicken and garnish with fresh thyme and rosemary sprigs.

Nutrient analysis per serving: *712 kcalories, 64 grams protein, 60 grams carbohydrate, 23 grams fat, 5 grams saturated fat, 180 milligrams cholesterol, 6 grams fiber, 478 milligrams sodium*

Exchanges: *4 starch, 7 lean meat*

Roasted Chicken with Spiced Apples and Onions

Northern Europeans have long been cooking chicken with apples and onions for warming winter meals. Try this exotic version of a homey staple, accented with Indian and Chinese spices; it comes from Aquavit in New York (see Appendix A). The blend of spices means you can omit the salt and not miss it. Make this dish a day ahead when you anticipate having a busy schedule. The flavors will meld over night.

(continued)

The Yogurt Rice (see next recipe) is a perfect starch complement. Just add a green or yellow vegetable for a colorful, complete meal.

Preparation time: *45 minutes*

Cooking time: *1 hour and 40 minutes*

Yield: *6 servings*

The vegetables:

1 medium sweet potato, cut into ½-inch cubes

2 Granny Smith apples, peeled, cored, and cut into ½-inch cubes

1 onion, cut into ½-inch cubes

2 shallots, cut into ½-inch pieces

1 clove garlic, chopped

Leaves from a sprig fresh thyme

Leaves from a sprig of fresh mint, chopped

1 tablespoon olive oil

2 tablespoons water

The spice mixture:

½ teaspoon ground cinnamon

⅛ teaspoon ground cardamom

2 whole star anise

2 whole cloves or ⅛ teaspoon ground cloves

4 white peppercorns

2 black peppercorns

The chicken:

1 3½-pound chicken

1 Preheat oven to 350 degrees Fahrenheit.

2 *For the vegetables*: Bring saucepan half full of water to a boil. Add cubed sweet potato and blanch 2 minutes. Drain, rinse with cold water, and drain again.

3 In a mixing bowl combine blanched sweet potato, apples, onion, shallots, and garlic. Add thyme and chopped mint leaves.

4 In a small bowl, combine olive oil with 2 tablespoons water and add to vegetable mixture, stirring to evenly coat.

5 *For the spice mixture*: Place ground cinnamon and cardamom in a small bowl. Using a mortar and pestle (shown in Figure 13-2), or an electric spice grinder, lightly crush together the star anise, cloves, white peppercorns, and black peppercorns, along with salt to taste, and add to bowl.

6 Add half the spice mixture to the vegetables and reserve the rest for Yogurt Rice.

7 *For the chicken*: Rinse chicken with cool water and pat dry with paper towels.

Figure 13-2: Crush herbs and spices with a mortar and pestle.

8 Stuff chicken lightly with some of the vegetable mixture. Place the remaining vegetables in a layer on the bottom of a roasting pan. Set a rack into the pan, over the vegetables. Place the chicken on the rack.

9 Place the pan in oven and roast for about 1 hour, until the vegetables are tender. Check the pan occasionally, adding water if it becomes dry. Remove the vegetables from the pan and reserve.

10 Return the chicken to the oven and roast another 50 minutes or until the internal temperature of the thigh meat reaches 160 degrees Fahrenheit.

11 When chicken is cooked, remove vegetables from cavity and add to reserved pan vegetables.

12 Carve chicken, cover securely with foil, and keep warm.

13 Add enough water to pan juices to make 1 cup, stirring well to deglaze the pan, using a wooden spoon to dislodge any browned bits stuck to the bottom. Use vegetables and pan juices for making Yogurt Rice.

14 Serve carved chicken with Yogurt Rice (or with the vegetables as a side-dish).

Note: *You'll need to momentarily remove the roasting pan from the oven and set it on a work surface. Using a carving fork, skewer the chicken and transfer it to a platter. Lift the rack and spoon the vegetables into a bowl and keep warm in second oven. Alternatively, reserve these in a baking dish and microwave to reheat before serving.*

Nutrient analysis per serving: *310 kcalories, 24 grams protein, 22 grams carbohydrate, 14 grams fat, 3.5 grams saturated fat, 91 milligrams cholesterol, 3 grams fiber, 74 milligrams sodium*

Exchanges: *1 starch, ½ fruit, 3 medium-fat meat*

(continued)

Yogurt Rice

This recipe, which uses basmati rice, the standard rice of India, is meant to accompany the preceding recipe for Roasted Chicken with Spiced Apples and Onions from Aquavit in New York (see Appendix A). If you can't find basmati rice in your local markets, white rice may be substituted. Even better, use whole-grain, unrefined brown rice, or brown basmati rice, now widely available in specialty food markets. These grains are an excellent source of magnesium, needed for heart health. Be sure to follow the package instructions, because whole grains require more cooking liquid and longer cooking times.

Preparation time: *10 minutes*

Cooking time: *20 minutes*

Yield: *6 servings*

1 cup basmati rice

1 cup water

½ teaspoon salt (optional)

1 cup cooking liquid from Roasted Chicken with Spiced Apples and Onions, or chicken broth

The reserved vegetables from Roasted Chicken with Spiced Apples and Onions

½ cup plain yogurt

Reserved spice mixture from Roasted Chicken with Spiced Apples and Onions recipe, or 2 teaspoons curry powder

1 tablespoon chopped chives

1. In a medium saucepan, combine the basmati rice with 1 cup water, and salt, if desired. Bring to a boil, reduce heat, and simmer, keeping covered, until the rice is almost tender and the liquid is almost gone, about 10 minutes.
2. Add the cooking liquid and reserved vegetables from the roasted chicken. Stir in the reserved spices. Cover and continue cooking until the rice is tender, 5 to 10 minutes, and liquid is absorbed. Remove from heat and fold in the yogurt and chives. Keep covered.
3. Serve with carved chicken.

Nutrient analysis per serving: *133 kcalories, 4 grams protein, 26 grams carbohydrate, 2 grams fat, 1 gram saturated fat, 7 milligrams cholesterol, 0 grams fiber, 55 milligrams sodium*

Exchanges: *2 starch*

Safety measures for handling poultry and game

Poultry and game birds are sold with the skin, where bacteria are most likely to multiply. When you bring poultry home from the market and remove its wrapping, check to see whether the bird has a sulfur smell or feels slimy, both signs of advanced bacterial contamination. Packaged poultry, wrapped in plastic, is especially prone to spoiling. If you even suspect that the poultry you've bought has spoiled, immediately throw it out or return it to the store. You don't want to risk salmonella bacterial poisoning.

If you plan to cook the poultry within a day or two, keep it fresh by removing its packaging and keeping it in a covered dish in the refrigerator. If you won't be using it right away, remove the original packaging and rinse the poultry. Then repackage it in freezer wrap and freeze it.

Good Reason to Gobble Up Turkey!

A standard 3½-ounce serving of white meat turkey, without the skin, has only 1 gram of saturated fat, which is even less than the same size serving of breast meat chicken. Turkey is also a good source of B vitamins and many minerals, including iron, potassium, selenium, and zinc, especially in the dark meat.

Buy turkey parts so you won't be stuck with Thanksgiving-scale leftovers. Bake a turkey breast for making sandwiches, a far healthier alternative than turkey luncheon meat, which is high in fat and sodium, and also contains preservatives and other added chemicals. Or make a hearty turkey soup, starting with a turkey leg. To remove the fat, put the cooked soup in the refrigerator overnight. The fat will float to the top and harden, making it easy to lift out with a spoon the next day.

Avoid buying self-basting turkeys. Fat or oil is inserted under the skin of the breast of the turkey before it is packed or frozen. As the turkey cooks, the added fat bastes the bird when it melts and oozes out — not a pretty picture.

Another way to enjoy turkey is to eat it ground like hamburger. In many markets, you'll find it right next to the ground beef. Sometimes you have your choice of ground white meat, ground dark meat, or a mix. Ground turkey also makes a tasty meatloaf. Try this one!

Turkey Loaf with Portobello Sauce

When you've had your fill of chicken breast, switch to turkey! Meatloaf is a homey food that became chic in recent years. You'll find it served in trendy gourmet restaurants, a witty addition to elaborate menus. This recipe is a dressed-up version, topped with fancy portobello mushrooms, those meaty giants you can now find in the produce section of most supermarkets. Have this meatloaf for dinner and then in a sandwich the next day for lunch.

Preparation time: *25 minutes*

Cooking time: *60 minutes*

Yield: *4 servings*

The meatloaf:

Nonstick cooking spray

1 medium yellow onion, minced

1 stalk celery, minced

1 pound lean ground turkey

¼ cup chopped parsley

¼ cup fine bread crumbs

¼ cup skim milk

1 egg white, lightly beaten

1 clove garlic, minced

1 teaspoon dried thyme leaves

¼ teaspoon nutmeg

¼ teaspoon black pepper

The sauce:

2 teaspoons unsalted margarine (see note)

1 large portobello mushroom, cleaned and cut into small pieces (about 1 cup)

1 cup low-sodium chicken broth

⅛ teaspoon each ground nutmeg, black pepper, salt

1. Preheat oven to 350 degrees Fahrenheit.
2. For the meatloaf, coat a large skillet with cooking spray and place over medium heat until hot. Add onion and celery. Sauté, stirring often, until translucent, about 5 minutes.
3. Meanwhile, in a large bowl, combine turkey, parsley, bread crumbs, milk, egg white, garlic, thyme, nutmeg, and pepper. Add onion and celery and mix well.
4. Form into a loaf and place in a well-coated loaf pan. Bake 50 minutes or until internal temperature is 165 degrees Fahrenheit.
5. For the sauce, melt the margarine in a saucepan placed over medium heat. Add mushrooms. Sauté, stirring, until tender.
6. Remove from heat. Add chicken broth, nutmeg, pepper, and salt. Return to heat. Cook until fragrant and slightly thickened, 5 minutes.

7 When the meatloaf is cooked, unmold, slice, and place portions on warmed dinner plates.

8 Ladle mushroom sauce over sliced turkey loaf.

Note: *Look for brands of margarine that are not made with hydrogenated oils, which contain transfatty acids.*

Nutrient analysis per serving: *219 kcalories, 32 grams protein, 11 grams carbohydrate, 4 grams fat, 1 gram saturated fat, 66 milligrams cholesterol, 2 grams fiber, 266 milligrams sodium*

Exchanges: *1 starch, 4 very lean meat*

Cook Up Game Birds as a Special Treat

Game birds include quail, pheasant, duck, and easy to cook squab. These delicacies may be costly, but certainly will make a dinner guest feel special. You are more likely to find these sold frozen, but some specialty stores carry fresh birds or can order them.

TIP

When selecting a fresh bird, look for a plump, firm appearance. The skin should be fresh-looking, not dull or dry. In addition, the bird should have no off odor.

Squab alla Piemontese

Barbetta in New York City (see Appendix A) sent us this delightful recipe for squab, featured in the color section of the book. Squab is a domesticated pigeon, one that has never flown and therefore is very tender (although, one imagines, personally unfulfilled). This grounded bird is ready for market at 4 weeks old and usually weighs about a pound or less. Gourmet markets sell fresh squab in the summer months, and in some areas of the country year-round; frozen squab is available throughout the year. You can also ask your butcher to order some.

These small birds are a treat when you have time to nibble the meat off their tiny bones. If squab isn't available, you can substitute Rock Cornish hens, a miniature chicken that is a hybrid of White Rock and Cornish chickens. Cornish hens are sold frozen.

Squab takes well to any recipe for cooking chicken. A common way of preparing squab is to roast it, as the Italians do in this recipe.

(continued)

Preparation time: *30 minutes*

Cooking time: *45 minutes*

Yield: *6 servings*

6 1½-pound fresh squabs, innards and excess fat removed, rinsed and patted dry

1 tablespoon olive oil

1 tablespoon butter

4 celery stalks, diced

2 leeks, white part only, thinly sliced

4 medium carrots, diced

1 cup white wine

½ teaspoon rosemary leaves

6 sage leaves

1 cup reduced-sodium chicken stock or consommé

salt and pepper to taste

1 Preheat oven to 350 degrees Fahrenheit.

2 Salt interior of birds and truss them as shown in Figure 13-3.

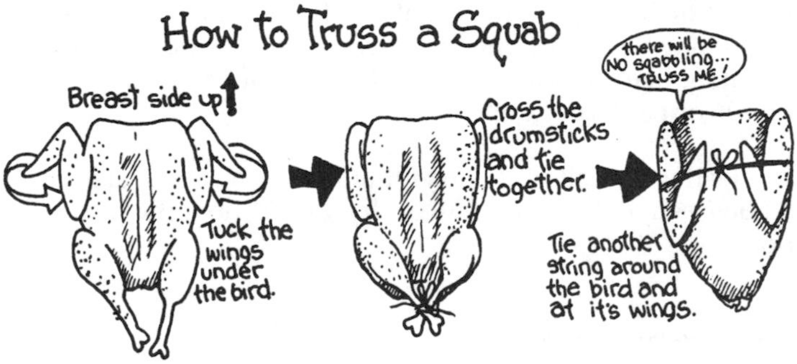

Figure 13-3: Follow these steps for trussing squab.

3 Heat olive oil and butter in a large, heavy saucepan over medium-high heat. Place trimmed squab and the wings in the saucepan and cook until golden brown; turn and cook until browned on the other side. Transfer squab to a large plate.

4 Add the vegetables to the pan and cook, stirring often, until lightly brown, about 5 minutes. Add the wine, rosemary, and sage and stir with a wooden spoon, scraping to dissolve the flavorful particles adhered to the bottom of the pan.

5 Reduce the wine to 2 to 3 tablespoons, return the squabs to the pan, and then add ½ cup of the stock. Bring to a boil. Cover the saucepan and place in the preheated oven. Cook for 40 to 45 minutes using the remaining stock to baste (see note).

6 When squabs are done, remove the wings and discard and transfer the squabs to serving plates. Spoon off the fat from the surface of the sauce, and then distribute sauce and vegetables over squabs.

Note: *If you are not comfortable using a saucepan in the oven, transfer the squab and sauce to an oven-proof casserole and place in oven.*

Nutrient analysis per serving: *265 kcalories, 21 grams protein, 10 grams carbohydrate, 15 grams fat, 4.5 grams saturated fat, 70 milligrams cholesterol, 2 grams fiber, 321 milligrams sodium*

Exchanges: *2 medium-fat meat, 2 vegetable, 1 fat*

Chapter 14

Creating Balanced Meals with Meats

In This Chapter

- Making wise meat choices
- Minimizing fat with proper cooking techniques
- Cooking with moist heat
- Splurging wisely

Recipes in This Chapter

- Loin of Pork Glazed with Roasted Vegetable Salsa
- Char-Grilled Double-Cut Pork Chop with Black-Eyed Pea Relish and Sweet Potato Fries
- Grilled Beef Tenderloin with Spicy Balsamic Vinaigrette
- Roast Leg of Lamb Scented with Coriander
- Truffled Wild Mushroom Gravy
- Stewed French Lamb Shanks with White Beans
- Cheese-Stuffed Beef Tenderloin with Charred Tomato Poblano Sauce

Protein is an ideal food for people with diabetes because it contains only minimal carbohydrate and, consequently, does not raise blood glucose levels significantly under normal circumstances. Every time you eat, you need to be sure to include some protein to balance the fat and carbohydrate in your diet. Meals that contain protein, as well as fat and starch, help stabilize blood glucose and can give you a more consistent supply of energy.

Your body uses protein to build and repair tissues. Meat is an excellent source of protein for this purpose because it contains all nine *essential* amino acids, those that must be obtained through diet. Your body uses these to manufacture the other *nonessential* amino acids. Plant foods also contain amino acids, but building tissue from the protein in plants is a less efficient process because, in any particular food, certain amino acids may be low or missing. For example, beans are low in the essential amino acid, methionine, and corn is low in the essential amino acid, lysine. Consequently, you need to eat plant foods in the right combination — thus the great tradition in Latin American cooking of eating beans with corn tortillas! Recent research shows that you don't need to eat all the needed amino acids in a single meal, just over several meals. For example, you can have rice for lunch and baked beans for dinner.

Meat is also a source of B vitamins and many minerals needed for good health. In particular, it is an excellent source of vitamin B12, essential for normal functioning of the nervous system, and iron for transporting oxygen to the cells.

Where There's Meat, There's Fat

Although meats offer the advantage of being a source of high quality protein, they unfortunately also contain fat, including saturated fats that can raise cholesterol levels and contribute to heart disease. Loin and round cuts of meat, such as pork loin (used in the following recipe) are the leanest cuts. Buy meats that are graded Choice or Select instead of Prime, which has more fatty marbling. (Also take a look at Appendix B for a list of very lean, lean, medium-fat, and high-fat meats.)

Loin of Pork Glazed with Roasted Vegetable Salsa

Loin of pork is preferred for oven-roasting because slicing it for serving is so easy. However, loin of pork can easily become dry. This recipe specifies loin of pork with the bone left in, which yields moister, more flavorful meat and gives you more flexibility in timing.

Preparation time: *15 minutes*

Cooking time: *1½ to 2 hours*

Yield: *6 servings or more*

1 3- to 4-pound pork loin roast, bone-in

⅓ cup Roasted Vegetable Salsa

⅓ cup Dijon-style mustard

2 cloves garlic, minced

2 teaspoons minced fresh sage leaves or 1 teaspoon dried sage

½ teaspoon sea salt and freshly ground black pepper to taste

2 pounds potatoes, peeled and cut into 1-inch cubes

2 tablespoons olive oil, plus more as needed

1 Preheat the oven to 450 degrees Fahrenheit.

2 In a small bowl, mix together the garlic, sage, salt, and pepper.

3 Arrange the potatoes in a roasting pan that is also large enough to hold the pork. Toss the potatoes with 1 teaspoon of the garlic-sage mixture and olive oil. Place pan in the heated oven while you prepare the pork.

4 In a bowl, combine Roasted Vegetable Salsa and mustard. Spread the mixture over the pork.

5 Take the potatoes out of the oven, place the pork loin on top of the potatoes or alongside them, and put the pan back in the oven. Roast undisturbed for 30 minutes.

6 Remove roasting pan from the oven. Stir potatoes, using a spatula to scrape them off the bottom of the pan if necessary. Lower the heat to 325 degrees Fahrenheit and continue to cook, stirring the potatoes every 15 minutes or so.

7 After 1¼ hours total cooking time, check pork for doneness by inserting an instant-read thermometer into several places in the meat. When the thermometer reads 145 degrees Fahrenheit, remove roasting pan from the oven. Transfer the pork to a platter and let it rest for 10 to 15 minutes before carving. During the resting time, the temperature should continue to rise to 155 degrees Fahrenheit, leaving only a trace of rosiness in the center of the meat. (Cook pork to an internal temperature of 150 degrees Fahrenheit and a resting temperature of 160 degrees Fahrenheit if you prefer pork well done.)

8 Return the potatoes to the oven to keep warm, lowering the heat to 325 degrees Fahrenheit.

9 Carve the meat and serve the potatoes. Enjoy with a green vegetable such as sautéed zucchini. Savor the pork the next day in a sandwich, along with sautéed onions and more salsa.

Roasted Vegetable Salsa

Preparation time: *30 minutes*

Cooking time: *20 minutes*

Yield: *2½ cups*

1 pound ripe tomatoes

2 medium poblano chilies

2 red onions, sliced ¼-inch thick

4 garlic cloves, peeled

2 teaspoons extra-virgin olive oil

½ cup tomato puree

2 tablespoons chopped fresh cilantro

2 teaspoons fresh thyme leaves

½ teaspoon salt

2 teaspoons cider vinegar

1 Place tomatoes and chilies over the hot fire of a grill or in a broiler pan and grill or broil on all sides until they are charred and blackened. Remove from grill or broiler and transfer to a large bowl. Loosely cover and set aside.

2 Heat oven to 425 degrees Fahrenheit.

(continued)

3 Drizzle onions and garlic with 2 teaspoons olive oil. Toss them together to coat and then spread them in one layer on a baking sheet. Roast them, stirring occasionally, until the onions are soft and brown and the garlic is soft and lightly browned in spots, about 15 minutes. Remove and cool at room temperature.

4 Peel the charred tomatoes and remove cores, catching any juice in a bowl, and add the peeled, cored tomatoes to the juice. Set aside. Peel chilies, remove seeds and stems, and cut into ¼-inch dice. Place chilies in a medium-size bowl.

5 Place roasted onion and garlic in a food processor fitted with a metal blade and process until moderately finely chopped. Add to the bowl with the diced chilies and stir. Put the grilled tomatoes in the processor and process coarsely. Add chopped tomatoes, tomato puree, cilantro, and thyme to the bowl.

6 Season tomato salsa with salt. Stir in vinegar. Cover and refrigerate for a couple of hours to allow flavors to develop. Taste again before using and adjust flavors.

Nutrient analysis per 4-ounce serving: *398 kcalories, 36 grams protein, 26 grams carbohydrate, 16 grams fat, 4 grams saturated fat, 90 milligrams cholesterol, 3 grams fiber, 384 milligrams sodium*

Exchanges: *4 lean meat, 2 starch, 1 fat*

When you read promotional material describing the value of eating different types of meat and praising their low fat content, don't take these numbers as gospel. Before the fat was measured, it's likely that every last smidgen of visible fat was trimmed away, which is not likely to happen in a home kitchen.

Cooking Techniques That Minimize Fat

If you've ever roasted a leg of lamb, you're already familiar with one of the dry-heat methods of cooking that involves no added fats. In addition, the fat in the meat drains away during the cooking process. Grilling and broiling work in the same way. Obviously, the technique of deep-frying meats, such as spareribs, doesn't offer the same advantages!

The following sections describe each of these healthful techniques individually.

Grilling

Grilling is the darling of lean cuisine. Lean meats, such as well-trimmed pork chops, can be cooked quickly over the high heat, without drying out. And the charring that naturally occurs delivers great flavor. No rich sauces are required! In the old days, a steak may have been served with a buttery béarnaise sauce. Today, slices of grilled meat come with slimming salsa made with vegetables or fruit and a touch of vinegar and spices. This type of dish is common fare on gourmet restaurant menus, and home cooks have also learned to make salsa. Experiment with the one in the following recipe.

Char-Grilled Double-Cut Pork Chop with Black-Eyed Pea Relish and Sweet Potato Fries

This recipe, shown in the color section, comes from Capitol Grill in Nashville (see Appendix A). It's a simple summer dish with plenty of Southern charm, thanks to the addition of black-eyed peas and sweet potatoes, two staples of Southern cooking. Be sure to buy double-cut pork chops, an unusual cut that is extra generous, and have your butcher prepare these from the center-cut loin. This chop has a distinct "eye" of meat, with little meat elsewhere. If you like, brush the pork chops with your favorite barbecue sauce prior to grilling.

Preparation time: *30 minutes*

Cooking time: *1 hour 5 minutes*

Yield: *6 servings*

3 large sweet potatoes, peeled and cut into large wedges

¼ cup olive oil

Optional salt and pepper to taste

¼ cup finely diced red bell pepper

¼ cup finely diced onion

¼ teaspoon chopped garlic

1½ cups cooked black-eyed peas

½ cup finely diced tomato

1 teaspoon sugar

1 ounce sherry vinegar (2 tablespoons)

1 teaspoon fresh parsley, chopped

½ teaspoon dried sage

½ cup chicken broth (or beef or vegetable broth)

6 double-cut (thick) pork chops (about 10 ounces each)

1 *For the potatoes:* Preheat oven to 450 degrees.

2 Toss sweet potatoes with half the olive oil.

(continued)

3 Place the sweet potatoes evenly in a shallow baking dish and bake them for 15 minutes. Reduce heat to 375 degrees and cook another 15 to 20 minutes, until crisp and golden brown.

4 Remove from oven and season with salt and pepper.

5 *For the relish:* While the potatoes cook, place the remainder of the oil in a medium saucepan and heat.

6 Add red pepper, onions, and garlic and sauté until softened, about 4 minutes.

7 Add peas, tomato, sugar, vinegar, parsley, sage, and broth, and cook until most of the liquid is evaporated, about 20 minutes.

8 Add salt (optional) and pepper to taste. Remove from heat and keep warm.

9 *For the pork chops:* Preheat charcoal grill to medium heat and lightly oil grill rack.

10 Season pork chops with pepper and place them on grill about 5 inches from the heat. Cook for about 9 to 10 minutes and then turn pork chops and cook the other side another 9 to 10 minutes to reach 155 degrees (medium).

11 Arrange pork chops on individual plates with relish and sweet potatoes.

Nutrient analysis per serving: *445 kcalories, 39 grams protein, 30 grams carbohydrate, 18.5 grams fat, 4.6 grams saturated fat, 92 milligrams cholesterol, 5 grams fiber, 161 milligrams sodium*

Exchanges: *5 lean meat, 2 starch*

Serving grilled meat with an interesting vinaigrette is another way to give a flavor accent without increasing the amount of saturated fat in the final dish. Start with olive oil, a source of monounsaturated fats that promote heart health, add vinegar, and — here's something you might not have thought of — a rich meat broth, as in the next recipe.

Grilled Beef Tenderloin with Spicy Balsamic Vinaigrette

Chef Gordon Hamersley of Hamersley's Bistro in Boston (see Appendix A) created an intriguing vinaigrette, incorporating olive oil, vinegar, and meat broth in this preparation for beef tenderloin.

To appreciate the richness of the beef flavored with this very spicy sauce, it is best to serve the tenderloin with a simple mixed green salad and accompaniments such as grilled vegetables seasoned with olive oil and balsamic vinegar. If one 6-ounce serving is too much protein for your meal plan, save some from dinner and enjoy a cold beef sandwich the next day.

Preparation time: *25 minutes*

Cooking time: *40 minutes*

Yield: *4 servings*

½ cup beef stock

½ cup red wine

2 tablespoons balsamic vinegar

½ teaspoon coriander seeds

½ teaspoon fennel seeds

½ teaspoon cayenne pepper

¾ tablespoon paprika

½ teaspoon cumin

½ teaspoon fresh chopped thyme

¼ cup olive oil

½ teaspoon salt

½ teaspoon black pepper

1 tablespoon warm water (if necessary)

1½ pounds beef tenderloin, cut into four pieces

2 tablespoons vegetable oil

Pepper to taste

1 In a small saucepan combine beef stock, red wine, balsamic vinegar, coriander seeds, fennel seeds, cayenne, paprika, cumin, and thyme. Bring to a boil and then simmer until ¼ cup remains.

2 Transfer contents of saucepan to a blender. With the blender motor running, add olive oil in a very slow, steady stream, until it is incorporated. Add salt and pepper. If the vinaigrette is too thick, add a few drops of warm water. Reserve in a warm place until ready to serve.

3 Preheat grill to medium heat.

4 Rub each piece of beef with vegetable oil and salt and pepper. Place the beef on the grill and cook until medium rare, turning once or twice. Remove beef from the grill and let rest for a minute before serving. (Total cooking time depends on how hot the grill is and how thick the steaks are, but they will probably take about 8 minutes.)

5 Divide the warm vinaigrette among the plates. Place the beef on the sauce and serve.

Nutrient analysis per serving: *511 kcalories, 46 grams protein, 0 grams carbohydrate, 35 grams fat, 10 grams saturated fat, 144 milligrams cholesterol, 0 grams fiber, 646 milligrams sodium*

Exchanges: *6 lean meat, 3 fat*

TIP: When grilling meat, you can also add calorie-free flavor by adding special woods such as mesquite, herbs, or grapevine trimmings to the fuel so that their perfume scents the food being cooked.

Broiling

The essential difference between grilling and broiling is that while the heat source is located below the food in grilling, it is above the food in broiling. When broiling, allow the fat to easily drain from the meat as it cooks, place the meat on a broiler tray fitted with a rack.

One good reason to broil rather than grill is that when meat is grilled, the fat melts and drips down on the charcoal or wood chips. It heats to an extremely high temperature and then undergoes a chemical change and produces a carcinogenic compound. Rising smoke carries this compound to the meat and, when you eat the meat, you're exposed to this carcinogen. Eating grilled meats occasionally is fine, but for everyday cooking, broiling is better.

TIP: For a really snazzy look, whether you are grilling or broiling, as you cook the meat on the first side, give it a quarter turn. You'll be making a criss-cross pattern with the heated rods of the grill. Then turn over the meat to continue cooking it until it is done to your taste.

Roasting

Roasting is a simple technique that requires little effort. Season meat with herbs and spices and cook it in the oven until it reaches a desired degree of doneness. You just need to ensure that the meat doesn't dry out, a possibility with this dry-heat method of cooking. Here are some suggestions:

- Slow-roast meat at a low temperature, 350 degrees Fahrenheit and below.
- Wrap meat in foil for the majority of cooking time and remove only for the last half hour of cooking to allow the meat to brown.
- Give meat a bread-crumb coating.
- Cook roasts with the bone still attached, as in the following recipe.

Roast Leg of Lamb Scented with Coriander

The delectable natural juices of this meat make a simple sauce that's hard to beat. Enjoy this leg of lamb, as the French would say, *au jus.*

Preparation time: *10 minutes*

Cooking time: *About 1½ hours*

Yield: *6 servings or more*

2 tablespoons coriander seeds

1 large clove garlic, minced

½ teaspoon sea salt

1 teaspoon freshly ground black pepper

1 leg of lamb, about 5 to 7 pounds, with as much surface fat removed as possible and preferably at room temperature

1 Preheat oven to 425 degrees Fahrenheit.

2 Put coriander seeds in a plastic bag and crush seeds with a rolling pin.

3 In a small bowl, mix crushed coriander with garlic, salt, and pepper.

4 Using a thin-bladed knife, cut several small slits in the lamb. Press spice mix into these cuts and rub the remaining spices all over the outer surface of the meat. Set aside in the refrigerator for an hour or more to blend flavors.

5 Spray a large nonstick roasting pan with cooking spray. Put pan on stove and place lamb in pan. Cook lamb over medium-high heat, turning to sear and brown all sides.

6 Move lamb in pan to oven, roast the lamb for 30 minutes, and then lower the heat to 350 degrees Fahrenheit. Cook another half hour and check the internal temperature of the lamb with a meat thermometer. Continue to check every 10 minutes until the desired temperature is reached. (An internal temperature of 130 degrees Fahrenheit indicates medium-rare and of 135 degrees Fahrenheit is medium. It is also a good idea to check in several places for doneness. Total cooking time will be less than 1½ hours.)

7 Before carving the lamb roast, let it rest for a few minutes. Serve with the pan juices.

Nutrient analysis per 3-ounce serving: *162 kcalories, 24 grams protein, 0 grams carbohydrate, 7 grams fat, 2 grams saturated fat, 76 milligrams cholesterol, 0 grams fiber, 252 milligrams sodium*

Exchanges: *3 lean meat*

Sautéing

Although sautéing can require you to first add a little butter or oil to the pan to keep the food you are about to cook from sticking, calorie-counting chefs do sauté some meats using as the lubricant the fats that are naturally in the meat. As the meat cooks, the fats and juices coat the cooking surface in the pan. Medallions of pork can be cooked this way.

You can also cook virtually without oil in a well-seasoned pan. An aluminum pan lined with stainless steel is a good choice. You can "season" such a pan just before cooking meat by following these three steps:

1. **Scour the pan with salt to remove debris and to create a smooth surface.**
2. **Spray a light film of cooking oil such as safflower into the pan.**
3. **With absorbent toweling, rub the pan to remove any excess oil and to coat bare spots.**

Cast-iron pans are also ideal for this technique. To create a nonstick, rust-proof finish on iron cookware, here's what to do:

1. **Wash the pan with hot, soapy water and a stuff brush, and then rinse and dry completely.**
2. **Oil the cookware inside and out with cooking oil.**
3. **Cover the bottom rack of an oven with aluminum foil. Preheat oven to 350 degrees Fahrenheit.**
4. **Place pan upside down on the top rack of the oven. The foil will catch any excess drippings.**
5. **Bake the cookware for 1 hour at 350 degrees.**
6. **Let the cookware cool slowly in the oven.**
7. **When the pan cools, store it, uncovered, in a dry place.**

Slices of veal can be cooked in a well-seasoned iron skillet. Give this dish a try and top with the following luxurious sauce. And good news: In terms of the Food Exchange Lists for diabetes, this sauce is free!

Truffled Wild Mushroom Gravy

This gravy recipe comes from Cafe Allegro in Kansas City (see Appendix A). It goes very well over veal or poultry. If a mushroom broth is not available, substitute with a chicken or vegetable broth. Truffle oil can be found in specialty food stores. You can use any of a number of mushrooms for this gravy; several varieties are shown in Figure 14-1.

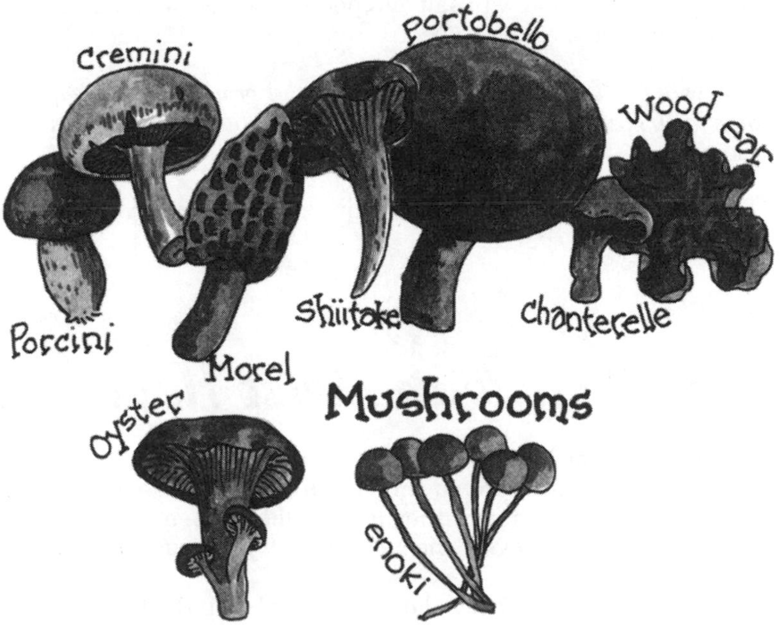

Figure 14-1: Many varieties of mushrooms will work for this gravy recipe.

Preparation time: *40 minutes*

Cooking time: *60 minutes*

Yield: *1 quart*

1 tablespoon olive oil

1 cup assorted wild mushrooms (shiitake, cremini, black trumpet, hedge hog, lobster, oyster, morel, and so on)

½ leek, thinly sliced white part only

Pinch of salt

¼ stalk celery, diced small

1 tablespoon garlic, minced

1 cup mushroom stems

½ cup white wine

¼ potato, peeled and chopped

3½ cups mushroom broth (Prepare the recipe for Wild Mushroom Broth in Chapter 8 or substitute chicken or vegetable broth.)

Salt and pepper to taste

1 tablespoon truffle oil

(continued)

1 Heat olive oil in a large saucepan over medium heat. Add mushrooms and sauté, stirring occasionally, until mushrooms are cooked. Remove mushrooms and set aside.

2 In the same pan, add a little more oil and sauté the leek over low heat with a pinch of salt. Add celery, garlic, and mushroom stems and continue to cook over medium heat for about 5 minutes. Add white wine and cook for 1 more minute. Add potato and broth. Bring to a boil and then simmer for 45 minutes.

3 Remove from heat and cool. Pour mixture into a food processor and purée. Strain through a fine strainer. Season with salt and pepper. Mix back in the sautéed mushrooms and add truffle oil.

Nutrient analysis per ¼-cup serving: *33 kcalories, 1 gram protein, 3 grams carbohydrate, 2 grams fat, 0 grams saturated fat, 0 milligrams cholesterol, 0 grams fiber, 55 milligrams sodium*

Exchanges: *Free*

Cooking Meats with Moist Heat

If you want to make sure that meat is moist and tender when it's finished cooking, invest in a Dutch oven. This is a large pot or kettle, often made of cast iron, that has a tight-fitting lid. The lid is essential to keep the steam inside, helping to prevent the meat from drying out.

TIP

Shop for a pot with a heavy lid. Gravity will help the lid fit tightly. Alternatively, if you have a pot that leaks steam, cut a square of heavy aluminum foil large enough to cover the lid of your pot. When the lid is on the pot, wrap the foil over the lid and tuck it under the lip of the pot. Most of the steam will stay where you want it.

Lamb shanks take well to stewing and are especially succulent cooked this way. In the following recipe, they are cooked with beans, a combination that is a French invention.

Stewed French Lamb Shanks with White Beans

You can find lamb shanks already packaged in the meat section of supermarkets, but these will need the fat trimmed before they are ready to cook. Alternatively, ask your butcher for lamb shanks and request that the fat be trimmed and also the silver skin removed. This membrane can be tough to chew. These French-style lamb shanks, which are shown in the color section, are delicious served with a crisp green salad to create a little feast.

Preparation time: 20 minutes

Cooking time: 3 hours

Yield: 4 generous servings

2 tablespoons extra-virgin olive oil

4 lamb shanks, trimmed of fat and silver skin

1 large onion, chopped

4 cloves garlic, chopped

¼ cup finely chopped fresh parsley

1 tablespoon minced fresh rosemary

1 14-ounce can lowfat, reduced-sodium chicken stock

1 20-ounce can cannellini or other white beans, rinsed and drained

1 bay leaf

Freshly ground black pepper to taste

1 In a heavy Dutch oven with a tightly fitting lid, heat olive oil over medium heat. Add the lamb shanks and brown well on all sides. Transfer lamb to a platter and set aside. Pour off all but 2 tablespoons of fat in the Dutch oven.

2 Add onion, garlic, parsley, and rosemary. Sauté over medium heat, stirring often, until onion is tender, about 5 minutes; do not let the garlic burn. Whisk in chicken stock, scraping up any browned bits. Stir in beans, bay leaf, and pepper.

3 Return lamb to the pot and cover tightly. Reduce heat to maintain a low simmer and cook for 2½ hours. Halfway through the cooking time, turn the lamb shanks over. At this point, if stew is too liquid, remove the lid and simmer until slightly thickened.

4 To serve, ladle lamb and beans into wide soup bowls and serve with a green salad and a whole-grain country loaf of bread.

Nutrient analysis per serving: *386 kcalories, 34 grams protein, 26 grams carbohydrate, 20 grams fat, 6.5 grams saturated fat, 92 milligrams cholesterol, 7 grams fiber, 602 milligrams sodium*

Exchanges: *2 starch, 4 medium-fat meat*

Special handling

Many people these days are opting for "clean meat," that is, meat from animals raised without added hormones or routine doses of antibiotics. The demand for organic meat, from animals raised on organic feed, is also growing dramatically.

If you decide to make the switch, be aware that such meats require special preparation because they can be leaner, firmer, and chewier. Serve cuts such as steak or leg of lamb on the rare side to keep the meat tender, and cook stew meats at a low temperature for a longer time.

Breaking the Rules

Suppose that you're traveling. You've made dinner reservations at the Anasazi in Santa Fe, and you have a ravenous appetite. You scan the menu, and the dish that you select Cheese-Stuffed Beef Tenderloin with Charred Tomato Poblano Sauce. Why not? It's the chef's specialty, and you are interested in gourmet food. Yes, this dish is high in fat, but you can fit this type of food into a diabetic diet if you have a smallish portion and cut back on fats in your meal plan the rest of the day or the day following this meal.

TIP

A recommended serving of protein for diabetes can be as little as 2 to 3 ounces, depending on the individual. An average serving of meat is about 4 ounces, about the size of a pack of cards. This is the portion size in the following recipe for tenderloin.

Cheese-Stuffed Beef Tenderloin with Charred Tomato Poblano Sauce

A gourmet way of preparing a cut of meat is to cut a small hole and fill it with stuffing. In this sumptuously rich recipe from Anasazi Restaurant in Santa Fe (see Appendix A), steak is stuffed with cheese. It can snow in Santa Fe, and this high-fat dish would certainly taste wonderful on a wintry night (One virtue of fat is that it can function as insulation, keeping the body warm.) Because this dish is low in carbohydrate, enjoy it with tortillas or corn bread.

Preparation time: *45 minutes*

Cooking time: *1 hour*

Yield: *4 servings*

3 large tomatoes

1½ tablespoons olive oil

½ cup red onion, ¼-inch dice

3 tablespoons minced garlic, divided use

½ tablespoon cumin powder

¼ cup chicken broth

¼ cup veal demi glacé (available in some supermarkets or gourmet specialty stores)

¼ cup poblano chilies, roasted, peeled, and diced (you may substitute Pasilla or canned whole chilies)

¼ cup chopped cilantro, divided use

Lime juice to taste

½ cup jalapeño jack cheese

¼ cup light sour cream

2 tablespoons bread crumbs

4 tablespoons minced shallots

4 4-ounce center-cut filet mignon

1 tablespoon vegetable oil

1 *For the sauce:* Arrange broiler rack so that it is 3 to 4 inches from the heat source. Preheat broiler.

2 Core tomatoes and cut in half. Rub with ½ tablespoon of olive oil. Place cut side down on roasting pan and broil until skin becomes dark, 3 to 5 minutes. Remove skin and any black spots and purée in blender or food processor. Set aside.

3 Heat 1 tablespoon olive oil in heavy-bottomed saucepan. Add diced onion and 1 tablespoon minced garlic. Sauté 2 minutes, stirring constantly, and then add cumin, tomato purée, chicken broth, and veal demi glacé. Bring to a boil; reduce heat and simmer for about 30 minutes, stirring occasionally. Add diced poblanos, 2 tablespoons of chopped cilantro, and lime juice to taste. This recipe makes 1 cup.

4 *For the cheese stuffing:* While the sauce simmers, prepare the stuffing: Combine jalapeño jack cheese, sour cream, bread crumbs, 3 tablespoons minced garlic, minced shallots, and the remaining chopped cilantro. Mix until well combined.

5 Preheat oven to 450 degrees Fahrenheit.

6 In top center of each fillet, cut a small hole with a knife (see Figure 14-2). Using your finger, hollow out a space big enough to hold about 2 tablespoons of cheese stuffing. Pack the stuffing into the pocket in the meat until full. Season meat with salt and pepper if desired.

7 Heat vegetable oil in an ovenproof sauté pan. Sear meat cheese side up until well browned. Turn and sear the other side for 2 minutes. Turn again and place in oven 6 or 7 minutes for medium rare. Remove and let rest while assembling garnishes.

8 To serve, place each meat portion in center of individual dinner plates, spoon 2 tablespoons of Charred Tomato Poblano Sauce over top, and garnish with cilantro sprigs.

Cheese-Stuffed Beef Tenderloin with Charred Poblano Sauce
In top center of each filet, cut a small hole in, with a knife.
Use your finger to hollow out a space big enough to hold about 2 table-spoons of the cheese stuffing.
Pack the stuffing in until FULL!

Figure 14-2: How to stuff a beef tenderloin.

Nutrient analysis per serving: *404 kcalories, 31 grams protein, 10 grams carbohydrate, 26 grams fat, 10 grams saturated fat, 100 milligrams cholesterol, 2 grams fiber, 370 milligrams sodium*

Exchanges: *1 starch, 4 medium-fat meat, 1 vegetable, 3 fat*

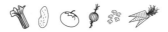

Chapter 15

Having a Little Bite

In This Chapter

- Enjoying a sandwich instead of a meal
- Keeping your blood glucose steady by eating scaled-down meals
- Savoring bruschetta — dressed-up toast
- Preparing your own fast food
- Making a mini-meal of hors d'oeuvres
- Splurging on fancy foods

Recipes in This Chapter

- Mediterranean Tuna Burger
- Moose's Moroccan Spiced Swordfish Sandwich
- Feta Bruschetta
- Chicken and Cheese Quesadillas
- Herbed Vegetarian Cornmeal Pizza
- Black Bean and Rice Burritos
- Spinach Pie
- Shrimp Cakes

In addition to eating regular meals, you may need to eat a small snack between breakfast and lunch and between lunch and dinner in order to maintain a steady level of blood glucose. You may also find that having a bite to eat at bedtime helps you maintain glucose levels throughout the night.

All this food may sound like a lot to you, certainly enough to put on pounds! But the key is eating smaller portions, a subject we cover in Chapter 2. For example, if you decide to have a between-meal snack, consider these suggestions:

- Two crackers and a small wedge of cheese
- Slice of apple and five almonds
- Small scoop of tuna salad and six grapes
- Slice of turkey on a rye-crisp with a bit of mustard
- Smear of peanut butter on a couple slices of banana

If you eat four or five times a day, you also need to watch how much you eat during regular meals. For example, if you want a light lunch and you've saved some leftovers from last night's dinner, have a chicken leg, a serving of rice pilaf, and enjoy three or four spears of cooked asparagus as a salad, served with vinaigrette. This amount of food isn't likely to add pounds but is enough to be satisfying.

Everyone has assembled private little meals like this one, eating a little leftover spaghetti from here and some mushroom soup from there, a couple of raw string beans, and the like. Maybe you wouldn't serve this menu to company, but such combinations can taste just fine when you are hungry and not in the mood to cook. Another option is to create a simple but satisfying meal from scratch.

This chapter is all about scrumptious sandwiches and mouth-watering morsels that are little meals in themselves. Eight recipes follow that will get you started thinking about cooking in this way. Make one dish and you're finished — a modern approach to cooking. How often do you have time to cook yourself a full-course meal, anyway?

These dishes are also great to order in restaurants. Scan the appetizers, which are usually plentiful in upscale or gourmet restaurants, and you're sure to find something you like. Look for fish cakes, such as the shrimp cakes that Papillon Café in Denver serves (the recipe appears later in this chapter), or spinach pie, a standard starter dish in Greek restaurants (another recipe in this chapter). These dishes usually can supply you with protein, fat, and carbohydrates, which are the three macronutrients that can give you a steady supply of glucose. You may also want the house green salad with dressing on the side. This starter course, too, is in keeping with a diabetic diet.

REMEMBER

You have no obligation to your waitperson to order a main course!

Turning a Sandwich into a Meal

If you add enough protein to a sandwich, it can stick to your ribs and be as satisfying as any meal laid out horizontally! Of course, you can always eat a hamburger, but what about a more healthful and slimming variation: a fish burger. Many fast-food restaurants have added fish sandwiches to their menus to offer their customers an alternative to red meat, which is high in saturated fat. Unfortunately, the fish is usually deep-fried and wedged between nondescript white bread buns slathered with mayonnaise. But fish sandwiches needn't be this dismal if you do the following:

- Make your fish sandwich with the finest quality fish possible: fresh salmon, tuna, red snapper, or shellfish (such as crab, lobster, or shrimp).
- Use fresh-cooked fish, still warm from the sauté pan or grill.
- Toast the sandwich bun or the sandwich bread to add some appetizing crunch, needed to complement the softer texture of the fish.
- Use tomato shrimp cocktail sauce, rather than high-fat mayonnaise, to flavor the sandwich, or add a smear of mustard mixed with chopped fresh dill.

- Include vegetable condiments in the sandwich or served on the side, for example, raw or cooked onion, fresh or vinegared cucumbers, or pickled ginger.
- When you make a fish patty, combine the fish with inventive ingredients, such as raisins or nuts to add a little texture.

Why not begin by making the following burger made with fresh ahi tuna, which has flesh that is pale pink and a flavor slightly stronger than albacore tuna. (The most expensive canned tuna is albacore and, like all canned tuna, is precooked.)

Mediterranean Tuna Burger

Chef Terence Feury of Striped Bass in Philadelphia (see Appendix A) devised this recipe, made with fresh tuna, preferably *ahi,* the meaty tuna that is as satisfying as beef. This sandwich deserves an elegant presentation. No bun is necessary here, only toast points, plus a green salad served on the side.

Preparation time: *25 minutes*

Cooking time: *15 minutes*

Yield: *2 servings*

½ cup finely chopped onions

1 teaspoon garlic, minced

Pinch of saffron (optional)

2 tablespoons chopped golden raisins

10 ounces raw tuna

1 teaspoon olive oil

½ tablespoon chopped pine nuts

1 tablespoon chopped parsley

½ tablespoon chopped chives

¼ teaspoon salt

1 teaspoon canola oil

1 In a small skillet, heat olive oil over medium heat. Add the onions and garlic and cook, stirring often, until softened, about 3 minutes. Add saffron and raisins and cook on low heat for 10 minutes.

2 Transfer onions to a mixing bowl to cool. Meanwhile, chop raw tuna and then add it to cooled onion mixture along with the pine nuts, parsley, chives, and salt. Form into patties and refrigerate 10 minutes or until ready to cook (maximum of 4 hours).

3 Heat canola oil in a nonstick skillet over medium heat. When hot, add the tuna patties and cook for 2 minutes on each side, until browned and medium-rare.

(continued)

Wondering about pine nuts?

You may not be familiar with pine nuts, called *pignoli* in Italian. They are a standard condiment in Italian cooking. Pine nuts grow inside pine cones. The removal of the nuts, which involves heating the pine cone, is a labor-intensive process, hence the high price of pignoli.

Pine nuts, or piñon, were also a staple food of Native Americans who depended on forest foods. If the season is right and you happen to be passing through a pine forest, you may find a local shop selling piñon that is absolutely fresh. Otherwise, look for pignoli in the nut section of upscale supermarkets and specialty food stores.

Pine nuts from Italy are torpedo-shaped and have a light, delicate flavor. Chinese pine nuts, which are less expensive, have a squat, triangular shape. Their flavor is more pungent and can easily overwhelm other foods. Pine nuts, which have a high fat content, must be stored in the refrigerator or freezer to keep them from going rancid. In the refrigerator, they last up to 3 months, and frozen up to 9 months.

Nutrient analysis per serving: *234 kcalories, 34 grams protein, 12 grams carbohydrate, 5 grams fat, 1 gram saturated fat, 64 milligrams cholesterol, 2 grams fiber, 348 milligrams sodium*

Exchanges: *5 very lean meat, 1 fruit*

Swordfish is another fish that is high in fat (the healthy type of fat, which you can read about in Chapter 12) and makes a great sandwich that satisfies in the same way that hamburger does. Its rich flavor works well with spices, such as charmoula, a spice mixture used in Moroccan cooking. Charmoula is a combination of cumin, garlic, lemon zest, parsley, cilantro, paprika, olive oil, and lemon juice, a mixture that sounds like it would be good on just about anything! The following recipe gives you a chance to use it on fish.

Moose's Moroccan Spiced Swordfish Sandwich

Moose's restaurant in San Francisco (see Appendix A) contributed this delightful recipe. Be sure to allow the fish to marinate for several hours to allow the flavors of the charmoula to blend with the flavor of the fish. Although this recipe calls for one serving of charmoula, the ingredients for the charmoula mix are enough for six to seven portions (save the extra for other Moroccan dishes). This sandwich is served open-faced so you can see the tantalizing ingredients.

Preparation time: *15 minutes (plus 3 to 5 hours for marinating)*

Cooking time: *5 minutes*

Yield: *1 serving*

4 tablespoons extra-virgin olive oil, divided use

3 teaspoons lemon juice, divided use

1 teaspoon chopped fresh cilantro, divided use

Salt and freshly ground black pepper to taste

10 leaves arugula

½ teaspoon ground cumin

½ teaspoon chopped garlic

½ teaspoon lemon zest

½ teaspoon dried parsley

¼ teaspoon paprika

6 ounces swordfish, cut into ½-inch slices

1 slice sourdough French bread, sliced ¼-inch thick and toasted

¼ medium roasted red pepper, julienned

1 In a small bowl, whisk together 2 tablespoons olive oil, 1 teaspoon lemon juice, ½ teaspoon cilantro, salt, and pepper. Add arugula leaves and toss. Set aside.

2 *To make charmoula:* In a bowl, combine cumin, garlic, lemon zest, parsley, ½ teaspoon cilantro, paprika, 2 tablespoons olive oil, and 2 teaspoons lemon juice. Pour into a large, shallow bowl or small baking dish.

3 Add swordfish, turning slices to coat. Marinate swordfish slices for 3 to 5 hours in the charmoula.

4 Heat grill to moderate heat. Grill fish about 2 minutes per side.

5 On sourdough French bread, arrange roasted peppers and dressed arugula leaves. Top with grilled fish.

Nutrient analysis per serving: *460 kcalories, 25 grams protein, 17 grams carbohydrate, 33 grams fat, 5 grams saturated fat, 42 milligrams cholesterol, 2 grams fiber, 255 milligrams sodium*

Exchanges: *1 starch, 3 medium-fat meat, 3 fat*

Creating Scaled-Down Meals

The multicourse meal is a thing of the past in everyday eating. We prefer one really good dish, served with perhaps a salad or dessert. This way of eating is well suited to a diabetic diet because a moderate amount of calories and carbohydrates are likely to be consumed. Feasting on a grander scale can drive up blood glucose levels.

If you want to add stand-alone dishes to your cooking repertoire, you have many to choose from, including some of the more nutritious specialties served in fast-food eateries as well as a wide range of ethnic dishes featuring traditional ingredients. Browse through the following recipes for a quick introduction.

Dressing up toast

One of the tastiest little morsels to come into fashion in recent years is *bruschetta*, a form of garlic toast but with added condiments. In Italian, the word *bruscare* means to "roast over coals." To make bruschetta, toast small pieces of bread sliced from a baguette, rub the bread with garlic, and drizzle them with extra-virgin olive oil, which gives a distinctive olive flavor. Add salt and pepper to taste, and then once again warm the bread before serving. Many restaurants that feature Mediterranean cuisine offer bruschetta as an appetizer. The cook usually adds tomato and basil to the topping, and perhaps some feta cheese. If you want a sample of this delicious combo, try the following recipe.

Feta Bruschetta

Bruschetta, or toasted bread with flavorful toppings, is loved by more than just Italians these days, and tasty variations abound. This one with feta cheese is quick to prepare using crisp, thin French bread. You can use Italian bread if you like if you find a long, thin loaf. This recipe is featured in the color section of this book.

Preparation time: *15 minutes*

Cooking time: *5 minutes*

Yield: *4 servings*

8 large slices French bread

2 teaspoons extra-virgin olive oil

2 garlic cloves, coarsely crushed

Nonstick cooking spray

2 plum tomatoes, finely chopped

⅓ cup fresh basil, chopped

4 ounces feta cheese, crumbled

Salt and freshly ground black pepper to taste

1 Preheat oven to 500 degrees Fahrenheit.

2 Brush bread with oil. Rub soft side with garlic. Arrange bread in one layer on a baking sheet coated with cooking spray. Bake at 500 degrees until bread is lightly toasted, about 3 to 5 minutes.

3 In a bowl, combine tomatoes, basil, and feta cheese. Divide mixture and spoon onto each slice of toasted bread. Sprinkle with salt and pepper and serve warm.

Nutrient analysis per serving: *185 kcalories, 7 grams protein, 19 grams carbohydrate, 9 grams fat, 5 grams saturated fat, 25 milligrams cholesterol, 2 grams fiber, 636 milligrams sodium*

Exchanges: *1 starch, 1 medium-fat meat, 1 fat*

Bruschetta is also yummy with other toppings. Here's a list of possible variations:

- Black-olive paste or tapenade (see the recipe for Black Olive Pesto in Chapter 7)
- Mashed white beans
- Cooked spinach or other greens such as kale or broccoli rabe
- Grilled vegetables such as zucchini and eggplant
- Leftover cooked, chopped seafood
- Prosciutto or another type of ham

Making your own fast food

Sometimes, nothing hits the spot like fast food! Fast food offers entertaining flavors, lots of crunch, and irresistible salt and fat — not to mention the convenience of running into an eatery, being fed in less than 5 minutes, and leaving with lunch accomplished in only 10 minutes. However, the menu usually includes a significant number of deep-fried foods that are at odds with a diabetic diet geared to be heart healthy and slimming. (See Chapter 18 to find good choices in fast-food places.)

Many on-the-run foods are staples of Mexican cooking. For example, quesadillas are turnovers made with flour tortillas and cheese. The tortilla is placed flat and topped with fillings, and then folded in half and cooked on a griddle or fried. However, the following quesadilla recipe improves on this method, using much less cooking fat. All you need to do is spray the pan with oil.

TIP

Instead of using a nonstick cooking spray, buy a spray can designed to hold cooking oil and fill it with the oil of your choice. You can buy this clever kitchen accessory in department stores that have a housewares department and in gourmet kitchen supply shops.

Chicken and Cheese Quesadillas

This recipe gives you a gourmet version of quesadilla, thanks to the addition of tropical fruit and yogurt. Cook this dish once and then invent your own variations! Just remember to include some protein to turn this snack food into a little meal.

Preparation time: *10 minutes*

Cooking time: *25 minutes*

Yield: *4 servings*

2 chicken breasts (split), thinly sliced

Water (in nutrional analysis) or low-sodium chicken broth to cover chicken

⅓ cup lowfat plain yogurt

1 mango, chopped

4 tortillas, each 10-inch

1½ apples, chopped fine

1 cup shredded reduced-fat provolone cheese

Nonstick cooking spray

1 In a medium pot, simmer chicken breast in water or chicken broth for 15 to 20 minutes, until meat is no longer pink. Cool in the broth to retain moistness.

2 Combine yogurt and mango.

3 Spray a 12-inch nonstick skillet with cooking spray and place it over medium heat.

4 Lay out tortillas on a flat surface. Spread equal parts of yogurt mixture on each tortilla. Top each tortilla with ¼ of chicken breast, ¼ of chopped apples, and ¼ cup of cheese. Roll up tortillas.

5 Place tortillas in heated skillet. Cook on each side until golden brown.

Nutrient analysis per serving: *452 kcalories, 34 grams protein, 50 grams carbohydrate, 12 grams fat, 5 grams saturated fat, 66 milligrams cholesterol, 4 grams fiber, 1790 milligrams sodium*

Exchanges: *4 lean meat, 2 starch, 1½ fruit*

Who doesn't like pizza, in any form? The following recipe omits the standard pizza crust and substitutes cornmeal instead, to add to the variety of grains in your diet.

The lowdown on lowfat

Many of the recipes in this book make use of lowfat dairy products, such as the reduced-fat provolone cheese in the Chicken and Cheese Quesadillas. Reduced-fat and fat-free cheeses are made either partially or completely with nonfat milk, plus various additives to enhance texture and flavor.

Unfortunately, lowfat cheese has its drawbacks. Fat is a flavor carrier, so the lower the fat content in a cheese, the less flavor it has. In addition, when you heat lowfat cheese, its texture can turn rubbery. And, thanks to the low fat content, lowfat cheese doesn't readily melt. However, shredding it first, as in the quesadilla recipe, can help.

Imitation cheese is another creature altogether. It's usually a concoction of tofu, calcium caseinate (a milk protein), rice starch, lecithin, and various additives. Imitation cheese is a nonfat, noncholesterol product sorely lacking in flavor. Don't use this in cooking and waste good ingredients on an imposter.

Herbed Vegetarian Cornmeal Pizza

This recipe for homemade pizza can take its place in a diabetic meal plan — a great meal solution when you need to feed a young person who has diabetes.

Preparation time: *30 minutes*

Cooking time: *10 additional minutes*

Yield: *4 servings*

1 cup yellow cornmeal

1⅓ cups cold water

2 tablespoons freshly grated Parmesan cheese

1 teaspoon freshly chopped oregano

1 teaspoon freshly chopped basil

Nonstick cooking spray

1 small red onion, thinly sliced

1 clove garlic, crushed

1 small green pepper, cored, seeded, and thinly sliced

4 mushrooms, thinly sliced

⅛ teaspoon freshly ground black pepper

1 cup shredded part-skim mozzarella cheese

3 plum tomatoes, thinly sliced

1 Preheat oven to 375 degrees Fahrenheit.

(continued)

2 In a small bowl, mix cornmeal with ⅔ cup of water. In a small saucepan, bring the other ⅔ cup water to a boil. Gradually add cornmeal mixture to boiling water, mixing with a fork until thick, 2 to 3 minutes. Remove from heat and stir in Parmesan cheese, ½ teaspoon each of oregano and basil. Let cool slightly. Spray a 12-inch pizza pan or baking sheet with cooking spray. With wet hands, spread cornmeal mixture evenly onto pizza pan or, if using a baking sheet, spread mixture to form a circle, 12 inches in diameter and about ½-to ¼-inch thick.

3 Bake crust, uncovered, for about 20 minutes, until golden brown.

4 Coat a medium skillet with cooking spray and place over medium heat until hot. Add onion, garlic, and green pepper, and sauté for 2 minutes. Add mushrooms and black pepper and sauté for 5 minutes, stirring often, until they are lightly browned and their water has evaporated.

5 Sprinkle mozzarella cheese evenly over crust. Arrange tomatoes over cheese. Cover tomatoes with remaining cooked vegetables. Sprinkle remaining oregano and basil.

6 Bake uncovered for 10 minutes, until cheese melts.

Nutrient analysis per serving: *249 kcalories, 13 grams protein, 37 grams carbohydrate, 7 grams fat, 4 grams saturated fat, 19 milligrams cholesterol, 3 grams fiber, 344 milligrams sodium*

Exchanges: *2½ starch, 1 medium-fat meat, 1 fat*

The following recipe prepares another fast food from south of the border: a vegetarian combo of beans and rice to yield a complete and nourishing protein.

Black Bean and Rice Burritos

This tasty entrée makes a substantial meal. Although the beans and cheese do supply some protein, most of the calories come from carbohydrate. Keep your starch intake to a minimum in other meals the day you enjoy this dish, or have just a half portion and add some chicken or fish.

Preparation time: *40 minutes*

Cooking time: *25 minutes (in preparation)*

Yield: *4 servings*

Salsa

½ cup chopped tomato

2 teaspoons jalapeño peppers, minced

1 tablespoon green onions, sliced, white part only

3 tablespoons freshly squeezed lime juice

1 tablespoon chopped fresh cilantro

1 In a bowl, combine all ingredients.

2 Chill.

Burrito

1 cup rice

1½ cups water

1 teaspoon garlic powder

¼ teaspoon ground cumin

1 can (15 ounces) black beans, undrained

4 tortillas, 10-inch

1 cup shredded reduced-fat cheddar cheese

4 tablespoons thinly sliced green onions

4 tablespoons salsa

4 tablespoons plain lowfat yogurt

1 Rinse rice. Combine with water in small saucepan. Bring to boil. Reduce heat. Cook on low heat, covered, for 20 minutes, until all water is absorbed and rice is cooked tender.

2 Combine garlic powder, cumin, and black beans in a saucepan. Bring to a boil, then simmer, uncovered for 5 minutes. Stir occasionally. Remove from heat. Stir in rice.

3 Spread out tortillas on a flat surface. Spoon equal parts of the bean and rice mixture down the center of each tortilla. Top each tortilla with ¼ cup of cheese, 1 tablespoon green onions, 1 tablespoon salsa, and 1 tablespoon yogurt. Roll up tortillas.

Nutrient analysis per serving: *510 kcalories, 20 grams protein, 85 grams carbohydrate, 9 grams fat, 4 grams saturated fat, 21 milligrams cholesterol, 7 grams fiber, 765 milligrams sodium*

Exchanges: *5 bread/starch, 1 medium-fat meat*

Snacking on hors d'oeuvres

Go to most ethnic restaurants and you can see listed on the menu lots of little side dishes, any one of which would make a perfect mini-meal or snack. For example, Thai cuisine offers chicken *sate* (skewered pieces of chicken with a peanut dipping sauce). From Russia come *piroshki*, small turnovers filled with meat, seafood, cheese, or mushrooms. And Greek cooking also offers a wonderful repertoire of hors d'oeuvres, such as stuffed grape leaves, feta cheese and olives, and *spanakopita* (or spinach pie). The following recipe is a tasty version you can make in your own kitchen.

Spinach Pie

Who says you can't get a good vegetable into a delicious snack? You can fill an omelet with sautéed sweet peppers and onions, or grill tomatoes and onions to serve with smoked fish and breads the way the English do. A serving of this spinach pie has the further advantage of being low in fat. Whet your appetite by checking out the photo of it in the color section.

Preparation time: *15 minutes*

Cooking time: *50 minutes*

Yield: *4 servings*

Nonstick cooking spray

1 package (10 ounces) frozen chopped spinach, thawed

1 medium yellow onion, thinly sliced

1 medium carrot, peeled and grated

1 cup low-sodium chicken broth

¼ teaspoon dried marjoram, crumbled

2 egg whites, lightly beaten

1 whole egg, lightly beaten

1 cup skim milk

1 cup shredded Swiss cheese

¼ teaspoon black pepper

1 Preheat oven to 350 degrees Fahrenheit.

2 Coat a 9-inch pie pan with nonstick cooking spray.

3 Squeeze all the water from spinach. Set aside.

4 In a small saucepan, cook onion and carrot with chicken broth and marjoram, uncovered, at low boil, stirring occasionally, until all liquid has evaporated and vegetables are nearly glazed, about 20 minutes. Spread vegetables out on a sheet pan to quickly cool.

5 In another bowl, whisk together egg whites and the whole egg. Add spinach and cooled onion and carrot, milk, cheese, and pepper.

6 Pour mixture into pie pan and bake uncovered, 25 to 30 minutes, until filling is set. Remove and cool.

Nutrient analysis per serving: *83 kcalories, 7 grams protein, 8 grams carbohydrate, 3 grams fat, 1 gram saturated fat, 7 milligrams cholesterol, 3 grams fiber, 129 milligrams sodium*

Exchanges: *3 vegetable, ¼ high-fat meat*

Savoring fancy foods

If you're bored with what you are eating, maybe what you're eating is boring! Try something new. Go to gourmet stores and buy specialty foods such as roasted red peppers (which come in a bottle), or creamed herring (which is sold in jars). And occasionally you may decide to treat yourself to more expensive items such as fresh figs, raspberries, buffalo meat, crabmeat, or shrimp. You don't have to wait to go on a cruise to eat these fancy foods! Have these shrimp cakes and you'll feel like you're dining with the captain.

Shrimp Cakes

Papillon Café in Denver (see Appendix A) contributed this recipe, pictured in the color section of this book. These cakes go well served with cocktail sauce and a mixed field green salad with vinaigrette or as wonderful finger food at a buffet. Asian markets carry Japanese bread crumbs, called *panko* on packages, and rock shrimp are just another type of shrimp, like jumbo, tiger striped, and popcorn.

Preparation time: *35 minutes*

Cooking time: *25 minutes*

Yield: *4 servings*

(continued)

1½ stalk celery

½ small carrot

2 tablespoons fresh chives, chopped

1 tablespoon fresh dill, chopped

1 tablespoon fresh basil, chopped

1 tablespoon fresh celery leaves, chopped

1 tablespoon mayonnaise

¼ cup half-and-half

1 cup Japanese (white) bread crumbs

½ pound cooked large shrimp

½ pound raw large shrimp

½ cup corn, frozen, cooked

½ pound rock shrimp, chopped (if unavailable, substitute with ½ pound uncooked large shrimp)

¾ cup heavy cream

1 tablespoon lemon juice

Cayenne pepper to taste

Salt and black pepper to taste

2 tablespoons olive oil

1 Preheat oven to 350 degrees Fahrenheit.

2 In a food processor, chop celery and carrot. Remove from processor and place in the middle of a clean kitchen towel. Squeeze out excess water, and then transfer to a medium bowl. Add to the bowl chives, dill, basil, celery leaves, mayonnaise, half-and-half, and bread crumbs. Mix well.

3 In a food processor fitted with a metal blade, process both the cooked and raw shrimp until they are in little pieces (do not purée). Add to the vegetable and herb mixture in the bowl. Add corn and mix well.

4 Place rock shrimp in food processor and chop. Add cream to make a thick mousselike consistency. Add this shrimp mixture to the first shrimp mixture. Mix well and add lemon juice, cayenne pepper, salt, and black pepper.

5 With wet hands, form 4 large oval or round cakes. Add more bread crumbs if consistency is too moist. Place each cake in bread crumbs to create a slight crust.

6 Heat oil in a large skillet over medium heat. When hot, place cakes in skillet and brown, about 4 minutes each side. Remove cakes from skillet and place on a flat baking pan, and bake for 15 minutes. Serve hot with lemon wedges.

Nutrient analysis per serving: *568 kcalories, 52 grams protein, 15 grams carbohydrate, 32 grams fat, 14 grams saturated fat, 437 milligrams cholesterol, 1 gram fiber, 625 milligrams sodium. (Note: this calculation is based on a total of 16 ounces of shrimp.)*

Exchanges: *1 starch, 7 medium-fat meat*

Chapter 16

Smart Ways to Include Dessert in a Diabetic Diet

In This Chapter

- Ending a meal with fruit
- Flavoring fruit with wine and spirits
- Making fruit ices
- Boosting nutrients in baked goods
- Getting creative with dessert sauces

Recipes in This Chapter

Even though diabetes is a disease that involves impaired metabolism of carbohydrates, you can still enjoy desserts that contain starches and sugar. You just need to select your ingredients wisely and eat reasonably modest portions. But don't waste time feeling guilty because you can't stay away from sweets. Sweet is one of the basic tastes, just like sour and salty, and craving sweet foods is normal.

Of course people crave sweets such as cookies, jelly donuts, pies, and candy made with refined white flour and white sugar, which provide little nutrition. Enriched white flour has had a significant portion of the nutrients in the original whole grain removed, and white sugar contains no vitamins or minerals at all. However, you can create appealing desserts that feature nutritious ingredients, and this chapter shows you how.

Finishing a Meal with Fruit

If you want to eat something sweet, fruit is a better choice than downing some form of baked goods that is full of sugar. While white table sugar supplies calories, it contains no vitamins or minerals. In contrast, fruit is an excellent source of these nutrients, and the sweetest, ripest fruit contains the highest levels. In selecting fruit, choose a variety of colors to give yourself a range of nutrients.

Fruit is also less likely to send blood glucose levels higher when eaten at the end of a meal. Protein and fat in the foods that make up the primary part of the meal help balance the carbohydrates that are virtually always in desserts. Having some sweet is fine as part of a well-managed diabetic diet, but *when* the sweet is eaten is very important. Eating a sugary slice of pineapple on its own can overburden an individual's ability to break down and store the sugars in the fruit. Of course, the type and scheduling of diabetes medication also plays a pivotal role in the management of blood glucose, but it's a good idea also to pay attention to how you pace the different types of food you eat.

TIP

If you want sweetness without calories, you can choose from several noncaloric sweeteners. We describe these in Appendix D.

Inventing Luscious Fruit Desserts

You can always end a meal with a plain piece of fruit, perhaps served with a small wedge of cheese and a couple of crackers to add protein and fat to balance the carbohydrate in the fruit. However, fruit can also be combined with many other flavorings and foods. Wonderful desserts and mouth watering nibbles can be concocted using luscious fruit and adding a special ingredient or two. You can use all sorts of herbs, spices, and nuts to enhance the flavor of fruit. For example:

- Top a slice of honeydew melon or cantaloupe with grated ginger.
- Cut the flesh of a mango into pieces and add a squeeze of lime juice and a sprinkling of cayenne.
- Poach fresh peaches in water or wine to which you've first added fresh mint leaves.
- Peel a banana and freeze it, and then purée the banana in a food processor, along with some almond or peanut butter, and you'll have a fruit version of ice cream.
- Sprinkle orange slices with nutmeg, put under the broiler to cook until they are lightly golden, and then top with a scattering of shredded coconut.

TIP

When shopping for shredded coconut, check the label. Buy plain coconut without added sugar.

- Poach mixed dried fruits in water along with a few whole cloves and a dash of cinnamon and serve topped with a dollop of yogurt and a sprinkling of slivered almonds.

Another intriguing combination of flavoring and fruit is the following dessert, originating from Italy, made with vinegar and berries.

Balsamic Strawberries

A wonderful, traditional Italian way to serve fresh berries is to sprinkle them with vinegar. The full-bodied, slightly sweet flavor of balsamic vinegar is especially good with fruit.

Preparation time: *10 to 15 minutes, plus 2 hours to sit*

Cooking time: *None*

Yield: *4 servings*

2 pints (1 quart) fresh strawberries

4 to 6 teaspoons sugar

1 tablespoon balsamic vinegar

1 Clean strawberries by placing them in a colander or sieve and running cool water over them. Immediately wipe dry. Or you can wipe them with a damp paper towel. Do not immerse them in water because you will dilute their flavor.

2 Hull strawberries and halve or slice them. Place in a shallow bowl or pan (a 10-inch glass pie pan works well) and sprinkle with the sugar.

3 Cover tightly with plastic wrap and marinate berries for 2 hours, stirring them occasionally, if serving immediately. If the berries are to be served later, refrigerate and then let them come to room temperature before serving.

4 Sprinkle on the vinegar within a half hour of serving. Serve in small, individual bowls.

Note: *Treat yourself to organic strawberries and you can avoid a common source of pesticides.*

Nutrient analysis per serving: *69 kcalories, 1 gram protein, 16 grams carbohydrate, 0 grams fat, 0 grams saturated fat, 0 milligrams cholesterol, 3 grams fiber, 2 milligrams sodium*

Exchanges: *1 fruit*

About balsamic vinegar

Balsamic vinegar has enjoyed a great deal of popularity in recent years and can be found on most grocery store shelves. This type of vinegar is made from white Trebbiano grape juice and acquires its dark color and pungent sweetness from aging in barrels for several years.

If vinegared fruit seems too exotic for your palate but you want to make a simple fruit dessert, you can always resort to making that homey classic: baked apples. The following recipe for baked apple is sweetened with fruit sugar from various sources — raisins, orange juice, apple juice, and the apple itself.

TIP

Apples contain pectin, a form of soluble fiber, which slows the absorption of food and helps control blood glucose levels.

Orange Baked Apple

If you are cooking a roast for dinner, make some room in the oven and add a baking dish full of these apples, to enjoy a warm dessert at the end of your meal. Baked apples are good anytime, so make enough! Leftovers will be a welcome treat at breakfast.

Preparation time: *15 minutes*

Cooking time: *50 minutes*

Yield: *4 servings*

4 large Macintosh apples

4 cinnamon sticks

¼ cup raisins

Nonstick cooking spray

½ cup freshly squeezed orange juice

¼ cup dry sherry

Zest of one orange

½ cup apple juice concentrate

⅛ teaspoon each nutmeg, cinnamon, ginger

1 Preheat oven to 375 degrees Fahrenheit.

2 Core apples almost completely through, leaving the bottom of the apple intact. Put 1 cinnamon stick and equally divided raisins in the center of each apple and place them in a baking dish coated with nonstick spray.

3 In a bowl, combine orange juice, sherry, orange zest, apple juice concentrate, nutmeg, cinnamon, and ginger. Fill each apple with this mixture and pour remaining mixture over apples.

4 Bake for 45 minutes or until a knife easily pierces the flesh.

5 To reduce the liquid that remains after baking the apples, pour these juices into a small saucepan and simmer until reduced by half to concentrate the flavor. Pour the sauce over the apples.

Note: *A serving of these baked apples supplies virtually the entire carbohydrate allotment for an average meal. If the meal you eat along with this dessert provides some carbohydrate, have a half portion or less of these apples.*

Nutrient analysis per serving: *193 kcalories, 1 gram protein, 45 grams carbohydrate, 1 gram fat, 0 grams saturated fat, 0 milligrams cholesterol, 6 grams fiber, 4 milligrams sodium*

Exchanges: *3 fruit*

Serving Fruit with Wine and Spirits

To turn fruit into a quick dessert for company, you can always resort to your wine cellar or liquor cabinet for a solution. You can hardly miss! Sauté tropical fruits such as papaya, mango, pineapple, and banana in a little butter. Then, when they are golden, add a few tablespoons of rum to the skillet before serving this delectable mixture. This advice applies even if you have only grapefruit in the fridge. Drizzle grapefruit halves with rum and broil. Fruit is also tasty accented with sherry, one of the ingredients in the recipe for Orange Baked Apple.

Opting for organic

You do yourself a favor when you purchase organic fruit rather than buying fruit that has been commercially raised. By definition, organic fruit is raised without the use of synthetic herbicides, pesticides, and fertilizers. In addition, organic fruit is not treated with fumigants, waxes, or artificial colors. The term *certified organic* means that the produce has been raised on land where prohibited chemicals have not been used on the soil or crops grown there for at least 3 years. In addition, an independent and knowledgeable third party (not the farmer) guarantees that this is so.

Consider using organic fruit in all your recipes. Strawberries rank as one of the most contaminated crops. Most of the apples sold in supermarkets have been given a wax coating. And orange zest, tiny strips of the outer surface of orange peel, may carry chemicals sprayed on the fruit at some point during production.

Alternatively, make sure to wash conventionally raised produce thoroughly. A good solvent is a solution of a few drops of dish soap mixed with a pint of tap water, which is more effective than plain water. Adding salt or vinegar to the water, however, does not help.

The flavor of various liqueurs also blends well with fruit. Although liqueurs are high in sugar, their intense flavor goes a long way, so you'll only need to add a teaspoon or two to flavor several servings.

Experiment with these liqueurs:

- Amaretto (almond-flavored)
- Cointreau (orange-flavored)
- Crème de menthe (mint-flavored)
- Drambuie (scotch-flavored)
- Framboise (raspberry-flavored)

Fruit is also lovely poached in wine. The classic example is a gift from French cuisine: pears poached in wine. Use red or white wine — whichever appeals to you. The final product contains little alcohol. By the time the pears are finished cooking, most of the alcohol in the wine has evaporated.

TIP

Cook only with wines that are good enough to drink. Your dish will not be successful if it's made with a vinegary wine you wouldn't swallow if it were presented in a glass.

Pears Poached in Red Wine

This recipe is a classic but hardly boring. The pears will have a lovely tint from the red wine, which can be made darker by leaving them in the syrup longer. When you want an easy but elegant dessert, pears poached in wine and garnished with mint leaves is always a winner. To ensure tidiness, core the pears with a melon baller.

Preparation time: *10 minutes*

Cooking time: *35 minutes*

Yield: *4 servings*

2 tablespoons sugar

1 cup red wine

½ cinnamon stick, 1½ inches long

2 whole allspice berries

Pinch freshly grated nutmeg

1 whole clove

2 firm Bosc pears (each 8 ounces), peeled, halved, and cored

1 Preheat oven to 350 degrees Fahrenheit.

2 Combine all ingredients except the pears in a small saucepan and bring to a boil over medium-high heat. Reduce heat and simmer 5 minutes.

3 Arrange pear halves in baking dish, core side up. Pour liquid over pears, as shown in Figure 16-1, cover with lid or foil, and bake 10 minutes. Remove from oven and uncover. Turn pears over and spoon the cooking juices over the fruit. Re-cover and return to oven for another 10 to 15 minutes (if pears are ripe or soft, cooking time will be shorter).

Poached Pears
Arrange pears in a baking dish, core side up
Pour liquid over pears.

Figure 16-1: Place pear halves in the baking dish and pour the liquid over the pears.

4 Remove from the oven and uncover. Let pears cool in syrup, turning or basting with the syrup for a deeper color. Serve each ½ pear with about 2 tablespoons syrup poured on top.

Nutrient analysis per serving: *129 kcalories, 1 gram protein, 23 grams carbohydrate, 1 gram fat, 0 grams saturated fat, 0 milligrams cholesterol, 3 grams fiber, 4 milligrams sodium*

Exchanges: *1½ fruit*

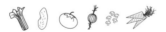

Removing the alcohol in wine and spirits

Many people make the assumption that by boiling wine or spirits for a few minutes, they can remove all the alcohol. However, this is not the case. Water boils at 212 degrees Fahrenheit and alcohol at 173 degrees Fahrenheit. A mixture of the two boils somewhere between these two temperatures, allowing some but not all of the alcohol to evaporate into the air. In actuality, cooked food may contain from 5 to 85 percent of the original alcohol. How much is retained depends on how and at what temperature the food was heated, the cooking time, and the source of the alcohol. The best advice for anyone who must avoid even a trace of alcohol is not to have any dish that includes wine or spirits as one of the ingredients.

Turning Fruit into an Ice

A fruit ice is like a sorbet, but made by hand rather than churned in an ice cream maker. A version of fruit ice, *granita,* is sold everywhere in Italy, in a vast selection of fruit flavors. The beauty of ices and sorbets is the immediacy of their flavor, unobscured by fat. Fresh fruit flavor is all you taste.

Although ices usually are made with sugar, the following recipe relies only on orange juice and the pineapple for sweetening. You may also want to experiment with this recipe and substitute other fruit. Lemon flavor is also excellent in ices.

Pineapple Ice

This refreshing ice gains volume as air is beaten into the fruit mixture. The addition of egg white, the basis for airy meringues, helps preserve the texture. Even so, the shelf life of fruit ice is short. This ice is best when made an hour or so before serving.

Preparation time: *15 minutes plus an hour and a half in the freezer*

Cooking time: *None*

Yield: *4 servings*

1 egg white, or 1 ounce pasteurized egg whites (Pappetti is one brand name)

2 tablespoons orange juice

1 tablespoon freshly grated orange rind

1½ cups undrained crushed pineapple

1 Combine all the ingredients in a large bowl. Place in freezer until slightly frozen, about ½ hour. Remove from freezer and beat until fluffy.

2 Pour into serving dishes and return to freezer for 45 minutes to 1 hour, or until firm, but not hard. If made in advance, allow to soften in the refrigerator 30 to 40 minutes before serving.

Nutrient analysis per serving: *65 kcalories, 1 gram protein, 16 grams carbohydrate, 0 grams fat, 0 grams saturated fat, 0 milligrams cholesterol, 1 gram fiber, 15 milligrams sodium*

Exchanges: *1 fruit*

TIP

If you are serving a specially cooked meal and want to be sure that the flavors of each course are fully appreciated, serve this ice between courses to refresh the palate. It's a very gourmet touch!

Making Healthy Baked Goods

The pleasure of eating fruit only increases when you add a little pastry! Of course, regular pastry comes with plenty of fat and is usually not recommended as part of a diet meant to keep you from gaining weight. But there is an alternative. Pie crust can be made with a mixture of cereals that you press into the bottom of a pan and then use the remainder to top the fruit. No need to go find your rolling pin.

Start with your favorite granola, add nuts, and maybe include some oats. You can create a dish of such nutritional value that you can legitimately eat it for breakfast! The following recipe even calls for nutrient-packed whole-wheat flour, a worthwhile staple to keep in your kitchen.

Apple Crisp

This lighter, healthier version of an old favorite is made without white sugar or fat. As a finale for dinner, have a little apple crisp to satisfy your sweet tooth, but because this dessert is full of carbohydrates, skip bread or other carbohydrate sources at this meal.

Preparation time: *25 to 30 minutes*

Cooking time: *50 to 55 minutes*

Yield: *8 servings*

3 large apples

½ cup rolled oats

½ cup whole-wheat flour

¼ cup Grape Nuts cereal

1½ teaspoons cinnamon, divided use

¾ cup plus 3 tablespoons unsweetened apple juice, divided use

½ cup raisins

1 tablespoon lemon juice

2 teaspoons cornstarch

2 tablespoons margarine, at room temperature

1 Preheat oven to 350 degrees Fahrenheit. Spray or lightly grease a 9-inch pie dish.

2 Using a sharp paring knife, quarter the apples. Then, using a potato peeler or paring knife, peel the apples, and cut out the core (see Figure 16-2). Set aside.

(continued)

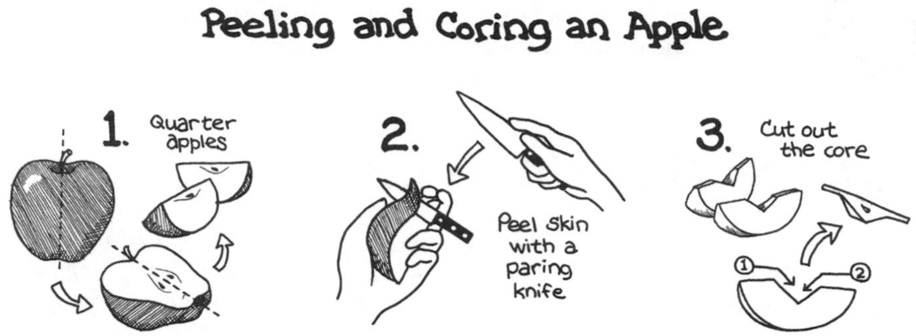
Peeling and Coring an Apple
1. Quarter apples
2.
Peel skin with a paring knife
3. Cut out the core
①
②

Figure 16-2: Quarter, peel, and core apples before slicing them.

3 *To make filling:* Whisk the cornstarch into ¼ cup of the apple juice. In a large sauté pan, combine the apple juice–cornstarch mixture, ¾ cup of apple juice, the apples, raisins, ¾ teaspoon cinnamon, and lemon juice. Bring to a boil over high heat, and then reduce heat and simmer about 7 minutes, gently stirring occasionally to cook evenly. (Apples should be only slightly tender.) Remove apples and raisins with slotted spoon and place into the pie dish. Increase heat under sauté pan and maintain a low boil until sauce becomes syrupy. Pour sauce over apples and raisins.

4 *To make topping:* Combine rolled oats, whole-wheat flour, Grape Nuts, margarine, and ¾ teaspoon cinnamon in a medium bowl. Stir in up to 3 tablespoons of the apple juice, until the mixture holds together. Evenly dot over filling.

5 Bake for 30 minutes, until apples are bubbly and crust is lightly browned. Cool slightly, and serve at room temperature or warm.

Nutrient analysis per serving: *226 kcalories, 3 grams protein, 46 grams carbohydrate, 5 grams fat, 0 grams saturated fat, 0 milligrams cholesterol, 5 grams fiber, 83 milligrams sodium*

Exchanges: *2 starch, 1 fruit*

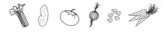

Decorating with Dessert Sauces

You can make a sauce simply by puréeing fruit. Pick one that is colorful, such as rosy raspberries or bright green kiwi. Then call on the artist within you and have some fun. Here are some ideas:

- Use a colorful sauce as a background. Place a large spoonful of fruit sauce in the middle of an individual dessert plate. Arrange slices of fruit and berries in an attractive pattern on top of the sauce.

- Put sauce in a plastic bottle fitted with a nozzle. Draw some doodles on a plate before you place the food you're serving on it, or place the food and then make some sort of design.
- Create a sauce zigzag that fills the entire plate.
- Make a scalloped border around the edge of the plate.
- Make big polka dots.
- Create a design in two colors using two different sauces.

Have fun and let yourself be artistic.

Being Adventurous with Flavor

Rich dessert sauces, such as chocolate and butterscotch, are loved with good reason. But they also supply plenty of carbohydrates and calories. However, other taste treats await! How about a spicy dessert sauce? Just as the flavor of main-course dishes can be enhanced with spices rather than fat, dessert, too, can be brought to life with these special flavorings.

The following recipe incorporates mustard seeds, cumin, and fennel. Healthful yogurt, rather than oil, holds together the dressing's many ingredients.

Fresh Fruit Plate with Sweet and Hot Dressing

This could be a salad, but can also be an elegantly beautiful dessert. Try different combinations, depending on the season. An attractive selection of fruit is two pink grapefruit, one papaya, and one d'anjou pear, the assortment used to tally the nutritional analysis of this recipe. Combinations — such as peaches, cherries, and melon, or apple and banana slices with mini clusters of grapes — are also delicious and eye-catching.

Preparation time: *10 to 15 minutes to make the dressing, 10 to 20 minutes to assemble the fruits*

Cooking time: *None*

Yield: *8 servings*

(continued)

2 tablespoons poppy seeds

2 tablespoons sunflower seeds

2 tablespoons sesame seeds

2 teaspoons mustard seeds

½ teaspoon cumin or fennel seeds

Pinch of celery seeds

½ cup pineapple juice

⅔ cup plain nonfat yogurt

4 teaspoons orange juice concentrate

3 pounds assorted fresh fruits

A few sprigs mint or watercress for garnish

1 Toast all the seeds in a heavy skillet over low heat, stirring often, until they give off a roasted aroma (up to 5 minutes).

2 Remove from heat and transfer the seeds to a food processor or spice grinder. Grind to a coarse meal, using quick pulses. Transfer to a small bowl and whisk in remaining ingredients except fruits and mint garnish. Mix well, cover, and refrigerate until serving time.

3 To serve, slice the fruit and arrange on a platter or 8 individual plates. Garnish with sprigs of mint. Drizzle 2 tablespoons dressing over each serving, or pass it in a small pitcher.

Nutrient analysis per serving with 2 tablespoons dressing: *150 kcalories, 4 grams protein, 25 grams carbohydrate, 5 grams fat, 0.7 grams saturated fat, 1 milligram cholesterol, 4 grams fiber, 22 milligrams sodium*

Exchanges: *1½ fruit, 1 fat*

Part III
Eating Out for the Person with Diabetes

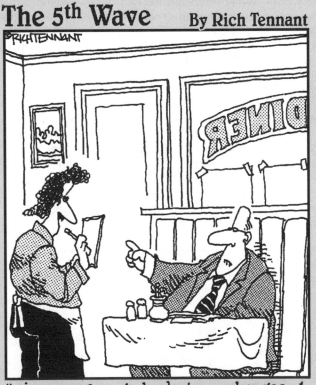

The 5th Wave By Rich Tennant

"Give me 2 carbohydrate exchanges, 1 protein exchange, and if I have any room left, I'll take a ½ fat exchange."

In this part . . .

You may believe that — because you have diabetes — you can no longer enjoy the creative cuisines and the wonderful atmospheres and service of great restaurants. This part puts that misinformation to rest with a resounding *bon appétit,* French for "You are about to be treated to a great restaurant meal." The chefs and restaurant owners in this book are interested in good nutrition as well as delicious food. They agreed to work with us for that very reason. They also want their customers to come back.

Unfortunately, we can't guarantee that the recipes will always be exactly as you find them in this book if you order them in the restaurant that provided them. Chefs change often in restaurants and ingredients are not always exactly the same. The chef may use regular-salt chicken stock instead of low-salt chicken stock, for example. The best you can do is ask that the food be prepared in the way that you expect.

Chapter 17

Eating Smart While Eating Out

In This Chapter

- Preparing to go to a restaurant
- Taking your seat
- Checking the menu
- Managing your eating at each meal and in different kinds of restaurants
- Enjoying your food
- Considering dessert

People eat many of their meals in restaurants these days, so integrating restaurant eating into a nutritional plan is essential for a person with diabetes. The restaurant business is booming, and creative chefs have the same celebrity status as famous sports stars. And they deserve it. They are using fresh ingredients to produce some of the most delicious and unique tastes imaginable. Unfortunately, nutrition is not always uppermost in their minds. Our experience with the many chefs in this book proves that interest in good nutrition is increasing, but you're still on your own most of the time when selecting healthy foods. This chapter helps you ensure that your restaurant eating fits well into your nutritional plan.

Your situation may be much like the plight of the customer who called the waiter over and said, "Waiter, taste this soup." The waiter replied, "Is there something wrong with it?" "Never mind," said the customer, "just taste the soup." "But it smells and looks okay," said the waiter. "That's all right, just taste the soup," replied the customer. "But sir, there's no spoon," said the waiter. "Aha," said the customer. The point is that you are ultimately responsible to ensure that you eat healthy foods.

Planning for Restaurant Dining

If you live in (or are visiting) one of the cities that contains a restaurant we reference in this book (see Appendix A), the task of finding a restaurant that is appropriate for a person with diabetes is much easier for you. You just need to go to that restaurant and select an entrée that has the letters MD next to it. *MD* means *meal for diabetes,* and the presence of those letters next to a menu item means that we have prepared and analyzed that recipe. We can guarantee that it will provide the carbohydrates and the exchanges (see Chapter 2) that we list with that recipe in this book. In general, these recipes will be lower in fat and lower in salt.

REMEMBER

We vouch only for the recipes marked with an MD. The rest of the menu may contain food that you can eat, but you will have to make that evaluation by questioning your waitperson carefully. Even if the balance of energy sources is right, you will probably receive too much food and should take some home or leave some on your plate.

Because this book is limited to 14 cities and 17 restaurants, you may often find yourself having to choose a restaurant where you don't know the contents of the food. How do you go about choosing a restaurant in this situation? Here are a few suggestions:

- No particular kind of food is better or worse than any other, with the exception of fast food (we discuss this issue in the next chapter). You may think that vegetarian food is better than animal sources, but a dish of pasta in a creamy sauce is no better than a piece of fatty steak. Often, restaurants have several menu items that fit into your nutrition plan.
- Consider choosing a restaurant that you can walk to and from. The exercise you get will offset the extra calories you may consume.
- Many restaurants now publish their menus on the Internet. Before deciding to visit a particular restaurant, go to the establishment's Web site and make sure that they provide food you can eat.
- Don't go to the restaurant if the catch of the day is fish sticks.
- Call ahead and find out whether you can substitute items on the menu. Nonfranchise and non-fast-food restaurants are much more likely to let you substitute menu items. Fast-food restaurants are able to serve large numbers of people at lower prices by making the food entirely uniform. On the other hand, as the next chapter explains, this uniformity makes it easier to know the exact ingredients and methods of preparation. You need to ask only a few questions to know whether a restaurant will be accommodating. Ask whether the staff will
    - Substitute skim milk for whole milk and margarine for butter.
    - Serve gravies, salad dressings, and sauces on the side.
    - Bake, broil, and poach instead of frying or sautéing.
- An older restaurant has the advantage of having experienced and well-trained staff who know what the kitchen staff are willing to do for you, based on what has been done before.

- Find out whether the restaurant already has special meals or entrées for people with chronic diseases such as heart disease. They are much more likely to be health conscious in their cooking.
- When you choose a restaurant, consider what you have already eaten that day. For example, if you have already eaten your daily limit of carbohydrate, then the choice of a restaurant where pasta or rice are the major ingredients may not be a good one. The choice of a restaurant is often made days in advance, so on the day of your visit, prepare for the restaurant by eating less of the major ingredients you will find there.
- Drink water or have a vegetable snack before you go to the restaurant so that hunger won't drive you to make bad choices.
- If you know that the restaurant serves huge portions of everything, don't go there unless you plan to share your meal or take part of your meal home.

Mrs. Wilson, who has type 2 diabetes, decided to go to a well-known delicatessen before she attended a musical play. She knew that they served huge portions, but she also knew that she could order a mini-version of many of the items. At the restaurant, she ordered a mini-Reuben sandwich, expecting to get half or less of the usual entrée. What arrived was the entire Reuben sandwich without the usual potato salad and coleslaw. She couldn't take half of it home because she was going directly to the show. She knew that she'd feel bad leaving part of such a delicious sandwich, so she ended up eating most of it. Her blood glucose level later that night reflected the huge excess in calories that she had consumed.

You can see from the information in this section that you can do plenty, even before you reach the restaurant, to prepare for dining out. Your preparation may make the whole experience much more satisfying and less frustrating.

Beginning the Dining Experience

As you sit down to enjoy your meal, you can take many steps to make the experience of eating out the pleasure that it ought to be. A few simple considerations at this point allow you to enjoy the meal free of the concern that you are wrecking your nutritional program. Among the steps that you can take are the following:

- Ask your waiter not to bring bread or to take it off the table if it is there already. That goes for chips and crackers as well.
- Check your blood glucose before you order so you will know how much carbohydrate is appropriate at that time.
- If you arrive early, avoid sitting in the bar with cocktails before you move to your table to eat your meal.

- Ask for raw vegetables without a dip, what the restaurant menus call *crudités,* so you can munch on something before you order.
- Ask the reservationist to seat you promptly so you don't have to wait and get too hungry or even hypoglycemic.
- Wait to administer your short-acting insulin until you can be sure of the food delivery time.

Mr. Phillips, a 63-year-old man with type 2 diabetes, was trying to understand, with the help of his dietitian, why his blood glucose had risen to 386 mg/dl after a meal at a local Mexican restaurant. "I knew the portions were large, so I ordered a bean tortilla, and I didn't even eat the whole thing. I left half of it on my plate. I ate very little of the rice as well." The dietitian asked him if he had arrived early at the restaurant. "Oh yes, I forgot. We had to wait in the bar and I had a virgin margarita." "That," said the dietitian, "explains your high blood glucose. The margarita is all carbohydrate."

Ordering from the Menu

The menu and the "specials" are arranged to encourage you to order a big meal. One of the more interesting things that we learned as a result of working with the chefs whose recipes are found in this book, especially the European chefs now cooking in the United States, is the expectation of large portions on the part of U.S. restaurant-goers, compared to Europeans. The chefs were amazed at how much food they had to put on each plate in order to satisfy U.S. tastes. When you order meat, fish, or poultry, you are often getting at least twice as much as the serving in the diabetic exchange lists. Considering how frequently people eat out in the United States, it's no wonder the population is getting fatter.

Your strategy for ordering from the menu should include the following:

- Plan to leave some food or take home half your order, because the portions will almost always be too large.
- Consider using an appetizer as your entrée.
- If you decide to have wine, order it by the glass. A bottle of wine will always be finished, and unless eight of you share the bottle, you will drink too much.
- Consider a meal of soup and salad. They can be delicious, filling, low in calories, and low in carbohydrates.
- Feel free to get a complete description, including portion size, of an appetizer or entrée from the waitperson so that you aren't surprised when the food arrives. Pay particular attention to how the food is cooked — in fat or butter, for example.

- Order clear soups rather than cream soups.
- Ask for salad dressings and sauces on the side if possible. This way, you are in control of the amount you consume.
- Order a dish to be shared with another person.
- You are probably wise to choose fish more often than meat, both to avoid fat and for the cholesterol-lowering properties of fish. Remember, however, that fried fish can be as fat-laden as a steak.
- Watch out for vegetarian dishes. They are often high in carbohydrates and made with a lot of dairy products that contain saturated fats.
- Let your server know that you need to eat soon. If there will be a delay in getting food to you because the kitchen is slow or busy, insist that vegetable snacks be brought to the table.

The description of an entrée usually offers clues that tell you whether or not it's a good choice for you. These words, in particular, indicate that the preparation keeps fat to a minimum:

- Broiled
- Cooked in its own juice
- Poached
- Grilled
- Blackened
- Baked

On the other hand, the following words point to a less desirable high fat entrée:

- Buttered or in butter sauce
- Creamed or in cream sauce
- Deep fried
- Escalloped
- Fried
- In a plum sauce
- In cheese sauce
- Sautéed
- Sweet and sour
- With peanuts or cashews
- Battered
- Golden brown

Does it really matter if you order one kind of sauce versus another? Here are the calorie counts per tablespoon for various salad dressings. Remember that the energy in food is properly expressed in kilocalories, not calories, which are a thousand times smaller:

- Blue cheese: 82 kilocalories
- Creamy Italian dressing: 52 kilocalories
- Lowfat French dressing: 22 kilocalories
- Red-wine vinegar: 2 kilocalories

Planning at Each Meal and in Specific Kinds of Restaurants

You can make good choices at every meal, whether it's breakfast, lunch, or dinner. Every kind of food offers you the opportunity to select a lowfat, low salt alternative. You just need to think about it and be aware of the possibilities. Helping you choose healthy meals is the purpose of this section.

Breakfast

The good choices at breakfast are fresh foods, which usually contain plenty of fiber. Fresh fruit and juice are good ways to start the meal, followed by hot cereals such as oatmeal or Wheatena, or high fiber cold cereals such as shredded wheat or bran cereals. Always add skim milk instead of whole milk. Enjoy egg whites but not yolks, or make an omelet with two whites for every yolk.

Less desirable choices are foods such as quiche, bacon, fried or hash brown potatoes, croissants, pastries, and doughnuts.

Appetizers, salads, and soups

Raw and plain food beats those cooked and covered with butter or sour cream, and that rule applies to appetizers, salads, and soups, too. Raw carrots and celery can be enjoyed at any time and to almost any extent. Clear soups are always healthier. Salsa has become a popular covering for crackers instead of a high fat dip. A delicious green salad is nutritious and filling.

By contrast, olives, nachos, and avocados have lots of fat. Nuts, chips, and cheese before dinner add lots of calories. Fried onion appetizers are currently very popular, and they're often dripping with fat. Watch out for the sour cream dips and the mayonnaise dips, since they, too, are full of fat.

Seafood

Most fish are relatively low in fat and can be a healthy choice. But even the best fish can compromise your nutrition plan when they are fried. Fish that stand out in the lowfat category are cod, bass, halibut, swordfish, and tuna in water. Most of the shellfish varieties are also lowfat. Stay away from herring, tuna in oil, and fried anything.

Chinese food

You can eat some great Chinese food and not have to worry about upsetting your diet plan. Stick to vegetable dishes with small amounts of meat in them. Avoid fried dishes, whether they are meats, tofu, or rice and noodles. Pot stickers, an appetizer often found on the menu, and sweet-and-sour pork will really throw off your calorie count and your fat intake. Stay away from the almond cookies that often follow Chinese meals.

Indian food

Rice and pita bread are good carbohydrate choices, but avoid foods made with coconut milk. Meat, fish, and poultry cooked in the Tandoori manner are fine, but Indian chefs like to fry many foods; keep those to a minimum. Curries are fine as long as they are not made with coconut milk.

Italian foods

Stick to tomato-based sauces, and avoid the creamy, buttery, cheesy sauces. Minestrone soup is a hearty vegetable soup that is low in fat. Pasta in general is fine as long as the sauce is not fatty. Sausage is a poor choice, whether served with pasta or placed on pizza. Pesto sauce can be made with little fat. If you love the taste of basil, as Dr. Rubin does, ask for a lowfat version of this classic sauce. Ask whether the kitchen staff will make garlic bread with roasted garlic alone, without the butter that often accompanies it. You will be delighted with the delicious taste.

Japanese food

Japanese food is generally fine to eat, particularly sushi, miso soup, and broiled fish. Stay away from the tempura, which is deep-fried. Limit your rice intake to a maximum of two-thirds of a cup at a meal.

Mexican food

Mexican food has become increasingly popular, but Mexican restaurants offer many temptations to slip from your healthy eating plan. Have salsa, not guacamole, as an appetizer. Stay away from *refried;* it means just what the word says. Avoid all dishes laden with cheese as well as dishes heavy in sausage. Tortillas, burritos, and tostadas are delicious and good for you as long as you avoid the addition of a lot of cheese, sour cream, or guacamole. And it doesn't hurt to keep in mind the importance of moderation. Mexican restaurants are known for large servings, so take some home.

Enjoying Your Food

After you have been so conscientious in planning this delicious restaurant meal, you deserve to really enjoy the food. But you aren't done with your preparations yet. All the great planning can come undone if you are careless at this point. Think about the following advice as you eat:

- If you have a glass of wine, consider the number of calories.
- After you have carefully controlled the intake of food on your plate, don't add significant calories by tasting or finishing your eating partner's food.
- Try using some behavior modification to prolong the meal and give your brain a chance to know you have eaten: Eat slowly, chew each bite thoroughly, and put your fork down between each bite.
- Remember that the meal is a social occasion. Spend more time talking to your companions and less time concentrating on the food.
- Remove the skin if you are eating poultry, and allow the sauce to drip off the morsel of food on your fork if you are eating a dish cooked in a sauce.

Finishing with Dessert

For many people, the early parts of a meal are just a prelude to their favorite part, which is dessert. Most people have a "sweet tooth," and dessert is often the way that they satisfy that need. The Italians don't call the part of the menu that features the desserts the *dulci* without reason. The word means *sweets*. Dessert, in many restaurants, has become a showpiece. The pastry chef tries to show how sweet he or she can make the dessert while creating a culinary work of art. The term *decadent* is often used in describing the richness of these desserts.

Does this mean that you can't have any dessert at all? No, making a wise choice simply requires a certain amount of awareness on your part. You need to ask yourself the question, "Is the taste of this dessert worth the potential damage it will do to my blood glucose and calorie intake?" If you can answer this question with a "yes," then have the dessert, but check your blood glucose and adjust your medications as needed after eating it, and return to your nutritional plan without spending a lot of time regretting your lapse. You might even do a little extra exercise to counteract the calories.

On the other hand, if you want to answer the question with a "no," here are some considerations that may help you avoid temptation:

- Do you really need or want the dessert?
- Will you remember it 10 minutes later when you are at the theater?
- Could you share the dessert or just taste it?
- Is a fruit dessert available that you could enjoy?

Chapter 18

Stopping for Fast Food

In This Chapter

- Enjoying burgers and pizza on the way to Yosemite
- Starting with breakfast on a trip to Lake Tahoe
- Choosing food carefully between San Francisco and Los Angeles
- Crossing the road for chicken on a gambling junket from L.A. to Las Vegas
- Seeking sun and good nutrition on the way from L.A. to Phoenix

Haven't you always wanted to tour California, the Golden State? Here is your chance. You have been invited by Dr. Rubin and Fran Stach to travel with them on the highways and byways of California and nearby states. You can stop along the way at some of the best known fast-food restaurants in the country. Luckily, you are with Fran, who knows the contents of all the foods in these restaurants, and Dr. Rubin, who is there to make sure that you enjoy yourself while staying on your eating program. If you want to get the details on these trips, you can refer to Frommer's very popular travel guides. We will give you just the bare essentials here.

We have selected these specific restaurants because they are usually the most common examples of a particular class of fast-food restaurants. In no way do we mean to recommend them above others in their class.

People used to say that at fast-food restaurants you could get more nourishment from biting your lip than eating the food. This is definitely no longer the case. Because everyone is conscious of good nutrition these days, it is possible to find something healthful to eat in any fast-food restaurant.

The reason these establishments are called fast-food restaurants is that they have food preparation, ordering, and serving down to the least amount of time possible. Because we are in a hurry and don't want to stop for a long time, there's nothing wrong with enjoying that convenience, but we want to make sure that the food is right for you.

Of course, some of these places are not meant to rush into and out of. They are sit-down places, but the food is standardized and is prepared pretty fast, so the result is about the same. This chapter discusses those kinds of restaurants, too.

One advantage of franchise restaurants is that a hamburger in a Denny's in California is almost exactly the same as a hamburger in a Denny's in New Mexico or Oregon. You know exactly what you are getting, which makes the meal easier to fit into your diet. On the other hand, the quick serving and eating often doesn't allow your brain enough time to recognize that your body has eaten enough calories; and you might be tempted to order more food. Don't.

In this chapter, we hit the high spots, the most commonly visited fast-food places. One chapter isn't enough space to cover the hundreds of different fast-food franchises all over the country. In general, a burger in McDonald's looks like a burger at Burger King, but there *are* major variations.

TIP

If you want to be sure of the nutritional content of various fast foods, refer to *The American Diabetes Association Guide to Healthy Restaurant Eating* (written by Hope S. Warshaw, MMSc, RD, CDE, and published by the American Diabetes Association; to order, call 800-232-6733), which covers a lot more, but definitely not all, of the available restaurant chains. You can find a great deal of information about fast-food restaurants on the World Wide Web. Visit your favorite search engine and enter the name of a specific franchise.

Stopping on the Way to Yosemite

Yosemite National Park is the crown jewel of the national park system and a trip there is a must. It's a ride of about 214 miles from San Francisco (see Figure 18-1). We are leaving about 11:30 a.m., so we won't be driving long before stopping for lunch. You are driving, and Fran and Dr. Rubin are sitting back relaxing. You checked your blood glucose before we started, and it was fine. Just after noon you decide that you are hungry. The insulin that you took before breakfast is starting to actively lower your blood glucose. We are on I-580 ("I" for interstate highway), and you notice a lot of restaurants at the next exit, which is Exit 27, Hopyard Road, Pleasanton. So you pull off the interstate.

In front of us, we have numerous choices. Among them are

- Arby's
- Burger King
- Buttercup Pantry Restaurant

- Denny's
- El Molino
- Hungry Hunter
- In-N-Out Hamburgers
- Nations Hamburgers
- Pleasant Asian Quisine
- Taco Bell

How do we choose from such a full plate? Fortunately, Fran knows the menu at Denny's and can help you make good choices, so we pull into Denny's. Denny's is a good representative of the sit-down restaurant group, which also includes Applebee's, Bennigan's, Big Boy restaurants, Bob Evans Farms, Coco's, Fresh Choice, Hometown Buffet, Perkins' Family Restaurants, Ruby Tuesday, and on and on.

We sit down after a bathroom stop and look at the menu. The first thing Fran points out is that the menu offers some healthy choices. For example, the Charleston Chicken Dinner has about 325 kilocalories (kilocalories is the correct measurement, not calories, which is a much smaller number), although 50 percent of them are fat calories, 20 percent carbohydrate calories, and 30 percent protein calories. It contains about a gram of sodium, and the fat is 20 percent saturated, so the dish is not ideal. You will have to reduce your fat intake at other meals and increase your carbohydrates, but at least the total calorie count and the salt content are acceptable. This choice has 1 starch, 3 lean-meat exchanges, and 2 fat exchanges. It contains 16 grams of carbohydrate.

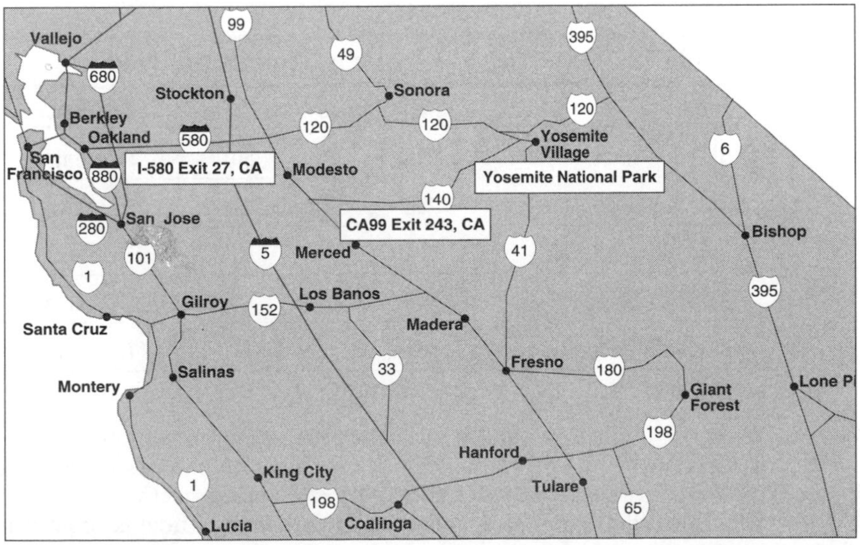

Figure 18-1: San Francisco to Yosemite.

Looking further down the menu, Fran points to the Grilled Chicken Breast Dinner, which is only 130 kilocalories. The breakdown is 28 percent fat and 72 percent protein with a little more than ½ gram of sodium. You can add some carbohydrate in the form of a small potato or a slice of bread. This addition would add 15 grams of carbohydrate and 3 grams of protein. Now you have 210 kilocalories with 17 percent fat, 30 percent carbohydrate, and 53 percent protein. Again, you will need to balance the high protein by taking less at other meals. The meal has 3 very lean meat exchanges plus a starch, or a total of 15 grams of carbohydrate if you have the bread.

Fran wants to offer you a few more choices, so she suggests the Grilled Alaskan Salmon Dinner. This selection contains 210 kilocalories with 17 percent of calories as fat, 2 percent as carbohydrate, and the rest as protein. This dish contains only small amounts of salt and saturated fat. You may want to add a slice of bread, bringing the kilocalorie count up to 290 and the breakdown to 12 percent fat, 29 percent carbohydrate, and 59 percent protein. This meal provides 4 very lean meat exchanges and a starch exchange.

Finally, you might like the Senior Pot Roast. It has only 218 total kilocalories with the small potato to give you a bit of carbohydrate. The fat content is 6 grams (2 of them are saturated), and there are 800 milligrams of sodium. The energy breakdown is 25 percent fat, 38 percent carbohydrate, and 37 percent protein. With this choice, you are approaching the good balance of energy sources that we prefer. It adds 3 lean meat exchanges and 1 starch exchange to your nutrition plan. There are a total of 21 grams of carbohydrate.

You decide on the Senior Pot Roast. Fran has the Grilled Chicken Breast, and Dr. Rubin has the Alaskan Salmon Dinner. As we eat, Fran points out some of the really bad choices on the menu (see Table 18-1).

Table 18-1 Menu Choices to Avoid

Food	*Kilocalories*	*%Fat*	*Sodium*
Buffalo Wings	856	60	5½ grams
Mozzarella Sticks	756	43	5½ grams
Onion Ring Basket	824	55	2 grams
Sampler of above	1,405	51	5⅓ grams
Bacon Cheddar Burger	935	61	1.7 grams

WARNING!

What the choices in Table 18-1 all have in common is the high calorie, fat, and salt content. But you can't say that you have no choices. The menu contains plenty of choices, but you have to choose wisely. You won't usually travel with your dietitian, but bring along this book. It's the next best thing.

Let's get back on the road. Yosemite awaits. But we are taking in the sights along the way, so a few hours go by and we find ourselves only 60 miles further when it's time for dinner. You pull off at Exit 243 on CA 99, Carpenter Road, Briggsmore Avenue, and we are again confronted with many choices, including

- Albertos Molcasalsa
- Bakers Square Restaurant
- Black Angus
- Burger King
- Denny's
- Domino's Pizza
- El Pollo Loco
- Fresh Choice
- Hometown Buffet
- IHOP
- Imperial Garden
- Jack in the Box
- Kirin
- McDonald's
- Olive Garden
- Outback Steakhouse
- Taco Bell
- Taco Shop
- Teriyaki King
- TOGO'S

You can even find a Wendy's if you want to cross under the highway to the other side.

Everyone is in the mood for pizza, so Domino's Pizza wins out. We agree to share a 12-inch (eight slices), medium cheese, deep-dish pizza with peppers and mushrooms as the toppings. Peppers and mushrooms add very little to the calorie count and you don't need to consider them in your food plan. Two slices of the pizza provides about 480 kilocalories, with 22 grams of fat and about 1 gram of sodium. You end up with 40 percent fat, 45 percent carbohydrate, and 15 percent protein. The pizza provides a bit too much fat and too little protein, but your choice at lunch balances out your fat, carbohydrate, and protein intake. The exchanges work out to 3 starches, 1 carbohydrate, 1 medium-fat meat, and 3 fats. The carbohydrate consists of 55 grams. A small green salad with a fat-free dressing provides a satisfying, low calorie addition.

If you take insulin, you have to balance your short-acting insulin dose with the number of grams of carbohydrate in your meal. See Chapter 2 for help in doing this.

Don't forget that you need to leave two slices of the pizza on the table when you depart.

Most of the vegetable toppings can be added without adding calories, but we recommend that you avoid certain toppings because they contain too much fat. These include

- Bacon
- Cheddar cheese
- Sausage
- Pepperoni

It's nice to know that you can enjoy pizza if you have a little advance knowledge about what goes into it. The preceding information holds true for most of the fast-food pizza places along the road.

We continue on to Yosemite and enjoy the magnificent valley, including Half Dome, El Capitan, the waterfalls, and the rest of the beautiful park.

Stopping for Breakfast on the Way to Lake Tahoe

For our second trip, we are going to glorious Lake Tahoe, a magical place surrounded by high mountains, many of which still have their winter coating of snow. It's a trip of about 225 miles from San Francisco (see Figure 18-2), and we are getting an early start so that we can enjoy the scenery for at least half the day. Dr. Rubin is driving. We left without breakfast because he knows that a Starbucks is less than 20 miles down the road.

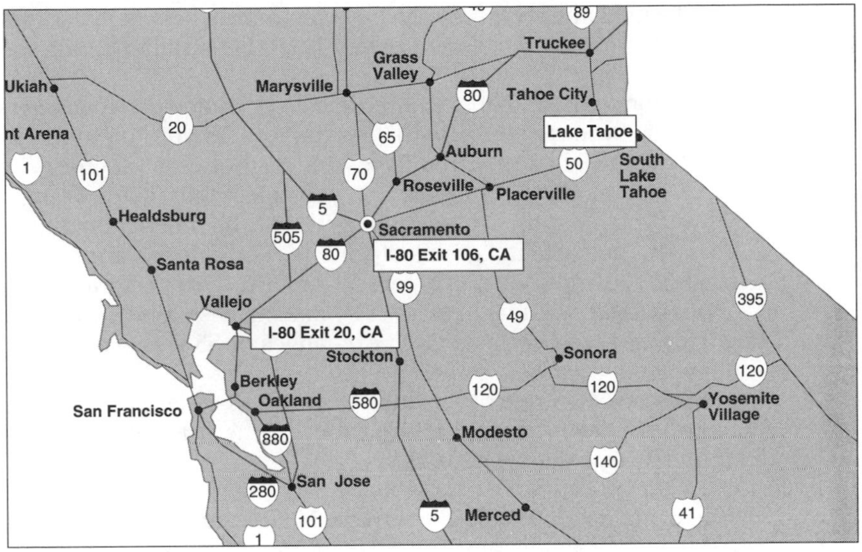

Figure 18-2: San Francisco to Lake Tahoe.

He exits from I-80, Exit 20, Appian Way, El Sobrante. We are again confronted with numerous choices, including McDonald's on the north side of the road and Burger King, Carl's Jr. Hamburgers, and Wendy's on the south side, but we proceed to Starbucks, also on the south side of the exit.

Starbucks is a good example of the breakfast group, which includes Dunkin' Donuts, Manhattan Bagel Company, and many others. You usually can get a coffee drink and a muffin. The bagel places offer many varieties of bagels.

If you stick to the coffee drinks with nonfat milk, you will drink about 120 kilocalories for a Caffe Latte. Using whole milk — which the coffee shop usually does unless the customer specifies nonfat — will just about double that calorie count and add saturated fat. You can really rev up the calories if you have a Caffe Mocha with whole milk and whipping cream. Now you are taking in 340 kilocalories and 55 percent of that is fat. Skip that drink and enjoy the nonfat Caffe Latte. It has 1 gram of fat, 17 grams of carbohydrate, and 12 grams of protein.

You have a choice between muffins or croissants to go with your beverage. Remember that Starbucks doesn't bake its own pastries, so some variation in the nutrient content may occur from place to place, but the calorie counts are generally about the same.

Fran tells us that a croissant, even a plain one, is between 250 and 350 kilocalories and almost 60 percent of that is fat. Let's skip the croissants.

We move on to the muffins, where we have a choice between lowfat and regular muffins. Because you're with your doctor and your dietitian, you naturally choose the lowfat variety. You have a choice between blueberry or cranberry. You're in the mood for cranberry, so you select that flavor. Fran points out how well you have chosen and tells you that the muffin contains about 240 kilocalories and 380 milligrams of sodium. The calories are 8 percent fat, 87 percent carbohydrates, and 5 percent protein. This is not a good breakdown for you, but you will make up for it by making wise food choices later in the day. This meal gives you 3 starch exchanges or 53 grams of carbohydrates.

If you had selected one of the Starbucks shop's other pastries, such as a bow tie or a bear claw, you would have eaten at least 300 kilocalories and 40 percent of that would have been fat.

On the other hand, if we had spotted a Manhattan Bagel Company place, you could have had almost any bagel except the Everything (which has too much salt) and the Salt bagel (which gives you a jolt of up to 7,000 milligrams of sodium). The rest of the bagels generally provide about 260 kilocalories. Adding 2 tablespoons of cream cheese, you have to count an additional 100 kilocalories unless the cheese is lowfat. The cream cheese has 100 kilocalories, of which 80 to 90 percent is fat, so you end up with a total of 360 kilocalories. The breakdown is 28 percent fat, 59 percent carbohydrate, and 13 percent protein, not a bad division. This bagel with cream cheese has 3½ starch exchanges and 2 fats. The carbohydrate count is 53 grams.

Well, we've had breakfast and are eager to drive. Beautiful Lake Tahoe awaits, offering all kinds of camping, hiking, swimming, and even some indoor diversions. Why don't we just drive the rest of the way?

Eating Well between San Francisco and Los Angeles

Today, we are heading down to the movie capital, Los Angeles. The ride is a bit less than 400 miles, most of them on I-5 (see Figure 18-3). We may take in Disneyland while we are there, and we will certainly visit Universal Studios. Fran is driving. We had breakfast at home, and it's about time for a morning snack. Fran says that she knows a Baskin-Robbins not too far ahead, where we can get a snack that will not be high in calories or fat.

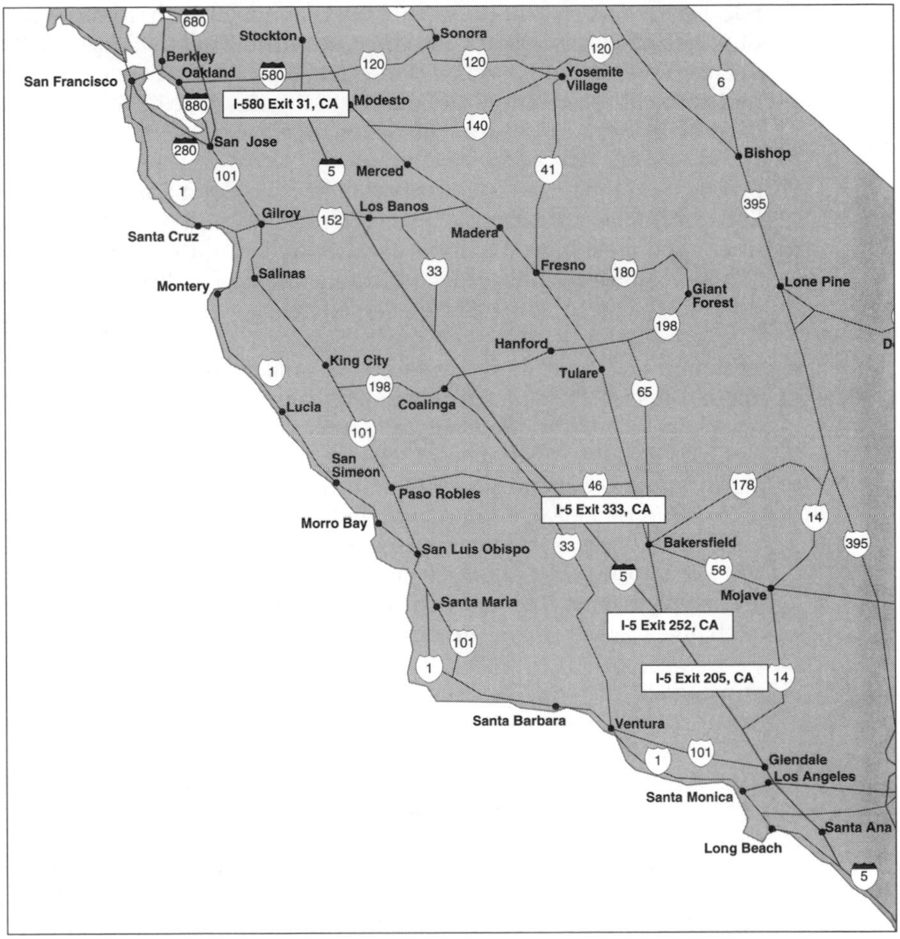

Figure 18-3: San Francisco to Los Angeles.

Fran pulls off I-580 at Exit 31, Colier Canyon Road, Airway Boulevard. On our side of the freeway are Beeb's Sports Bar and Grill and Cattleman's. We cross over to the other side where a Wendy's is the only competition for the Baskin-Robbins we have stopped for.

Baskin-Robbins is one of the leaders of the dessert group. Others in this group include Carvel Ice Cream Bakery, I Can't Believe It's Yogurt, and TCBY. If you choose nonfat frozen yogurt or limit yourself to a half cup of ice cream, you will stay within your nutritional plan, and either choice makes a pretty good snack. As always, the key is moderation.

For example, at Baskin-Robbins, Fran recommends that you share the Cappuccino Nonfat Blast with her. It provides 270 kilocalories with 60 grams of carbohydrate and 9 grams of protein. It would be especially good if you had eaten little carbohydrate earlier in the day. The exchange breakdown is 3 carbohydrate and 1 fat-free milk exchange.

If you are in the mood for a smoothie, try the Copa Banana soft serve or the Sunset Orange soft serve. They come in at 280 and 300 kilocalories, respectively, and most of that amount is carbohydrate, about 60 grams in each. They each also have 8 grams of protein and no fat. They contain 3½ carbohydrate exchanges and 1 fat-free milk exchange.

Baskin-Robbins has a few lowfat ice creams such as Caramel Apple AlaMode and Espresso 'N Cream. From ½ cup of these you get only 100 kilocalories, mostly carbohydrate — about 20 grams — and 3 grams of protein. Baskin-Robbins also offers a bunch of ice cream flavors that contain no added sugar and provide about the same 100 kilocalories, 20 grams of carbohydrate, and 3 grams of protein. Even the regular deluxe ice creams are not too damaging to your eating plan if you limit yourself to ½ cup. They provide about the same 170 kilocalories with about 10 grams of fat, 20 grams of carbohydrate, and 2 grams of protein. They are considered to contain 1 carbohydrate and 2 fat exchanges. Avoid the ice creams with the word "butter" in the name.

You can see that you don't need to avoid these dessert places. Just be careful about what you choose and try to eat in moderation.

After a quick snack, we are back on the road to L.A. We travel another couple of hours and it's lunchtime. Fran seems to know all the exits. She pulls off of I-5 at Exit 333, CA 198, Lemoore and Hanford. She wants to give us a choice, and we find plenty of them here. On the east side of the highway is the Harris Ranch Restaurant. The other side has Burger King, Carl's Jr. Hamburgers, Denny's, Garden Room, McDonald's, Oriental Express, Red Robin Restaurant, and Taco Bell. Fran suggests that we check out the McDonald's and the Taco Bell for a possible choice for lunch.

McDonald's is, of course, a member of the burger group, which includes places such as Burger King, Carl's Jr. Hamburgers, Hardee's, In-N-Out Hamburgers, Jack in the Box, Rally's Hamburgers, Wendy's, Whataburger, and numerous others.

TIP

Watch for a few key words that warn you not to order a particular item in these restaurants. If the food is called a double, big, jumbo, monster, or the ultimate, stay away from that selection. Also avoid any menu item with bacon.

A McDonald's hamburger is not a bad selection. It has 270 kilocalories made up of 9 grams of fat, 34 grams of carbohydrate, and 13 grams of protein. The breakdown of sources of energy is 30 percent fat, 50 percent carbohydrate, and 20 percent protein. Isn't it curious that a meat source such as a hamburger has less protein than anything else? The hamburger has about a half-gram of salt and represents 2 starch exchanges, 1 medium-fat meat exchange, and 1 fat exchange.

Another good choice at McDonald's is the Chicken McNuggets (four pieces). One serving is only 190 kilocalories and provides 11 grams of fat, 10 grams of carbohydrate, and 12 grams of protein. The breakdown is 53 percent fat, 21 percent carbohydrate, and 26 percent protein. The sodium is relatively low at ⅓ of a gram. The exchanges for this meal are ½ starch, 2 lean meat, and 1 fat.

A Garden Salad with a lowfat dressing can accompany either of your choices without adding many calories. Even a small order of French Fries doesn't hurt your nutrition plan. It provides 210 kilocalories from 10 grams of fat, 26 grams of carbohydrate, and 3 grams of protein. It contains 2 starch and 2 fat exchanges.

So you see that you can eat at McDonald's and stay within your nutritional guidelines. What about going over to Taco Bell and checking them out before deciding where we are going to eat?

Taco Bell is a prime representative of the Mexican group of fast-food restaurants. They are particularly popular in California and the southwestern United States. Taco Bell restaurants offer some advantages:

- They feature many varieties of dishes with beans that add fiber and provide spicy sauces that add flavor without calories.
- You can keep the high fat items such as sour cream and cheese off your dishes.
- They tend to have less protein and more carbohydrates in their food.
- They fry in vegetable oil and not lard.

On the other side are the disadvantages:

- They refry their beans, adding more fat.
- They add a lot of cheese.
- Many items contain a high salt content.
- Fruits and vegetables are rarely seen in a Mexican fast-food meal.

You can make some good choices at Taco Bell, and Fran will help us pick them out. She points to the Chili Cheese Burrito containing 330 kilocalories, made up of 13 grams of fat, 37 grams of carbohydrate, and 14 grams of protein. The energy breakdown is 36 percent fat, 46 percent carbohydrate, and 18 percent protein — not too bad. It is relatively high in sodium at 870 milligrams. The exchanges are 2½ starch, 1 medium-fat meat, and 1½ fat.

Moving along on the menu, we come to a Tostada. Its 300 kilocalories come from 15 grams of fat, 31 grams of carbohydrate, and 10 grams of protein. The sources of energy are 45 percent fat, 41 percent carbohydrate, and 14 percent protein. It has less than a gram of salt, an accomplishment for this group. The exchanges work out to 2 starch, 1 medium-fat meat, and 2 fat exchanges.

A Taco and Taco Supreme, as well as a Soft Taco and Soft Taco Supreme, round out this restaurant's good choices. Their kilocalories are between 200 and 260, with 50 percent of them coming from fat, 30 percent from carbohydrates, and 20 percent from protein. The carbohydrate is between 14 and 23 grams. There are 1 to 1½ starch exchanges, 1 medium-fat meat exchange, and 1 or 2 fat exchanges. They don't contain a lot of salt.

All of us are in the mood for Mexican food, so we stay here and enjoy a tasty meal. For a beverage, we drink water to avoid additional calories.

Heading to Las Vegas to See the Shows

Now that we are in Los Angeles, it's not a big trip to Las Vegas, the site of some of the best entertainment in the country. We are going to see the Cirque du Soleil, a group of amazing acrobats and clowns. We may take advantage of some of the other indoor activities as well.

The ride is 280 miles, mostly on I-15 (see Figure 18-4). Dr. Rubin is doing the driving. He drives a little fast, but safely. Lunchtime is approaching, so he pulls off from I-15 at Exit 176, Lenwood Road. Plenty of restaurants are available to choose from, including Arby's, Baskin Robbins, Carl's Jr. Hamburgers, Del Taco, Denny's, In-N-Out Hamburgers, KFC, Wendy's, and McDonald's. Dr. Rubin is interested in a sandwich, so he chooses Arby's.

Arby's is a good representative of the sandwich group. This group includes Au Bon Pain, Blimpie, and Subway. These places have the advantage that you get to choose exactly what to put into your sandwich. They often have light menus that contain your best choices. They offer clear soups as well as salads with lowfat dressing.

Walking into Arby's, Fran homes in on the light menu. The Roast Beef Deluxe and the Roast Chicken Deluxe sandwiches are good choices. They have 280 to 300 kilocalories each. The Roast Beef Deluxe has about 4 more grams of fat than the Chicken Deluxe. They break down into about 31 percent fat, 45 percent carbohydrate, and 24 percent protein, which isn't bad at all. They have about 800 milligrams of sodium per sandwich. Each selection has 33 grams of carbohydrate (that total will help you determine your appropriate insulin dosage). The Roast Beef Deluxe has 2 starches and 2 medium-fat meat exchanges, while the Chicken Deluxe has 2 starches and 2 lean-meat exchanges.

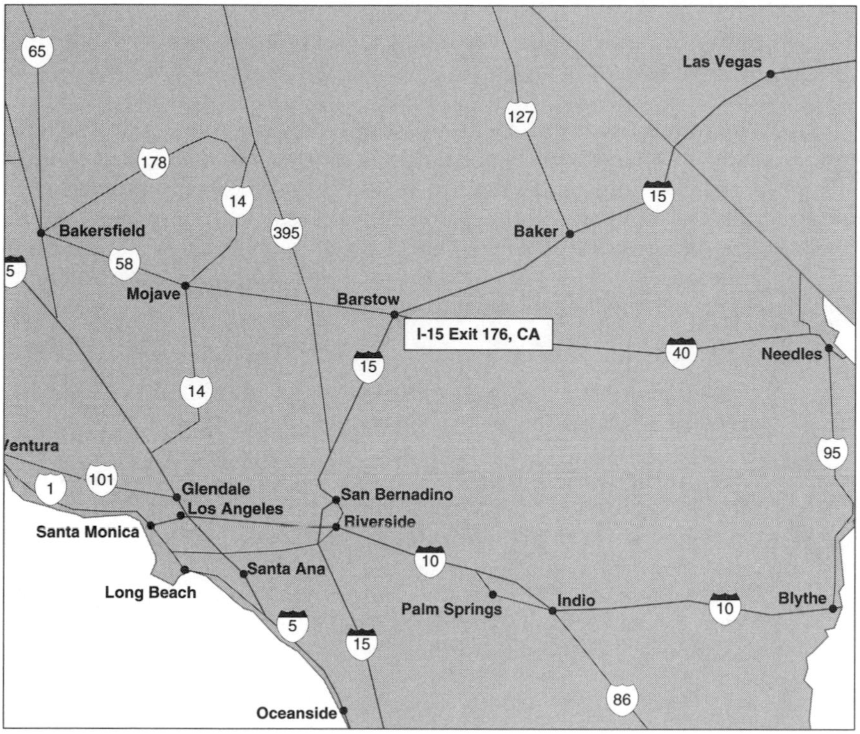

Figure 18-4: Los Angeles to Las Vegas.

From the other sandwiches, Fran recommends the Junior Roast Beef. It has 324 kilocalories with 14 grams of fat, 35 grams of carbohydrate, and 17 grams of protein. This breakdown produces 39 percent fat, 44 percent carbohydrate, and 17 percent protein. This sandwich contains almost 800 milligrams of sodium. The Junior Roast Beef gives you 2 starches, 2 medium-fat meats, and 1 fat exchange.

After making our selection and enjoying the meal, we are on the road again. We find ourselves close to Las Vegas when we decide to get off the highway again and have dinner. Dr. Rubin pulls off at I-15, Exit 37 in Nevada, the Tropicana Avenue exit.

Because this exit is so close to Las Vegas, the restaurants are even more numerous than usual. Some are in the big hotels. There are several fast-food places, including Burger King, In-N-Out Hamburgers, Jack in the Box, KFC, McDonald's, Taco Bell, and Wendy's. It's your turn to choose, and you select KFC because you are in the mood for chicken.

KFC is the best known representative of the chicken group of fast-food restaurants. The other popular restaurants in this group include Boston Market, Church's Chicken, Kenny Rogers Roasters, and Popeye's Chicken and Biscuits. They all feature chicken that is coated with batter and fried, which isn't good for you. Some restaurants now sell roast chicken, which is much better for your health, especially if you remove the skin of the chicken (which gets rid of a lot of fat).

The difference in calories when the skin is removed is dramatic. A roasted chicken breast with skin is 251 kilocalories, and skinless it is 169 kilocalories. A roasted chicken drumstick without skin is only 67 kilocalories. A roasted thigh without skin is only 106 kilocalories. Practically every calorie is protein. The carbohydrate is negligible. Therefore, a breast without skin provides 5 very lean meat exchanges, a drumstick supplies 2 very lean meats, and a thigh has 2 lean-meat exchanges.

You can order a piece of corn to give you 2 starch exchanges or have a piece of bread. Alternatively, you can have a corn muffin or rice pilaf. A side of green beans adds few calories while it fills you up.

When you buy food at chicken restaurants, stay away from large fried chicken pieces that are high in calories, fat, and sodium. Make sure that gravies and dressings are served on the side. One chicken should yield four servings.

Now it's time to get to our hotel and enjoy some of the great shows that are found in Las Vegas and nowhere else. They actually build the structure with the show in mind. Some of the shows are expensive, but they are worth every dollar.

Finding the Sun in Phoenix

For our final trip, we are going after heat and desert sun. We are driving from Los Angeles to Phoenix, an excursion of 381 miles (see Figure 18-5). On this trip, we are going to try to stop at a couple of other burger places so we can compare them with McDonald's. On any trip you take, you can bet that you will find either McDonald's, Burger King, or Wendy's, the last two being the ones we will visit on the way to Phoenix.

You are doing the driving. After about 115 miles, you pull off of I-10 at Exit 129, Thousand Palms, Rancho Mirage, and Palm Desert. We find not only Burger King but also Carl's Jr. Hamburgers, Del Taco, Denny's, In-N-Out Hamburgers, and McDonald's. You pull into Burger King, and we all take a look at the menu.

Fran compares a McDonald's hamburger with a Burger King hamburger. The Burger King has more fat, less carbohydrate, and more protein. In comparison with the McDonald's product, the Burger King sandwich supplies one additional medium-fat meat exchange, and the sodium content is about the same.

Unfortunately, the rest of the menu is doubles and bigs, all of which you should avoid because they are filled with salt and fat. You can add some bulk with a Side Salad and lowfat dressing.

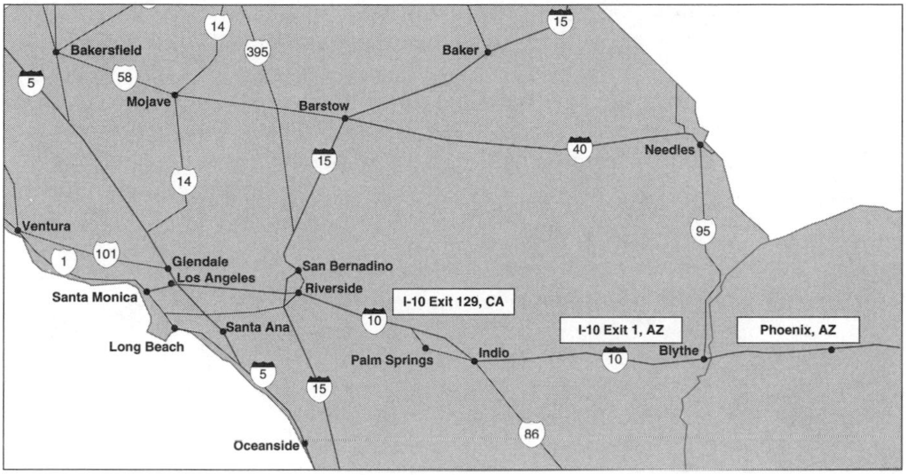

Figure 18-5: Los Angeles to Phoenix.

We all have a hamburger and continue driving. We tour along the way and arrive at out next stop just about dinnertime. You exit I-10, Exit 1 in Arizona. The exit is called Ehrenburg, Parker, and it's about 118 miles further along I-10.

Not many restaurants are here, but we're looking for a Wendy's and find it. The rest include a Silly Al's Pizza & Burgers (no relation to Dr. Rubin) and Thad's Restaurant.

Wendy's hamburger for kids is almost identical to McDonald's hamburger, providing 2 starch and 2 medium-fat meat exchanges. The chicken pieces for kids, which Wendy's calls Chicken Nuggets, are exactly like the four pieces of chicken at McDonald's.

Wendy's does have a small Chili plate, which provides 210 kilocalories with 15 grams of carbohydrate. It has 800 milligrams of sodium, and the exchange count is 1½ starch and 1 medium-fat meat. You can round it off with a Side Salad and reduced-fat dressing. Wendy's offers a salad bar that includes reduced-fat dressing as well. Be very careful about portions at the salad bar. There are lots of high calorie items that add up fast.

Fran points out that Wendy's has some nice Salads-to-Go that are low in calories. The Caesar's Side, Deluxe Garden, Grilled Chicken, and Side Salad are all good choices, especially if you select Italian salad dressing with reduced fat and calories, the Hidden Valley Ranch with reduced fat and calories, or the Fat Free French. Any of these salad choices with dressing yield about 150 kilocalories, 10 grams of carbohydrate, 2 vegetable exchanges, and 1 medium-fat meat exchange. The exception is the Grilled Chicken Salad, which contributes 2 additional lean-meat exchanges.

So Wendy's actually offers plenty of choices, and we don't go away hungry. But we all agree that we have had enough of fast-food restaurants.

REMEMBER

No one should say that a person with diabetes can't go to this type of restaurant and remain on his or her nutritional plan. But there are many seductive and unhealthy choices. You need to plan in advance what you are going to choose. You can't go wrong if you stick to the selections that we talk about in this chapter.

Part IV
The Part of Tens

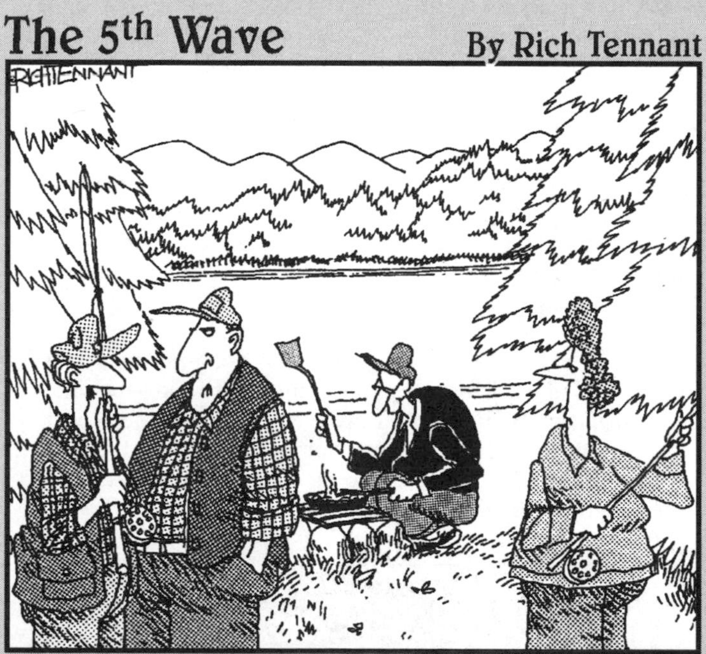

"Don't use that excuse on me, Wayne. Ain't no good reason why a man with diabetes can't help himself to some of Earl's fried mealworms."

In this part . . .

This part shows you that major improvements can arise from minor changes. It takes you through some basic steps to improve your diet, none especially difficult by themselves. You will realize the tremendous impact that substituting more healthful ingredients can have on your overall nutrition.

You can also find some essential techniques to normalize your blood glucose and thus prevent complications of diabetes. Many of these tips don't relate to diet, but approach blood glucose normalization from a general lifestyle perspective.

This part also offers information on managing the special problems of healthy eating for a child with diabetes. In this situation, you are not only trying to keep the blood glucose normal, but allow for normal growth and maturation. This balance requires some special considerations, and we try to offer them.

Chapter 19

Ten Simple Steps to Improve Your Diet

In This Chapter

- Keeping a food diary
- Avoiding missing a meal
- Using water for many purposes
- Cooking with half the fat
- Adding salt at the last minute
- Flavoring with condiments, herbs, and spices
- Including vegetables in all meals
- Sitting down for meals
- Stripping away fat wherever possible
- Cooking by the B's — braising, broiling, boiling, and barbecuing

Following a nutritional plan sometimes seems so complicated. But really, if you follow the few simple rules outlined in this chapter, you can make the process much easier. This chapter provides you with ten simple things you can do today. None of them cost anything other than time. Doing them one at a time makes a big difference in your calorie and fat intake. Adding one after another makes the results huge. Your weight, blood pressure, and blood glucose all fall. Who could ask for anything more?

Maintaining a Food Diary

Try this little diversion: For the next two days, write down everything you eat and drink. Before you go to bed on the evening of the second day, take a separate piece of paper and try to reconstruct what you have eaten for the past two days without looking at your original list. Then compare the two lists.

The differences in the lists will startle you. The point of this exercise is to show you that you are doing a lot of mindless eating. Trying to follow a nutritional plan from memory doesn't work.

A food diary not only shows you what you are eating all the time but also makes it easy to select items to reduce in portion size or eliminate altogether. When you go to your doctor, the fact that your diary lists birdseed for every meal helps confirm your statement that you eat like a bird.

You might even include something in your diary about how you are feeling and what you are doing. This information, besides turning your diary into a more personal statement, allows you to see the associations between your mood and your food. Keeping your exercise record in the diary makes it even more useful, reminding you of when you did (or did not) exercise.

Finally, your dietitian can easily plug your food intake into a computer program to analyze such valuable information as calorie breakdown, amount of salt, levels of saturated fat, and amount of cholesterol.

Eating Every Meal

When you miss meals, you become hungry. If you have type 1 diabetes, you can't safely miss meals, especially if you have given yourself regular or lispro insulin. Rather than letting yourself become hungry, eat your meals at regular times so that you don't overcompensate at the next meal (or at a snack shortly after the meal you missed) when you are suffering from low blood glucose. Many people overtreat low blood glucose by eating too many sugar calories, which results in high blood glucose later on.

WARNING!

You should not miss meals as a weight-loss method, particularly if you take a drug that lowers blood glucose into hypoglycemic levels. A pregnant woman with diabetes especially should not miss meals. She must make up for the fact that her baby extracts large amounts of glucose from her blood. Both mother and growing fetus are adversely affected if the mother's body must turn to stored fat for energy.

TIP

Eating smaller meals and having snacks in between is probably the best way to eat because doing so raises blood glucose the least, provides a constant source of energy, and allows control of the blood glucose using the least amount of external or internal insulin.

The fact is, following your complete nutritional plan in less than three meals is extremely difficult.

Drinking Water Throughout the Day

Seventy percent of your body is water, and all your many organs and cells require water to function properly. Most people, especially older people, do not get enough water. Older people often have the additional disadvantage of losing their ability to sense when they're thirsty. The consequences may include weakness and fatigue, not to mention constipation.

Water can replace all the sodas and juice drinks that add unwanted calories to your day. You soon lose your taste for those drinks and discover that you don't need (or miss) the aftertaste of soda and juice that you took for granted. Those drinks also raise the blood glucose very rapidly and are often used to treat low blood glucose.

One of our patients admitted to drinking 10 to 12 cans of cola drinks daily. He had a high blood glucose that returned to normal when he broke his cola habit.

Make drinking water a part of your daily habits. Drink some when you brush your teeth. Drink more with meals and snacks. Many people don't want to drink much water close to bedtime because if they do, they'll have to wake up to go to the bathroom — all the more reason to make sure you get your water ration, which should be at least eight 8-ounce glasses, early in the day.

Reducing Added Fat

If you use recipes that have been handed down in your family, they often contain much unnecessary added fat. The same can be said for recipes created by chefs who are not conscious of the harmful effects of high fat intake. We carefully selected the recipes in this book to minimize added fat. You should try to do the same thing when you cook.

Cooking food doesn't generally require the extra fat. We can remember when a pancake recipe required a cup of vegetable oil, but we now know that you can make delicious pancakes without all that oil. While vegetable oil is better for you than animal fats like lard and butter, it still has plenty of calories — in fact, as many as animal fats. A gram of fat contains 9 kilocalories, no matter the source.

Try reducing the suggested fat by 50 percent. See whether the taste suffers or if preparing the food is more difficult.

How much difference does reducing the fat make in terms of kilocalories? A cup of oil is 8 ounces, and each ounce is 28.35 grams. Because each gram has 9 kilocalories, a cup of oil contains about 2,000 kilocalories. You get rid of 1,000 kcalories by reducing the fat in half. If your recipe serves four people, each person is getting 250 kilocalories less fat. Is that a worthwhile reduction? You bet!

Chapter 20 is full of great substitutions.

Leaving Out the Salt

For reasons that are unclear to us, most Americans like a lot of salt in their food. Consequently, these people taste mostly salt and not much of the food. Try getting rid of the salt in your recipes. You can always add it later on if you miss the flavor that salt adds. At first, you may think that the food tastes bland. Then you will begin to discover the subtle tastes that were in the food all along but were overpowered by the salt.

Why do we emphasize cutting salt levels? We know that salt raises blood pressure. Recent studies, particularly the United Kingdom Prospective Diabetes Study, have shown that you can slow or prevent diabetic complications by reducing blood pressure.

You can try the approach of slowly removing salt from the recipe. If it calls for a teaspoon of salt, add only three-quarters of a teaspoon. You won't notice the difference. Next time, try half a teaspoon. And so on. In the recipes in this book, we have tried to use less salt wherever possible, with the permission of the chefs who created the recipes. Most chefs have been very open to eliminating salt.

Adding Taste with Condiments, Herbs, and Spices

This section explores a case of getting something for almost nothing. If you like a lot of distinctive flavors in your food, try using various condiments, herbs, and spices to replace the flavors of fat and salt. Experimenting with these flavors can bring entirely new tastes to old favorite recipes. Surely, the new millenium is all about breaking free from old habits of eating, which may not be so good for you, and replacing them with new tastes.

Many of the chefs in this book — who are some of the most renowned chefs in the world — have achieved their fame by virtue of their willingness to go in new taste directions. They have combined foods that no one put together before and used spices not traditionally used in foods from their particular ethnic origin. The result has been an explosion of new tastes combined with better nutrition.

Foods that you associate with bland taste, such as some fish, come alive when you add the right herbs and spices. You may never have liked those foods before, but you will now. Not only do they taste different, but they will smell wonderful and exotic. They have the additional advantage of being very good for you.

Examples of condiments that will add great taste and few calories are salsa, hot sauce, mustard, and horseradish. Herbs that add flavor include rosemary, thyme, basil, and many others. They are best added toward the end of cooking to preserve their flavor if fresh, or at the beginning of cooking to bring out their flavor if dried.

Using Vegetables Throughout the Day

What makes you think that you can use only broccoli as a side dish with your dinner meat or fish? How can you possibly get in your daily three to five servings of vegetables if you think like this? What would happen if you drank vegetable juice for breakfast? Suppose you added vegetables to an omelet? How about a salad at lunch instead of that large sandwich containing way too much carbohydrate?

You can find so many different kinds of vegetables in the grocery, yet most people limit themselves to very few of them. Your whole meal can consist of vegetables with a small amount of protein thrown in just as a garnish. Try a vegetarian restaurant to see for yourself how delicious freshly prepared vegetables can be.

We are not talking about the starchy vegetables like beans, peas, and lentils that really belong in the starch list of exchanges, but rather the vegetables that contain much less carbohydrate. These vegetables include asparagus, bok choy, green beans, cabbage, carrots, cauliflower, chard, collards, onions, summer squash, turnips, and water chestnuts.

Use these vegetables in meals and for snacks. They fill you up but add very few calories. Some are just as good when frozen and defrosted (because they are flash frozen immediately after picking) as they are when fresh. Especially good snack vegetables include baby carrots, cucumbers, and pieces of sweet pepper.

Sitting Down for Meals

Eating food with others is one of the pleasures of life. As an added advantage, it also slows the pace of your eating, which allows your brain to recognize when you are full so you stop eating at the appropriate time. By sitting down and eating more slowly, you slow the absorption of carbohydrates, thus slowing the rise in your blood glucose.

Another advantage of sitting down and eating with others is that the other people serve as a brake on how much you eat. When people eat alone, they tend to eat more. In the company of others, you are restrained by social controls. By eating while sitting at the table, you see only the food on the table. When you stand and eat, you can easily walk to the kitchen, where all the rest of the food is (if you're not there already).

You usually limit the food served at the table to what is on your plate, so you are not exposed to excessive food. You can make sure that the only foods brought to the table are acceptable food choices, especially if they are prepared as attractively as possible. A lot of your eating is done because the food looks so good, so make the right foods the best looking foods.

Removing the Attached Fat

Many foods, such as sausage and luncheon meats, contain so much fat that lowering their fat content isn't possible. You should mostly avoid these foods. But other protein sources such as chicken, steak, roast beef, and pork have large amounts of visible fat attached to them. Remove this fat before you prepare the food. In the case of poultry, removing the skin removes most of the fat. Selecting white meat rather than dark further reduces the fat in poultry.

As fat cooks on a barbecue, it often flames, which causes the meat to burn. Removing the fat before you cook it makes the cooking process safer (because the burning fat won't spray around), and the resulting meat is much lower in calories.

Cooking by the B's

The best methods of cooking all begin with a *b,* such as braising, broiling, boiling, and barbecuing. These methods of preparation don't add fat and often remove of a lot of the fat within the food. Broiling a hamburger, for example, often eliminates as much fat from a moderate-fat hamburger as buying a reduced-fat hamburger to begin with. Frying, sautéing, and other methods that depend upon butter or fat add exactly the things that you want to remove.

TIP

If you must use fat, use a spray that keeps added fat down.

Chapter 20

Ten Easy Substitutions in Your Eating Plan

In This Chapter

- Making better carbohydrate choices
- Replacing "bad" fats with "good" fats
- Switching from larger to smaller portions

One of your major weapons in your lifelong battle against complications of diabetes is your ability to choose. You can choose to exercise every day. You can choose to take your medications. Perhaps your most effective resource is your skill at making the right food choices. The consequences of choosing the right foods are immediate and enormous.

First, when you eat right, you feel better in general. Your body, like any complicated machine, prefers the correct fuel. Next, you notice more normal levels when you test your blood glucose. As a consequence of those more normal levels, you sleep better, you don't have to go to the bathroom as often, and your sexual activity benefits because you feel better. If you are a woman, your vaginal infections come to an end, which benefits both your general health and your sexual activity. In the long run, people of both sexes avoid the complications of diabetes, such as eye disease, kidney disease, and nerve disease.

You can achieve all of these benefits by making the correct food choices, if you have type 2 diabetes (see Chapter 1). With type 1 diabetes, you have other considerations, but good food choices are very important as well. Take a look at the suggestions in this chapter. None of them is especially difficult to follow. With these suggestions, you generally save money. You usually lose weight. Do you need any further incentives?

Choosing Fruits to Replace Sweets

Trading fruits for sweets may seem difficult if you eat in restaurants frequently, but it doesn't have to be. In Chapter 16, you find several delicious recipes created by chefs who understand the importance of offering a lower calorie, lower fat choice for dessert. These recipes usually consist of unique ways to prepare fruits or mix fruits together for a delicious new taste. Look for similar offerings on the menus of the restaurants you visit, and try the recipes from this book at home.

At home, of course, you're in charge. The tradition of offering a bowl of fresh fruit at the end of a meal seems to have disappeared in the United States, but you can revive it for your family and guests. You can find fresh fruit 12 months a year, although the choices are fewer in the winter months compared to the summer. You don't have to limit fruit to the role of replacing dessert at the end of a meal, either. Starting a meal with grapefruit or melon is a delicious substitute for a plate of pasta or some other higher calorie appetizer. Ending the meal with a delicious peach or some grapes or plums can be just as satisfying as that sugary, fatty pie, cake, or ice cream.

How do you benefit from this change? If you end your meal with a typical piece of carrot cake, you take in 339 kilocalories, consisting of 11 grams of fat and 56 grams of carbohydrate. A dessert you sometimes find in restaurants called Chocolate Decadence has 340 kilocalories, made up of 15 grams of fat and 51 grams of carbohydrate. Choose a sweet peach instead, and you get only 60 kilocalories, consisting of 15 grams of carbohydrate and no fat.

We don't want to put the dessert chefs out of business. They're some of the most creative people in the culinary arts. But just as the chefs who create the entrees have switched to much more nutritious main dishes, as shown in this book, dessert chefs should be able to use the abundance of fresh fruits to prepare wonderful desserts.

Adding Fiber to Your Diet

Choosing fruits as described in the preceding section has another benefit: Fruits contain fiber. Why is fiber so desirable, especially for the person with diabetes? Although fiber is a carbohydrate, you can't break it down into nutrients that add calories. Fiber has many benefits, but the most important are the following:

- Soluble fiber can dissolve in water and lower blood glucose and fat levels.
- Insoluble fiber stays in the intestine where it helps to prevent constipation and probably cancer of the colon.

The next question is, how do you get more fiber? Breakfast is the easiest place to make a change:

- Eat whole-grain bread in place of refined breads like white bread.
- Eat unrefined cereals like oats in place of processed cereal.
- Eat muffins made with fruit and whole grains.

You can add more fiber at other meals by choosing pasta instead of potatoes and higher fiber rice like basmati instead of white rice. Even among fruits, those from temperate climates, such as apples and plums, provide more fiber than hot climate fruits like bananas.

Making the Right Fat Selections

REMEMBER

Vegetable sources of fat are always more healthful than animal fats.

Animal fats belong to a group called the *saturated* fats, which raise cholesterol. You don't want to raise cholesterol. Some animal fats are actually cholesterol itself, such as the fat in the yolk of an egg. These fats should rarely appear in your diet.

Even among the vegetable fats, some are better and some are worse. The better ones (like olive oil and canola oil) don't raise cholesterol. The worse ones (like corn oil, cottonseed oil, palm oil, coconut oil, and margarine) lower the good cholesterol. You don't want to lower the good cholesterol.

REMEMBER

Whether you eat animal fat or vegetable fat, all fats contain an enormous 9 kilocalories per gram. Fat is an efficient way for your body to store excess energy. You want to limit your daily fat intake to 30 percent or less of your total calories.

Finding a Cow That Makes Lowfat Milk

You would think that if scientists can clone sheep and send a man to the moon, they could produce a cow that can make lowfat milk. Unfortunately, as far as anyone knows, getting cows to produce lowfat milk can't be done yet, so we'll have to continue extracting the fat after milking. In any case, you benefit from the lower fat. If you drink regular milk now, start withdrawing yourself from the fat by changing to 2 percent for a while, then to 1 percent, and you may even go as low as skim milk.

You may think that you could never stand to drink skim milk. After you have used it for a while, however, you'll find that regular milk tastes too creamy.

When you order your morning cafe latte, unless you specify lowfat milk, the server makes it with regular milk.

Does drinking skim milk or regular milk really make a difference? Do bees like nectar? If you lower your milk fat from regular to 2 percent, you go from 72 kilocalories of fat to 45. Moving down to skim milk, of course, eliminates even those 45 kilocalories of fat.

Other dairy products that you can eat in a lowfat form include hard cheeses like cheddar, as well as softer cheeses like cream cheese. Yogurt is another popular food that you can purchase in a lowfat version.

Lowfat doesn't necessarily mean low calorie. Ingenious food manufacturers have found ways to entice you to buy their lowfat foods by adding lots of carbohydrate (sweetener), so the calorie count may still be major. Read the label!

Catching Fresh Fish

You've had a long day, and you want to pick up something to make for dinner. You stop in front of the frozen foods and find a breaded frozen fish fillet. The instructions to prepare it are simple, so you put the box in your basket. Don't! Put the package back neatly on its shelf and head over to the fresh fish department.

You can purchase a nice 4-ounce piece of swordfish, tuna, salmon, or Mahi Mahi, broil it with herbs for 10 minutes or less, and end up with the right amount of protein and far less fat and carbohydrate calories. The breaded frozen fish is much too large for a single meal and has excess calories that you simply don't need.

Your broiled fish will taste better, too. Frozen fish just can't duplicate the taste of very fresh fish.

Spilling the Beans

You know that your muscles are made of protein, so naturally, when you think of protein, you think of meat. The time has come to recognize that protein comes from many sources, however. Vegetables have proteins, too, and they don't have the fat that the meats provide.

People have suggested that you can't eat only vegetable protein sources because they lack some of the building blocks required for muscle growth, and that you can find those building blocks only in animal protein. As always, an exception breaks that rule: the soybean. Soybeans contain all the different building blocks you need to build your own protein.

Even without soybeans, you can get all the building blocks you need by eating several different vegetable protein sources together, such as rice and beans or yogurt with chopped nuts.

The best non-meat sources of protein are legumes like dried beans and peas. Other protein sources include nuts and seeds, but these contain quite a bit of fat, so the calorie count swells. The following vegetable protein sources provide the equivalent of 1 ounce of animal protein:

- ½ cup of cooked dry beans
- ¼ cup of seeds (like sunflower seeds)
- ⅓ cup of nuts (like pecans and peanuts)
- ½ cup of baked beans
- ½ cup of tofu

Choosing the Least Fatty Meats

You are sick of beans, and your spouse spends more time finding new deodorants for the house than showering you with affection. You need real meat. At this point, you can make some very good choices that save you plenty of fat and calories.

If the cut of beef's name contains the word "round" or "loin," you are choosing a lower fat selection. Cuts from the leg also tend to have lower fat content. Examples are top sirloin, ground round, or top round and leg of lamb. For help in selecting lowfat meats, ask your butcher.

The difference between lean cuts and fatty cuts can be as much as 70 kilocalories per ounce. If you eat the higher fat meat, you get an extra 200 kilocalories or more, almost all of it in the form of saturated fat — the equivalent of 40 minutes of walking exercise.

REMEMBER

Poultry and wild game like pheasant, goose, and duck can also be lowfat meat alternatives, *if you remove the skin.*

Playing with Portions

Many restaurants offer the same food items as appetizers and main dishes. The fact is, the quantity served as an appetizer is generally the right amount of food for your nutritional plan, while the main dish may be twice as much or more. In addition, the main dish costs at least three times as much as the appetizer. So we heartily recommend that you order the appetizer for your main dish.

Some restaurants have a children's menu containing the same food as the main menu but in smaller portions. We know of no federal law that prohibits an adult from ordering off the children's menu. Never mind the annoyed facial expression of your server, who rapidly calculates the loss in tip.

If you have ever ordered a tasting menu in a restaurant, you know that you get a large number of different foods but very little of any of them. The chefs know that you don't need enormous quantities, but you do want the feeling that you're getting a lot. Your appetizer–main dish comes on a small plate and psychologically satisfies you.

One of our patients had dinner in a restaurant known for its large portions. Wisely, she shared a meal with her spouse. Unwisely, she felt that she could order a dessert since she had eaten so little of her main dish. She ordered a piece of pumpkin pie that was served, for some reason, on a large plate. Although the piece was enormous, she had the feeling that she had received only a small portion and went ahead and ate it all. Needless to say, her blood glucose suffered.

Snacking on Lowfat Foods

We encourage you to have snacks during the day to smooth out your glucose control and prevent coming to meals in a hungry state. Your choice of snacks can add a lot of calories, especially fat calories, or it can satisfy you without damaging your nutritional plan.

Instead of high fat potato chips, choose air-popped popcorn. Instead of a glass of apple juice, choose an apple. Other satisfying snacks that don't mess up your plan include three breadsticks, one matzo, three rice cakes, or five saltines.

You can really improve your snack satisfaction by using the microwave oven to warm or cook the snack. An apple in the microwave becomes a baked apple — somehow more delicious than a raw apple but no more caloric. Just make sure you don't also have a baked worm.

Finding Free Foods

With free foods, we aren't referring to foods that you can tuck into your shopping basket and expect to leave without paying. We mean foods that have so few calories that you can eat them and not have to list them in the food diary we propose in Chapter 13.

A long list of free foods exists, including the following:

- Black coffee, tea, club soda, sugar-free drinks, and bouillon
- Salad greens
- Sugar-free varieties of candy, gum, and jam for the regular candy, gum, and jam that is full of sugar
- Cranberries and rhubarb
- Cabbage, celery, cucumber, green onions, and mushrooms
- Seasonings and condiments (discussed in Chapter 13)

Enjoy these foods with meals, as snacks, or any way you want.

REMEMBER

These free foods have so few calories that they are useless as a treatment for low blood glucose.

Chapter 21

Ten Strategies to Normalize Your Blood Glucose

In This Chapter

- Knowing your blood glucose level
- Exercising down the glucose
- Taking medications as recommended
- Keeping a positive attitude
- Planning for unexpected situations
- Reacting immediately to foot problems
- Maintaining dental health
- Staying aware of new developments
- Using expert help
- Avoiding what doesn't work

In *Diabetes For Dummies*, Dr. Rubin describes the management of diabetes in detail. In this chapter, you find the highlights of that extensive discussion. While this book is about eating, controlling your blood glucose requires much more from you. Everything we suggest here is directed toward normalizing your blood glucose.

REMEMBER

Doctors consider your blood glucose *normal* when it is less than 110 mg/dl (6.1 mmol/L) if you have eaten nothing for 8 to 12 hours. If you have eaten, your blood glucose is normal if it is less than 140 mg/dl (7.8 mmol/L) 2 hours after eating. If you never see a blood glucose level over 140, you are doing very well, indeed. See Chapter 1 for a full explanation of mg/dl (milligrams per deciliter) and mmol/L (millimoles per liter).

You can use many tricks to achieve this level of control. In this chapter, you find the best of the lot. All of our patients can remember receiving and using some advice that made a huge difference in their life with diabetes. If you have a tip that you want to share, let us know at `mellital@ix.netcom.com`. We'll try to get it into the next edition of this book.

Knowing Your Blood Glucose

No excuse is adequate for you to not know your blood glucose at all times, although we've heard some pretty far-out excuses over the years — close to "The dog ate my glucose meter." The ability to measure blood glucose accurately and rapidly is the greatest advance in diabetes care since the discovery of insulin. Yet many people don't track their blood glucose.

Sure, sticking your finger hurts, but laser devices now make it painless, and even the needles are so fine that you barely feel them. How can you know what to do about your blood glucose if you don't know what it is in the first place?

The number of glucose meters you can choose is vast, and they are all good. Your insurance company may prefer one type of meter, or your doctor may have computer hardware and software for only one type. Other than those limitations, the choice is yours.

If you have very stable blood glucose levels, test once a day — some days in the morning before breakfast, other days in the evening before supper. Varying the time of day you test your blood glucose gives you and your doctor a picture of your control under different circumstances. If your diabetes requires insulin or is unstable, you need to test at least before meals and at bedtime in order to select your insulin dose.

Using Exercise to Control Your Glucose

When people are asked how much exercise they do, about a third say that they do nothing at all. If you are a person with diabetes and consider yourself a part of that group, you aren't taking advantage of a major tool — not just for controlling your blood glucose, but for improving your physical and mental state in general.

Don't think that exercise means hours of exhaustion followed by a period of recovery. We're talking about a brisk walk, lasting no more than 20 to 30 minutes, every day. If you want to do more, that's fine, but just about anyone can do this much. People who can't walk for some reason can get their exercise by moving their arms.

A few of the benefits of exercise include

- Lowers the blood glucose by using it for energy
- Helps with weight loss
- Lowers bad cholesterol and triglyceride fats and raises good cholesterol
- Lowers blood pressure

- Reduces stress levels
- Reduces the need for drugs and insulin shots

When we see a new person with diabetes, we give him or her a bottle of pills. These pills are not to be taken by mouth; they're to be spilled on the floor and picked up every day. It's our way of making sure that a new patient gets at least a little exercise every day.

Taking Your Medications

You have the advantage of having some of the best drugs for diabetes available to you, which was not true as recently as five years ago. A few years ago, as specialists in diabetes, we struggled to keep our patients in good control to avoid complications of diabetes. Now, with the right combination of medications (and by using some of the other tools in this chapter), just about any patient can achieve excellent control. But no medication works if you don't take it.

The word *compliance* applies here. Compliance refers to the willingness of people to follow instructions — specifically, taking their medications. People tend to be very compliant at the beginning of treatment but, as they improve, compliance falls off. Diabetic control falls off along with it.

The fact is, as you get older the forces that contribute to a worsening of your blood glucose tend to get stronger. You want to do all you can to reverse that tendency. Taking your medications is an essential part of your overall program.

Maintaining a Positive Attitude

Your mental approach to your diabetes plays a major role in determining your success in controlling the disease. Think of diabetes as a challenge — like high school math or asking out your first date. As you overcome challenges in one area of your life, the skills you learn are available to other areas. Looking at something as a challenge allows you to use all your creativity.

When you approach something with pessimism and negativity, you tend to not see all the possible ways you can succeed. You may take the attitude that "It doesn't matter what I do." That attitude leads to failure to take medications, failure to eat properly, failure to exercise, and so forth.

REMEMBER

Simply understanding the workings of your body, which comes with treating your diabetes, probably makes you more healthy than the couch potato who understands little more than the most recent sitcom.

Planning for the Unexpected

Life is full of surprises — like when you were told you have diabetes. You were probably not ready to hear that news. But you can make yourself ready to deal with surprises that may damage your glucose control.

Most of those surprises have to do with food. You may be offered the wrong kind of food, too much food, too little food, or the timing of food does not correspond to the requirements of your medication. You need to have plans for all these situations before they occur.

You can always reduce your portions when the food is the wrong kind or excessive, and you can carry portable calories (like glucose tablets) when food is insufficient or delayed.

Other surprises have to do with your medication, like leaving it in your luggage — which is on its way to Europe while you are headed to Hawaii. Again, your ability to think ahead should prevent this from ever occurring.

Not everything is going to go right all the time. However, you can minimize the damage by planning ahead.

Seeking Immediate Help for Foot Problems

One error that leads to a lot of grief in diabetes is failure to seek immediate help for any foot problems. Your doctor may see you and examine your feet only once in two or three months. You need to look at your feet every day. At the first sign of any skin breakdown or other abnormality (such as discoloration), you must see your doctor. In diabetes, foot problems can go from minor to major in a very brief time. We don't pull punches in this area because it is so important — major problems may mean amputation of toes or more.

You can reverse most foot problems, if you catch and treat them early. You may require a different shoe or need to keep weight off the foot for a time — minor inconveniences compared to an amputation.

Things you can do besides inspecting your feet every day include

- Testing bath water with your hands to check its temperature, because numb feet can't sense if the water is scalding hot
- Ensuring that nothing is inside your shoe before you put it on
- Wearing new shoes only a short time before checking for damage

Brushing Off Dental Problems

Keeping your teeth in excellent condition is important for anyone, but especially if you have diabetes. "Excellent condition" means brushing them twice a day and using dental floss at the end of the day to reach where the toothbrush never goes. It also means visits to the dentist on a regular basis for cleaning and examination.

We have seen many people with diabetes have dental problems as a result of poor dental hygiene. As a side effect, controlling the blood glucose is much harder. After patients cure their teeth, they require much less medication.

People with diabetes don't have more cavities than non-diabetics, but they do have more gum disease if their glucose isn't under control. Gum disease results from the high glucose that bathes the mouth — a perfect medium for bacteria. Keeping your glucose under control helps you avoid losing teeth as a result of gum disease, as well as the further deterioration in glucose control.

Becoming Aware of New Developments

The pace of new discoveries in diabetes is so rapid that keeping on top of the field is difficult even for us, the experts. How much more difficult must it be for you? You don't have access to all the publications, the drug company representatives, and the medical journals that we see every day.

You can keep current in a number of ways. Begin by taking a course in diabetes from a certified diabetes educator. Such a course gives you a basis for a future understanding of advances in diabetes. Get a copy of Dr. Rubin's book *Diabetes For Dummies*, which explains every aspect of diabetes for the nonprofessional. Join a diabetes organization, particularly the American Diabetes Association, which you can find on the Internet at `www.diabetes.org`. You will start to receive their excellent publication, *Diabetes Forecast*, in the mail, which often contains the cutting edge of diabetes research as well as available treatments. Finally, don't hesitate to question your doctor or ask to see a diabetes specialist if your doctor's answers don't satisfy you.

The cure for diabetes may be in next week's newspaper. Give yourself every opportunity to find and understand it.

Utilizing the Experts

The available knowledge about diabetes is huge and growing rapidly. Fortunately, you can turn to multiple people for help. You should take advantage of all of them at one time or another, including the following people:

- Your primary physician, who takes care of diabetes and all your other medical concerns
- A diabetes specialist, who is aware of the latest and greatest in diabetes treatment
- An eye doctor, who must examine you at least once a year
- A foot doctor, to trim your toenails and treat foot problems
- A dietitian, to help you plan your nutritional program
- A diabetes educator, to teach you a basic understanding of this disease
- A pharmacist, who can help you understand your medications
- A mental health worker, if you run into adjustment problems

Take advantage of any or all of these people when you need them. Your insurance company is enlightened enough to pay for them if you use them.

Avoiding What Doesn't Work

Not wasting your time and money on worthless treatments is important. When you consider the almost 20 million people with diabetes in the United States alone, they provide a huge potential market for people with "the latest wonder cure for diabetes." Before you waste your money, check out the claims of these crooks with your diabetes experts.

You can find plenty of treatments for diabetes on the Internet. One way you can be sure that the claims are based on science is to look for verification from the Health on the Net Foundation, which you can find at `www.hon.ch/HomePage/Home-Page.html`. Their stamp of approval means the site adheres to principles that every legitimate scientist agrees with. One place you can be sure that the information is accurate is at Dr. Rubin's Web page at `www.drrubin.com`. He has provided the addresses of the best sites on the Internet for diabetes information, and you can click on those sites from his page.

REMEMBER

Don't make any substantial changes in your diabetes management without first discussing them with your physician.

Chapter 22

Ten Tactics for Teaching Children with Diabetes Healthy Eating Habits

In This Chapter

- Setting an example
- Teaching eating skills
- Using outside resources

An epidemic of excessive weight and obesity has taken hold among children, resulting in more type 2 diabetes in children than ever before. Several factors are responsible for this epidemic, including

- Consuming high fat foods
- Drinking large amounts of high calorie fruit drinks and other caloric beverages
- Increasing time spent in front of the TV and the computer and not exercising

Children pay a high price for their overweight condition in the form of low self-esteem and less acceptance by their peers, not to mention the risk of developing type 2 diabetes.

For overweight children, the old joke about being too short for your weight really is true. Children often grow out of their overweight condition. As a parent, your job is to help them maintain their weight until they grow older and taller, not necessarily to help them lose weight.

This chapter describes how you can help your child with diabetes to achieve healthy eating habits. You are an enormous force in your child's life and can do a great deal, as he or she grows up, to create a person with a life of quality as well as quantity.

Setting an Example

Children resemble their parents not just because of the physical resemblance but also because children pick up their parents' mannerisms. Your children are constantly studying you. They follow the example you set with your eating. If they observe you overeating and dieting, they assume that is the appropriate way to eat.

You set a dietary example by eating the same foods that you want your child to eat. You set an example by keeping the quantities of food you eat moderate and by choosing food that is low in fat and salt and high in fiber. You set an example when your child observes that exercise is a part of your daily routine.

Involving Children in Food Preparation

When you ask children to describe their earliest memories, they often talk happily about helping their grandmother make some kind of food. Many of the chefs in this book began cooking by their grandmother's or mother's side.

Preparing food together can be a great bonding experience between you and your child, which also provides you with the opportunity to teach good nutrition. If you follow a recipe and tell your child to measure half the fat listed in the recipe or to leave out the salt altogether, that lesson stays with the child for life.

Have your child create his or her own nutrition plan for a day and discuss every part of it, pointing out what is carbohydrate, protein, and fat, the balance among those foods, and how they affect his or her diabetes. Use the food guide pyramid (see Chapter 2 for more information on the food guide pyramid) or the child's nutrition plan as a guide for planning.

Engaging Children in Shopping

Taking your child to the market is a great opportunity to teach good food-buying habits. Let your child read the nutrition labels (see Chapter 5 for a full explanation of nutrition labels) and explain to him or her what each type of nutrient means. Point out that you're looking for foods low in total fat, saturated fat, cholesterol, and salt. Have your child compare carbohydrate and protein content of foods as well as the other substances named on the label, especially fiber but also calcium, iron, vitamin A, and vitamin C. Explain how each of these substances plays a part in their nutrition. Let your child look at labels together, like those on a bottle of fruit drink compared with a container of lowfat milk. Or compare regular and lowfat milk.

If you purchase foods without labels (like fresh fruits and vegetables), be prepared to explain the contents of those foods. Create a food basket that mirrors the government food pyramid so your child can see the amounts of each food group that should make up a diet.

Teach your child how the market entices you to buy high calorie, low nutrition food, especially at the checkout counter where you don't have time to change your mind and put it back. (Look for more information on this topic in Chapter 5.)

Ensuring Good Restaurant Eating

If you eat at fast-food places with your kids, review Chapter 18 so that you are prepared to point out the best selections on the menu. If the foods for the restaurant you frequent are not in the chapter, find out where you can get nutritional information. To find this information, you can visit the fast-food company's Web site or you can write to the company if you get the address at the fast-food restaurant that you go to. Alternately, publications exist that list the food in these restaurants with their nutrient content.

If you go to individual restaurants, encourage your child to find out what is in the food he or she orders. Considering what you pay for the food, you are entitled to know what you're getting. Point out the fact that portions, even children's portions, are usually too large. Set an example in the restaurant by ordering appetizers rather than main dishes or taking half of your food home.

WARNING!

Don't tell your child how much time to take to eat — that is a decision best left to your child, who knows when he or she is full. If your child leaves food on the plate, don't point out that starving people in some remote country would love to get their hands on the leftovers. Don't try to regulate your child's food intake by telling him or her to stop eating or to keep eating. Rather, set an example by stopping when you know you have had enough. If your child has type 1 diabetes, discuss the need for enough carbohydrate at each meal.

Missing No Meals

Your child must know that missing meals is not appropriate for many reasons. If he has type 1 diabetes, a missed meal is a fairly certain prelude to a *hypoglycemic* (low blood glucose) reaction. Breakfast is especially important because he or she is going from the fasting (sleeping) state, when energy needs are minimal, to the state of activity, when calories are essential. Your school-age child will have trouble with morning classes when no food energy is available.

A second problem associated with a missed meal is the extreme feeling of hunger that leads to overcompensating during the next meal. Overeating at that meal can make your child go from low to very high blood glucose very rapidly.

Finally, the lesson that your child receives when he or she misses meals is that irregular eating is acceptable. The best way to encourage weight control is to teach regular eating of smaller meals and snacks, which is a program that anyone can follow for life and be fairly certain of getting good, balanced nutrition. After the initial weight loss, people rarely continue to succeed when their weight loss program calls for missing meals.

Involving the Child with the Dietitian

The dietary needs of growing children are complicated enough, but when you factor in diabetes as well, the situation may be beyond the knowledge of a parent. When you feel overwhelmed, call on the dietitian, but always with the child present. A nutritional plan for diabetes is not something you impose upon your child, but something you work out together with your child.

You and the dietitian must take your child's food preferences into consideration. If you don't, your child will not likely follow any plan that you devise with the dietitian.

Keeping Problem Foods Out of Sight and Good Foods in Easy View

If potato chips or creamy cookies sit on the kitchen counter, can you blame your child (or yourself) for grabbing a handful every time he or she goes by? Don't buy these foods in the first place, but if you do, keep them out of sight. You know what happens when you walk up to a buffet table. You can more easily avoid what you don't see.

On the other hand, keep fruits and vegetables in plain sight, along with other acceptable snacks like air-popped popcorn. Having a special device for drinking water is a good idea, too, because it makes water into something special and, therefore, more desirable. Even having a pitcher of water in the refrigerator beats going to the sink, where the association is with washing hands and dishes rather than nutrition.

Again, your child follows your example. If you raid the freezer for ice cream, don't be surprised to see your child do the same thing. The great benefit to you when you set an example for your child is the excellent nutrition that you get.

Monitoring TV Food Ads with Your Child

Like it or not, your child spends a certain amount of time in front of the television every day. The ads that he or she views are most likely for high calorie, high sugar, high fat snack foods. Sitting with your child for some of the viewing time and discussing the nutritional content of the food is important and valuable. Even if you keep that kind of food out of your food basket and your house, your child will eventually go to a friend's home and find that food.

If you have discussed the food in advance, your child is in a position to turn it down or at least to know how eating it affects his or her nutritional plan. You should not expect your child to be perfect with food at home or away. Are you? We confess that we sometimes stray from perfect eating ourselves.

Your child should learn from poor food choices by seeing the effect upon his or her blood glucose. Such an observation may be enough to prevent your child from making that particular choice again. On the other hand, you never want to nag your child about eating off the nutritional plan. Rather, you should accept the misstep and tell the child to move back to appropriate eating with the next meal.

Utilizing the Experts

You can make use of expert advice to help with your child's nutrition. The American Diabetes Association and the Juvenile Diabetes Foundation both offer plenty of food-related materials, as do many other organizations. They can be found through Dr. Rubin's Web page at `www.drrubin.com`.

Probably one of the most valuable resources is the American Dietetic Association, which also has a Web site (available through Dr. Rubin's site). They can provide nutrition plans, recipes, nutritional analysis of foods, and other useful information.

Teaching the Meaning of Portions

Your child has no more idea of the meaning of portions than you did before you read this book. In Chapter 1 we show you how to recognize a portion of various kinds of foods. Teach this information to your child so that he or she can readily select the amount of food that corresponds with a portion. Thinking in terms of a tennis ball representing a medium fruit or a domino representing an ounce of cheese is much easier for a child than thinking in terms of measurements. These terms also introduce a certain amount of fun in the process of selecting how much to eat.

Part V
Appendixes

"Well, yes, my blood sugar is a little low..."

In this part . . .

In Appendix A, you can read about the great restaurants that contributed recipes to this cookbook.

Appendix B shows you how to use diabetic exchanges to figure out a proper diabetic diet. The exchanges help you know what and how much food should be eaten to maintain normal weight and normal blood glucose levels, the key to prevention of diabetes complications.

Appendix C is a cooking glossary that defines terms that you find in this book.

Appendix D offers a handy list of weights and measures so you can convert any quantity in a recipe to another system of measurement.

Appendix E shows you where you can find great recipes for a person with diabetes, both in books and on the Internet.

Appendix A
Restaurant Descriptions

After you have had a chance to look over and try some of the wonderful dishes in this book, you will never again think that people with diabetes can't enjoy terrific meals. The chefs who have contributed these recipes are health- and nutrition-conscious, and you will probably be able to find other choices on their menus that also will fit your nutritional plan very well. However, note that we have tried to reduce calories by reducing fat and sugar intake as much as possible — with the agreement of the chefs — as well as keeping salt intake on the low side.

The meal you receive in the restaurant may not be exactly what you find here, especially because chefs change often; also, chefs sometimes cook for 100 or more people, and their measurements may not be exact every time. Most food must be prepared rapidly in a restaurant and not the same way. You will also receive a portion that is generally too large, so be prepared to take some home.

The restaurants that contributed recipes for this book are all fine restaurants that have been given the stamp of approval by various testing organizations. You will not be disappointed no matter what you eat in these establishments, but the calories and the distribution of carbohydrates, protein, and fat may not fit your nutritional plan perfectly. You need to adjust other meals and snacks to get your overall nutrition plan to conform to the guidelines for a full day (see Chapter 2).

The difficulty of preparation for the recipes in this book varies greatly. For a couple of reasons, we have included some recipes that are more labor-intensive and time-intensive than usual. First, many of you are excellent cooks and will try these recipes despite the difficulties because they are delicious and worth the time. Second, even if you choose not to try specific recipes, you'll find wonderful tips about foods and techniques to incorporate into whatever you cook. Third, you'll get an idea of what goes into the magical foods that our fine restaurants are turning out, and you can choose to order that dish if you go to that restaurant. Whatever your pleasure, bon appétit!

Restaurant Descriptions

The following sections introduce the restaurants in this book and the recipes they contributed. Each establishment offers innovative cuisine and a quality dining atmosphere.

Anasazi Restaurant

113 Washington Avenue, Santa Fe, New Mexico, 505-988-3030

Anasazi Restaurant, the restaurant of the Inn of the Anasazi in Santa Fe, New Mexico, serves culinary legacies of the Southwest featuring Native American, northern New Mexico, and American cowboy cuisine. Dishes are made with naturally healthy ingredients, including locally grown organic produce. This cuisine, along with the restaurant's décor and service, has earned Anasazi numerous awards, including the Condé Nast Traveler Gold List Award and the Mobil Four Star Award for 1999, as well as recognition by the *ZAGAT Survey* as one of America's top restaurants.

Executive chef Randall J. Warder began working in restaurants in Birmingham, Michigan, at the age of 14. He received formal training at Michigan State University and the University of Texas at Dallas, but obtained most of his skills on the job, particularly at the famous Mansion on Turtle Creek in Dallas. He is passionate about the flavors of the American Southwest. He loves to experiment with new combinations of ingredients and seasonings.

Anasazi Restaurant contributed the following recipes for this book:

- Wild Mushroom Tacos (Chapter 7)
- Black Bean Soup with Salsa Mexicana (Chapter 10)
- Cowboy Shrimp with Jalapeño Cornsticks (Chapter 12)
- Cheese-Stuffed Beef Tenderloin with Charred Tomato Poblano Sauce (Chapter 14)

Anthony's Fish Grotto

1360 Harbor Drive, San Diego, California, 619-232-5103

Anthony's Fish Grotto has been serving fresh seafood in San Diego County since 1946. It is a family-owned business that purchases only the highest quality fish and shellfish. The fish is hand-filleted and portioned by weight. Anthony's serves the largest variety of fresh seafood in Southern California, with a list of seasonal catches that changes daily. Anthony's scrumptious appetizers, Mama Ghio's famous Clam Chowders, crisp seafood salads, and delicious entrees delight more than 100,000 guests annually in the four Fish Grotto locations around San Diego. Anthony's prides itself on its ability to accommodate guests with special dietary needs, so a person with diabetes should find no trouble eating a wonderful meal at Anthony's establishment.

Anthony's Fish Grotto contributed the following recipes to this book:

- Field Greens with Bay Shrimp (Chapter 9)
- Greek Salad with Swordfish (Chapter 9)
- Panko Sautéed Alaskan Cod (Chapter 12)

Aquavit

13 West 54th Street, New York, New York, 212-307-7311

Aquavit was opened in 1987 by Hakan Swahn, who had a simple mission: to serve the finest Swedish cuisine available. The overwhelming success of the restaurant from the beginning is clear proof that he has succeeded. Located in a former Rockefeller family brownstone, the restaurant is understated on the outside and grand on the inside. A bar near the entrance provides samples of traditional Swedish appetizers, accompanied by one of several flavored *aquavits,* an icy neutral spirit from which the restaurant derives its name. The Atrium dining room creates the feeling of a Scandinavian forest glade with its white birch trees and fountain.

Only 28 years old, executive chef Marcus Samuelsson already has more accolades than most chefs receive in a lifetime, including Best Rising Star Chef in 1999 from the James Beard Foundation and an award as one of the Great Chefs of America from the Culinary Institute of America. Born in Ethiopia, he was adopted by a Swedish couple and raised in Sweden, where his grandmother taught him to cook from age 6. He studied at the Culinary Institute in Goteborg, coming to Aquavit in 1994. His approach is to combine traditional Swedish cuisine with his modern innovations. As he says, "I want to ensure that each guest has the ultimate three-star experience and leaves Aquavit feeling like they've taken a little trip to Scandinavia without leaving New York."

Aquavit contributed these recipes to this book:

- Cold Poached Salmon with Fresh Fruit Chutney and Herb Sauce (Chapter 12)
- Roasted Chicken with Spiced Apples (Chapter 13)
- Yogurt Rice (Chapter 13)
- Sautéed Breast of Chicken with Smoke-Flavored Tomato Sauce and Grilled Spring Vegetables (Chapter 13)

Barbetta

321 West 46th Street, New York, New York, 212-246-9171

Barbetta is the oldest restaurant in New York still run by its founding family. It was started in 1906 by Sebastiano Maioglio, the father of the current owner, Laura Maioglio. Laura has transformed her restaurant into New York's first truly elegant Italian dining destination. Located in the middle of the theater district, it has an enchanting outdoor garden for warm-weather dining. Just as Laura is responsible for the beautiful décor of the restaurant, she is very involved in the kitchen, and all the recipes featured in this book reflect her taste. She has worked with many different chefs over the years to create a cuisine that is true to the flavors of Italy, particularly the area of Piemonte, the northwestern region. It is an award-winning cuisine, achieving awards such as four stars in the *Mobil Travel Guide* and the maximum one star from Fodor. Good nutrition is important to Laura Maioglio, and the following recipes from Barbetta confirm her focus on health (Laura developed the dessert recipe, Red Fruit Soup, with her pastry chef, Alvaro Ojeda):

- Pumpkin Soup (Chapter 8)
- Red Fruit Soup (Chapter 8)
- Cool Minestrone Soup (Minestrone Freddo) (Chapter 10)
- Braised Fennel (Finocchio) (Chapter 11)
- Tagliarini alla Primavera (Chapter 11)
- Squab alla Piemontese (Chapter 13)

Cafe Allegro

1815 West 39th Street, Kansas City, Missouri, 816-561-3663

Cafe Allegro is an intimate bistro-style restaurant located in the heart of the chic 39th Street dining district of Kansas City. It has exposed brick walls, warm mahogany accents, and an eclectic art collection that together create a casually elegant atmosphere and a warm dining experience. The restaurant emphasizes contemporary seasonal cuisine and an extensive collection of world-class wines and liqueurs. The establishment is the creation of chef/owner Stephen Cole, who learned his skills both in fine restaurants and in business administration at the University of Denver.

Chef de cuisine Ted Habiger was hired by Stephen Cole in 1995 and rapidly assimilated all the skills needed to keep Cafe Allegro in its number-one ranking in Kansas City, according to the *ZAGAT Survey*. Habiger personally chooses the finest organic produce available in the local markets and turns them into the delicious specials served that evening. With Stephen Cole, he makes certain that his guests are fully aware of what they are about to eat and that the food is not only delicious but low in saturated fat and calories. These are the recipes from Cafe Allegro:

- Roasted Butternut Squash Soup (Chapter 8)
- Farmer Tomato Gazpacho (Chapter 8)
- Braised Leek and Shiitake Hot and Sour Soup (Chapter 8)
- Wild Mushroom Broth (Chapter 8)
- Snapper Veracruzana (Chapter 12)
- Grilled Black Grouper with Middle Eastern Couscous (Chapter 12)
- Truffled Wild Mushroom Gravy (Chapter 14)

Capitol Grill

In the Westin Hermitage Hotel, 231 6th Avenue North, Nashville, Tennessee, 615-345-7116

Capitol Grill is located in the historic Hermitage Hotel, the oldest Grand Hotel in Nashville. The hotel was built in 1916. Executive chef Perry Seal, who has worked there since 1996, runs the restaurant. Chef Seal is a Vermont native who graduated from the New England Culinary Institute's advanced placement program in 1993. He began his restaurant cooking in Williamsburg, Virginia, as a pastry chef, and then returned to Vermont to become executive chef at the Capitol Plaza Hotel in Montpelier. He was asked to come to work at the Café Milano in Nashville and finally chosen for his current position a few years later.

The Capitol Grill contributed the following recipe to this book:

- Char-Grilled Double-Cut Pork Chop with Black-Eyed Pea Relish and Sweet Potato Fries (Chapter 14)

Erna's Elderberry House

48688 Victoria Lane, Oakhurst, California, 559-683-6800

Erna Kubin-Clanin — owner of The Estate by the Elderberries and its restaurant, the Elderberry House, as well as chef in the restaurant — says she has a simple philosophy: "I have the simplest of tastes; I want only the best." Opened in 1984, the restaurant was patterned after Erna's love for the French countryside of Provence. Since its opening, it has garnered numerous awards for its culinary achievements, including the Mobil Five Star Award and the highest rating from the *ZAGAT Survey* as one of America's top restaurants.

At the age of 30, Executive chef James Overbaugh already has more than 15 years of culinary experience. He graduated from the Culinary Institute of America in Hyde Park, New York, in 1989 and has rapidly ascended the culinary ladder to his current position. Together with Erna, James produces six new *prix fixe* dinners (complete meals at a set price) every night. The fame of the restaurant is enhanced by the cooking school, which has been teaching the finest culinary skills for over 15 years.

Erna's contributed the following recipe to this book:

- Carrot Soup with Leek and Blood Orange (Chapter 8)

Hamersley's Bistro

553 Tremont Street, Boston, Massachusetts, 617-423-2700

Hamersley's Bistro has consistently been ranked among the best restaurants in Boston by such varied observers as *Boston Magazine, Food and Wine, Gourmet,* and *The New York Times.* The *ZAGAT Survey* also ranks Hamersley's as one of Boston's top restaurants year after year. The restaurant features the freshest seasonal New England ingredients to create both traditional and French inspired food, as well as contemporary American bistro fare.

Chef and owner Gordon Hamersley began to cook in Boston while he was a university student. He moved to Los Angeles, where Wolfgang Puck helped him hone his skills as a chef, and then went to France to learn the intricacies of French cooking. Returning to Boston, Gordon and his wife, Fiona, opened a small version of Hamersley's Bistro, but the restaurant's rapid success forced them to look for a larger space. They settled at their current address, and Hamersley's has been winning awards ever since. Among them are *Food and Wine's* Ten Best New Chefs of 1988, the James Beard Award: Best Chef Northeast, and a four-star rating from *The Boston Globe.* Gordon loves to produce hearty dishes but is very conscious of the nutritional value of the food he prepares. He teaches his skills in cooking classes at Boston University and around the country.

Here are the recipes contributed by Hamersley's:

- Salad of Smoked Salmon with Horseradish Dressing (Chapter 7)
- Zucchini Soup with Herbs and Spices (Chapter 8)
- Grilled Lobster with Green Bean, Corn, and Tomato Salad (Chapter 9)
- Cabbage, Bean and Bacon Soup (Chapter 10)
- Gordon Hamersley's Hearty Lentil Soup (Chapter 10)
- Roast Chicken with Red Onions and Potatoes (Chapter 13)
- Grilled Beef Tenderloin with Spicy Balsamic Vinaigrette (Chapter 14)

Heartbeat

149 East 49th Street, New York, New York, 212-407-2900

Located in the stylish W New York Hotel at 541 Lexington Avenue at 49th Street, Heartbeat offers an innovative menu that reflects the hotel's philosophy of balance and well-being. Renowned Executive Chef Michel Nischan has put together a menu that focuses on accenting the natural flavors of food. To achieve this objective, Heartbeat shuns the use of butter and heavy dairy products, which mask food's natural flavors.

Michel Nischan came to his role as Executive Chef after serving as Corporate Consulting Chef for famed restaurateur Drew Nieporent's Myriad Restaurant Group, where he was responsible for overseeing some of their most respected restaurants. Additionally, he owned the highly acclaimed Miche Mache, where he was named "the best chef in Connecticut" by *Connecticut Magazine*.

Heartbeat contributed the following recipes to this book:

- Simple Green Salad with Citrus and Herbs (Chapter 9)
- Carmelized Cauliflower (Chapter 11)

Moose's

1652 Stockton Street, San Francisco, California, 415-989-7800

Whenever a list of the best restaurants in San Francisco is prepared, Moose's is usually at or near the top. Proprietors Mary Etta and Ed Moose are San Francisco originals who combine an appreciation for fine food and a lively bar with backgrounds in theater, journalism, and politics. The result is a refuge for clientele ranging from North Beach neighbors and Bay Area power brokers to national media players.

The food is the responsibility of executive chef and managing partner Brian Whitmer. His extensive background includes Montrachet in Manhattan and the Highlands Inn in Carmel, but his Sicilian grandmother is his real inspiration. *Esquire* magazine has called him "One of America's finest chefs." He seems to sense what people want to eat and is able to give it to them in a uniquely beautiful and delectable form.

Moose's contributed the following recipes to this book:

- Cappellini with Moose's Winter Tomato Sauce (Chapter 10)
- Moose's Barbecued Tuna (Chapter 12)
- Moose's Coddled Wild King Salmon (Chapter 12)
- Moose's Moroccan Spiced Swordfish Sandwich (Chapter 15)

Osteria Del Mondo

1028 East Juneau Avenue, Milwaukee, Wisconsin, 414-291-3770

Osteria del Mondo means "the gathering place of the world." It specializes in authentic regional Italian cuisine. It has been garnering praise since it was opened in 1994 by chef/owner Marc Bianchini. It is consistently listed as one of the top 25 restaurants in Milwaukee by local food critics and was rated one of the top five in the state by the *ZAGAT Survey* in 1998.

Marc Bianchini, only 29 years of age, has the resume of a chef many years older. He graduated with honors from the Culinary Institute of America in 1990 and spent the next several years in Italy at the finest restaurants there, followed by more on-the-job training at fine restaurants in New York City. He went to Chicago and enjoyed the Midwest so much that he decided to stay and open Osteria in Milwaukee. His cuisine reflects the great training he has enjoyed.

Osteria Del Mondo contributed these recipes to this book:

- Chicken Salad with Gorgonzola Mayonnaise and Walnuts (Chapter 9)
- Basil and Onion Pea Soup (Chapter 10)

Papillon Café

250 Josephine, Denver, Colorado, 303-333-7166

Opened in 1995, Papillon Café was immediately greeted by stunning reviews. The restaurant features the finest French cooking because the chef and owner, Radek Cerny, learned his craft from some of the great French chefs. Amazingly, Radek comes from Czechoslovakia, but left there to work in some of the best restaurants of Italy and France. After leaving Europe he went to Denver, Colorado, where he established himself as one of the most creative chefs in the city, winning numerous awards and the most important award of all, a dedicated and consistent clientele. He opened a series of restaurants where the emphasis has always been on the highest quality cooking and the most elaborate presentations in a very pleasant setting, with a focus on service.

Papillon Café provided these recipes for this book:

- Black Olive Pesto (Tapenade) (Chapter 7)
- Spicy Eggplant Tomato Sauce (Chapter 10)
- Shrimp Cakes (Chapter 15)
- Feta Bruschetta (Chapter 15)

The Dining Room at the Ritz-Carlton, San Francisco

500 Stockton at California, San Francisco, California, 415-296-7465

The Dining Room at the Ritz-Carlton, San Francisco, offers great cuisine in a setting that has won numerous awards for elegant dining and fine service. It receives the highest ratings from the *ZAGAT Survey* and many others year after year. The American Automobile Association has given it the highest Five Diamond Award for the last three years in a row. *Gourmet* magazine has given it the Top Table in San Francisco Award for the last two years along with its #1 award for Top Authentic Local Cuisine and its #4 award for Tops for Elegant Dining.

Chef Sylvain Portay is no stranger to awards for his masterful cooking. In Monte Carlo he teamed with Alain Ducasse to earn a three-star Michelin rating for Le Louis XV restaurant, and then he went to Le Cirque for four years before coming to the Ritz-Carlton. He prepares dinner only and emphasizes the freshest of ingredients and local produce.

The Dining Room at the Ritz-Carlton contributed the following recipe for this book:

- Riviera Salad (Chapter 9)

Spiaggia

One Magnificent Mile, 980 North Michigan Avenue, Chicago, Illinois, 312-280-2750

In its 15th year as the premier Italian restaurant of Chicago, Spiaggia has undergone a dramatic renovation to its dining room, with its spectacular views of Lake Michigan. Over the years, the restaurant has won all the major culinary awards including America's Top Tables Award from *Gourmet* magazine, the Distinguished Restaurants of North America Award, and recently, the Insegna del Ristorante del Mondo from the president of Italy.

Chef Paul Bartolotta graduated from a restaurant and hotel management program and then went on to work at some of the finest restaurants in Italy. He returned to the United States in 1987 to work at San Domenico in New York, where he raised it to a three-star restaurant. Bartolotta brought this skill to Spiaggia, where he earned the James Beard Best Midwest Chef award in 1994. Chef Bartolotta emphasizes a cuisine that features the best of contemporary as well as traditional Italian cooking.

Here are the recipes that Spiaggia contributed to this book:

- Risotto with Seasonal Green Vegetables (Risotto con Verdure) (Chapter 10)
- Braised Sea Bass in a Garlic Tomato Broth (Branzino all'Acqua Pazza) (Chapter 12)
- Clam and Leek Soup with Parsley (Brodetto di Vongole e Porri al Prezzemolo)
- Chicken with Lemon, Spinach, and Ham (Saltimbocca di Pollo alla Limone con Spinaci) (Chapter 13)

Star Canyon

3102 Oak Lawn Avenue, Number 144, Dallas, Texas, 214-520-7827

Star Canyon combines a sophisticated Texas ranch look with contemporary Western décor. The custom interiors were all done by artisans from Texas using local natural resources. The items on the menu reflect the seasonal offerings found in nearby markets. These features, along with the cuisine, are the reason that Star Canyon was named the restaurant that Best Reflects Dallas in the July 1999 *Wine and Food* restaurant poll and one of the top five new restaurants in America by the James Beard Foundation.

Chef and owner Stephan Pyles is acknowledged as one of the founding fathers of southwestern cuisine and was the first Texan inducted into *Who's Who of Food and Wine in America.* He is the recipient of numerous awards including the AAA Five Diamond Award for multiple years. He has written several important cookbooks, especially, *The New Texas Cuisine.* The list of dignitaries for whom he has cooked is a tribute to his achievements.

Star Canyon contributed these recipes to this book:

- Jícama-Belgian Endive Salad with Tequila-Orange Vinaigrette (Chapter 9)
- Mango-Tortilla Salad (Chapter 9)
- Shrimp and Papaya Enchiladas with Avocado-Tomatillo Salsa (Chapter 12)
- Grilled Red Snapper with Black Bean–Roast Banana Mash (Chapter 12)

Striped Bass

1500 Walnut Street, Philadelphia, Pennsylvania, 215-732-4444

Striped Bass combines style and ambience in the heart of Philadelphia's most upscale shopping and dining district. The restaurant features an all-seafood menu that has earned it numerous awards, including *Gourmet* magazine's America's Top Tables and a four-star rating from the *Mobil Travel Guide* since 1995. It was opened 6 years ago by owner Neil Stein, who has over 30 years of experience in the restaurant industry.

Executive chef Terence Feury is passionate about cooking with seafood. He comes to Striped Bass from a number of fine restaurants, having begun his culinary education at the Academy of the Culinary Arts in New Jersey. He trained with great chefs at places such as Peacock Alley at the Waldorf-Astoria Hotel and Le Bernardin, both in New York City. He is bringing in new and unique fish to enhance the already exciting Striped Bass menu.

Striped Bass provided the following recipes for this book:

- Lemon Sole with Brussels Sprouts (Chapter 12)
- Seared Scallops in Basil Lemon Broth (Chapter 12)
- Mediterranean Tuna Burger (Chapter 15)

Vij's Restaurant

1480 West Eleventh Avenue, Vancouver, British Columbia, 604-736-6664

Located just around the corner from the newly refurbished Stanley Theatre in Vancouver, Vij's Restaurant has the subtitle "curry art gallery." Vikram Vij, the owner and chef, opened his first restaurant nearby and was immediately successful, quickly requiring more space in his current location. The food combines the best of South Asia with Pacific tastes and flavors. The restaurant now resides in the top-20 list for Vancouver in *Gourmet* magazine year after year.

Vikram Vij learned hotel management in Austria and then came to Canada, where he trained at Bishop's and Rain City Grill in Vancouver. The recipes are the creation of Vikram and his wife. They change the small list of delicious entrees every three months.

Vij's Restaurant contributed these recipes to this book:

- Spiced Chopped Kale and Potatoes (Chapter 11)
- Chicken in Cilantro, Mint, and Serrano Pepper Curry (Chapter 13)
- Kalongi Chicken (Chapter 13)

A City-by-City Restaurant Travel Guide

So that you can use this section as a kind of travel guide, we have listed the restaurants by cities, which are in alphabetical order.

Boston

Hamersley's Bistro

Chicago

Spiaggia

Dallas

Star Canyon

Denver

Papillon Café

Kansas City

Cafe Allegro

Milwaukee

Osteria Del Mondo

Nashville

Capitol Grill

New York

Aquavit

Barbetta

Heartbeat

Oakhurst, California

Erna's Elderberry House

Philadelphia

Striped Bass

San Diego

Anthony's Fish Grotto

San Francisco

The Dining Room at the Ritz-Carlton, San Francisco

Moose's

Santa Fe

Anasazi Restaurant

Vancouver

Vij's Restaurant

Appendix B

Exchange Lists

In this appendix, you can find the Food Exchange Lists for Diabetes that are the basis of a popular meal-planning approach to help you eat the right number of calories from the correct energy sources. Dietitians recommend certain foods, but the patient has the choice to use whatever foods he or she wants. For more information on how to use the exchange method of balancing your diet, see Chapter 2.

Listing the Foods

Thousands of different foods are available, and each one can be grouped on the basis of the energy source (carbohydrate, protein, or fat) that is most prevalent in the food. Fortunately, the food content of one type of fish — salmon, for example — is just about the same as another type of fish, such as halibut. Therefore, a diet that calls for one meat exchange can use any one of a number of choices or exchanges. You can exchange one for the other, so your diet is never boring.

Listing all food sources in this space isn't possible. But for a list of just about all available foods, purchase *The Official Pocket Guide to Diabetic Exchanges* from the American Diabetes Association at 800-232-6733 or through the ADA Web site in Appendix E.

Starch list

Tables B-1 and B-2 list starch exchanges. Each exchange contains 15 grams of carbohydrate plus 3 grams of protein and 0 to 1 grams of fat, which amounts to 80 kilocalories per exchange. Foods containing whole grains have about 2 grams of fiber.

Table B-1 Starch Exchanges

Cereals, Grains, Pasta	*Bread*	*Dried Beans, Peas, Lentils (Higher in Fiber)*
Bran cereals, ½ cup	Bagel, ½	Beans and peas, ⅓ cup (cooked)
Cooked cereals, ½ cup	Breadsticks, 2	Lentils, ½ cup (⅔ ounce total) (cooked)
Grape-Nuts, 3 tablespoons	English muffin, ½	Baked beans, ¼ cup
Grits (cooked), ½ cup	Frankfurter bun, ½	
Pasta (cooked), ½ cup	Hamburger roll, ½	Lima beans, ½ cup
Puffed cereal, 1½ cups	Pita, 6 inches across, ½	Peas (green), ½ cup
Rice (cooked), ⅓ cup	Raisin bread, 1 slice	
Shredded wheat, ½ cup	Tortilla (1 slice), 6 inches	
	White bread, 1 slice	
	Whole wheat bread, 1 slice	

Table B-2 More Starch Exchanges

Crackers/Snacks	*Starchy Vegetables*	*Starchy Foods with Fats*
Animal crackers, 8	Corn, ½ cup	Chow mein noodles, ½ cup
Graham crackers, 3	Corn on the cob, 1	Cornbread, 2 ounces
Matzo, ¾ ounce	Potato (baked, 3 ounces), 1	French fries, 10
Melba toast, 5 slices	Potato (mashed), ½ cup	Muffin, 1
Popcorn (no fat),	Squash (winter), ¾ cup	Pancakes (2), 4 inches 3 cups

Crackers/Snacks	Starchy Vegetables	Starchy Foods with Fats
Pretzels, ¾ ounce	Yam (sweet potato), ⅓ cup	Waffle, 4½ inches, 1
Whole wheat cracker, 4		
Saltine-type cracker, 6		

Meat and meat substitutes list

Meats are divided into very lean, lean, medium-fat, and high-fat lists based upon the fat they contain. They all contain no carbohydrate and 7 grams of protein. The fat content changes the kilocalorie count for each exchange as follows:

	Fat (grams)	Kilocalories
Very lean	0-1	35
Lean	3	55
Medium-fat	5	75
High-fat	8	100

Very lean meat and substitutes:

- Poultry: Chicken or turkey (white meat, no skin), 1 ounce
- Fish: Fresh or frozen cod, flounder, haddock, halibut, trout, fresh tuna or tuna canned in water, 1 ounce
- Shellfish: Clams, crab, lobster, scallops, shrimp, imitation shellfish, 1 ounce
- Game: Duck or pheasant (no skin), venison, buffalo, ostrich, 1 ounce
- Cheese with 1 gram of fat or less per ounce, nonfat or lowfat cottage cheese ¼ cup, fat-free cheese, 1 ounce
- Other:
    - Processed sandwich meats with 1 gram or less fat per ounce, 1 ounce
    - Egg whites, 2
    - Egg substitutes, ¼ cup
    - Hot dogs with 1 gram or less fat per ounce, 1 ounce
    - Kidney, 1 ounce
    - Sausage with 1 gram or less fat per ounce, 1 ounce

Count the following as one very lean meat and one starch:

- Beans, peas, lentils, ½ cup

Lean meat and substitutes:

- Beef: USDA Select or Choice grades of lean beef trimmed of fat, such as round sirloin and flank steak; tenderloin; roast (rib, chuck, rump); steak (T-bone, porterhouse, cubed); ground round, 1 ounce
- Pork: Lean pork, canned, cured, or boiled ham; Canadian bacon; tenderloin, center loin chop, 1 ounce
- Lamb: Roast, chop, or leg; 1 ounce
- Veal: Lean chop, roast, 1 ounce
- Poultry: Chicken, turkey (dark meat, no skin), chicken white meat (with skin), domestic duck or goose (well-drained of fat), no skin, 1 ounce
- Fish:
  - Herring, 1 ounce
  - Oysters, 6 medium
  - Salmon (fresh or canned) or catfish, 1 ounce
  - Sardines (canned), 2 medium
  - Tuna (canned in oil, drained), 1 ounce
- Game: Goose (no skin), rabbit, 1 ounce
- Cheese:
  - 4.5% fat cottage cheese ¼ cup
  - Grated parmesan, 2 tablespoons
  - Cheeses with 3 grams or less fat per ounce, 1 ounce

Medium-fat meat and substitutes list:

- Beef: Ground beef, meatloaf, corned beef, short ribs, Prime grades of meat trimmed of fat such as prime rib, 1 ounce
- Pork: Top loin, chop, Boston butt, cutlet, 1 ounce
- Lamb: Rib roast, ground, 1 ounce
- Veal: Cutlet (ground or cubed, unbreaded), 1 ounce
- Poultry: Chicken (dark meat with skin), ground turkey or ground chicken, fried chicken (with skin), 1 ounce
- Fish: Any fried fish, 1 ounce

- Cheese: With 5 grams or less fat per ounce
  - Feta or mozzarella, 1 ounce
  - Ricotta, ¼ cup
- Other:
  - Egg, 1
  - Sausage with 5 grams or less fat per ounce, 1 ounce
  - Soy milk, 1 cup
  - Tempeh, ¼ cup
  - Tofu, 4 ounces or ½ cup

High-fat meat and substitutes list:

- Pork: Spareribs, ground pork, pork sausage, 1 ounce
- Cheese: All regular such as American, cheddar, Monterey Jack, Swiss
- Other:
  - Processed sandwich meats with 8 grams or less fat per ounce such as bologna, pimento loaf, salami, 1 ounce
  - Sausage such as bratwurst, Italian, knockwurst, Polish, smoked, 1 ounce
  - Hot dog (turkey or chicken, 10 per pound), 1
  - Bacon (20 slices per pound), 3 slices

High-fat meat plus one fat exchange:

- Hot dog (beef, pork, or combination), 1

High-fat meat plus two fat exchanges:

- Peanut butter, 2 tablespoons

Fruit list

Each exchange in Table B-3 contains 15 grams of carbohydrate (60 kilocalories) but no protein or fat. The list includes fresh, frozen, canned, and dried fruit and juice.

Table B-3 Fruit Exchanges

Fruit	*Dried Fruit*	*Fruit Juice*
Apple, 4 ounces	Apple, 4 rings	Apple, ½ cup
Applesauce, ½ cup	Apricots, 8 halves	Cranberries, ⅓ cup
Apricots, 4	Dates, 2½	Grapefruit, ½ cup
Apricots (canned), ½ cup	Figs, 1½	Grape, ⅓ cup
Banana (9 inches), ½	Prunes, 3	Orange, ½ cup
Blackberries, ¾ cup	Raisins, 2 tablespoons	Pineapple, ½ cup
Blueberries, ¾ cup		Prune, ⅓ cup
Cantaloupe, ⅓ melon (5-inch diameter) or 1 cup cubes		
Cherries, 12		
Cherries (canned), ½ cup		
Figs, 2		
Fruit cocktail, ½ cup		
Grapefruit, ½		
Grapes, 15		
Honeydew, 10 ounces or 1 cup cubes		
Kiwi, 1		
Mango, ½		
Nectarine, 1		
Orange, 1		
Papaya, 1 cup		
Peach, 1		
Peaches (canned), ½ cup		
Pear, 1 small		
Pears (canned), ½ cup		

Fruit	Dried Fruit	Fruit Juice
Persimmon, 2		
Pineapple, ½ cup		
Pineapple (canned), ⅓ cup		
Plum, 2		
Raspberries, 1 cup		
Strawberries, 1¼ cups		
Tangerine, 2		
Watermelon, 1¼ cups		

Milk list

Each exchange has 12 grams of carbohydrate and 8 grams of protein. Each exchange may have 0 to 8 grams of fat, so the kilocalorie count is 90 to 150.

Skim and very lowfat milk list: Add 0 kilocalories for fat content.

- Skim milk, 1 cup
- ½-percent milk, 1 cup
- 1-percent milk, 1 cup
- Nonfat or lowfat buttermilk, 1 cup
- Evaporated skim milk, ½ cup
- Dry nonfat milk, ⅓ cup dry
- Plain, nonfat yogurt, ¾ cup
- Nonfat or lowfat fruit-flavored yogurt sweetened with alternative sweetener, 1 cup

Reduced fat milk list: Add 45 kilocalories for fat content.

- 2-percent milk, 1 cup
- Plain lowfat yogurt, ¾ cup
- Sweet acidophilus milk, 1 cup

Whole milk list: Add 72 kilocalories for fat content.

- Whole milk, 1 cup
- Evaporated whole milk, ½ cup
- Goat's milk, 1 cup
- Kefir, 1 cup

Vegetable list

Each exchange has 5 grams of carbohydrate and 2 grams of protein, which equals 25 kilocalories. Vegetables have 2 to 3 grams of fiber. Remember that starchy vegetables such as lentils, corn, and potatoes are on the starches list earlier in this chapter. The serving size for all is ½ cup of cooked vegetables or 2 cups of raw vegetables.

- Artichoke (½ medium)
- Asparagus
- Beans (green, wax, Italian)
- Bean sprouts
- Cabbage
- Carrots
- Cauliflower
- Eggplant
- Greens (collard, mustard)
- Kohlrabi
- Okra
- Onions
- Pea pods
- Peppers (green)
- Rutabaga
- Sauerkraut
- Summer squash
- Turnips
- Water chestnuts
- Zucchini

Fats list

These foods have 5 grams of fat and little or no protein or carbohydrate per portion. The calorie count is, therefore, 45 kilocalories. The important thing in this category is to identify the foods that are high in cholesterol and saturated fats and avoid them. See Table B-4.

Table B-4 Fat Exchanges

Unsaturated Fats	***Saturated Fats***
Avocado, ⅛ medium (1 ounce)	Butter, 1 teaspoon
Salad dressing, 1 tablespoon	Bacon, 1 slice
Margarine, 1 teaspoon	Coconut, 2 tablespoons
Salad dressing (lowfat), 2 tablespoons	Cream, 2 tablespoons
Margarine (diet), 1 tablespoon	Cream, sour, 2 tablespoons
Mayonnaise, 1 teaspoon	Cream, heavy, 1 tablespoon
Almonds, 6	Cream cheese, 1 tablespoon
Cashews, 1 tablespoon	Salt pork, ¼ ounce
Pecans, 2 whole	
Peanuts, 10 large	
Walnuts, 2 whole	
Seeds (pine nuts, sunflower), 1 tablespoon	
Seeds (pumpkin), 2 teaspoons	
Oil (corn, olive, soybean, sunflower, peanut), 1 teaspoon	
Olives, 10 small	

Other carbohydrates

This list contains cakes, pies, puddings, and other foods with lots of carbohydrate (and often fat). They have 15 grams of carbohydrate. Because the protein and fat content is so variable, the total kilocalories in each item varies as well. Examples are too numerous to list but include, for example:

- Ice cream, ½ cup
- Brownie, 2-inch square

Free foods

These foods contain less than 20 calories per serving, so you can eat as much of them as you want without worrying about overeating and without worrying about serving size.

- **Condiments:** Catsup (1 tablespoon), horseradish, mustard, pickles (unsweetened), low-calorie salad dressing, taco sauce, and vinegar
- **Drinks:** Bouillon, sugar-free drinks, club soda, coffee, and tea
- **Fruit:** Cranberries, unsweetened, and rhubarb
- **Nonstick pan spray**
- **Salad greens:** Endive, any type of lettuce, and spinach
- **Seasonings:** Basil, celery seeds, chili powder, chives, cinnamon, curry, dill, flavoring extracts (vanilla, for example), garlic, garlic powder, herbs, lemon juice, lemon, lime, mint, onion powder, oregano, paprika, pepper, pimiento, soy sauce, spices, wine (used in cooking), Worcestershire sauce
- **Sweet substitutes:** Sugar-free candy, sugar-free gum, sugar-free jam or jelly, and sugar substitutes such as saccharin and aspartame
- **Vegetables:** Cabbage, celery, cucumber, green onion, hot pepper, mushroom, and radish

Using Exchanges to Create a Diet

Foods in exchange lists make it easy to create a diet with great variation. You can find typical diets in *The Official Pocket Guide to Diabetic Exchanges* from the American Diabetes Association, but remember that they generally permit more carbohydrate than we do. The menus in this section have been adjusted to reflect the lower carbohydrate and higher protein that we recommend. Table B-5 shows our exchange amounts for diets of 1,500 kilocalories. Table B-6 offers a sample menu.

This diet provides 150 grams of carbohydrate, 125 grams of protein, and 45 grams of fat, keeping it in line with the 40-percent carbohydrate, 30-percent protein, and 30-percent fat program.

You can have the total menu in Table B-6 on one day.

Table B-5	1,500 Kilocalories
Breakfast	***Lunch***
1 fruit exchange	3 lean-meat exchanges
1 starch exchange	1 vegetable exchange
1 medium-fat meat exchange	2 fat exchanges
1 fat exchange	1 starch exchange
1 lowfat milk exchange	2 fruit exchanges
Dinner	***Snack***
4 lean-meat exchanges	1 bread exchange
2 starch exchanges	½ lowfat milk exchange
2 vegetable exchanges	1 lean-meat exchange
1 fruit exchange	
2 fat exchanges	
½ lowfat milk exchange	

Table B-6	A Sample Menu at 1,500 Kilocalories
Breakfast	***Lunch***
½ cup apple juice	3 ounces skinless chicken
1 piece of toast	½ cup cooked green beans
1 teaspoon margarine	4 walnuts
1 egg	1 slice bread
1 cup skim milk	1 cup applesauce
Dinner	***Snack***
4 ounces lean beef	¼ cup cottage cheese
1 piece of bread	½ English muffin
½ cup peas	½ cup skim milk

(continued)

Table B-6 *(continued)*
Dinner
1 cup broccoli
⅓ cantaloupe
2 tablespoons salad dressing
Salad of free foods
4 ounces lowfat yogurt

Table B-7 shows the exchange amounts for an 1,800 kilocalorie diet. This diet provides 180 grams of carbohydrate, 135 grams of protein, and 60 grams of fat, which maintains the appropriate 40:30:30 division of calories.

Table B-7	1,800 Kilocalories
Breakfast	***Lunch***
1 fruit exchange	3 lean-meat exchanges
1 starch exchange	1 vegetable exchange
1 medium-fat meat exchange	2 fat exchanges
2 fat exchanges	2 starch exchanges
1 lowfat milk exchange	2 fruit exchanges
	½ lowfat milk exchange
Dinner	***Snack***
4 lean-meat exchanges	2 bread exchanges
2 starch exchanges	2 lean-meat exchanges
2 vegetable exchanges	½ lowfat milk exchange
1 fruit exchange	
3 fat exchanges	

Using the example of the 1,500 kilocalorie diet, you should be able to make up an 1,800 kilocalorie diet.

Appendix C

A Glossary of Key Cooking Terms

al dente: Cook to slightly underdone with a chewy texture, usually applied to pasta.

bake: Cook with hot, dry air.

barbecue: Cook on a grill using charcoal or wood.

baste: Spoon melted butter, fat, or other liquid over food.

beat: Mix solid or liquid food thoroughly with a spoon, fork, whip, or electric beater.

bind: Add an ingredient to hold the other ingredients together.

blanch: Plunge food into boiling water until it has softened to bring out the color and loosen the skin.

blend: Mix foods together less vigorously than beating, usually with a fork, spoon, or spatula.

boil: Heat liquid until it rolls and bubbles.

bone: Remove the bone from meat, fish, or poultry.

braise: Brown foods in fat, and then cook slowly in a covered casserole dish.

bread: Coat with bread crumbs.

broil: Cook by exposing directly to high heat.

brown: Cook quickly so the outside of the food is brown and the juices are sealed in.

caramelize: Dissolve sugar and water slowly and then heat until the food turns brown.

chop: Cut food into small to large pieces.

curdle: Cause separation by heating egg- or cream-based liquids too quickly.

deglaze: Pour liquid into a pan of meat — after roasting or sautéing and after removal of fat — to capture the cooking juices.

degrease: Remove fat from the surface of hot liquids.

devein: Remove the dark brownish-black vein that runs down the back of a shrimp.

dice: Cut into cubes the size of dice.

dilute: Make a liquid, such as a sauce, less strong by adding water.

drain: Remove liquid by dripping through a strainer.

drippings: The juice left after meat is removed from a pan.

dust: Sprinkle lightly with sugar or flour.

emulsify: Bind hard-to-combine ingredients, such as water and oil.

fillet: Cut meat, chicken, or fish away from the bone.

fold: Mix together without breaking.

fry: Cook in hot fat over high heat until brown.

garnish: Decorate food.

grate: Shred food in a grater or food processor.

grease: Lightly cover a pan with fat to prevent food from sticking.

grill: Cook on a rack over hot coals or under a broiler.

hors d'oeuvres: Bite-sized foods served before dinner.

infusion: Extract flavor from a food into a hot liquid.

julienne: Cut vegetables and other foods into matchstick-sized strips.

knead: Work dough to make it smooth and elastic.

leaven: Cause to rise before and during baking.

marinate: Place in a seasoned liquid to tenderize.

meringue: Egg whites beaten with sugar and baked at 300 degrees to 325 degrees Fahrenheit.

mince: Chop food very fine.

pan-broil: Cook on top of the stove over high heat, pouring off fat or liquid as it forms.

parboil: Partially cook food in boiling water.

pare: Remove skin from a fruit or vegetable.

phyllo: A tissue-thin layer of dough.

pickle: Preserve food by submerging in a salty brine.

pilaf: A rice dish seasoned with herbs and spices, combined with nuts, dried fruits, poultry, and vegetables.

pinch: The amount of food you can take between two fingers.

poach: Submerge food in a liquid that is barely boiling.

proof: Test yeast — to find out whether it's active — by mixing with warm water and sugar.

purée: Break food into small particles (examples are applesauce or mashed potatoes).

reduce: Boil down a liquid to concentrate the taste of its contents.

roast: Cook in dry heat.

sauté: Brown food in very hot fat.

shred: Tear or cut into very small, thin pieces.

simmer: Cook over low heat, never boiling.

skim: Spoon off fat that rises to the surface.

soufflé: A baked food made light by egg whites.

steam: Cook food over a small amount of boiling water.

steep: Place dry ingredients in hot liquid to flavor the liquid (tea is an example).

stew: Slowly cook meat and vegetables in liquid in a covered pan.

stir-fry: Quickly cook meat or vegetables in a wok with a little oil.

sweat: Cook over low heat in a small amount of fat (usually butter), to draw out juices to remove rawness and develop flavor.

toast: Brown by baking.

vinaigrette: A dressing of oil, vinegar, salt, pepper, and various herbs and spices.

whip: Beat rapidly to add air and lighten.

zest: The outermost colored peel of an orange or other citrus fruit.

Appendix D

Conversions of Weights, Measures, and Sugar Substitutes

Do you know how many tablespoons are in a cup? How many grams are in a pound? And how do you choose between all those sugar substitutes on the market? This appendix offers some helpful information.

Conversions

The following list provides some common measurement conversions.

1 teaspoon = ⅓ tablespoon

1 tablespoon = 3 teaspoons

2 tablespoons = ⅛ cup (1 ounce)

4 tablespoons = ¼ cup

5⅓ tablespoons = ⅓ cup

8 tablespoons = ½ cup

16 tablespoons = 1 cup

1 cup = ½ pint

2 cups = 1 pint

2 pints = 1 quart

4 quarts = 1 gallon

1 pound = 16 ounces

1 fluid ounce = 2 tablespoons

16 fluid ounces = 1 pint

Table D-1 explains how to convert specific measurements. For example, if you have 3 *ounces* of mushrooms, how many *grams* of mushrooms do you have? To find out, multiply 3 by 28.35 (you have 85.05 grams).

Table D-1 Conversion Methods

To Convert	*Multiply*	*By*
Ounces to grams	Ounces	28.35
Grams to ounces (dry)	Grams	0.035
Ounces (liquid) to milliliters	Ounces	30.00
Cups to liters	Cups	0.24
Liters to U.S. quarts	Liters	0.95
U.S. quarts to liters	Quarts	1.057
Inches to centimeters	Inches	2.54
Centimeters to inches	Centimeters	0.39
Pounds to grams	Pounds	453.59

Sugar Substitutes

The new approach to nutrition for people with diabetes doesn't emphasize the elimination of sugar from your diet entirely as long as you count the kilocalories that you are consuming. When a recipe calls for only a few teaspoons of sugar, you may want to use table sugar. When the recipe calls for ¼ cup of sugar or more, then substitution with a noncaloric sweetener of your choice will definitely save you kilocalories. There are also sweeteners besides glucose that do contain kilocalories but offer other advantages, such as not raising the blood glucose as fast. We discuss your sweet options in the following sections.

Kilocalorie-containing sweeteners

These sweeteners contain kilocalories that are added into the total kilocalorie count. They are absorbed differently than glucose, so they affect the blood glucose differently.

- **Fructose, found in fruits and berries:** Fructose is actually sweeter than table sugar *(sucrose)*. It's absorbed more slowly from the intestine than glucose, so it raises the blood glucose more slowly. It's taken up by the liver and converted to glucose or triglycerides.
- **Xylitol, found in strawberries and raspberries:** Xylitol is similar to fructose in terms of sweetness. It's taken up slowly from the intestine so that it causes little change in blood glucose. Xylitol doesn't cause tooth cavities as often as the other nutritive sweeteners, so it's used in chewing gum.
- **Sorbitol and mannitol, sugar alcohols occurring in plants:** Sorbitol and mannitol are half as sweet as table sugar and have little effect on blood glucose. They change to fructose in the body.

Sweeteners without kilocalories

Non-nutritive or artificial sweeteners are often much sweeter than table sugar. Therefore, much less of this type of sweetener is required to accomplish the same level of sweetness as sugar. The current artificial sweeteners include

- **Saccharin:** This sweetener is 300 to 400 times sweeter than sucrose. It's rapidly excreted unchanged in the urine. Brand names are Sucaryl, Sugar Twin, and Sweet 'n Low. It can be used in baking and cooking.
- **Aspartame:** This sweetener is more expensive than saccharin, but many people prefer its taste. It's 150 to 200 times sweeter than sucrose. Brand names are Equal and Sweetmate. Aspartame loses its sweetening power when heated, so it can't be used successfully in food that you need to cook for more than 20 minutes.
- **Acesulfame-K:** This type of sweetener is about 200 times sweeter than sugar and is used in baking and cooking. The brand name is Sweet One.
- **Sucralose:** This sweetener, made from sugar, is 600 times sweeter than its parent, sucrose. The brand name is Splenda. It does not lose its sweetness when heated.

If you are planning to substitute another sweetener for sugar, check out Table D-2 to find the measurements needed to achieve equal sweetness.

Table D-2 Amount of Sweetener Necessary to Produce Equally Sweet Taste

Sugar	*Fructose*	*Saccharin*	*Aspartame*	*Acesulfame-K*
2 teaspoons	⅔ teaspoon	⅕ teaspoon	1 packet	1 packet
1 tablespoon	1 teaspoon	⅓ teaspoon	1½ packets	1¼ packets
¼ cup	4 teaspoons	3 packets	6 packets	3 packets
⅓ cup	5⅓ teaspoons	4 packets	8 packets	4 packets
½ cup	8 teaspoons	6 packets	12 packets	6 packets
⅔ cup	3½ tablespoons	8 packets	16 packets	8 packets
¾ cup	¼ cup	9 packets	18 packets	9 packets
1 cup	⅓ cup	12 packets	24 packets	12 packets

Appendix E

Other Recipe Sources for People with Diabetes

So many cookbook recipes are available for people with diabetes that this book would not have been written if it didn't offer a special feature, namely the recipes of some of the finest chefs in the United States and Canada. You can find a number of excellent books and even more recipes on World Wide Web sites. You can generally count on the recipes in books to contain the nutrients they list, but Web recipes may not be as reliable; you need to evaluate the site before accepting the recipes. You can trust the sites that we list here. You can find them by typing in the address or by going to Dr. Rubin's Web site at `www.drrubin.com`.

When you get to Dr. Rubin's Web site, click on the Useful Addresses link, where you can find links to all the sites we mention here.

Cookbooks for People with Diabetes

No book like this one exists on cooking for people with diabetes. Those listed in this section offer recipes for home-grown meals, not the creative work of the great chefs. However, plenty of useful information and tons of good recipes appear in the books we list here.

American Diabetes Association, *Month of Meals Series,* American Diabetes Association, 1998.

Cross, Doris, and Alice Williams, *Real Food for People with Diabetes,* Prima Publishing, 1997.

Geil, Patti, and Ross, Tami, *The Complete Step by Step Diabetic Cookbook,* Oxmoor House, 1995.

Donkersloot, Mary, R.D., *The Simply Gourmet Diabetic Cookbook,* Three Rivers Press, 1998.

Gaines, Fabiola Demps, R.D., L.D., and Roniece Weaver, R.D., L.D., *The New Soul Food Cookbook for People with Diabetes,* American Diabetes Association, 1999.

Geil, Patty B., *Diabetes Meals on $7 a Day or Less,* American Diabetes Association, 1999.

Grunes, Barbara, *Meatless Diabetic Cookbook***,** Prima Publishing, 1998.

Hess, Mary Abbott, *The Art of Cooking for the Diabetic,* NTC/Contemporary Publishing, 1998.

Little, Billie, *Recipes for Diabetics, Penguin,* U.S.A., 1999.

Marton, Beryl M., *The Great Chicken Book for People with Diabetes,* American Diabetes Association, 1999.

Polin, Bonnie Sanders, and Frances Towner Giedt, *The Joslin Diabetes Gourmet Cookbook,* Bantam Books, 1993.

Stanley, Kathleen, C.D.E., R.D., M.S.E.R., and Connie Crawley, M.S., R.D., L.D., *Quick & Easy Diabetic Recipes for One,* American Diabetes Association, 1997.

Wedman-St. Louis, Betty, *Fast & Fabulous Diabetic Menus,* Contemporary Publishing, 1998.

Woodruff, Sandra, *Diabetic Dream Desserts,* Avery Publishing Group, 1996.

Ten Recipe Web Sites for People with Diabetes

In this section, we list the best of the currently available Web sites. Things change so frequently on the Web that it's difficult to stay up-to-date. Look for newer listings on Dr. Rubin's Web site at `www.drrubin.com`.

- The nutrition section of the American Diabetes Association Web site begins at www.diabetes.org/nutrition. Here you find discussions of nutrition as well as lots of recipes.
- Planet Rx offers plenty of information about diet and exercise together. Their Internet site is found at www.diabetes.com/health_library/diet_ and_exercise.html. The site provides information about restaurant dining as well.
- OnHealth Diabetes Center has a file of recipes through ww1.onhealth.com/conditions/condctr/diabetes/index.asp.
- Children with Diabetes includes a large amount of information on meal planning, sugar substitutes, and the food guide pyramid, as well as many recipes at www.childrenwithdiabetes.com/d_08_000.htm.
- The Joslin Diabetes Center points out that "there is no such thing as a diabetic diet" among many other topics on nutrition at its Web site www.joslin.org/education/library/index.html.
- The Web page Ask NOAH About Diabetes supplies links to many important articles about diabetic nutrition as well as diabetic recipes at www.noah.cuny.edu/diabetes/diabetes.html#PREVENTION.
- Olen Publishing has a Food Finder site that lists the nutritional values for the food in about 20 major fast-food restaurants at www.olen.com/food.
- The Vegetarian Resource Group maintains a large site filled with information for vegetarians who have developed diabetes at www.vrg.org/journal/diabetes.htm.
- The Food and Drug Administration provides a long article about diabetic nutrition at vm.cfsan.fda.gov/~lrd/cons1194.txt.
- *Diabetic Gourmet Magazine* offers a valuable site that contains information about diagnosis and treatment as well as numerous recipes that you can use at www.diabeticgourmet.com.

Index

Symbols

• A •

• B •

• C •

• D •

• E •

• F •

• G •

• K •

• L •

• M •

• N •

• Q •

• R •

• W •

• X •

• Y •

• Z •

Notes

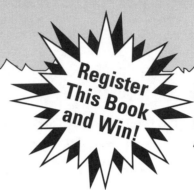

Includes recipes from America's top chefs

IDG BOOKS WORLDWIDE

Don't let diabetes stop you from eating well — enjoy every meal!

Leading diabetes expert Dr. Alan Rubin teams up with great chefs and respected dietitians to show that it is possible to live with diabetes while savoring delicious dishes at home and at fancy restaurants and fast food places. In this must-have companion to *Diabetes For Dummies®*, you'll find great ideas for eating well at every meal, plus inspiring recipes to tempt you into the kitchen.

Alan L. Rubin, M.D., a pioneer in diabetes treatment for 25 years, teaches about diabetes to medical professionals and the public around the world.

Discover how to:

- *Cook flavorful meals for every occasion*
- *Make diabetes-smart choices when eating out*
- *Stay in control while on vacation*
- *Avoid food-shopping pitfalls*
- *Understand the health values of what you eat*

$19.99 US
$27.99 CN
£14.99 UK
7 85555 02276 8 Cooking
ISBN 0-7645-5230-9
51999
9 780764 552304

Get smart!
www.dummies.com